The War Vice-President, HANNIBAL HAMLIN.

Eastern Maine and The Rebellion

Being An Account of The Principal Local Events In Eastern Maine During The War.
And
Brief Histories of Eastern Main Regiments.

Contains Accounts of Mobs, Riots, Destruction of Newspapers, War Meetings, Drafts, Confederate Raids, Peace Meetings, Celebrations, Soldiers' Letters, and Scenes and Incidents at The Front, Never Before In Print.

R. H. Stanley and Geo. O. Hall

Heritage Books
2008

HERITAGE BOOKS
AN IMPRINT OF HERITAGE BOOKS, INC.

Books, CDs, and more—Worldwide

For our listing of thousands of titles see our website
at
www.HeritageBooks.com

Published 2008 by
HERITAGE BOOKS, INC.
Publishing Division
100 Railroad Ave. #104
Westminster, Maryland 21157

Copyright © 1887, 2002 R. H. Stanley & Geo O. Hall

All rights reserved. No part of this book may be reproduced or transmitted in any form or by any means, electronic or mechanical, including photocopying, recording or by any information storage and retrieval system without written permission from the author, except for the inclusion of brief quotations in a review.

International Standard Book Numbers
Paperbound: 978-0-7884-2230-0
Clothbound: 978-0-7884-7600-6

DEDICATION.

In compiling this volume, we have necessarily sought the columns of the Press, for the years 1861-66; the admirable reports of Adjutant General Hodsdon, for the same years; private journals and memorandums, as well as personal correspondence.

To Major Small, and the Sixteenth Regiment Association, we are under great obligations, for the use of the four cuts belonging to them.

For the universal courtesies extended us when in search of information, and especially for the uniform kindness and interest manifested by those connected with that admirable institution, the Bangor Public Library, we wish to return our sincerest thanks.

TO THE PRESS OF EASTERN MAINE,

WHICH HAS SO OFTEN AND SO FREELY GRANTED US FAVORS,

WE DEDICATE THIS BOOK,

Trusting that one and all, may find within its pages, some new and instructive facts, regarding the darkest days of our Country's history.

THE AUTHORS.

INTRODUCTION.

IT HAS been our endeavor in these pages, to depict the scenes and incidents occuring at home, during the Rebellion, rather than the giving of a minute description of the varied experiences of the thousands, who marched away from Eastern Maine, at their Country's call.

We lay no claim to high literary merit, simply placing before you, in condensed form, the facts; believing that as the memories of the older readers are quickened, and the younger generation learn of the experiences of fathers and mothers, in their efforts to preserve the Union, all will find something of deep interest.

R. H. STANLEY.
GEO. O. HALL.

CONTENTS.

CHAPTER I. Page 17

The News From Fort Sumter—How It Was Received In Bangor—President Lincoln's Proclamation—General Veazie Offers Fifty Thousand Dollars—A Grand Rally at Norombega Hall—Dangers Which Menaced Bangor Shipping—"Panicky" Times.

CHAPTER II. Page 21

Bangor's Proud Boast—She Raises The First Company of Volunteers That Enlisted in The United States—To Put Down The Rebellion—The First Recruiting Office—The Riot In Baltimore, and Washington In Danger—The First Company Elect Officers—The "Grattan Guards" and "Bangor Light Infantry"—Capt. Meinecke Opens an Office in the Gymnasium—Doings of The City Council—The Big Relief Fund and Who Gave It—Daniel Chaplin Raises a Company—Other Offices Opened.

CHAPTER III. Page 33

Enlistments Continued—The Ex-Tiger And Amory Associates—The Home Guards—"Bangor May Now Fearlessly Face A Frowning World"—The Cavalry And The Sons Of Temperance—Maine On A War Footing—The First Regiment—The Governor's Proclamation—Division And Regimental Orders—Maj. Gen. Butler, of Maine—He Issues A Corpulent Proclamation—The Towns' Round About—Grand Meetings, Stirring Speeches, And Odd But Earnest Resolutions.

CONTENTS.

CHAPTER IV. Page 39

States Rights Men, Timid Men and Copperheads—The Stars And Stripes Everywhere—Forming of The First Regiment—Captain Chaplin's Company Organize—Arrival of The Castine Company—A Grand Military Display—Forming of The Second Regiment. Complete List of Officers—A Sketch of Each Company.

CHAPTER V. Page 46

The Second Maine In Camp—How The Men Lived—Preparations For A Southern "Tour"—Wheelwright & Clark Contract To Furnish Uniforms—The Women Give Substantial Aid—Extracts From The Daily Press—What Each Soldier Had—The Camp On Essex Street—Military Ardor In Business Circles—Red, White And Blue Letter Paper—Odd Advertisements—Linen Handkerchiefs And Bandages—The Regiment Ordered To The Front.

CHAPTER VI. Page 51

Off For The War—Presentation Of The Flag—Vice-President Hamlin's Address—Scenes At The Station—Reception At Augusta—The Trip To New York—A Grand Reception There—On Board The Transport—Measles Break Out—In Camp At Willett's Point—Trouble Regarding Enlistment Papers—On To Washington.

CHAPTER VII. Page 58

In Camp At Washington—A Letter From Col. Roberts—Preparing To Strike The Decisive Blow—A Visit From Secretary Seward—Scenes And Incidents—Going To The Front.

CHAPTER VIII. Page 62

Continuation Of The Scenes In Bangor—The Sixth Regiment—The Independent Volunteers Organize—The Temperance Volunteers—The Jam Breakers Of Oldtown—Rebels Capture Bangor Ships—Troops Disbanded And Paid Off—Great Disappointment—Rifling Cannon At Bangor—Death Of The Bangor Union—Buying Horses For Government—Ass't Surgeon Hamlin At Home—Deaths In The Second Maine—Departure Of The Sixth Maine Battallion—Their Officers—Additional Recruits For The Second—The Sixth Maine To The Front—Regimental And Company Officers.

CHAPTER IX. Page 71

The Battle of Bull Run—How The News Was Received at Home—Intense Anxiety And Excitement—A Few Telegraph Headings—Letters From The Second Maine.

CHAPTER X. Page 83

Destruction Of The Bangor Democrat—Infuriated Citizens, Maddened By Its Bitter Attacks Upon The Government—Throw Type, Cases And Press Into The Street And Burn Them—Editor Emery Has A Narrow Escape—What The Press Said—Interviews With Bangor Men Who Took Part In The Raid—The Trial At Belfast—Issue Of The Democrat Extra—Editor Emery Addresses The People.

CHAPTER XI. Page 98

The Fourth Maine—A Gallant Regiment Hampered By Some Poor Material—One Company Reorganized—Deserters Numerous—Some Brilliant Engagements—The Regiment Nearly Annihilated—General Berry Of Rockland—Col. Marshall Of Belfast.

CHAPTER XII. Page 103

"All Quiet On The Potomac"—A Few Battles In The West—Formation Of Other Maine Regiments—A Big War Meeting—A National Fast In September—Sharp Shooters Wanted—What Was Required Of Them—Chas. Hamlin, Esq., Opens A Recruiting Office—Penobscot County And Bangor Bear Off State Honors—Gen. Jameson Commands A Brigade—Col. Roberts In Command Of Several Forts—The Banks Suspend Specie Payment—The Close Of The Year—The Soldiers In Winter Quarters—Some Of The Stories They Told.

CHAPTER XIII. Page 111

The State Guards—A Company In Each Ward—One Or More In Each Town—The Officers—The Orders To Drill—The First American Boycott—A Great Rally—An Immense Crowd In Bangor—Gen. Howard Arrives—Serious Accident At Norombega Hall—The Platform Gives Way—Many Ladies Injured—The City Council Increases The Bounty—"Excursion" To Richmond.

CHAPTER XIV.   Page 118

History Of The Second Mainê Regiment, From The Spring Of '62—They Leave Hall's Hill—Ordered To Yorktown—Siege Of Yorktown—They Receive The Thanks Of Gens. McClellan And Porter—Chickahominy—Battle Of Hanover Court House—Gaine's Mill—Malvern Hill—The Camp At Harrison's Landing —On To Fredricksburg—They Give Battle To The Enemy At Manassas—Picket Duty At Stone Bridge—The Battle Of Fredricksburg—Close Of The Year.

CHAPTER XV.   Page 124

History Of The Sixth Maine—Chain Bridge—On The March—Lewinsville— Fort Griffin—Col. Burnham—The New Officers—Much Fighting—A Singular Combat—The Axe Brigade—Sleeping On Their Arms—Much Fighting And Great Losses—Daring Deeds By Co. "D"—Col. Burnham Ordered To Maine —Lieut. Harris In Command—Rappahannock Station—Col. Harris Seriously Wounded And Maj. Fuller Takes Command—Defending Washington—Arrival At Portland—Mustered Out.

CHAPTER XVI.   Page 137

The Eighteenth Maine—Organized At Bangor And Ordered To Washington— Changed To The First Maine Heavy Artillery—Twelve Months Of Idleness— They Join The Army Of The Potomac—The First Fight—The First Great Slaughter—They Are Mowed Down By Ranks—Placing The Blame—Death Of Col. Chaplin—His Last Words—His Military Career—Forty Days Under Fire—A Gallant Charge—The Winter Before Petersburg—At Amelia Springs —They Capture Artillery, Colors And Men—Back To Bangor.

CHAPTER XVII.   Page 154

Northern Politics—The Three Parties In Maine—Union Republicans, War Democrats And Breckenridge Democrats—The Last Also Called Copperheads— What They Did In 1861—A Thrilling Appeal For Volunteers—Politics In 1862—Eastern Maine "Locals."—Thousands Of Deserters North—McClellan's Address To The Press—Gloom And Despair Everywhere—Close Of The Year.

CHAPTER XVIII.   Page 161

In 1863—Return Of The Second Maine—The Military Escort—The Speakers At Norombega—Vice-President Hamlin's Second Address To Them—Local Events.

CHAPTER XIX. Page 169

The Draft—How It Was Avoided In '62—Patriotic Appeals And Odd Advertisements—Elijah Low Is Appointed Provost Marshal—What He Did—He Has A Row With The Maine Central—And Is Ordered To Take Possession And Run It At Government Expense—The Travel To Canada Becomes Large—A Patten Rebel Defies Uncle Sam—And Comes To Grief—Capt. Low Exposes A Defaulter—The Draft In Houlton—Bells Tolling For Lincoln And Clanging For Victory Over Lee—The Hunt In Maine For The Assassin Booth.

CHAPTER XX. Page 183

In 1864—Another Call For Troops—And Another Draft Ordered—The "Soldiers Rest"—The Big Sanitary Fair—The Elections—The Close Of The Year—Gold And Merchandise—Its Rise And Fall—How Fortunes Were Made—How Some Lost Them—The Boom In Groceries, Cotton And Woolen Goods—Boots, Shoes And Clothing At War Prices—Something About Hardware—Fools And Their Folly—A. T. Stewart & Co. Are Caught—Sliding Down And Sliding Out—Making Change With Veazie And Hersey Scrip.

CHAPTER XXI. Page 190

In 1865—The Draft Continues—Glorious News From The Army Of The Potomac—Victory All Along The Line—Twelve Thousand Prisoners In Three Days—Surrender Of Lee And His Army—Great Rejoicing At Home—What The People Did—A Great Day For Maine—Interesting Accounts From An Old Journal—A Procession Forms In Bangor And Many Calls Made—What Was Said And Done.

CHAPTER XXII. Page 202

The Nation In Mourning—Another Great Crime Of The Slave Power—President Lincoln Assassinated—A Nation In Tears—Terrible News—The President's Case Hopeless—Almost Miraculous Escape Of Grant.

CHAPTER XXIII. Page 207

The First War Meeting In Rockland—Flag Raisings—Rockland Votes To Raise Ten Thousand Dollars For Aid Of Soldier's Families—Elijah Walker Opens A Recruiting Office—Arrival Of The Companies For The Fourth Regiment—The Work Of The Ladies—The Departure Of The Fourth Regiment—Meeting At Camden—The News From Bull Run—The Ward Companies—The Draft.

CONTENTS.

CHAPTER XXIV. Page 217

Presentation Of Silver Service To Gen. Berry By His Officers—Rockland Ships Seized By The "Alabama"—Funeral Of Gen. Berry—Vice-President Hamlin's Opinion Of The Man—The Harbor Batteries—Return Of The Fourth Regiment—Rockland Raises Thirty Thousand Dollars To Fill The Quota—Capture Of The "Rouen"—The Coast Guards—The Fall Of Richmond—Death Of Lincoln—Close Of The War—Return Of The Soldiers.

CHAPTER XXV. Page 229

Belfast And Surrounding Towns During The Rebellion—The Early War Meetings—The First Enlistments—Stealing The Flag From The Custom House—Searsport Responds—Militia Attend Church—News From Bull Run—Building The Gunboat—Something From "Old Troy"—The Draft In 1863—Names Of Those Drawing Tickets—The Searsport Unfortunates.

CHAPTER XXVI. Page 236

Building Belfast Batteries—Excitement In Mercantile Circles—Dixie Prices—A Landlady Buys Largely—An Editor Arrested—The Killing Of a Waldo Sheriff In Wesley—A "Hard Gang" Resist The Belfast Officers—Deserters Stealing Horses—They Are Pursued—They Shoot Chief Of Police Charles McKenney—Additional Men Join In The Pursuit—One Of Them Shot Through The Heart—They Are Finally Captured—And Are Beaten To Death—News Of Lee's Surrender—Belfast Celebrates And Burns A Building—Men Blown From A Cannon's Mouth—The People Nearly Hang An Innocent Man—Copperheads Go Fishing—The Death Of Lincoln—Belfast Of To-Day.

CHAPTER XXVII. Page 246

The First Cavalry—They Were Never "Rattled"—The Organization—The Officers From Eastern Maine—"Dashing" Spurling—Why Col. Goddard Resigned—How The Band Got Even—Leaving For The Front—Scenes Of Inactivity—Douty Gains Command—Raiding And Skirmishing—They Save The Army Of Banks—The Gallant Fight At Brandy Station—Another At Aldie—The Fall Of Douty—The History Of The Regiment To The Close Of The War—Coming Home.

CHAPTER XXVIII. Page 259
CALVIN S. DOUTY.

CHAPTER XXIX.   Page 267

War Matters In Dexter—A Strong Union Sentiment—And A Large "Secesh" Element—Local Matters—The Great Peace Conventions—Fifteen Thousand People Gather—"Seven Barrels Of Doughnuts"—A Monster Procession—Sentiments Hostile To The Union—The Dexter Band "Play It" On The Democrats—Interviews With Men Who Participated—Scenes At Barton's Grove—Treasonable Talk—The Dinner Cooked On The Vice-President's Stove.

CHAPTER XXX.   Page 278

The History Of The Twenty-Second Regiment—To Fortress Monroe—Newport News—New Orleans—Up The Mississippi—Baton Rouge—Disease And Death—Donaldson—Irish Bend—Quelling Negro Insurrections—A Gallant Charge—Port Hudson—Jerrard In Command—He Is Placed Under Arrest—Banks Again Displays His Dislike Of Maine Officers—Capture Of Port Hudson—Return Of The Regiment—The Twenty-Sixth—An Extensive Tour—A Little Fighting—Some Guard Duty—Returning Home—The Third Battery—The Twenty-Eighth—Account Of The Formation—Sleeping In Beecher's Church—To The Front—Regimental History.

CHAPTER XXXI.   Page 284

The Eighth Regiment—Its Organization—The Capture Of Hilton Head—Colonel Strickland Resigns—Capture Of Fort Pulaski—The First Emancipation Proclamation—Capture Of Jacksonville, Fla.—The Furlough—Presentation To Colonel Rust—Again At The Front—Drury's Bluff—Cold Harbor—In Front Of Petersburg—Bermuda Hundred—Forts Gregg and Baldwin—Appomattox C. H.—Killed And Wounded—Return Of The Regiment.

CHAPTER XXXII.   Page 292

The Eleventh Regiment—Its Organization And Officers—To The Front—Siege Of Yorktown—The Battle Of Seven Pines—In The Rifle Pits—Honorable And Dangerous Duty—The Best Axe-Men Of The Army—The Mathews County Invasion Destruction Of The Salt Works—Twenty-One Days Afloat—Presentation To Colonel Plaisted—At Morris Island—The Florida Trip—On To Richmond—Death Of Lieutenant Colonel Spofford—To New York—Clover Hill—Patrol Duty—Return Of The Eleventh.

CONTENTS.

CHAPTER XXXIII. Page 299

Ellsworth And Hancock County---The First Meeting---Ringing Resolutions---Money For Soldiers Aid---The First Flag Raising---Jesse Dutton Opens Recuiting Office---The Hancock Giants---Rebels Cut Down The Liberty Pole At Blue Hill---The Rifle Company---The Noble Work Of The Ladies--Ellsworth Men In The Navy---Return Of Wounded Soldiers---Death Of Lieutenant Rice---The Ward Companies---The Ellsworth Band---Recruiting Continues---The Dirigo Club---Lee's Surrender---Close Of The War.

CHAPTER XXXIV. Page 306

The Second Cavalry---Its Formation---The First Detachment At New Orleans---Its Battles----Arrival Of The Main Regiment----To Florida --Raids And Skirmishes---Return To Augusta---The Thirty-First Regiment---Its Organization---Its Battles---Tolopotomoy Creek---Cold Harbor---Bethesda Church---Weldon Railroad---In Front of Petersburg---Arrival Home.

THE LOSS OF THE "EMMA JANE," - - - - - Page 387

CONTENTS.

BIOGRAPHICAL SKETCHES.

Major Gen. Hiram G. Berry,	Page 311
Major Whiting S. Clark,	" 320
Captain Benj. F. Hunter,	" 321
Brig. Gen. Thomas W. Hyde,	" 322
Lieut. Wm. R. Newenham,	" 322
Brevet Brig. Gen. Llewellyn G. Estes,	" 323
Lieut. Col. George Fuller,	" 324
Brevet Brig. Gen. John D. Rust,	" 325
Captain John H. Ballinger,	" 330
Surgeon John Benson,	" 331
Asst. Surgeon William R. Benson,	" 332
Captain Billings Brastow,	" 332
Brev. Brig. Gen. Charles W. Roberts,	" 333
Captain C. A. Boutelle,	" 334
Brig. Gen. Hiram Burnham,	" 338
Captain Samuel W. Daggett,	" 345
Captain William R. Currier,	" 347
Captain Henry Crosby,	" 347
Dr. A. C. Hamlin,	" 349
Lieut. George W. Grant,	" 350
Brevet Brig. Gen. Charles D. Gilmore,	" 350
Lieut. Israel H. Washburn,	" 351
Brev. Brig. Gen. George Varney,	" 352
Capt. Francis W. Sabine,	" 352
Lieut. Col. Daniel F. Sargent,	" 354
Col. Augustus B. Farnham,	" 355
Brevet Brig. Gen. Charles Hamlin,	" 356
Brevet Maj. Gen. Cyrus Hamlin,	" 360
Brig. Gen. Charles D. Jameson,	" 361
Lieut. Col. Winslow P. Spofford,	" 364
Major Joel A. Haycock,	" 365
Brevet Brig. Gen. Harris M. Plaisted,	" 367
Col. Jasper Hutchings,	" 376
Lieut. W. H. H. Rice,	" 377
Capt. F. A. Cummings,	" 378
James W. Clark,	" 379
Adjut. Gen. John L. Hodsdon,	" 382
Brevet Brig. Gen. Jos. Sewell Smith,	" 383
Hon. Hannibal Hamlin,	" 385

CHAPTER I.

The News From Fort Sumpter—How It Was Received In Bangor—President Lincoln's Proclamation—General Veazie Offers Fifty Thousand Dollars—A Grand Rally at Norombega Hall—Dangers Which Menaced Bangor Shipping—"Panicky" Times.

On the twelfth of April, 1861, at four o'clock in the morning, the batteries on Sullivan's Island, Morris Island, as well as those along the shores of Charleston Harbor, opened fire on Fort Sumpter. At a late hour that day the news reached Bangor, causing consternation and indignation. Although the daily papers had kept our citizens informed of the doings of our government as well as the Southern States, and although war had been declared inevitable, yet our people could hardly realize that the blow had fallen, and that the soil of the South that for years had yielded bountiful harvests, was soon to be made red with the life blood of thousands ere peace again spread her white wings over our land.

At once there came to the minds of the patriotic sons of the North the one thought that the Rebellion must be subdued, and the citizens of Maine, and especially those of Bangor, waited with feverish impatience the action of the authorities at Washington. They had not long to wait. On the 15th of April, President Lincoln called forth the militia of the United States to the number of 75,000 men, and his words in the proclamation show he had little conception of the magnitude of the war which had been inaugurated. He said:

"I deem it proper to say that the first service assigned to the forces will probably be to repossess the forts, places and property which have been seized from the United States; and in every event the utmost care will be observed consistently with the object aforesaid, to avoid any devastation, any destruction of or interference with property, or any disturbance of peaceful citizens in every part of the country."

As soon as this proclamation was issued a feeling of relief was experienced, and every one felt that the right step had been taken, and all looked for a speedy suppression of the rebel element. From all the loyal States came offers of men and money, and the people of Bangor, as well as those in the surrounding towns being possessed of a patriotic spirit, were anxious to enlist at once. Rousing meetings were held, where resolutions upholding the Government were passed, while one wealthy citizen—Gen. Samuel Veazie —offered to advance fifty thousand dollars "for the defence of the Union and the Constitution."

As soon as possible after the proclamation the Secretary of War made a requisition on Governor Washburn for a regiment for immediate service. Governor Washburn replied: "Maine will respond promptly," and thereupon issued his proclamation; "to convene the Legislature of this State" April 22d; "then and there to consider and determine on such measures as the condition of the country and the obligations of the State may seem to demand." The same night there was a grand rally at Norombega Hall, which was attended by an immense number of our citizens. This meeting was called to order by Gen. S. P. Strickland, and by his motion Hon. Samuel H. Blake was called upon to preside, after which the following vice presidents were chosen: Samuel Veazie, George W. Pickering, James Dunning, Isaiah Stetson, Solomon Parsons, Hastings Strickland, Thomas N. Egery, Charles W. Roberts, F. Meinecke, S. H. Dale, I. S. Bartlett, A. C. Smith, James O'Donohue, Jonathan Young, J. S. Wheelwright, Aaron A. Wing, Joseph Porter, David Bugbee, Geo. A. Cummings, Michael Boyce, H. H.

HON. ISRAEL WASHBURN, JR.,
THE FIRST WAR GOVERNOR.

Fogg, Israel B. Norcross, Patrick Golden, Sidney Thaxter, W. H. Smith, Robert Carlisle, Luther H. Eaton, M. Gilligan, John S. Ricker, A. L. Simpson, F. Muzzy, Benj. H. Mace. The secretaries were F. A. Wilson, T. H. Garnsey and Frank Garland. At this gathering speeches, all breathing intense loyalty, were made and the following resolutions adopted:

"*Resolved*,—That it is the duty of every American citizen in the present alarming and dangerous crisis of the American Union, to give an earnest, patriotic and hearty support to the General Government, and that Maine ought and will respond to the utmost of her ability, both in men and money, to maintain the liberty of the country and the union of the States; and we believe the time has come when the whole power of the Government, and of the loyal people of all the States, be unhesitatingly and vigorously exerted to crush the rebellious and revolutionary madmen who seek to overthrow the Goverment." This meeting closed a day of intense excitement in Bangor.

There was a faction here who, if they did not speak out for the Confederacy would say nothing against it, and the patriotic citizens began to display flags at their places of business and residences. Collector Wingate, of the Custom House, had received that morning an American flag, which he hoisted at the top of the building. It was the only flag ever displayed there save one, which was hoisted on the occasion of a Fourth of July celebration. Immediately a crowd gathered on the southerly side accompanied by the Bangor Cornet Band, and after the music, speeches were made by Wm. H. McCrillis, Charles W. Crosby and Joseph Bartlett. "The Times," a democratic paper, as well as "The Bangor Union," then issued from Wheelwright and Clark's block, also displayed the national flag. That day, too, the monied men were busy, and the directors of the Market Bank voted to offer Governor Washburn a loan of twenty-five thousand dollars to the State, "if wanted for present emergencies."

During these exciting days the business men were very busy. Many of them saw—or thought they saw—chances to reap harvests by putting in large stocks, and they purchased liberally. Some were owners of vessels of great value, and just what to do with them became a serious question. Quite a number were in southern ports or on their way there, while still others were loading for New Orleans, Mobile, Charleston and other important cotton points. In many cases owners made haste to order them home, or their captains were instructed to secure freights for foreign ports, little dreaming that before the war was over their crafts would be sought for by Confederate vessels, even to the uttermost part of the world. Their anxiety was heightened by a proclamation issued by Jefferson Davis, April 17th, "inviting all those who may desire, by armed service in private armed vessels on the high seas, to aid this government, to make applications for commissions or letters of marque and reprisal to be issued under the seal of these Confederate States."

As regards business, the hopes of the merchants were not realized. Contrary to expectation everything dropped in price, and for a long time there was a decided feeling of uneasiness. A panic was feared and, once started, no one could tell where it would end. Some had their all invested in business, but they were stout of heart and confided in each other, and in this way averted what at one time seemed to menace the entire business interests of the city. In 1862 there was a marked advance in values, and those who held on reaped bountifully. In '63 there were still greater advances, and many of the fortunes now being enjoyed by the later generation were made at that time.

CHAPTER II.

Bangor's Proud Boast—She Raises The First Company of Volunteers That Enlisted in The United States—To Put Down The Rebellion—The First Recruiting Office—The Riot In Baltimore, and Washington In Danger—The First Company Elect Officers—The "Grattan Guards" and "Bangor Light Infantry"—Capt. Meinecke Opens an Office in the Gymnasium—Doings of The City Council—The Big Relief Fund and Who Gave It—Daniel Chaplin Raises a Company—Other Offices Opened.

The first Company to enlist in Bangor was that known as "Capt. Emerson's Company." Emerson had been on the police force, but in April, 1861 was out of business. Just before the fight in Charleston harbor, James Dunning Esq., had arrived home from Washington and Baltimore, and from what he had seen and heard in those cities, was convinced that war must ensue and so stated to Emerson and others. Emerson replied that he should like to raise a Company, and Mr. Dunning agreed to assist him. Immediately on receipt of the news of the opening of hostilities, Mr. Dunning sought out Mr. Fisk, of the firm of Fisk and Dale, and requested the key of the Bethel, promising to send Mr. Emerson after it. Later, when Emerson applied for it, both Fisk and Dale told him it was folly to suppose volunteers would be wanted, and intimated that both he—Emerson—and Dunning were insane. Emerson reported to Mr. Dunning, who immediately secured the room over Finson's market, and opened an office for recruits. While Emerson was erecting a flag staff which he had hewn out, Mr. Dunning sought out Mr. Heath, a well known drummer, who at once repaired to the place and began to "drum up" recruits. Mr. Dunning next visited Mr. John B. Foster, then in an insurance office, who prepared enlistment papers; drawing lines for name, date, town and number, after which he wrote across the head the following:

"We the undersigned, citizens of the city of Bangor, in the first Division of the Militia of Maine, agree to form ourselves into a Company of Volunteers, and do severally enlist and bind ourselves to preform all the duties and be subject to all the requirements and provisions of an act, entitled "an act to organize and disciplin the Militia;" approved April 9th, 1851. And humbly pray your honorable body to grant our petition for the same according to the provisions of said act.

Enlistments began at once. As fast as men applied they were examined by two physicians, Dr. Mason and another whose name is unknown, after which, if they met the physical requirements, they were allowed to sign. This was on April 18th. On the morning of the 19th, the following advertisement appeared in the daily press:

VOLUNTEERS!

"A volunteer company is now forming for the purpose of offering their services to the Governor. Able bodied men who wish to serve their country, can report themselves at the Taylor store Office, over Finson's Market, Mercantile Square, Bangor."

In the same paper was printed the following local:

"Volunteers Ready.—It is hoped that the authorities at Augusta will order recruiting offices opened as soon as possible. Volunteers in large numbers are waiting for the opportunity to enlist; and it is felt that Maine's quota of troops ought not to be last in the field. Another call will probably be made in a short time, and several additional regiments ought to be enrolled and in readiness."

On the 18th five men only signed the paper, these being:

1. Levi Emerson, Bangor.
2. James M. Adams, "

3.
4. William Lyon,   Bangor,
5. Hiram E. Brackett,   "
6. Hiram B. French,   "

On the next day, however, the company was filled as follows:

7. Henry Warren,   Bangor.
8. Joshua Ray,   "
9. Geo. A. McClure,   "
10. Sabin Jordan,   "
11. Geo. M. Carlisle, Jr.,   "
12. Hall J. Libby,   "
13. Henry M. Cushman,   Brewer.
14. Horace B. Washburn,   "
15. C. W. Graves,   Bangor.
16. Frederick Burns,   "
17. Ruel Jewett,   "
18. Calvin S. Chapman,   "
19. Cyrus Rogers,   "
20. O. W. Pratt,   "
21. A. F. Barden,   "
22. Sam'l Dearborn, Blacksmith, Bangor.
23. E. L. Sterling,   "
24. George Barton,   Monroe.
25. Thomas Foster,   Bangor.
26. Abner Boden,   Brewer.
27. Freeman Norton,   Jonesport.
28. Elden Keen,   Bangor.
29. Henry Roach,   "
30. Abiathar Sandborn,   "
31. Otis F. Hooper,   "
32. Warren Day,   Veazie.

33. Geo. H. Phillips,   Veazie,
34. Harvey Emery,
35. Frank L. Sawyer,
36. John Toray,
37. Lyman E. Richardson, Wayne.
38. John O. Mara, 2d,   Bangor.
39. Philip Riley,   "
40. S. Wilson Smith,   St. Albans. (erased).
41. C. L. Downs,   Brewer.
42. George York,
43. R. W. Hall,   Knox.
44. Geo. S. Sullivan.
45. H. P. Crowell,
46. Roscoe G. Wally,
47. James Cambell,
48. John Moore,
49. C. N. Whitney.   Bangor.
50. John McNeil,
51. Albert S. Russ,   Oldtown.
52. Samuel Niam,
53. C. Barrett,   Hermon.
54. A. L. Page, Drummer, Brewer.
55. Washington I. Martin, Herman.
56. Daniel Tibbetts, Jr.,   "
57. Albert G. Furbush,   Hampden.
58. Albert J. Otis,   Nashua, N. H.
59. Charles A. Woodbury, Hermon.
60. William Berry,   Orington.
61. William Crocker,   Alton.
62. H. S. Willis, Jr.,   "
63. A. J. Snow,   Brewer.

64.	B. F. Willey,	Alton.
65.	H. V. Whitcomb.	
66.	Franklin Buliers,	Lewiston.
67.	Stephen W. Dawson.	
68.	Michael Hogan,	Bangor.
69.	Galen Worcester,	"
70.	Patrick Peters,	"
71.	Robert Quimby.	
72.	Philip Harback,	Bangor.
73.	Alexander Chase,	"
74.	John R. Thurston.	
75.	Ruel S. Clark,	Bangor.
76.	Charles W. Merrill,	"
77.	Alonzo B. Luce,	Newport.
78.	C. R. Robinson,	Sebec.
79.	John G. Joy,	"
80.	John P. Drummond,	Bangor.

These names have been taken from the original papers, each signature being different from all the others, and the spelling and names of towns are as they appear there. The papers are full, and there is no doubt but what on the night of April 19th, 1861, just seven days after the battle of Fort Sumpter, there was an entire company of able bodied men enlisted for the suppression of the rebellion. The author claims for Bangor the high honor of being the first city to offer a company of volunteers for the defence of the Union, for immediately on the completion of enlistments, a telegram was sent to Governor Washburn informing him of the fact that a company was ready and asking him if the State would provide quarters. Immediately came the reply:

"Rendezvous the troops, the State will pay."

Signed, ISRAEL WASHBURN, JR.

This roll varies somewhat from the Adjutant General's report, as two or three men dropped out when other papers were presented, while some were added, but the changes were slight and did not effect the Company as an organization. Immediately on receipt of the telegram from Gov. Washburn, Mr. Dunning secured an unoccupied store near the recruiting office, owned by Wiggins Hill, Esq., and here the new recruits repaired and entered upon their life as soldiers. The next day, April 20th, was fair and warm, all nature seemed gay, but the news from Washington and Baltimore were most discouraging. The Sixth Massachusetts had had a fight in the street of Baltimore, and it was reported that the Confederate forces were near Washington and the Capital was in danger. That day business was generally suspended, while men gathered about the corners, in stores and offices, and, with grave countenances discussed the situation. Was the Confederate army really a powerful one? If they should take Washington could they not march upon New York and Philadelphia? Had the North underated the strength of the enemy? These and other similar questions presented themselves to the minds of all, but did not swerve the determination of the patriotic men of the North to subdue the South. At three o'clock that afternoon the new Company left their barracks and marched, as only raw recruits can march, to the City Hall. The whole town was out to see them, and cheer after cheer went up as they passed through the streets. At the hall they were addressed by Hon. Wm. H. McCrillis and Representative Jewett. The people remained about the streets long after the soldiers had returned to their quarters, eagerly discussing every bit of news. The Bangor Band came out early in the evening, and, repairing to the roof of Wheelwright & Clark's block played "Yankee Doodle," "The Star Spangled Banner" and other national airs, which were loudly cheered.

There were in Bangor at this time, two Companies of State Militia: an Irish Company, known as the "Grattan Guards," and the "Bangor Light Infantry." The former wore gray uniforms while the latter had red coats and huge bear skin hats, the pants being of two kinds; one for service in the street and at musters, and the other for dress occasions. This Company was composed of a class of men, that would, in these days of quaint expressions, be termed the "top knots" of the town, or "tony." Both of these organizations early considered the question of enlistment, but the impulsive Irish blood which ran through the "Grattans" caused them to decide with but little deliberation. On April 22d, William Connors, their first lieutenant, called a meeting for that evening, "to transact business of vital importance." What is now known as "Merrill's stable on Columbia street was then known as the Gymnasium, and here the second recuiting office was opened, the advertisement reading as follows:

VOLUNTEERS
AT THE
GYMNASIUM.

A company of Volunteers will be formed immediately at the Gymnasium Hall, and drilled *day and night* by the best officers in the city.

While these events were transpiring the City Council had been busy. The Saturday night previous they had authorized the Mayor to draw on the contingent fund for furnishing barracks and providing enlisted men with supplies, and steps were at once taken to put the arsenal on Essex street in good condition. The "Grattan Guards" did have "business of vital importance" for that night; they elected as officers:

Captain, John Carroll; 1st Lieut., Henry Casey; 2d Lieut., M.

J. Sweeney; 3d Lieut., P. Hurley, and then these patriotic Irishmen voted *unanimously* "to tender their services for the defence of the country."

While men were eagerly coming forward to enlist, others, possessed of wealth, were giving freely. A queston was raised as to how the wife and children of a man should be cared for in his absence. It was quickly settled. Samuel D. Thurston, Esq., and others, drew up and circulated the following paper.

"The subscribers hereto agree to pay the amounts severally subscribed to raise a fund for the benefit of the families of the persons volunteering for present emergencies of the country, and we hereby appoint S. P. Strickland, Aaron A. Wing, J. B. Foster and George Stetson, as a committee to collect and disburse the funds."

BANGOR, April 20th, 1861.

The following named persons gave two hundred dollars each:

George Stetson, Isaiah Stetson, Jas. O'Donohue, Timothy Field, G. K. Jewett, S. P. Strickland, W. P. Wingate, Jason Weeks, Abram Woodard, Sam'l F. Hersey, Thos. A. White, John S. Chadwick, S. Blake, Charles Stetson, G. W. Pickering, E. L. Hamlin, Wiggins Hill, Wheelwright & Clark, Sam'l Veazie, Estes & Whittier.

The following gave one hundred dollars:

Sam'l H. Dale, Sam'l H. Dale, Pres., James Dunning, A. A. Wing, Palmer & Johnson, Henry E. Prentiss, F. Muzzy & Co , Jas. B. Fiske, Thos. J. Stewart, W. A. Blake, W. H. Smith, Michael Schwartz, Morse & Co., David R. Stockwell, Jonathan Eddy, Jas. Littlefield, C. P. Brown, M. Giddings, N. C. Ayer & Co., John Wyman, Thos. N. Egery, Thurston & Metcalf, H. Strickland, Timothy Crosby, Nath'l Harlow, John Lane, Wm. Adams.

Contributors to the fifty dollar list were:

Sylvanus Rich, Charles Hayward, Chas. E. Phillips, D. Bugbee, Manson & Williams, T. W. Baldwin, Thos. A. Taylor, Sidney Thaxter, A. P. Atwood, Nathan Hopkins, B. B. Farnsworth, S. J. Murphy, Jabez True, James S. Rowe, H. M. Plaisted, Albert W. Paine, John A. Peters, Joseph Carr, Stickney & Roberts, Burleigh Pease, Geo. C. Pickering, Albert Emerson, Caleb Billings, S. P. Bradbury & Co., R. G. A. Freeman, Jas. McLaughlin, Mrs. Gilbert Atwood, Lydia A. Bartlett.

Smaller sums ranging from fifty dollars down to one dollar were given by:

E. A. Upton, W. S. Dennett, J. N. Bowler, Geo. L. Phillips, E. N. Fogg, F. M. Sabine, James Walker, Wm. T. Pearson, E. H. & H. Rollins, James Thissell, Eben Blunt, G. P. Smith, R. Davis, D. H. Kimball, J. O. B. Darling, Shaw & Merrill, A. G. Wakefield, O. R. Patch, J. M. & R. Hodgkins, Wm. Arnold, F. H. Hodgman, Jas. Bartlett, Chas. K. Miller, John L. Crosby, J. W. P. Frost, H. Bartlett, Wm. Boyd, H. G. Thaxter, E. T. Fox, Seth Paine, W. J. Loud, Wheeler & Lynde, Abram Moor, S. S. Stevens, Howe & Yeaton, H. B. Stewart, A. Woodard, S. H. Boardman, M Gilligan, S. B. Morrison, A. Leighton & Co., Farris & Webb, C. S. Bragg, Sam'l B. Stone, S. T. Pearson, I. Parsons, I. R. Clark, B. F. Bradbury, A. R. Hallowell, E. F. Duren, H. H. Fogg, F. A. Wilson, E W. Flagg, Patrick Wall, Amos Stickney, N. H. Colton, G. W. Stevens, S. C. Hatch, J. C. White, E. C. Smart, G. W. Larrabee, E. D. Godfred, I. S. Johnson, A. Thompson, R. H. Hitchborn, Geo. Palmer, W. O. Ayer, Charles Hale, Z. S. Patten, Cyrus Arnold, Thompkins & Morris, P. M. Whitman, George Fitz, Taylor Durgin, James Allen, Henry A. Butler, A. Drummond, Gardner Bragdon, A. Holton, David Fuller, V. L. Catinaud, John S. Kimball, N. S. Harlow, Dr. McRuer, Fred S. French,

Hooper Chase, A. P. Guild, Jas. Smith, Jr., Jonas Cutting, J. F. Robinson, A. S. French, A. C. Flint, Chas. B. Abbott, Thos. J. Witherly, Jno. Batchelder, J. P. Wyman, Dillingham & Smith, S. T. Chase, Lemuel Bradford, Geo. Wellington, D. P. Wingate, Jas. Bryant, C. F. Smith, Sam'l Gurnsey, Albert Smith, N. H. Parsons, N. Kittredge, M. T. Stickney, N. H. Dillingham, W. L. Whitney, G. W. Whitney, J. P. Veazie, John L. Cutler, Geo. Chalmers, Henry Garland, N. P. Pendleton, T. W. Porter, J. Bright, Geo. H. Bartlett, F. Garland, Elias Merrill, Chas. Hight, Wm. H. McCrillis, N. D. Folsom, Geo. A. Thatcher, Josiah Towle, J. Mason, J. B. Foster, J. C. Mitchell, Jona' Gilman, E. G. Thurston, R. B. Dunning, Edwin Chick, Nathan W. Chase, T. S. Dodd, C. H. Dunning, Solo' Parsons, Samuel Fletcher, S. F. Jones, Aaron Babb, John Goodell, Jr., W. T. Pierce, N. H. Bishop, Sam'l Reynolds, A. S. Sweet, Dickey & Fifield, Amos Jones, Seth Emery, J. N. Boynton, J. H. Clergue, E. Call, Cyrus Goss, Isaac M. Bragg, John E. Godfrey, T. A. Hill, Ira Goodhue, S. F. Humphrey, Jacob McGaw, Amory Battles, C. C. Everett, Wm. T. Hilliard, A. K. P. Small, Ira Chamberlain, G. W. Thompson, J. G. Dummer, Thos. Trickey, W. F. Brann, W. H. Perry, Thos. Mason, John Patten, R. Haskins, O. P. Sawtelle, W. S. Pattee, J. S. Patten, J. & G. Hemmingway, J. P. Bent, M. H. Tarbox, C. G. Porter, W. S. Hellier & Co., J. N. Downe, George Shepard, Enoch Pond, Wm. Mann, D. T. Smith, Sam'l Harris, A. Dalton, Ira Dunbar, John Webster, I. Goodwin, G. W. Spratt, J. Forbes, John Andrews, S. Lawton, L. Stockwell, E. G. Gilman, Henry Gillan, C. P., B. Plummer, John Dole, J. A. Bacon, John B. Carr, James McLaughlin, Addie V. Merrill, A. F. Chase, Sam'l G. Harlow, Wm. S. Whitman, L. E. Sabine, Wm. Flowers, Benj. Ireland.

This list contains the names of nearly all of the business men of Bangor, who could give and who were in sympathy with the Government. As the names are read over, some idea of the work of "Old Father Time" in twenty-five years, can be gained. Others yet living have moved to distant parts, yet have a home here in the hearts of their associates, during the dark days of '61, '62 and '63.

If it were possible, the women of Bangor were more excited than the men. Their husbands, fathers, brothers and lovers were enlisting and making active preparation to leave for the South. While they shed many tears in secret, they were all courage in public, and rendered much assistance. Many articles of clothing were needed, which neither the State nor the United States could furnish at that time, and the patriotic women worked with willing hands to furnish them. The following notice was issued.

LADIES ATTENTION!

All ladies wishing to enlist to make up clothing for the volunteers, are requested to meet at rooms over Fenno & Hale's store, at any time during Tuesday, April 23.

MRS. S. F. HERSEY,
MRS. T. N. EGERY.

Charles Hale kept then at 24 Main street, and here accommodations were furnished for fifty ladies and free use of sewing machines tendered. For a long time all available space was occupied, while other ladies made generous contributions of material. Think of it! Delicate women sat there, day after day, gradually forming from the shapeless mass of cloth, garments for loved ones; garments soon to be rent by the bullet or the bayonet, and drenched, may be, with the life current of him so dear to the maker. No wonder the men of the land were fighters! How could they be otherwise when the women set them such an example of heroism?

When the war broke out, Daniel Chaplin was a clerk in the store of Thurston and Metcalf. During the forenoon of Monday, April 22, he tendered his resignation, saying he was going over to Exchange street and open a recruiting office. He did so, establishing himself next to Phillips & Witherly's store. Previously he had held a commission as Captain in the State Militia, under Governor Fairfield. Wednesday noon, or about forty-eight hours after opening the office, his company had its required number. About the same time, Capt. Michael Boyce, once Commander of the Grattan Guards, established an office. There were now in all seven recruiting offices open, including the ex Tiger and Amory Associates. The country round about had heard the news of war, and stalwart men were coming in from all directions, anxious to join the ranks. Soon after the meeting of the Legislature, there arrived from Augusta papers authorizing the enlisting of men in the name of the State of Maine. Previous to this, such men as had been enrolled, were volunteers only, waiting to be accepted. Thomas A. Taylor seems to have been the one commissioned by Gov. Washburn, as State enlisting officer, as he issued the following:

ATTENTION!
VOLUNTEERS WANTED
BY
AUTHORITY OF THE STATE.

When mustered into the service of the United States, a bounty of $22.00 will be paid, and one month's pay.

Call at Taylor's old store, Mercantile Square, and at Boyce's, corner State and Exchange streets.

T. A. TAYLOR, Enlisting Officer.

CHAPTER III.

Enlistments Continued—The Ex Tiger And Amory Associates—The Home Guards—"Bangor May Now Fearlessly Face A Frowning World"—The Cavalry And The Sons Of Temperance—Maine On A War Footing—The First Regiment—The Governor's Proclamation—Division And Regimental Orders—Maj. Gen. Butler, of Maine—He Issues A Corpulent Proclamation—The Towns' Round About—Grand Meetings, Stirring Speeches, And Odd But Earnest Resolutions.

Enlistments continued and volunteers were plenty. Among other bodies of men who offered their services, were the Ex-Tiger and Amory Associates. This organization was formerly the "Tiger" hand engine company, but, owing to some trouble with the Marshal, had been disbanded as such, but kept up their organization, and early in April met in their rooms in Exchange Block, voted to fill their ranks and tender their services. A recruiting office was opened at their rooms, and at an election of officers held later, Daniel Sargent, of Brewer, was made Captain; Edward L. Getchell 1st Lieut.; Ralph Morse 2d Lieut., and Wm. H. S. Lawrence, Orderly. They entered the Second Maine as Company "G."

Strange as it may now appear, there seemed to have been good reasons for the establishment of a Home Guard, and with this object in view, citizens gathered at City Hall April 20th, to talk the matter over. Samuel D. Thurston, Esq., called the meeting to order, after which Charles Hayward, Esq., was chosen Chairman with John L. Crosby, Esq., as Secretary. On motion of John B. Foster, Esq., a committee of seven, consisting of John B. Foster, Lewis Goodwin, John P. Bent, T. W. Porter, J. D. Thurston, Charles P. Stetson and David Bugbee were appointed to make all necessary arrangements "for forming the Company, equipping the same, and putting it on a war footing forthwith, with instructions to report at the next meeting." S. D. Thurston made a motion which was carried: "that the company go into drill at once—that is, the company now present—and A. Kirkpatrick was chosen Captain; John P. Bent, 1st Lieut.; Dr. N. S. Harlow, 2d Lieut. The *Whig*, of the following day, said of the drill: "The Company were drilled according to Scott's Tactics, and the evolutions were performed with remarkable precision. With such a defense Bangor may fearlessly face a frowning world." It is quite evident that they were in earnest, for on April 23 they published the following advertisement:

"All persons who have signed the papers agreeing to meet as citizens, and, under the competent drill officer, practice and learn Military Tactics, are hereby notified to meet for preliminary business at City Hall, Tuesday P. M., at 4 o'clock. Signed: S. D. Thurston, T. J. Stewart, S. H. Dale, J. S. Wheelwright, J. B. Foster, B. B. Farnsworth, James Littlefield, N. S. Harlow, J. B. Fiske, Sidney Thaxter, Charles Haywood, and 90 others. The same day, Company "A" of the cavalry, voted to tender their services, and the Sons of Temperance, then a strong body, voted to raise a company, and soon after opened a recruiting office in Johnson's Hall.

It will be remembered that Governor Washburn had issued a proclamation calling upon senators and representatives to meet in their respective chambers in the Capitol, April 22d. At this session Maine was put on a war footing, and a bill was passed authorizing Governor Washburn to call out ten regiments, not exceeding one thousand men each, to be enrolled for two years, to be in constant readiness to move at a moments warning. The act also authorized the raising of one million dollars, if necessary, for military purposes; authorized cities and towns to relieve the families of soldiers without the usual disabilities in such cases; also staying pending suits and forbade future suits against volunteers until the close of the war. Existing laws were so amended as to enable the Governor to order the State Militia, in case of emergency, to any point out of the State. Governor Washburn immediately issued his proclamation calling for 10,000 volunteers—Companies not to have less than fifty, nor more than eighty-five privates—these to be over eighteen and under forty-five years of age, and captains were ordered to fill their ranks at once, discharging all who could not meet the age requirements or who were not physically competent. He also gave notice that the first ten companies organized as above—except that no company would be allowed over sixty-four privates—would be immediately concentrated at Portland where equipment would be completed, after which they would be mustered into the service of the United States as a regiment of Infantry.

The State of Massachusetts had a General Butler and Maine had one too. Nearly every resident of Bangor twenty-five years ago, knew Major General James H. Butler, of the Maine Militia, and, in order that the reader may understand just where he stood in military circles, his first Division Order is given.

STATE OF MAINE.

HEADQUARTERS FIRST DIVISION, BANGOR, April 20th, 1861. Division Order, No. 1.

The present and unprecedented emergency which calls into immediate exercise a portion of the physical powers of the United States, is too well known and understood to require any explanation to the troops composing this Division.

The President of the United States in the discharge of his duty, has called upon the Commander-in-chief of this State, to furnish him, without delay, with one Regiment of Infantry, and Riflemen, of ten Companies, and an order to detach a portion of the troops from this Division may be immediately expected, unless it should be rendered unnecessary by the alacrity and highly commendable zeal with which voluntary services are tendered.

The prompt action of the Commander-in-chief is delayed a few days, only on account of a defect in the Militia Law of the State. To remedy this defect, the Legislature will meet on the 22d, soon after which blank rolls for enlistment will be distributed, for the accommodation of all those who may wish to enroll their names upon the list of fame, and no suitable man need entertain fears of being rejected. They are assured that the Commander-in-chief has, in a manner highly becoming his important station and dignity of the State, tendered to the President of the United States, five full regiments, if so many should be needed.

Col. Chas. D. Jameson will forthwith promulgate this order throughout his command, and all detached companies in this Division, all of which, will be held in a constant state of readiness, prepared to carry into effect any subsequent order that may be issued by the Commander-in-chief.

Artillery Companies will hold themselves in readiness to serve as Infantry.

To this end he will cause to be promptly filled any and all vacancies of officers that now exist, and such as may happen from time to time within his command, without further orders from the Chief of Division.

The Major General, having appointed James Dunning, Esq., of Bangor, Division Inspector, with the rank of Lieut. Colonel, and Charles E. Dole, Esq., of Brewer, and Jos. L. Smith, Esq., of Oldtown, Aides-de-Camps, with the rank of Major, and each having been duly commissioned as such, they will be obeyed and respected accordingly.

By Major General JAMES H. BUTLER.

THOS. HERSEY, Division Quartermaster, Acting Orderly Aid.

This corpulent but patriotic document was productive of others, Order No. 2 reading as follows:

STATE OF MAINE.
FIRST DIVISION V. M. M. HEADQUARTERS,
BANGOR, April 24th, 1861.

Division Order No. 2.

To Charles D. Jameson, commanding First Regiment, First Infantry.

You will forthwith promulgate throughout your command the foregoing order, and cause it to be carried into effect immediately, and with the utmost energy. By order of the Major General.

CHARLES E. DOLE, Aide-de-Camp.

HEADQUARTERS FIRST REG., FIRST DIV., V. M. M.,
BANGOR, April 24th, 1861.

Pursuant to the foregoing Division Order, No 2, commanders of companies attached to this Regiment, tendering their services to the Commander-in-chief, will forthwith recruit their companies to the requisite number, and report the same to me, when they will be immediately ordered into camp of instruction.

C. D. JAMESON, Col. 1st Regiment V. M. M.

During this time the other cities and towns in Eastern Maine were equally busy; Calais voted to raise $5,000 in addition to $2,000 already given, and Messrs. Pike, Chase, Peabody, Whitney and Robbins were made a committee. Atkinson raised a flag pole, ninety-two feet in height, and on that occasion had music from the Charleston Band. Speeches were made by J H. Ramsdell, C. Brown and F. M. Marden. Oldtown voted $5,000, while Brewer gave the same day $3,000. Brewer also in one day subscribed $1,200 for a relief fund. Hampden had some grand rallies. On one occasion at Nealey's Corner, where a liberty pole was raised, the drummer—so the paper stated—" was a young lady who handled the sticks with science and enthusiasm." In another part of the town, Hon. Hannibal Hamlin addressed a meeting, saying: " While I deplore the sad condition of my country, yet I say there should be no temporizing, no going back in this contest between Law and Order, and Anarchy and Treason. I am willing to lay down my life should the sacrifice be necessary." At Exeter on a similar occasion, speeches were made by A. C. Smith, B. H. Mace and Thomas Garnsey, of Bangor, Lewis Barker of Stetson and others, and it was then *Resolved*—" That flinging our National banner to the breeze, we pledge ourselves to maintain its honor unsullied and to pray, pay or fight for the Union."

Resolved—"That he who is not for us is against us." Corinth was wide awake, and in one day 54 men enlisted there. John Morrison subscribed $1,000 for families of volunteers, and tendered the country the use of a six horse team. Ellsworth turned out one thousand strong April 29th, and listened to speeches by Arno Wiswell, J. S. Rice, Charles Hamlin, T. C. Woodman and N. K. Sawyer.

Resolved—"That we hold to-day the same contempt and scorn for Tories and Traitors of the North, as did our fathers those of 1776." There was a big Union meeting in Foxcraft, on the 27th, presided over by Hon. A. M. Robinson, with Joseph Chase, Hon. Thomas Pullen, Hon. Orias Blanchard, Plynn Clark, Timothy Hasseltine, Jas. M. Weymouth, Maj. C. H. B. Woodbury, Charles E. Kimball, Steadman Kendall, P. H. Rice, Hon. Nimrod Hinds and Stephen Drake as vice-presidents. Many speeches were made and strong resolutions adopted. While there, the Corinth Band voted to furnish music for flag raisings free at "any place this side of New Orleans. Houlton, Frankfort, Winterport, and in fact about all the towns held meetings with which nearly all the people were in full accord.

CHAPTER IV.

States Rights Men, Timid Men and Copperheads—The Stars And Stripes Everywhere—Forming of The First Regiment—Captain Chaplin's Company Organize—Arrival of The Castine Company—A Grand Military Display—Forming of The Second Regiment. Complete List of Officers—A Sketch of Each Company.

There was in this section, as well as in other parts of the North, a class of men known as "States Rights Men," who held to the idea that the South should be allowed to withdraw from the Union if they chose. Some of them no doubt were honest in their belief; others joined them thinking it better that a separation take place and thus avoid civil war, while still others, filled with a bitter hatred of Lincoln and his party, gave their sympathy and, during the long war which followed, substantial aid to the enemy. Many of the States Rights men and the timid ones afterwards marched to the "step of the Union," but the remainder, known as "Copperheads," continued to give their support all through the dark days to those seeking to overthrow the republic. These men and their families became marked people, were ostracized and ignored by the loyal sons and daughters of Eastern

Maine, and were made to feel, in various ways, that they were held in great contempt by the masses. In these times of peace it is hardly possible to realize to what a state of excitement our business men, as well as the mothers, wives and daughters of the city, were wrought. There was a mania for displaying the stars and stripes, and the absence of the red, white and blue, in or about a dwelling or store, made the place conspicuous, and at once stamped those controlling it as disloyal. The fever was caught by the children of our schools, and many of the little ones went daily to their studies, wearing, in some shape, the colors of the Union. April 25th, the young ladies connected with the High School, raised a flag in Abbott Square, and the attendance at the time seems to show the enthusiasm of the people. The Bangor Band was there and played national tunes, and between these J. J. Wingate's Flying Artillery fired salutes. The roar of cannon in those days seems to have been like the tunes of the band, sweet music to the ear.

The affair in Abbott Square took place at noon. At one o'clock the spectators, band and Artillery, marched down to the Penobscot Exchange, where Mr. Abram Woodward displayed the national flag, and speeches were made by Geo. W. Ladd and others. At two o'clock the same day, Mr. Chaplin's new company turned out, sixty-four strong, and marched to the head of Court street, where another flag was given to the April breeze, and speeches were made by A. W. Paine, Esq., J. W. Perkins and others. That day W. A. Blake, A. M. Roberts and Major Hayford raised flags, as did many others.

The State officials were very busy. It had been decided that the first regiment from Maine should be taken from Portland and the second from Bangor. Accordingly five Portland, two Lewiston companies, and one each from the towns of Auburn, Norway and Kittery were formed into what was known as the First Regiment, and orders were sent from Washington to hold themselves in readiness to march to Boston on Monday, the 29th. This was a disappointment to the Bangor men, who were filled with the commendable desire to be the first in the field, but although they were disappointed in this, it will be seen they were ahead of the First at the finish.

On the 25th of April, Chaplin's Company of volunteers was organized with full ranks. They chose the following officers: Captain, Daniel Chaplin; 1st Lieut., A. P. Wilson; 2d Lieut., Warren H. Boynton. They then sent the roll to the Governor and anxiously awaited United States orders. At this time they were in camp at the State Arsenal on Essex street, and with them were Capt. Emerson's company, the "Bangor Light Infantry," and Ex-Tiger and Amory Associates."

These formed the skeleton of what was afterwards the famous Second Maine. On Saturday, April 27th, the "Castine Light Infantry, 70 men, marched to Bucksport, where they were taken on board the steamer "M. Sanford" and brought to Bangor. They were under the command of Capt. S. K. Devreaux, and fourth Lieutenant, J. B. Wilson, the other positions not being filled. The Sanford was handsomely decorated with national flags, and, on her arrival was greeted with cheers from the immense crowd on the wharf. The "Bangor Light Infantry," "Grattan Guards," with the "Ex-Tiger and Amory Associates," all under the command of Major C. W. Roberts, and headed by the Bangor Band, the whole forming a solid body of nearly 400 men, did escort duty, and amid the booming of cannon, the cheering by the excited throng which followed, and the waving of banners, marched to the Arsenal. Up to this time the "Queen City" had never witnessed so warlike a display.

It stirred the already heated blood of many a youngster, and large additions were made that day on the rolls in the various recruiting offices. The company from Castine was joined the next day by twenty additional members, and was the largest on the field

Other companies were added until there were sufficient to form what was to be known as the Second Maine, and the following is the return of original Field and Staff officers, as well as commissioned and non-commissioned officers of each company:

CHARLES D. JAMESON, Colonel.
CHARLES W. ROBERTS, Lieut. Colonel.
GEORGE VARNEY, Major.
JOHN E. REYNOLDS, Adjutant.
CHARLES V. LORD, Quartermaster.
W. H. ALLEN, Surgeon.
AUGUSTUS C. HAMLIN, Asst. Surgeon.
JOHN F. MINES, Chaplain.
LUTHER A. PIERCE, Quarter Master's Sergeant.
EDWARD L. APPLETON, Sergeant Major.
ALDEN L. PALMER, Hospital Steward.

COMPANY A., SECOND MAINE.

Commissioned Officers.—Hermon Bartlett, Rinaldo B. Wiggin, James Deaneo.

Sergeants.—John Q. A. Lancey, Charles J. Hall, Charles W. B. Miller, William J. Deaneo.

Corporals.—Hartsorn P. Crowell, John C. Harmon, Samuel B. Hinckley, Warren H. Orcott.

COMPANY B.

Commissioned Officers.—Seth K. Deveraux, Charles W. Tilden, David D. Wardwell.

Brig.-Gen. Chas. D. Jameson.

Sergeants.—James C. Collins, Elisha S. Perkins, Geo. I. Brown, Joseph H. Sylvester.

Corporals.—Geo. E. Noyes, Richard Tibbetts, Simeon C. Murch, Charles Bridges.

COMPANY C.

Commissioned Officers.—Elisha N. Jones, John K. Skinner, Eliphalet S. Morrill.

Sergeants.—William R. Currier, Francis P. Hall, James Nicholson, Lincoln Graves.

Corporals.—James M. Simpson, Cyrus Swett, Edwin Currier, Charles W. Merrill.

COMPANY D.

Commissioned Officers.—John S. Sampson, Walter W. Sturtevant, Sumner R. Kittredge.

Sergeants.—Samuel V. Millett, Stephen D. Millett, James P. Kittredge, John H. Kittredge.

Corporals.—Richard A. Monroe, Lewis R. Haskell, John R. Stanchfield, Charles S. Leonard.

COMPANY E.

Commissioned Officers.—Levi Emerson, James W. Adams, Lyman E. Richardson.

Sergeants.—Thomas Foster, James L. Rowe, Colin L. Downes, John J. Randall.

Corporals.—Henry M. Cushman, Edwin L. Sterling, Ruel S. Clark, Hiram B. French.

COMPANY F.

Commissioned Officers.—Daniel Chaplin, Albion P. Wilson Warren H. Boynton.

Sergeants.—George W. Brown, Benjamin D. Whitney, Arthur C. Whitcomb, Charles Able.

Corporals.—George F. Whitney, Thomas H. Wooster, John S. Small, Jeremiah B. Atkins.

Company G.

Commissioned Officers.—Frederick Meinicke, Augustus Farnham, Frank A. Garnsey.

Sergeants.—George E. Holt, Albert M. Jackson, Horatio Staples, Joseph B. Forbes.

Corporals.—Stover B. Gross, Seth B. Ramsdell, John B. York, David Reevil.

Company H.

Commissioned Officers.—Daniel F. Sargent, Edward L. Getchell, Ralph W. Morse.

Sergeants.—William H. S. Lawrence, Daniel Quimby, Jr., William P. Holden, Christopher S. Gorham.

Corporals.—Charles Smith, Elbridge F. Haskell, Henry Schmell, Wm. H. Johnson.

Company I.

Commissioned Officers.—John Carroll, Henry Casey, Miles J. Sweeney.

Sergeants.—Richard Kelleher, Patrick J. Farrell, Michæl Crowley, Henry Granville.

Corporals.—Peter Mogan, William Twomey, William H. Boyce, Dennis Mahoney.

Company K.

Commissioned Officers.—Fernando C. Foss, Albert G. Fellows, Albert L. Cowan.

Sergeants.—John C. Quimby, William H. Hanson, George A. McLellan, Daniel Staples.

Corporals.—Charles J. Ellis, Americus W. Moore, Joseph A. Burlingham, Morison J. Folsom.

Company "A" contained eighty-one privates, thirty-seven of them being natives of Bangor, the balance coming from surrounding towns.

Company "B" was the Castine company, and contained sixty-five privates, four being from Bangor, while nearly all the rest came from Castine and towns along the coast.

Company "C" had sixty-one privates and two musicians, eleven being from Bangor. This company represented through its privates no less than twenty-four towns in the State. The first death that occurred in the regiment was that of Lorenzo Benner, a member of this company, a native of Palermo, this State, who died June 3d. Company "D" was the Milo company. All the officers and the single musician were from that town, as were also thirty-five of the eighty-four privates, the balance coming from adjoining places. They were large and finely formed men, inured to toil, and therefore well fitted for the hardships of the campaign upon which they were about to enter. Company "E," the first to enlist in Bangor, had ninety-one privates, new men having been taken in after the original company had been accepted. Company "F" had eighty-three privates, but only thirteen were Bangorians. This was the company raised by Capt. Chaplain in forty-eight hours, and in it were represented: Aurora, Hampden, Hermon, Carmel, Exeter, Veazie, Eddington, Bradford, Kenduskeag, Etna, Pittsfield, Glenburn, Leavant, Dixmont, Brewer, Winterport, Stetson, Bradley, Oldtown, Newport and Freedom, showing that the country lads were coming in from all directions at the time the company was formed. Company "G" had eighty-seven privates, forty being from Bangor as were also all of its officers. Company "H" had eighty-six privates, forty-six being from Bangor and twenty-three from Oldtown. Save Capt. Sargent all the officers were from Bangor. Company "I" was a Bangor company in every sense of the word. All officers were from that city, while of the eighty-five stalwarts who marched away, forty-eight claimed the Queen City as their home. Of the remainder, Bradley, Veazie, New York, Lincoln, Carmel and Etna furnished one each; Milford two; Portland eleven; Houlton eight, while the remainder are not credited to any town.

Company "K" was a miscellaneous collection of seventy-eight privates, about forty-three cities and towns being represented, while its officers were from Bangor, Oldtown and Stillwater. The whole force of the Second Maine when they marched away, was:

Field and Staff Officers,	11
Commissioned Officers,	80
Sergeants,	40
Corporals,	40
Musicians,	11
Privates,	840
Total,	972

CHAPTER V.

The Second Maine In Camp—How The Men Lived—Preparations For A Southern "Tour"—Wheelwright & Clark Contract To Furnish Uniforms—The Women Give Substantial Aid—Extracts From The Daily Press—What Each Soldier Had—The Camp On Essex Street—Military Ardor In Business Circles—Red, White And Blue Letter Paper—Odd Advertisements—Linen Handkerchiefs And Bandages—The Regiment Ordered To The Front.

Near the Arsenal on Essex street, barracks were erected for a portion of the troops, while others slept in the building which was lined along its sides with rude bunks. Each company had a company cook, and was supplied with provisions by the State. The officers had as caterer, an old and well known citizen of Bangor, named Murray, who owned for many years a famous restaurant. The men were kept well in hand, and, under the instructions of capable drill masters, made rapid progress. Adjutant John Reynolds was a proficient military man in those days, and he took charge of nine companies, while Lient. Palmer drilled Capt. Emerson's company. Few of the men had any idea of what was in store for them, yet they were anxious to learn, having a desire to make a good showing in the large cities which they expected to visit during their three months' "tour."

While they were thus engaged in perfecting themselves, Gov. Washburn and other State officials were very busy in providing clothing and arms. The firm of Wheelwright & Clark took a contract for uniforms, which were made of stout cadet grey, similar in color to that worn by the Confederates. As it afterwards proved, this similarity of appearance caused many awkward mistakes on the field of battle, as enemies often mingled together, or were near each other, each supposing themselves to be in the presence of their comrades. Messrs. Wheelwright & Clark sub-let contracts to all the tailors in the city, hired all available help, and then gave the balance to the lady volunteers sewing at City Hall. Here many of the leading women of Bangor gathered day after day. The hall was divided into sections, each being placed in charge of some competent person, and, by a tacit understanding, the money paid them was used to provide articles deemed necessary for the soldiers, but not furnished by the State.

A local in the Whig & Courier said: "There are thirty-two hundred garments, besides beds, &c., to be made for our soldiers. At the present rate of progress, more than a fortnight must elapse before the work is finished, and yet there are a large number of ladies at work, and some of those who began early are nearly sick with the labor and care which they have assumed. We are persuaded that this fact needs only to be known, to inspire hundreds of hearts in this city, and the neighboring towns, to offer their ready and willing help in the crisis."

"We presume it is understood that very good pay is offered by the Government for the making of flannel shirts, and, although this work is largely given out to the poor, yet more remain to be done than *can be hired*."

"Many more volunteers will be welcome to work at the City Hall, to work on cotton flannel shirts and drawers, the pants first designed to be made there having been withdrawn—and probably other halls in the city could easily be obtained for the purpose, if the City Hall should be full."

The State provided for each private, 1 cap and pompon, 1 eagle and ring, 1 pair trousers, 1 coat, 2 pairs grey flannel drawers and shirts, 1 pair shoes, 1 overcoat, 1 blanket, 1 knapsack with straps, 1 canteen with straps and 1 haversack; and one sash was allowed to the orderly of each company. No provision was made for uniforms for commissioned officers; they were allowed to draw from the Quartermaster's department, having the same charged to them.

Of course the camp of the regiment was an attractive spot, not only for the relatives and friends of the volunteers, but for the citizens in general and the small boy in particular. Each pleasant day large crowds gathered, and with much interest watched the movements of the men, witnessed the drill, and many an admiring glance was given the stalwart youths as they sauntered to and fro before their barracks, clad in their smart uniforms. When an officer, dressed in his new suit came down town, he at once became the centre of an admiring throng, and many of the stay-at-homes envied him. Alas! Many of them were never seen again, for before that summer had ended their bodies lay in unknown graves, or wasted away in rebel prisons.

Not only was the display warlike out on Essex street, but a military ardor prevaded the business and even the domestic circles. Men talked war, clamored for haste on the part of the Government, and even in the advertisements in the daily press the war was made a prominent feature. Here are some samples of advertising:

"The steamer M. Sanford will transport troops and munitions of war, and any authorized agents on business connected therewith, between Bangor and Boston, and all intermediate landings, *free of charge.*" LOOMIS TAYLOR, Agt.

* * * * * * *

"Red, White and Blue note paper for sale by,
E. F. DUREN."

* * * * * * *

"Envelopes with the United States Flag printed upon them for sale by, E. F. DUREN.

F. Meinecke headed an advertisement, "Victory or Death," and announced that he should dispose of his stock of embroidery cheap as he was "Going To War!"

Messrs. Stickney and Roberts declare the "Spirit of '76 still lives;" Thomas A. White had bales of "Mixed Twilled Flannel" for the army; Stone & Tenney say they are "Reinforced and Provisioned;" S. C. Hatch asks all to "Stand By The Flag;" while many other merchants employed cuts to attract attention and establish their loyalty. The following special notice will show that the boys of the Second Maine were given the best of everything.

"Ladies who are disposed to donate handkerchiefs, (all linen) and towels, for the use of the volunteers, are requested to leave them with the ladies of the Sewing Circle, over the store of Charles Hale, 24 Main street, at any time during the week."

There was also donated to the regiment, one to each man, officer and private alike, a little package not pleasant to contemplate, being suggestive of the grim side of war. These were known as "Pledgets" and "Bandages." The former was a piece of old linen or soft cotton, twelve or fifteen inches square, while the bandages consisted of a package of linen of the following shapes:

4 bandages 1 inch wide and 1 yard long,
6 " 2 " " " 3 " "
8 " 3 " " " 5 " "
4 " 4 " " " 7 " "

Many days did not pass before these came to be of use, for ere three months had rolled away, the men were hurled into a mighty battle—a battle of raw recruits, it is true—yet one in which human blood flowed freely, some of it blood that carried with it the life spark, and which could not have been checked by all these neat packages of bandages, even had the fair ones who made them in the far off Northern home, been there to have applied them.

On Saturday, May 11th, orders were received for the Second Regiment to leave by rail on Tuesday, May 14th, for New York, and it was understood that it would at once proceed to Washington. Gen. Hersey was commissioned as Paymaster, and on Monday paid the bounty money to the men. On the receipt of the order, the nature of which was quickly known throughout the city, the troops began preparations to leave. On Sunday, large numbers of our citizens gathered about Camp Washburn, while from the surrounding towns, relatives of the soldiers, as well as the curious, came in crowds. The city was full of strangers, and, as no one dreamed at that time of a long and bloody war, all were in a happy mood, save here and there some timid wife or loving mother, who, with sober face, talked of what "might happen." Many were the earnest prayers sent up to Him who held the destiny of the nation in His hand, by these loving ones, that all might return safe again, but, alas for them! All were not answered.

CHAPTER VI.

Off For The War—Presentation Of The Flag—Vice-President Hamlin's Address—Scenes At The Station—Reception At Augusta—The Trip To New York—A Grand Reception There—On Board The Transport—Measles Break Out—In Camp At Willett's Point—Trouble Regarding Enlistment Papers—On To Washington.

The morning of May 14 was a cloudy one, and the heavy leaden banks along the horizon suggested rain. At 8 o'clock the Second Maine Regiment, which then as now, held a warm place in the heart of every Bangorian, took up its line of march from Camp Washburn. Headed by the Bangor Cornet Band they, with steady step and proud bearing, marched down Essex and into Broadway as far as the First Parish Church. From the starting point to the church they marched along a lane of sad but exciting humanity. Although our city was soon to see other exciting and sad days—days when staid old men rushed through the streets half mad and crying aloud for vengeance—she had never before in her history been so wrought up as on that May 14th. The time had come. The war, heretofore, had been a thing of news, brought from a distance by the electric current and the mail. But now! The Second was going, yes, had already started for the front. Would they go into battle? Would they ever return, and when? Who among that gallant body of men were fated to die on Southern soil, and who would return and how? These were the questions asked by every thoughtful one. No wonder the people of Bangor were excited, yet little did they dream of the scenes of death and carnage through which their friends were to pass.

The house of Mrs. Jas. Crosby was handsomely decorated with flags that morning, and from its steps Miss McRuer made the regiment a present of a handsome American flag, after being introduced by Mayor Isaiah Stetson. Col. Jameson responded as he accepted it, and was followed by Vice-President Hamlin, who addressed the troops in a most earnest, eloquent and touching tribute to the patriotism of the people, "who have, with so wonderful a promptness and unanimity, sprung to the defence of the country in this hour of its greatest peril." He eloquently vindicated the cause of the country, and fired the hearts of the troops and of the immense throng of people with words of cheer and encouragement, and by referring the men with fervid tones to the righteousness of their cause, and to the truth that a man can peril his life in none more holy, or lay it down— if it should so happen to any—in a manner more worthy of his God-given humanity. He praised the devotion of the adopted citizens, whose loyalty is exceeded by none, and who rush into the ranks of the defenders of the best of governments. He believed that in such a cause, sustained by such noble men, there is no such word as fail. They would go with the best wishes and prayers of their friends, and they would return to them in due time with victory perched on their banner, and the integrity of the Government maintained and strengthened. "*It matters little when one throws off this mortal coil—but how and where it is important—and at no time and in no place can man better die, than when and where he dies for his country and his race."*

After cheering the Vice-President, Miss McRuer, Mayor Stetson, the ladies who gave the flag and others, the regiment marched to the station, where they were greeted with a salute by the Brewer Artillery. The rain was falling now, but the crowd was immense. The regiment was formed into line and fifteen minutes allowed for leave-taking. The scene cannot be described. Not all the drops that fell to the ground that morning came from the cold sky above. Hot, scalding tears rolled down the cheeks of old and young alike, and the scene moved thousands to tears who had come as spectators only. It was the first hard lesson which war teaches, and many a light hearted lad grew sad as he thought of the possibilities of the future. At 10.30 the men were ordered into the sixteen cars in waiting, and at a quarter before eleven, three locomotives drew them away amid the booming of cannon, the shrieking of whistles and the cheers of the multitude. With the prayers and blessings of the people, with cheers of encouragement, and tears of regretful partings, the gallant Second thus went forth to win success, as well as glory and honor, in their country's cause.

Although sorrow and sadness reigned at home after the departure of the regiment, the same cannot be said to have existed among the men on the train. Laughter and song, stories of past deeds and boasts of what would be done in the near future, mingled with cheers as the various stations were passed, engaged the attention of all until the Kennebec river was reached. The night previous the bridge owned by the railroad at Kendall's Mills had been burned, and the troops dis-embarked and marched over the County bridge, taking another train upon the westerly side, and continued the journey to Augusta. Here they formed into line and marched to the State House, where they were addressed by Gov. Washburn, after which all partook of a hearty meal and then continued on to Portland, where they arrived shortly after midnight. Wednesday morning they took the train for Boston, having, as an escort, while in Portland, a portion of the First Regiment, detailed for that duty. They marched at once to the depot of the Fall River Line, and late that night boarded the steamer State of Maine, arriving in New York at three o'clock the next afternoon.

Some four hundred citizens of New York, natives of Maine, were on hand to receive the regiment, and, under the chairmanship of R. P. Buck, Esq., attended to their wants, accompanying them on their march up town. This march, according to the "Commercial Advertiser," excited the admiration of the New Yorkers, many of whom declared the Second to be the finest body of men seen there. Along the whole line they were greeted with cheers, their marching favorably commented on, while the press the next day, without exception, devoted considerable space to a description of the "giants," as they were called. A grand supper had been prepared for the boys by their friends, but, before it could be partaken of the regiment was ordered into line and marched to one of the piers, where a transport was in waiting, ready to take them to Washington. That night they lay at anchor in the East river. In the morning, so it is stated by one of the regimental officers, Surgeon General Garcelon came on board, and, without consulting with Surgeon Allen, made a tour of the vessel, after which he went on shore and wired the authorities at Washington that the regiment was afflicted with the measles On receipt of this news, orders were issued for the Second to go into camp at Willett's Point, a charming spot, about ten miles up the

East river, where several New York regiments had been located. The next day they dis-embarked, and remained for some time. At this place the men enjoyed themselves hugely. The balmy May air made out-door life enjoyable. The residents round about contributed many luxuries, besides inviting many of the officers to their homes. One resident, a gentleman of wealth possessing an elegant home, made himself agreeable in many ways, and often entertained the regimental officers. In his family were several daughters, all beautiful girls, and one of them, it is said, gave her heart to one official, now a prosperous business man of Bangor. Indeed, it is claimed that several conquests were made among the fair sex, and had the stubborn rebels yielded in battle to the gallants of the Second, as freely as did the fair dames of Long Island, the war would have been early settled.

I deem it proper here to introduce a true statement of the facts regarding the enlistment papers which the men of the Second signed, together with their understanding regarding their time of service. In the haste incident to enrolling troops and getting them to the front, many blunders were made, not only by the U.' S. Government, but by the State authorities and the men. Undoubtedly a portion of the Second were wronged, this being due to a certain extent to the ignorance of men not familiar with the duties they had assumed. The following statement, carefully prepared by H. F. Hanson, M. D., now a resident of Bangor, private in the Second, is undoubtedly correct.

"Immediately after President Lincoln's call for seventy-five-thousand men for three month's service, recruiting offices were opened in various parts of Penobscot county. Several existing militia companies volunteered and many other companies were formed. The first papers signed were for three months. Soon after this call the State authorized the enlistment and organization of ten regiments for two years as State Militia. The men who had signed the first papers were requested to sign the latter also, which they did. The First Regiment of Portland, Col. Jackson, enlisted for two years, as did also the Second. The Second completed its organization first and started for Washington *before* the call for three year's men, expecting to answer the first call only. While in quarantine at Willett's Point a United States officer came to muster us in—May 28th 1861,—but declared he had no authority to muster in men for a less term than three years. Thereupon a large part signed new papers for three years, but a considerable number refused. All started, however, for Washington. At the end of three months the men who had not signed the long time papers expected, and some demanded their discharge. They had answered the first call, had participated in the battle at Bull Run and cited the First Regiment which had been sent home **without having been in battle.** Some 66 men, finding they could not gain a discharge refused to do duty, and these, together with some New York men, in a similar predicament were tried by court-martial in a lump, and ordered to be imprisoned at Dry Tortugas. On their way there the Second Maine boys concluded to re-enlist and were placed in the Second New York, then under Gen. Wool, where they did noble service. Before the expiration of the two years the survivors were returned to the regiment. At the end of the two years, by orders of Gen. Hooker, then in command of the army and the corps commander, Col. Varney took the regiment home leaving the three years' recruits to be divided up between the Twentieth Maine and certain Maine batteries. These recruits—or a certain part of them—refused to serve as orderd, claiming the implied contract was that they should return with the regiment. They afterwards submitted to the mild persuasions and kind treatment of Col.

Chamberlain. After the Second Regiment arrived home the Secretary of War thought that a mistake had been made, and ordered Col. Varney by telegraph to take his regiment back to Washington. Col. Varney and certain State officials went to Washington, represented the case as it was, when we were ordered to be discharged, and, considering our gallant fighting and the fact that but about two hundred of the eight hundred men remained, we were considered as having served our term of service. A congratulatory order was issued, a copy of which was given to each man, comparing them with the heroes of Austertitz, Waterloo, etc. Discharge papers read: "having been enlisted for three years are discharged by reason of expiration of time of service. July 28th, 1866, by equalization of bounty, $50 was to be paid two years' men, and $100 three years' men. The department has paid part of the men for two years and part of the men for three years; all men discharged by reason of wounds or disability being reckoned as three years men, while those who served in all the engagements, and were lucky enough to get home alive, were reckoned two years men, and paid accordingly."

Dr. Hanson was, at the outbreak of the war, living in Lee, in this State. He taught school in winter and drove logs in the spring, saving the money so acquired for a college course. When a paper containing the news of the battle in Charleston harbor was brought in to "the drive," young Hanson swam the brook, took the paper, and, seating himself upon a stump, read it aloud. Rising, he stuck his pickpole in a log, saying he was going to enlist. He did so at once, being the first man to enlist from Lee.

The regiment, having recovered its health, was now moved forward to Washington, where troops were being rapidly massed from all sections of the North.

CHAPTER VII.

In Camp At Washington—A Letter From Col. Roberts—Preparing To Strike The Decisive Blow—A Visit From Secretary Seward—Scenes And Incidents—Going To The Front.

On the arrival at Washington, the Second went into camp on Meridian Hill, and, under the instruction of competent officers, made rapid progress towards that efficiency so necessary to men who are to do battle. The following letter, written by Gen. Charles W. Roberts, will serve to show the condition and feeling of the men at this time.

CAMP SEWARD—MERIDIAN HILL,
HEADQUARTERS, SECOND REGIMENT, V. M. M.
JUNE 4TH.

In haste, I write to inform you that having finally squelched the measles, we have, after taking up our line of march from Willett's Point, passed through sullen, silent, yet unwilling Baltimore, without insult or injury, and through the kind efforts of Vice-President Hamlin, Gen. Strickland and other Maine friends have been permitted to pitch our tents upon this beautiful spot, one and a half miles from the city of Washington, and in full view of Arlington Heights, where some twenty thousand or more of volunteer troops are encamped. Six regiments are also in camp in our immediate vicinity, from the States of New York, New Hampshire and Rhode Island, thereby giving us disciples of Mars, diverse and sundry examples in military science, some of which we may follow, and many we shall not adopt.

By the way, intelligence has just reached us that General Butler, while on a scouting expedition in the vicinity of Fortress Mon-

BREVET BRIG.-GEN. CHAS. W. ROBERTS.

roe, has been taken a prisoner of war. The report is doubtless false, but the mere rumor serves to kindle up the *war spirit* in our boys, and the nearer we approach the lines of the enemy, the better, I find, they enjoy the soldier's life. Our companies today, although the weather with you would be considered oppressive, are briskly engaged in drilling "*a la* Hardee," this drill being universally adopted, as it is more simple and concise than any other now in vogue. We soon expect to leave our present *locale* for Arlington Heights, as none of the regiments arriving here of late have remained more than six or eights days, the column being rapidly moved forward, preparatory to a decisive blow, which will probably be struck within the lines of Old Virginia. That we might not be taken on a nip as to future movements, our field and staff officers have today made purchase of several fine bay horses, at a moderate sum, well bred to the saddle and apparently well trained in every respect. Owing to present troubles, "horse flesh" is much cheaper than at Bangor, consequently desirous of avoiding the risk and expense of transportation, we have concluded to let our favorites steeds remain at home, hoping that upon our return they may be better prepared to bear us about the familiar scenes we have left behind. On Friday afternoon last, the day of our arrival, we were honored by a call from Secretary Seward and daughter, and immediately after their departure our encampment received its present cognomen. On Thursday evening next, all of our commissioned officers are the invited guests of the Honorable Secretary and lady. This evening the Staff are invited to while away an hour or two at the residence of ex-Postmaster General Horatio King. Taking into consideration the manifold attentions showered upon us, one is led to exclaim "who wouldn't be a soldier?"

At Willett's Point, we unwillingly left in the extreme rear some of our command, in consequence of that very unsoldier-like disease, styled measles. Assistant Surgeon Hamlin and Hospital Steward Palmer were placed in charge of them, so we have no fears but that they will speedily join us, as nothing will be left undone in hastening their speedy recovery. While here Surgeon Allen has contrived to give us a *clean bill of health*, the only sickness being that which often arises from over fatigue. Several of our marches of late have been quite severe, and the sudden transition in climate, from cold to hot, has slightly debilitated our men. I notice, however, that other regiments have been more or less subjected to the same difficulty. As regards accidents, we have thus far only one to chronicle, which was at Willett's Point.

To the fair ladies of your city, with delicate hands but brave hearts, we tender the thanks of this regiment. Many an officer, as well as private, daily brings to light something carefully packed away—the result of their handiwork. No longer ago than yesterday, the remark was made by one of the troops, that a "Havelock" made by one of the Bangor gals, would be worth a gross of the miserable affairs purchased here. These articles constructed here, either by steam or lightning, with no particular regard to style or durability, present neither finely wrought stitches, nor a fabric over which much time and labor has been expended. One excuse is, however, that the demand exceeds the supply. We fear that this may be taken as a gentle *hint*, but if not responded to we shall not, on our return, order a court-martial over our best of friends and well wishers.

The First Maine Regiment, from Portland and vicinity, is expected to-day and will go into camp very near us. This regiment, we doubt not, will prove itself adequate to every emergency, having suffered more already in the way of chagrin and disappointment, than the trials and tribulations attendant upon the field of battle.

Being as yet in the dark as to where and when we shall next be ordered, we are not living in very elaborate style. Besides one thing being left behind at Bangor, viz: the Colonel's marquee, we are obliged to quarter in a house devoid of modern improvements. Col. Jameson, Major Varney, Adjutant Reynolds, Chaplain Mines, Sergeant Major Appleton and others have already selected the softest side of the hard-pine boards of which the floors are constructed, and having no better *trump card* to play, I must of course follow suit. However, the *sounds from home* which I hear around me, are the convincing proof that sleep is really a boon to weary mortals given, no matter where the night overtakes them. But "a soldier's life is always gay," and no fault to find have we.

Few regiments, we will venture to remark have overlooked little annoyances with a better grace than ours, and should our feeble efforts, whenever exercised, prove successful, we shall not on our return to the Dirigo State dwell long upon little defects which, possibly, might have been remedied had the antidote for the same been received in season.

As our regimental candle is fast expiring, I must for the present bid you adieu, promising at no distant day to give you a more faithful account of our stewardship.

CHAPTER VIII

Continuation Of The Scenes In Bangor—The Sixth Regiment—The Independent Volunteers Organize—The Temperance Volunteers—The Jam Breakers Of Oldtown—Rebels Capture Bangor Ships—Troops Disbanded And Paid Off —Great Dissapointment—Rifling Cannon At Bangor—Death Of The Bangor Union—Burying Horses For Government—Ass't Surgeon Hamlin At Home— Deaths In The Second Maine—Departure Of The Sixth Maine Battallion— Their Officers—Additional Recruits For The Second—The Sixth Maine To The Front—Regimental And Company Officers.

Leaving for a time the Second, in the full enjoyment of the hospitalities of friends, and in the pleasures incidental to camp life, which were to be replaced in six short weeks by scenes of blood and slaughter, let us once more return to the banks of the Penobscot. The patriotism of the men and women, and their efforts to promote the cause of the Union, did not abate with the departure of the Second. On the contrary, while they were yet in camp at Bangor, there had arrived the nucleus for other regiments, and these were receiving all the attention possible. Besides these troops there had been completed the organization known as the "Independent Volunteers," and these, too, were remembered by the workers. They had chosen the following officers:

David Bugbee, Captain; N. S. Harlow, First Lieutenant; J. B. Foster, Second Lieutenant; Charles P. Stetson, Third Lieutenant; Seth E. Benson, Fourth Lieutenant; with David Bugbee, A. D. Manson and S. D. Thurston, Standing Committee, and Fred E. Shaw, Clerk and Treasurer.

David Bugbee was well up in Scott's Tactics, then in general use, and rendered much assistance, not only to his own company but to U. S. volunteers. Regular drills of the Independent Volunteers were held in the Gymnasiam, while squad drills were over the store of J. S. Ricker. On May 18th, orders were received for all companies in the city to go into camp at once, which were obeyed. The Temperance Volunteers, Capt. Cass, voted to enlist under the three years call, and then voted to enlist for "ten years or longer if wanted." On the 22d, there were at Camp **Washburn**, companies from Ellsworth, Bucksport, Corinth, Oldtown and Brownville. The Oldtown company was composed of big men, they taking uniforms several sizes larger—on the average—than had ever been made, either in Maine or Massachusetts, and were styled the "Jam Breakers." Sixty-six of these men averaged six feet in height and one hundred and sixty-six pounds in weight. Many were river drivers and wood choppers by profession, and had reputation for skill and daring in breaking jams of logs when running them on the turbulent waters of the Penobscot and its branches, hence the very appropriate title which they bore. At this time a battalion of five companies was being made up at Eastport, and it was intended to combine them with the Bangor troops in the formation of a new regiment.

About this time the ship owners in the State of Maine began to feel the heavy hand of the Confederacy, and several rumors came regarding the loss of vessels on the seas, and it was asserted that Bangor owners, among them Capt. Sylvanus Rich, had lost heavily.

It would seem that the Government, notwithstanding their experience, still underrated the strength of the enemy and was confident that the army already gathered could conquer them, for, on May 27th there came orders to discharge and pay off all volunteers not already provided for with places in one of the six remaining regiments. There were at this time twenty-one companies of Eastern Maine men, over and above the regiments in camp. The Whig said: "F. M. Sabine, was yesterday to pay off Capt. Boynton's Newport company, at Newport, and Capt. Carlisle's and Capt. Cass' company in this city. Capt. Sawyer's company at Dixmont and Capt. Robert's company at Dexter were also to be paid off, and Capt. Chandler's company at Dover to-day. The names of the privates will be retained who are willing to enlist, if wanted, to fill up companies already designated."

Among the prominent firms doing business in Bangor at that time was that of Hinckley & Egery. When the State inspected its cannon, mostly brass field pieces, it was discovered that they were of the smooth-bore pattern, and it was at once ordered that they be rifled. There were twenty pieces to be so treated, and these were sent to Messrs. Hinckley & Egery, some coming from Portland on the steamer Daniel Webster.

In Wheelwright and Clark's block there were published two papers, "The Bangor Union" and "The Democrat." The support of the former was weak, and it expired early in June. In order to give an idea of the intensely loyal feeling pervading Bangor at the time, an editorial of the Whig and Courier, on its suspension, is given.

"DEATH OF THE BANGOR UNION."

"The daily organ of Secession in this city, the Bangor Union, expired on Saturday, as it should have expired, for want of breath. The editor calls it a 'suspension,' until the war is over and business revives—but we think its business will not soon revive. The simple truth is the people of this city would not sustain a paper which opposes the Government in its hour of vital peril, and sympathizes with traitors—and we trust the people of the country will take the same course to suppress the weekly publication from the same office, (The Democrat). The valedictory of the Union is a spiteful affair, but will scarcely move anyone except to laughter. The statement that certain respectable men have made every effort to suppress the paper by mob violence, excites a smile, when it is known that for months it has requird the earnest efforts of our leading citizens, to prevent that concern from being thrown into the river, and that the slightest encouragement from those whom the Union calls 'respectable citizens,' would have sealed its fate in five minutes. So of the curse which it calls down upon 'the men of property and standing, who have done all in their power to injure us.' Its curses will only come to roost upon the shoulders of their author. The business men of this city have simply done their duty, in refusing to aid in sustaining a traitorous organ in our city, and have taken precisely the right course to suppress it. If the Union had acted a loyal and manly part, and stood by the country instead of taking part with traitors, it would have received its share of support."

The Whig also paid attention to another organ of the same stripe as the Union. It says:

"The Standard, at Concord, one of the largest and vilest of the Secession organs of New England, has the impudence to send us a paper marked, "Please Ex." We would as soon exchange with the Court Journal of His Satanic Majesty, which, we take it, is edited by Judas Iscariot and Benedict Arnold."

Although the regimental officers had found horses in Washington, the Government officials commissioned Messrs. Stanley & Lang to purchase animals, both for the use of cavalrymen and the artillery. Accordingly, Acting Q. M. Gen. John L. Hodsdon inserted an advertisement, appointing days of purchase at Bangor, Skowhegan and Waterville. Horses must be some color other than white, well shod, sound and kind, etc. Good prices were paid, and many animals went to the war from this section.

On Thursday evening, June 13th, those who had friends in the Second, were glad to see Assistant Surgeon Hamlin, who came home on a ten day's furlough. He reported all the men who were left at Willett's Point as having joined the regiment, and, also brought the sad news of the death in camp of private Lorenzo D. Benner, of Brewer. On the day Surgeon Hamlin arrived home, a dispatch announced the death of Sergeant Charles F. Hall, of the Bangor Light Infantry company.

Monday June 24th, five companies before mentioned as being at Camp Washburn, left by rail for Portland, under command of Capt. Brown, of the Brownville company. The Oldtown band accompanied them, and, as was the case when the Second left, the citizens gave them a grand "send off." The companies were officered as follows: Company A, (Brownville) Capt. Moses W. Brown; 1st Lieut., Chas. H. Chandler; 2d Lieut., A. P. Buck. Company B, (Ellsworth) Capt. Isaac Frazer; 1st Lieut., Otis Kent; 2d Lieut., John D. McFarland. Company C, (Bucksport) Capt. Joseph Snowman; 1st Lieut., Franklin Pierce; 2d Lieut., Virgil P. Wardwell. Company D, (Corinth) Capt. Cyrus Brown; 1st Lieut., J. G. Roberts; 2d Lieut., Geo. Fuller. Company E, (Oldtown) Capt. A. G. Burton; 1st Lieut., Henry R. Sopher; 2d Lieut., L. H. Stinchfield. Few enlistments were made for a time, although Gen. Stevens received orders to recruit 250 volunteers to bring its standard to 1000 men.

There was a big celebration on the fourth of July, in which the people of the surrounding towns participated. On the sixth, the people had some interesting reading in addition to the account of Independence Day, given them by the press, it being that wonderful message of President Lincoln, wherein he shew that he, at least, realized the magnitude and power of the Confederacy, and called on the loyal States for four hundred thousand men, and four hundred million dollars. "These are big figures," said a Bangor man that day, "and when we are able to comprehend what they mean, we may be able to agree with Hon. A. G. Jewett, who said, at Belfast, the other day, that this war was not for days, nor months, but for years." While the people were considering the proclamation, President Lincoln and the Union generals were forwarding the campaign plans, which had been marked out. One misty July night, the citizens living in the outskirts of Washington, were awakened by a heavy jarring, which vibrated through their dwellings. Going to their windows they saw, much to their surprise, solid columns of troops marching by. They uttered no words, gave out no sounds, marched without music, yet in perfect step, and in the fog which had settled over their heads, as though nature was endeavoring to afford them a screen, as they advanced, they looked like huge spectres rather than men. Hour after hour they marched adown the streets, along the low lands and across Long Bridge to Virginia soil, and the morning light brightened the eastern horizon, ere the rear of the army departed. The Second, Third and Fourth Maine, accompanied by the Second and Third Connecticut regiments went over in the order named, and encamped at or near Falls Church. It now looked business like, and, as the boys lay there, knowing that within a few miles of them thousands of rebel troops were encamped, they began to think there was to be fighting after all.

At this time came news of the burning of the ship "Golden Rocket," built in Bangor in 1858, by James Dunning, and Charles E. Dole, of Brewer, and owned by Moses Giddings. She was captured and fired by the crew of the rebel steamer Sumpter. Her value was $30,000. In addition to this came news of the capture of the brig "Cuba," of Millbridge, brig "Machias," of Machias, and brig "Maria," of Portland. July 11th, the Sixth Maine, Col. Abner Knowles left for the front, and the First Maine, which had much political influence, but little else, was orderd home, having, according to the press of the day, "performed no service, gained no honors, and entitled to no particular credit. An unfortunate selection of officers, and a combination of unfavorable circumstances, rather than poor soldiers, have brought about the result." "We presume," said one paper, "that the better portion of the men will re-enlist, return to the war and earn a reputation worthy of Maine troops. The regiment was raised at an enormous expense, poorly uniformed and equipped, and have been unfortunate from the first."

The Sixth Maine, which was intended to replace the First, was really a better representative of Eastern Maine than the Second. With the exception of the Chaplain, every officer resided near the banks of the Penobscot or east of that river. During the war, as will be seen, it gained a wonderful reputation, and few regiments in the regular armies, of this or any other nation, have a grander record. Its officers were:

Colonel, ABNER KNOWLES, Bangor.
Lieut. Colonel, HIRAM BURNHAM, Cherryfield.
Major, FRANK PIERCE, Bucksport.
Adjutant, JOHN D. McFARLAND, Ellsworth.
Quartermaster, ISAAC STRICKLAND, Bangor.
Surgeon, E. F. SANGER, Bangor.
Asst. Surgeon, JOHN BAKER, East Machias.
Chaplin, ZENAS THOMPSON, Portland.
Quartermaster's Sergeant, PERCIVAL KNOWLES, JR., Bangor.
Hospital Steward, CHAS. A. McQUESTEN, Bangor.
Commisary's Sergeant, J. W. SNOWMAN, Bucksport.
Drum Major, Z. BUZZELL, Bucksport.
Fife Major, JOHN WASHBURN, Foxcroft.
Leader of Band, H. S. MOREY, Bangor.
The company officers were:

COMPANY A.

Capt.—Moses W. Brown, Brownville.
1st *Lieut.*—Chas. H. Chandler, Foxcrnft.
2d *Lieut.*—Addison P. Buck, Foxcroft.
Sergeants.—Sewall C. Gray, Exeter; Geo. W. Emerson, Brownville: W. G. Morrill, Williamsburg; Lyman H. Wilkins, Brownville; E. J. Jewett, Sangerville.

COMPANY B.

Capt.—Isaac Frazier, Ellsworth.
1st *Lieut.*—Otis W. Kent, Ellsworth.
2d *Lieut.*—John D. McFarland, Hancock.
Sergeants.—Milton Frazier, Albert M. Murch, Dan'l G. Meader, Geo. E. Thomas, A. T. Somerby, all of Ellsworth.

COMPANY C.

Capt.—Benj. F. Harris, Machias.
1st *Lieut.*—John H. Ballinger, Machias.
2d *Lieut.*—Chas. F. Stone, Machias.
Sergeants.—Fred A. Hill, Machias; B. A. Campbell, Pembroke; Wm. H. West, Machias; John L. Pierce, Machias; Wm. H. McCabe, Machias.

COMPANY D.

Capt.—Joel A. Haycock, Calais.
1st *Lieut.*—R. W. Furlong, Calais.
2d *Lieut.*—H. H. White, Calais.
Sergeants.—L. L. L. Bassford, Geo. W. McLain, B. F. Waite, Jr., Edward Williams, Geo. P. Blanchard, all of Calais.

COMPANY E.

Capt.—Jos. Snowman, Bucksport.
1st *Lieut.*—Benj. J. Buck, Bucksport.
2d *Lieut.*—V. P. Wardwell, Bucksport.
Sergeants.—Fred P. Ginn, Orland; Geo. C. Irvin, Bucksport;

C. E. Pillsbury, Bucksport; L. P. Abbott, Bucksport; Geo. Snowman, Bucksport.

Company F.

Capt.—Wm. N. Pysell, Pembroke.

1st *Lieut.*—John M. Lincoln, Pembroke.

2d *Lieut.*—Simon Pottle, 2d, Pembroke.

Sergeants.—Theo. Lincoln, Jr., Dennysville; J. C. Campbell, Pembroke; Chas. H. Bailey, Pembroke; Wm. H. Lincoln, Perry; Benj. Leland, Perry.

Company G.

Capt.—Ralph W. Young, Rockland.

1st *Lieut.*—Frank C. Pierce, Augusta.

2d *Lieut.*—Hiram B. Sproul, Cherryfield.

Sergeants.—Geo. W. Leighton, Columbia; A. L. Stevens, Steuben; L. W. Smith, Steuben; Geo. H. Jacobs, Cherryfield; John McGregor, Eastport.

Company H.

Capt.—Cyrus Brown, Corinth.

1st *Lieut.*—J. G. Roberts, Corinth.

2d *Lieut.*—Geo. Fuller, Corinth.

Sergeants.—Alex. Stevens, Bangor; Benj. F. Robinson, Sebec; A. J. Whittier, Corinth; Chas. Fitzgerald, Dexter; William H. Coan, Dexter.

Company I.

Capt.—Albert G. Burton, Oldtown.

1st *Lieut.*—Henry R. Soper, Oldtown.

2d *Lieut.*—Wm. H. Stanchfield, Milo.

Sergeants.—D. W. Freeze, Orino; Z. B. Putnam, Oldtown; L. Smith, Oldtown; J. H. Norris, Milford; Jas. S. Lane, Oldtown.

Company K.

Capt.—Theo. Carey, Eastport.

1st *Lieut.*—Thos. P. Roach, Eastport.

2d *Lieut.*—Charles Day, Eastport.

Sergeants.—John B. Waid, Eastport; Geo. H. Patterson, Eastport; Chas. T. Witherell, Eastport; Thatcher Vose, Robbinston; S. H. Wheeler, Eastport.

CHAPTER IX.

The Battle of Bull Run—How The News Was Received at Home—Intense Anxiety And Excitement—A Few Telegraph Headings—Letters From The Second Maine.

On the morning of July 22d, the people of Bangor were thrown into a state of great excitement by the arrival of news of a battle at Manassas, in which the Union Army was completely routed and had fled towards Washington. It was impossible in those days to get a correct account of a large battle at once, yet enough was at hand to convince our people that the hitherto despised rebels were by no means destitute of fighting ability, and however unholy their cause was, they had been successful, and that Washington was at their mercy. One not an eye witness can hardly realize the feelings of the patriotic sons and daughters of the North, nor can they imagine the suspense with which mothers and wives, sons, daughters and fathers waited to hear from their loved ones. The Second had been in the fight, and had carried themselves in such a manner as to reflect credit upon the old Pine Tree State. Beyond this, little could be learned. In those days one or two wires only were strung to Bangor, and consequently the telegraph service was slow and uncertain as compared with the present. Soon came the news that fourteen or more of the regiment were killed, and about sixty wounded or taken prisoners. This added to the agony, and other news was eagerly awaited, while the citizens, forgetting for a time business, gathered in groups about the city discussing the great calamity. During the day the following despatch was received:

WASHINGTON, JULY 22d, 1861.

"The Field and Staff Officers of the Second Maine Regiment are all safe, except Dr. Allen and his son, of Orono, who are supposed to be prisoners." HON. JOHN H. RICE.

Gradually the news came along, until at last the whole story had been told, and it was known that many of the gallant regiment had given themselves in defense of their country. As the survivors contemplated their dead heroes, did the words of Vice-President Hamlin, uttered to the regiment in Bangor on the day of their departure, come back to them?

"*It matters little when one throws off this mortal coil—but how*
"*and where it is important—and at no time, and in no place, can a*
"*man better die, than when and where he dies for his country and*
"*his race.*"

There are many survivors of that unfortunate day, and the author has been most kindly met when seeking information, and he presents below letters and reminscences of some of them.

Among our well known citizens, is Mr. Wm. H. S. Lawrence, then Sergeant in Company G, Second Maine. The following letter was written without any expectation of its ever meeting the public eye, but is nevertheless interesting reading:

ALEXANDRIA, VA., July 23d, 1861.

Dear Sister—I suppose that before this time you have heard about the late fight at Manassas, between our troops and the rebels, and that you and the rest of the family are on the "anxious seat" concerning the fate of your humble servant. Well, I am all right, but I will proceed with the particulars.

We left Falls Church last Tuesday afternoon, at two o'clock, and took up our march for Vienna, where we arrived at eight o'clock, the enemy leaving before us. The next morning we started for Fairfax Court House, our brigade consisting of three Connecticut regiments, the Second Maine regiment, and Varian's Battery of five pieces. When we got within a mile of Germantown, we formed a line of battle; the Second Connecticut and our regiment on the right, and the other two Connecticut on the left, with Sherman's and Varian's batteries right at the head of the Second Maine. In this manner we started, and after a short distance we came upon the breastworks of the enemy, behind which were concealed about 2,000 men. Sherman opened on them with his battery. After two or three shots they took to their heels and fled. If they had stayed they could have made a good stand. We pursued them all that day, and at night encamped about half way to Centreville. The next morning we overtook the rest of our division which had come in by the way of Fairfax.

The head of the column pressed on and engaged the enemy at Bull Run, about three miles this side of Manassas, but they were so completely concealed that our folks could not make much headway against them. We encamped on this side of Centreville Thursday and Friday. Friday afternoon, our company was detailed to help the sappers and miners, under Capt. Alexander, to build a bridge over Bull Run. We worked that night until dark, and the next morning we turned out at daybreak and went at it again. We finished it and loaded our teams by nine o'clock, and then joined the regiment again, which had by this time moved down to where we were.

About this time heavy fire commenced in front of us, telling us that a fight had commenced in earnest. We marched down with our brigade and halted about one-half mile from the battlefield. We waited there about an hour, at which time we were ordered to attack the enemy in the rear. To do this we started off to the right of where we were, at double-quick, which we kept up for a distantce of over three miles. The Second Connecticut were out as skirmishers, while we were held as a reserve. We had not been in line five minutes when we saw the stars and strips raised on one of the enemy's batteries, about one-half mile from us. We then had orders to advance at double quick, which we did, and at the same time the enemy opened on us from behind a fence directly in front, but *we gave it to them* and in less than five minutes they retreated; we rallied and followed. They retreated behind a lot of hay stacks when they stopped again, but we gave them all they called for and were driving them fast, when one of the masked batteries, which was to our left, opened on us a most deadly fire. We stood it without flinching until we were ordered by Col. Keyes to left flank into the woods. Capt. Sargent did not hear the order, and we stood there a long time after the rest had left—bound to show that the "Tigers" had grit, and I guess the enemy will remember us, for just as sure as one of them showed his head he was sure not to need his rations the next day. Our boys stood it like veterans. Col. Keyes soon came up and ordered us into the woods, where we went without showing our backs to the enemy at all. I think if we had had another regiment to back us, we would have taken that battery in spite of all the devils in the Southern Army.

We did not take any provisions, as we had orders from Capt. Sargent not to take any; there were some taken, however. It was an awful day for us. Our regiment was all cut to pieces when we advanced on that masked battery. We have lost a great many killed, wounded and taken prisoners. Of our company only some forty have reported themselves out of eighty.

About the middle of the action, Henry Holden, who was doing nobly, was wounded in the leg by a musket ball. It entered about six inches above the knee and passed through the leg, but did not break the bone nor touch the artery, so I think he will recover. The enemy kept up such a firing that it was almost sure death to go out after the wounded. Some of the Connecticut boys, as they were retreating, brought Henry off with them. I told Capt. Sargent I must go and look out for him, but as neither Lieutenants Morse nor Getchell were there with us, he could not spare me, but said he would send some men for him, which he did, sending six men to carry him to the hospital. We were then ordered to join the main body of the troops. I went and saw Henry before we started off; he stood it first rate and did not appear to be in much pain. We then proceeded to join the main body, the enemy keeping up a murderous fire in our rear.

As we were going over the field, I found one of our men who was wounded, trying to carry another off the field, who had a bad wound in the neck. I took six men, leaving only four with the captain, and started to carry him off with us. Going on we were joined by some of the Castine boys with a wounded man, and a party of the Bangor Light Infantry, carrying Wm. Deane. Deane was shot in the throat and was just alive. I don't think it possible for him to live. After we carried them two miles and a half, we got lost in the woods, and the troops that were passing by told us the enemy's cavalry was in our rear, taking all prisoners they could lay their hands on, and at the same time another body of men were flanking us to cut off our retreat. When we got this news we made all possible speed, being determined, however, not to leave our wounded in their hands; but we were well tired out after our day's work. At this time the party that had Holden came in sight, and as we were all beat out, we knew it was of no use to try to go farther, unless we could get assistance, as no one that was passing would as much as turn their hands over to help us. The boys wanted me to find our company and send some fresh men, so I started, but before I had got forty rods away, the enemy's cavalry came up to them and told them to surrender, which they had to do, only two or three escaping. I did not know of this till afterwards.

I could not see the main body, but kept on till I reached a house that was used as a hospital, where I found Dr. Allen and quite a number of wounded. I told the doctor what I came for, that I wanted him to send an ambulance after the wounded, but ours were all gone, and we could not get another for love nor money—and of the latter we had none. Just then I heard that the cavalry had taken them, so that it was useless to go back after them. The doctor told me the cavalry had been there, and that he had hung out a flag of truce. They told him that if we did not make any fight at the hospital our wounded should be well treated, but if we did they would have to take the consequences, and that I had better get all of the men that belonged to our regiment, and get them away as soon as possible, or they would shell the house. He told me that he was going to stay with the boys, and would take good care of Henry. I want you to tell Mrs. Holden this, as she will feel easier if she knows that he is well taken care of; and I don't think the rebels will dare to use them very roughly, as we have so many of their men prisoners. We cannot tell how much of a loss we have sustained, as our regiment is so scattered.

Of our company, I don't know of one who was killed outright.

Those that we know are wounded are Henry Holden; Sergeant Quimby, in the breast; Joseph Green, in the shoulder; Wm. Severance and Wm. Lovejoy are also known to be wounded, but have not been seen since the action. Of our company of eighty men there are but nineteen here besides commissioned officers. Capt Jones and one of the lieutenants of Company C, Brewer Artillery, were killed. Lieutenant Richardson, of Capt. Emerson's company, had his leg taken off by a cannon ball. Sergeant Staples, of Company H, Gymnasium Company, tells me that Fuller Orff was shot in the abdomen and bled internally, and that he was dying when he last saw him. I don't know half —but it is said that one-half of our regiment is killed, wounded and missing.

Our staff officers behaved nobly. I did not see much of any of them except Major Varney; tell Mr.——that the Major is a brick. I suppose we shall stay here for a day or two, and then we shall go back to Falls Church to recruit up. There is not a man in the regiment—or what there is left of it—that can walk without limping. We marched from Centreville here, the night after the action, without stopping. I think that Sunday and Sunday night we travelled over fifty miles, all on foot. We lost our blankets and rations, and a good many lost their coats; they threw them away on the battle-field, it was so warm.

I will not write more at this time, but the next time I write I will give all the particulars. All I wonder at is that there are any of us left; but I did not think of it at the time.

Your affectionate brother,

WILL.

From a letter dated Washington, July 26th, I take the following:

Poor Deane was killed while carrying the magnificent flag presented by the ladies of California. The ball struck the flagstaff and passed through his neck. His friends, while they mourn his loss, may derive some consolation in reflecting that he fell in defense of his country, and while clinging to its flag. This flag when poor Deane fell, was caught up by Quimby, an "ex-Tiger." Quimby was knocked down by the fragments of a shell, receiving a slight abrasion of the skin across the breast. He is not dangerously wounded. It was at this time that the fight commenced, over the flag, which at one moment was in the hands of the enemy, but was immediately recovered.

Young Rich, the son of Dr. Geo. Rich, escaped miraculously. He received a small bullet or buck-shot wound in the right cheek, It struck him obliquely, *passing through his cheek, and out between his teeth*, without damaging him in the least, any more than a puncture through the fleshy part of the cheek. His mouth must have been open at the time, as would naturally have been the case, with a person engaged in a conflict of this nature, so the old injunction, that a "closed mouth shows a wise head," does not hold good in all cases.

From another correspondent :

WASHINGTON, JULY 23d, 1861.

The loss of the Maine Second will not, I think, exceed fifty in killed and wounded. From the best information I can get, the killed will not exceed thirty. Capt. Jones of Brewer, was shot through the body. He was carried off the field by Lieutenant Skinner, who refused to leave his captain while alive, and was therefore taken prisoner. He was not wounded. Martin Jose, of Hampden, is spoken of in the highest praise by his felllow soldiers, for his coolness and daring. He fell in the front rank of one of the regiment's terrible charges on a 20 gun battery. Both his legs were shot off. His last words were:—"Have you carried the battery? Tell mother I fell fighting for my country." (His mother is a widow). Nearly all our wounded were left behind, and are now in the hands of the enemy; but doctor Allen is with them. He was taken prisoner with his son, and Dr. Palmer, who afterwards escaped. Dr. Palmer told me Dr. Allen might also have got away, but he said he would stay with the poor fellows and take care of them.

The bravery of our boys is the theme of every one. All fought well, it would seem—so well, it is difficult to particularize. But the boys speak so warmly of the conduct of Lieutenant Garnsey, Capt. Sargent, Lieutenant Casey and Peter Welch, I know it will give no offence to others to name them. Of young Garnsey the boys say he is a "little brick." The regiment charged up a hill on a 20 gun battery. At the top of the hill was a Virginia fence, only a few paces from the battery. Garnsey commanded the left wing of his company, and with a revolver in one hand and his sword in the other, he charged up the hill to the fence, on the top of which he leaped, and waving his sword, cried to his boys to follow him. Twice he led his men to the fence, but the murderous fire caused them to fall back, and throw themselves on the ground, behind an eminence to shield themselves from the storm of iron hail. It was by this battery that the Ellsworth Zouaves were cut up. I noticed that young Garnsey's clothes were covered with blood. His right-hand man was shot by his side. "Then," said he "I was mad, and would have reached that battery had we not been ordered back." Peter Welch, I am told, rushed in and took two prisoners, and brought them off, then went back under a terrible fire and brought off some of our wounded.

Such conduct, on the part of under officers and privates, could only have been inspired by the most gallant conduct of their superior officers. At one time, when the regiment was forced to retire after a charge, Col. Jameson said to his men: "Who will go with me to the rescue of the wounded?" Six brave fellows followed him, into the very jaws of death. Little can you imagine how our hearts swell towards our brave boys, for their heroic conduct in this great fight. Our State has not been disgraced, whatever may have been the conduct of the officers of some other States. All honor to the Second Maine and its brave officers. The State owes them a debt of gratitude she can never repay. HAL.

The Times had a correspondent, "Faust," who wrote his paper as follows:

"All accounts agree that our Maine Regiments behaved well. This was especially the case with the Second Maine. Col. Jameson led his regiment into action in gallant style, waving his sword over his head and rallying and encouraging his men in the bravest manner. So with Lieut. Col. Roberts. He showed the best kind of pluck, and maintained his self possession throughout." I hear most excellent reports of Adjutant John Reynolds, who, when the regiment got somewhat broken and confused in its desperate charge upon a battery, and mixed up with other disordered regiments, was heard above the din and noise shouting, "Second Regiment form in line!" "Second Regiment form in line!" and in this way succeeded in reforming a large number of his men.

A Washington correspondent of the Boston Journal thus speaks of the Second Maine: "This regiment was for a long time exposed to a hot fire. They were in Col. Keyes' brigade, and were in the column which pushed its way across Bull's Run and drove the enemy back to Manassas. When the cavalry charges were made, when all was confusion, Col. Jameson rallied his men, or what was left of them, and they were the last to leave the field.

There were five of his soldiers wounded lying close up to the enemy's batteries He sent back twenty-five men to bring them off, and all these were taken prisoners. Before his retreat six of his men were lying on the field where they made a charge. Grape and canister from the enemy's batteries were sweeping across the place. Col Jameson called for volunteers to go with him and bring them off; six men stepped forward. They went up upon the run and came to two rebels, when Col. Jameson covered them with his revolvers, took them prisoners and brought them in with the six wounded men.

THE FLAGS OF THE SECOND.

The regiment had three flags, one presented at Bangor, one at New York, and one that was given by ladies in California. There was considerable discussion about the latter. It appears that when it was sent from the Pacific. it was addressed to the "First Me. Regiment." The Second was first in the field, and the question arose as to whether it was intended for Regiment No 1. or the first regiment entering the service, and, to settle the matter the donors were asked to decide. There answer was: "Give it to the first regiment entering the service." Twenty-four hours before the battle it was given to the Second, and was carried in the Bull Run fight by Private Deane.

The Bangor Democrat had a word or two to say regarding the battle. The younger portion of our people can hardly realize that there was printed in our midst a paper whose whole sympathy was with the rebels, and which with no uncertain sound denounced the Northern patriots in their efforts to subdue the South. For a long time this sheet was allowed to have its say, although time and again men gathered together with the avowed intention of destroying it, but were pursuaded by the cooler heads to "wait." In the issue of July 30th, the Democrat printed an account of the Bull Run fight, using the following headlines:

"Total defeat and route of the Federal Army."

"President Davis's account of the great battle."

"Confederate loss 1,200."

"Federal loss 10,000."

In the article are these words:

"But alas! What was their errand? Could the God of our Fathers smile on their mission of subjugation and death?"

In speaking of future movements of the Federal army, Editor Emery said:

"Onward the shouting myriads will pour, until again met by the unequalled and invincible genius of Davis, Beauregard, Johnston and Lee, and the iron nerves of these noble men, who are defending their firesides and their homes, from the ruthless assaults of fanaticism and fury. Victory may again perch upon their banners for a short time, but long ere they will have reached Richmond, disaster will again have overtaken them, and, defeated and routed they will once more fly back to the Potomac in wild confusion, leaving the battle-field, and the wayside stained with the blood of thousands."

In another article was the following allusion to the loyal soldiers:

"On their own soil, and in defense of their own firesides and homes, they would be invincible; but in a civil war, so *Unjust* and *Cruel* as this, they can but meet with Defeat and Death."

CHAPTER X.

Destruction Of The Bangor Democrat—Infuriated Citizens, Maddened By Its Bitter Attacks Upon The Government—Throw Type, Cases And Press Into The Street And Burn Them—Editor Emery Has A Narrow Escape—What The Press Said—Interviews With Bangor Men Who Took Part In The Raid—The Trial At Belfast—Issue Of The Democrat Extra—Editor Emery Addresses The People.

Tuesday Aug. 13th, there appeared in the columns of the "Bangor Jeffersonian," the following:

"We stopped the forms of this paper from the press at one o'clock Monday, to announce, which we do with regret, that three or four men had entered the office of the 'Bangor Democrat' in the upper story of Wheelwright & Clark's block, while the most of the hands were at dinner, and in a few minutes threw the type, presses and fixtures out of the window into the square. An immense crowd of citizens soon gathered, but not until the work of destruction was nearly accomplished. Some boys soon piled the combustible portion of the fixtures in a heap and fired them. This week's edition of the paper had been partly worked off. In a few minutes the crowd suddenly moved towards the barber shop of Joseph Jones, in Taylor's new block, and the furniture of the shop was soon thrown into the street.

By this time Mayor Stetson had reached the spot and commanded the crowd to disperse, which they did immediately with deafening cheers. The provocation for the last act was, as we learn, Jones went into the street and asked John Wyman, Esq., to go into his shop—he wanted to see him. Mr. Wyman did not know who Jones was till he was told. Jones then grossly assaulted Wyman, striking him in his face several times, inflicting severe wounds. Mr. Wyman dealt back several blows, and left the barber sprawling on the floor. As soon as this assault became known, the crowd proceeded as above and cleared the shop. These things done, the streets were in a few minutes cleared and all was quiet."

The Whig and Courier of the same date says: "At a quarter before one, yesterday, an alarm of fire was given, and the engines passed up State street. No fire was found, but on the return of the people, a crowd was found gathered in West Market Square, and a large number of people in the office of the "*Bangor Democrat*," throwing the materials out of the windows. The office was completely gutted, and the stands, cases and newspapers afterwards burned in the square. The crowd subsequently cleared out the barber's shop of J. Jones, on Kenduskeag Bridge—the cause, we understand, was a personal attack made by Jones upon Mr. John Wyman, for remarks he had made in relation to the secession editors of the "*Democrat*." Jones met Wyman in the street, and invited him into his shop. Mr. Wyman complied, and after reaching the barber-shop, Jones asked what he meant by the remarks he had made. Mr. Wyman responded to the effect that he was not responsible to him, (Jones), for what he said. After some further remarks, Jones made an attack upon Wyman, striking him in the face, which was returned by Mr. Wyman. The excited crowd hearing of the collision, went into the shop, and threw the furniture into the street."

FROM "THE DAILY EVENING TIMES."

At a quarter to one o'clock this noon, while the employes of "*The Democrat*" office, situated in the fourth story of the Wheelwright and Clark block, were at dinner, and a very few persons in the neighborhood of the office, a number of persons entered the office and commenced the work of destruction by throwing the type, fixtures, presses, etc., out of the windows. The attack took every one by surprise, but in the course of a few minutes a large crowd collected, which was increased by an alarm of fire which had been given, probably in connection with the work of the mob. The office was completely emptied in the course of half an hour, the heavy cylinder press being thrown out upon the pavement along with the rest, while bonfires were kindled in West Market Square, and the inflammable materials committed to the flames. The large sign was also wrenched off from the building, leaving the upper portion with the head of Washington intact. While the work progressed the large American flag in the attic of the building was thrown out. Among the property destroyed was a large portion of to-morrow's edition of the "*Democrat.*"

Mr. Emery, editor of "*The Democrat*," returning from dinner to the office, attracted the attention of a crowd who pressed upon him, probably from motives of curiosity rather than from any design to injure him, and he found refuge in J. S. Ingraham's apothecary shop. The shop of Mr. Jones, the barber, on Kenduskeag bridge, was also cleaned out. We understand that he called a citizen into his office, and commenced an altercation with him, which resulted in the destruction of his effects.

We do not learn that there was any exhibition of violence, beyond that above described, and at 2 o'clock everything was quiet. The work of illegal violence was witnessed by citizens with varying emotions. Many were rejoiced, a few indignant, but we believe the sentiment of the cooler and wiser, while holding in abhorrence the course of the Democrat, was one of regret.

The above are the newspaper reports of the day, and are intended, evidently, to make as light of the matter as possible, but the facts of the case, as nearly as can be discoved from interviews with prominent citizens, who participated in the "event," are:

The editors of *The Democrat* had, from time to time, published editorials severely criticising the Government and its attitude in the war, and holding to the theory of "State Rights." Numerous leaders had appeared, denouncing the "Unholy War."

To give a slight idea of the character of the articles, we print an extract from its issue on the day of suppression:

"The loudest advocates of the existing deplorable war, in which the country has been involved, by the Abolition Republican party, are the political demagogues, the partisan priests, and the infamous speculators, who are coining fortunes out of the calamities of their country. The first want offices; the priests are for setting the niggers free; and the speculators are for the accumulating of pelf. The poor unfortunate people—the farmers, mechanics and workingmen—are to be first taxed to death, and then enslaved, as a consequence of all this infamous business."

This paper, from the first, with every means in its power, sought to cripple the Government and to alienate the people from it, by misrepresenting its objects, and the community. While the brave soldiers had gone out to peril their lives for their country, it declared the cause in which they were engaged an "Unholy War."

Small wonder then that the loyal citizens of Eastern Maine, holding that it was an evil that could not be reached by law, and that it was due to our brave soldiers in the field, that they be not subjected to a "fire in the rear," decided that "the Democrat" should not be tolerated at home.

With these their grounds for action, those engaged in the suppression, went at their work openly and at high noon, and showed themselves willingly responsible to the law for any damage they might commit.

"*The Times*" (dem.) of the next day, August 13th, says in an editorial on the matter:

"Of the treasonable and mischievous character of the obnoxious paper, there is no dissenting voice, except among the faction for which it spoke."

The *cause* now accounted for, I shall try to briefly place the *effect* before you. On the 12th day of August, 1861, at a quarter of one o'clock, and according to a pre-arranged plan, the bell of the First Parish church, on Broadway, began to ring a fire alarm, which was quickly taken up by the other bells in the city. Soon the engines, accompanied by a great crowd, might have been seen going over State street hill, in the supposed direction of the fire. In the meantime a small crowd collected in front of "The Democrat" office, and proceeded to enter it. The most of the crew of the paper were at dinner, as was the editor. The crowd immediately began to break up stands, cases and presses, and to throw them into the street. With the assistance of a brawny blacksmith and his sledge, the large cylinder press was broken into bits, and soon joined the rest of the outfit below. On the street was a large crowd now collected, (as it had been discovered that the fire alarm was a hoax, and the engines had returned by this time), who gathered together the inflammable materials, and soon had a roaring bonfire. The large sign was torn from the building, leaving the head of Washington, that surmounted it, and was also consigned to the flames. Large quantities of the next day's edition of the paper were found, and these joined the sign in keeping alive the Union bonfire.

Mr. Emery, the editor of the paper, soon returned from dinner, and on his arrival at the scene was immediately surrounded by a wild, and jostling crowd. Cries of "Lynch him!" "Hang him!" "Give him some tar and feathers," were heard, and but for the prompt aid of some of his friends he undoubtedly would have come to harm at the hands of the crowd.

He was hurried away from the infuriated multitude and into the drug store on the corner of Hammond and Central streets, then occupied by J. S. Ingraham, and from there he was taken out by a back door and hastily led to the Franklin House, on Harlow street. He was followed by the crowd into the drug store, but his guides by immediately taking him out the back way, baffled the pursuers, who then returned to the square.

The incensed crowd now entered the private office of Mr. Emery on the second floor of the block, and began to ransack his private papers, and prepare to destroy them, but owing to the clear headed arguments of Mr. John Wingate they were induced to cease the destruction of purely personal papers. Mr. Wingate then proceeded to gather up the documents and carried them to a place of safety. These were afterwards returned to Mr. Emery.

Let it not be understood that this gathering of representative citizens was in any sense an ordinary mob; on the contrary they were the better class of men who, in carrying on this destruction, did what they thought to be their duty to their country and to the good name of their fair city.

In an interview with Mr. B——, now a Main street merchant, he said:

"It was arranged that the signal to begin the work of 'dumping out' 'The Democrat,' was to be rung on the First Parish bell by Mr. D——. W——, (now dead), and I was to follow on the bell of the Episcopal Church. After ringing for three minutes we were to come down town, and we intended to have the job done before the engines returned. Our head rusher was a heavy built blacksmith named Tabor, and he was the man who broke up the big press. I am not one who believes in mob law or in violence, but in that case it was clearly necessary." "Why," he concluded, "Deacon —— even carried cases and trash to build that fire with, and he would not assist in anything that was not for the good of the city."

One of the most prominent men in the city at that time, signed a paper a few days before the act of destruction, agreeing to indemnify any man for loss of time or money, in consequence of his "throwing The Democrat" out of doors.

We can see from the above that it was not the ill-advised act of a few fanatics, but was accomplished by our best citizens, and considered by them a loyal and law-preserving necessity.

At a grand Union meeting at Norombega Hall on the Saturday before, resolutions were adopted of which the following are a part:

"*Resolved*,—That the rebel leaders' hope of success is founded mainly, on the aid and assistance which is promised them by the traitors of the North, who sympathize with them, and who are to act their part in the destruction of the Union, *by creating a reaction in Northern public sentiment, and this is to be accomplished by wilful and artful representations that this is an unholy war.*"

*　　*　　*　　*　　*　　*　　*　　*

"*Resolved,—That the newspaper called "The Democrat*," published in this city, by its unscrupulous advocacy of the legal right, and moral justness of the means, measures and ends of Southern secession, by its wilfully false and mendacious representations of the Rebellion, by its exaltations at all disasters, which happened to the National Union, and to our National Flag, is lending that aid and comfort to the armed enemies of our country, which *makes its editors, publishers and proprietors guilty of treason; and we brand all persons, connected with that pestilent sheet, as unworthy of public or private respect, or confidence.*"

The italics are our own, but the sentiment of this convention of the Union men of this county, must certainly show in what regard the paper was held at that time. Jones, who is spoken of in the same accounts in the papers of that day, only escaped by jumping from the awning, in front of his shop, to the street, where he was taken in the carriage of Mr. S. Walker and rapidly driven away. So sudden was his flight that he lost his hat, and the last seen of him for some time, was his disappearance, bareheaded, over State street, behind the flying horse.

The Trial.

In the report of the trial in the Supreme Judicial Court, Waldo County, held at Belfast, October 1866, appears the following:

There was evidence on the part of the plaintiffs tending to show the following facts: That they were owners of a printing establishment, being the chattels named in the writ, with which they executed job work, and printed a newspaper known as "The Democrat," of which the plaintiff, Emery, was editor; that the plaintiffs occupied, and carried on their business in the fourth and fifth stories of Wheelwright & Clark's block, so called, in Bangor, they occupying also a counting room in the second story. Wheelwright & Clark occupied the lower story, and the whole of the back of the building as a store, for their merchandise. The entrance to rooms of the plaintiffs was from West Market Square, and there was also an interior communication through the store of said Wheelwright & Clark, and the rooms were separated by a rough board partition and a door which was locked.

On the 12th of August 1861, the hands employed in the printing office left for dinner at the usual hour, but Emery was detained till about half past twelve, and soon after he left the church bells rang as for an alarm of fire; and about that time, a company of men, numbering from four to twelve entered the store of Wheelwright & Clark, armed with sledge hammers and other implements and were proceeding to go up the stairs in the direction of the plaintiffs room, when the said Clark put his hand upon the banister of the stairs, and forbade them proceeding farther. But they proceeded to the rooms of the plaintiffs, broke up the forms, destroyed their said property and threw it into the street; and immediately upon their reaching said rooms, a crowd began to collect in the streets, numbering from five hundred to two thousand, some of whom collected the materials, as they were thrown from the windows, into piles, and burnt them."

"There was evidence also tending to show that the defendants, Morse, Fifield, Arnold, Mann, Tabor, and Howe, were engaged in the work of breaking, destroying and throwing into the street, the property of the plaintiffs; and the defendants Ingalls, Harlow, Boyd and Rowe, were engaged in breaking up the materials; and defendants Dwinel and Dole, were aiding and assisting in the destruction of the property.

STATE OF MAINE.

Waldo, ss.

[L. S.] To the Sheriffs of our respective counties, or either of their Deputies. Greeting:

We command you to attach the goods, or estate of Rufus Dwinel, Oliver H. Ingalls, Llewellyn J. Morse, Noah S. Harlow, Isaac E. Fifield, Archibald L. Boyd, Marshall J. Egery, Orren Oliver, George H. Stiles, Frank M. Rowe, Jesse M. Arnold, James A. Robinson, Samuel S. Mann, all of Bangor, in the county of Penobscot; and Amasa Howe of Presque Isle, in the county of Aroostook, to the value of thirty thousand dollars, etc. etc.

*　　*　　*　　*　　*　　*　　*

who with force and arms wilfully and maliciously destroyed, without consent of the owners the following named goods, of the value of six thousand two hundred and thirty-four dollars and eighty-two cents."

Here follows a list of everything in the office, in it being mentioned five printing presses, weighing many tons, and valued at twenty-four hundred dollars.

William Thompson was a witness for the plaintiffs, and he testified to the selling of the property to the plaintiffs, and also as to its value.

Gorham L. Boynton was the next witness and testified to the fact that he was known as being a friend of the paper, and testified to its destruction, he being an eye witness. He was followed by Patrick Kelleher, who identified several persons who participated in the destruction and recollected seeing Morse at the window throwing out material. David Boynton saw Tabor at the window cheering. J. G. Clark testified that he tried to prevent the men from going into the office, and also that he had been informed by Dwinel some days previous, of the intended destruction of the office, and had urged Emery to move, and he (Emery) refusing, had given him legal notice to do so. One of the men demanded that a flag should be thrown out, and clerk Robinson being at dinner, I had to do it myself."

Payson C. Webber, Samuel Larrabee, President of the Mercantile Bank; Simon F. Walker Geo. W. Ladd, Cyrus E. Gould, Wm. McDonald, Elijah W. Hasey, Patrick Landers, Charles Gillispie, Benjamin Swett, Thomas W. Burr, Edward A. Buck and Editor Emery also gave, in detail, an account of the affair, after which witnesses for the defense were called.

James A. Robinson, N. S. Harlow, Isaac E. Fifield, Frank M. Rowe, James Dunning, Henry B. Farnham, George W. Whitney, Timothy T. Cates, Samuel S. Mann, Watson E. Plummer, John Trickey, William H. Smith, W. H. Harlow, John F. Patten,

George H. Stiles, J. J. Russell, W. H. H. Pitcher, Samuel Jewett and Thomas W. Burr, testified for defendants, after which the Judge charged the Jury.

The following is the verdict:

"The Jury find that Rufus Dwinel, Charles E. Dole, Oliver H. Ingalls, Llewellyn J. Morse, Noah S. Harlow, Isaac E. Fifield, Marshall J. Egery, Orren Oliver, George H. Styles, Frank M. Rowe, Jesse M. Arnold, James A. Robinson, Amasa Howe, Archibald L. Boyd, are not guilty, in manner and form, as the plaintiffs have declared against them; and that Samuel S. Mann, John Tabor are guilty, in manner and form, as the plaintiffs have declared against them; and assess damages for the plaintiffs, against the said Samuel Mann and John Tabor, in the sum of nine hundred and sixteen dollars and sixty-six cents."

"We have taken into account, the question of "*The Democrat*," of 1861, and find it was a nuisance, and should have been suppressed, or, in otherwise, it was, justifiable to destroy it. We find the property destroyed, over and above what was necessary, is $916.66.   HIRAM T. BLACK, Foreman.

A few days after the destruction of the office, Editor Emery prepared, and caused to be printed, "*The Democrat*—Extra," dated August 20th, 1861. This was a four page paper, about twelve inches long, by nine inches wide, and was printed by Mr. Samuel Smith, who, fearing the anger of the opposition party, had a written agreement with Mr. Emery, that it should be reported that it was printed in Portland. It is an exceedingly interesting number, as it shows, beyond doubt, that the Breckenridge Democrats *did* hold a convention on August 15th, and nominated county officers. This convention was first called to order in the office of Gorham L. Boynton, Esq., then, as now, on Central street, but the citizens brought out an engine, laid hose, and were preparing to play upon the office, when the inmates adjourned to the Bangor House. Major Marion B. Patten, Samuel McLellen, Henry P. Haynes, Benj. Swett, T. K. Holt, A. L. Barton, E. E. Brown, E. N. Stockman, M. G. Tuck, M. S. French, Marcellus Emery, Bradbury Robinson, Washington Weatherbee, Abraham Sanborn, D. F. Leavitt, Gilman Barley, Jabez Knowlton, W. M. R. Miller, and Isaac Dunning were among those who participated in the deliberations, or were chosen to office. A severe attack is made upon Adjutant General John L. Hodsdon, the course of "*The Democrat*" upheld, and then Editor Emery addresses the people as follows, giving his version of the destruction of the his office:

TO THE PEOPLE.

BANGOR, AUGUST 12TH, 1861.

"Ere this will have met your eyes, the telegraph will have announced the total destruction of The Democrat printing establishment by a lawless mob this afternoon. I owe it to myself and to you to give a brief statement of this outrage. On Wednesday afternoon last I was called on by Mr. Clark, of the firm of Wheelwright & Clark, who informed me that a mob spirit was again abroad in the city, and that an attack on my office was again contemplated. He said that he had great fears of the destruction of their building, in which my editorial and printing rooms were located, and requested me to remove my property. I told him I would reply to his request the following morning. He then stated that he had notified the Mayor, Isaiah Stetson, of the threats of the mob, and demanded his protection of the premises. During the next forenoon Mr. Clark again called, and was very urgent that I should have my property removed from his building that afternoon. I replied that his notice was very short, and that I must take until afternoon to consider the matter, adding that if he would do his duty as a citizen, and one of the proprietors of the building, his property could suffer no harm. When he again called on me in the afternoon, I told him that duty to myself as a citizen, duty to my associates in the ownership of the paper, and duty to the public required of me that I should not yield to the demands and pressure of a lawless mob. Subsequent interviews took place between Messrs. Wheelwright & Clark and myself in regard to the matter, the character of which I refrain from making public at this time.

On Saturday morning a call appeared in the Whig and Courier for a Union meeting in Norombega Hall, to be holden that evening. I was not present, but am credibly informed that William H. McCrillis, representative to the Legislature from this city, and Charles S. Crosby, County Attorney, made inflammatory speeches, and said all in their power to excite a mob. And here it should be said to the honor of Henry E. Printiss, Esq., that he attempted to make a speech opposing the efforts then and there being made to create a mob spirit, but his voice was powerless amidst a tempest of hisses. The meeting accomplished the object for which it was designed by those who originated it.

On Saturday and Sunday nights it became evident that my property was to receive no protection from the Mayor. I took such precautions as were necessary for its security. Today I proceeded, as usual on Monday, to print and mail my issue for the week. During the forenoon there were no indications that I saw of mob violence. I left my editorial room about 12.25 to go to my dinner, my boarding place being about half a mile distant. Whilst eating the fire bells were rung. After finishing my meal I set out to return to my office. The first person I met was William H. McCrillis, who was just turning into Broadway from Somerset street. He dropped his head as soon as he saw me, and for the first time since our acquaintance passed me without a salutation. Immediately after I met two gentlemen in a buggy, who informed me that my office had just been sacked, and all my property thrown into the street. Proceeding directly forward, on coming out of Central street I first saw the work of destruction, and there, too, I saw the first mob that had ever met my eyes. West Market Square and surroundings were filled with nearly two thousand people. In the middle of the square was a large fire, on which the multitude were engaged in heaping my tables, stands, cases, and other material. The Wheelwright & Clark blocks were surrounded with the wreck of what had, an hour before, constituted one of the largest and finest printing offices in Maine.

I made my way through the crowd to the stairway, which I found filled with the mob. They made no resistance to my ascending the long stairway. I found my office-door besieged by a large number of persons, armed with crow-bars, and like implements. As I approached the door they fell back. Whilst feeling for my key, one of their leaders, a man who had been honored with a position on our city police, demanded that I should instantly open the door. I then turned round and faced the mob, telling them that that office was rightfully under my control, but that if they saw fit to resort to violence, they could probably over-power me. I was unarmed. Before opening the door, I told them my object was to secure my account books, notes, bills, and private papers, and that I should give them the feeble protection in my power. I then opened the door and set about my business, the mob following me in, and indiscriminately seizing whatever they could lay their hands on, and throwing it out of the window into the street. The work of destruction was soon complete. I then left the office, the mob following me down the stairs. As I reached the sidewalk, there arose the infuriated cry of the mob, "Hang him! Tar and feather him! Kill him!" It was then I felt, how little there is of the terrors and threats of a mob for him who is conscious of having discharged his duty to the public and himself. The mad crowd were thirsty for the blood of one, who had been long and incessantly toiling to save them from the fetters that are being forged for their free limbs. His works may yet bear fruit.

As I made my way through the dense crowd, friend after friend gathered round me, for my protection. Their words of sympathy sank deep into my soul, whilst the demoniac cries for my blood fell unheeded on my ears. But one circumstance disturbed my equanimity, and that was like the sting of an adder. When I was beyond the danger and among friends, the Mayor, who regardless of his oath of office, would give me no protection for my property, who made no attempt to disperse the mob, who did not even order the reading of the riot act, who did not even lift a finger to preserve the peace of the city, although days and hours before warned of the threatened attack—when I was beyond danger, he suddenly conceived an anxiety for my personal safety, and suggested that I had better hurry away. Oh, the contemptibleness of cowardice; the baseness of treachery in high official position!

Thus hath the freedom of the Press been stricken down here in Maine, not from any patriotic impulse, but through the wicked instigation of a band of abandoned politicians who would willingly subvert all law and all order for the maintenance of a mere party dogma.

Though anarchy seems to be coming down upon our unhappy country like night, yet do I not despair. I still believe that there is yet virtue and intelligence enough in the people to maintain their liberties, and protect the free Press, which is their best guardian.

By this act of mob violence my all, the result of years of

unremitting toil, has been swept away; but I still have health, strength and youth, and a heart also, to struggle on in defence of the people's rights."

MARCELLUS EMERY.

Just how indignant Emery was at the conduct of the gentlemen alluded to in the above, is shown by the fact that he secured one of them to act as his attorney at the time of the trial.

Gentlemen now living who took part in the destruction declare to this day that it was a grand work, and convinced the men in the army that no "rear fire" would be tolerated.

CHAPTER XI.

The Fourth Maine—A Gallant Regiment Hampered By Some Poor Material—One Company Reorganized—Deserters Numerous—Some Brilliant Engagements—The Regiment Nearly Annihilated—General Berry Of Rockland—Col. Marshall Of Belfast.

Waldo, Knox, and Lincoln Counties were just as patriotic as those in the northern part of the State, and early in the war began to raise volunteers. It was decided by the authorities to raise the Fourth Regiment from that section, and orders were issued for it to rendevous at Rockland. The band numbered twenty-four members under the leadership of F. Singhi, of Rockland.

Co. "A" was from Belfast, and previous to the war had been known as the "Belfast Artillery," and was commanded by H. W. Cunningham. The record shows that it contained, when mustered in, June 15th, 1861, nineteen natives of Belfast only, while Bangor contributed ten, the balance coming from towns in Waldo County, with a few exceptions. Co. "B" was made up almost wholly of Rockland men, while Co. "C" came from that city and from Thomaston. Co. "D" also had a large number of residents from the city of lime rock and mud, with a sprinkling of men from the islands in Penobscot Bay. "E" was a miscellaneous collection, while "F" was raised in Waldo County, by Andrew D. Bean, of Brooks. "G" was from Wiscassett, "H" from Rockland, and was commanded under the old organization by G. J. Burns of that city, but, under the new organization, stood, Nov. 9th, 1861, under command of Wm. L. Pitcher, Albert L. Spencer and Geo. F. Bourne. "I" was from Searsport, Stockton and Winterport, with a few representatives of other towns thrown in to fill the ranks. "K" was from Belfast, and was formerly known as the "City Greys." Sixty-five of its members were from Belfast, the total number of privates being eighty-five. The author's first recollection of the war was a conversation held in his father's house regarding this company. One of the officers, at that time, rented a portion of the house, and often conversed with my parents regarding the company's action. There was a desire, on the part of some, to stay at home, yet they did not like to take the responsibility of refusing to enlist. Said one of these men to his comrades:

"The officers don't want to go. If we go down to-night and enlist, the officers won't sign, and we can then withdraw and throw the blame where it belongs."

This was done, and much to their surprise the officers signed too. That night the armory in Phœnix Row was broken open and search made for the papers, but Mr. Marshall had taken the precaution to carry them home, and the very few who wanted all the honors, and none of the dangers, were caught in a trap of their own setting. There were some boasters in their ranks.

One man, in a speech in Pierce's Hall, said he was going down into that Southern country, "and, if my courage be equal to my physical strength, *woe*—WOE—WOE be unto any rebel that gets into my hands." This man returned before the Bull Run fight, declaring he lay in his tent one night in Washington, spending the time in drinking ice water, and fanning himself without reducing his temperature, and could not stand the hot weather. However, the company was all right, and participated in the first great battle, where a number of men distinguished themselves. Before the end of the year, the captain had been promoted, the lieutenants had resigned, Lieutenant Carter, on account of deafness, caused by the roar of cannon at Bull Run, and the company was commanded by new men, two of whom had gone out as sergeants, while the other, Lieutenant Bisbee, had been taken from the ranks. When the regiment left Rockland it had, officers, musicians, wagoners, men and band, 1120 men. During the war many recruits were added to fill the places, so far as they could, of those killed, wounded and discharged, but such was the loss that at the end of three years, when the regiment returned, there were but three hundred and fourteen men to muster out. The regiment after leaving Washington on July 16th, marched to Centreville, and at the battle of Bull Run did grand work, being among the last to leave the field. "Ed" Redman, a member of company K, loaded and fired his gun until it became so heated as to blister his hands, and he was taken from the field by force, by his comrades. He was promoted after the battle to the position of Corporal. In the battle four officers were wounded or taken prisoners, seventeen privates killed and forty wounded.

After nine months at or near Washington, the Regiment participated in the siege of Yorktown, and after its evacuation was sent forward toward Williamsburg. From this place they went towards

Richmond, going into camp twelve miles from that place. They were from time to time engaged with the enemy, loosing more or less men each time, until their available force was reduced to two hundred and forty men, this being the number participating at Chantilly on the 1st of September. They were at this time on the retreat and later arrived near Washington. On the 15th they again crossed into Maryland and guarded the fords of the Upper Potomac. On the 12th of October they assisted in the attempt to intercept Stuart's Cavalry at Conrad's Ferry. On Nov. 22d they arrived at Falmouth, and left there on Dec. 13th to participate in the battle of Fredericksburg. They re-crossed the river on the 15th, returning to their old Falmouth camp, where they passed the balance of the winter. On the 26th of April, 1863, they crossed the Rappahannock, taking a prominent part in the battle of Chancellorsville. On June 11th they joined in the campaign resulting in the battle of Gettysburg, where on the second day of July, they lost in killed and missing eighty-six men with fifty-three wounded. Several other engagements were participated in, and when the army was re-organized under Grant, they were assigned to the Second Army Corps. On the 4th of May the Rapidan was crossed, and on the next day were heavily engaged at Torbet's Tavern, where they supported a brigade of the Sixth corps. That night they marched back to their division, and at daybreak on the 6th advanced on the enemy's works. They fought two days. This was the battle of the Wilderness, and here they lost officers killed, two; men killed, thirty-two; wounded one hundred and forty-seven, with three missing. From the 8th to the 23d the regiment was engaged in reconnoitering, building fortifications, etc., and then moved two miles to the front and took position in line of battle. The following day the regiment was relieved from duty in the army and ordered to proceed to Rockland, Me., where they arrived on the morning of the 25th. The men were furloughed until the 19th of July, on which day two hundred and forty-one officers and enlisted men were mustered out and discharged the U. S. service by Capt. Thomas C. J. Bailey, Seventeenth U. S. Infantry, the re-enlisted men and recruits whose term of service had not expired, having been transferred to the Nineteenth Regt. Me. Vols., before the departure of the regiment from the field.

The history of this regiment is not equal to many Maine bodies, for the reason that among the earlier enlistments were some poor material. Co. H. was re-organized and the record shows that a captain was dishonorably discharged, seventy-one men transferred to other companies or regiments, while no less than ten, or one out of every eight, deserted July 25th, 1861. In all there were thirty-eight desertions the first summer. The cause for much of this seeming disloyalty was identical with that which brought trouble to the Second Maine, and is fully described in the history of that organization. Two men, Col. Hiram Berry, of Rockland, and Col. Thomas H. Marshall, of Belfast, both at one time connected with the Fourth, deserve special mention. Col. Marshall died early in the war, while colonel of the Seventh, at Baltimore, the date being Oct. 25th, 1861. He was universally beloved by his comrades, was a gentleman of wealth and culture, and entered the army, not for honor or gain, but from motives which actuated every patriot. Belfast lost in his death, a noble citizen, and all felt that diseases contracted in the malarial low lands of Maryland, were powerful aids in cutting off the gallant men who had gone forth to do battle for the cause of Freedom. Of General Berry, his high standing as a man and his qualities as a soldier, are fully described under his "biographical sketch."

Col. THOS. H. MARSHALL.

CHAPTER XII.

"All Quiet On The Potomac"—A Few Battles In The West—Formation Of Other Maine Regiments—A Big War Meeting—A National Fast In September—Sharp Shooters Wanted—What Was Required Of Them—Chas. Hamlin, Esq., Opens A Recruiting Office—Penobscot County And Bangor Bear Off State Honors—Gen. Jameson Commands A Brigade—Col. Roberts In Command Of Several Forts—The Banks Suspend Specie Payment—The Close Of The Year—The Soldiers In Winter Quarters—Some Of The Stories They Told.

After the battle of Bull Run the opposing forces busied themselves in recruiting, repairing damages, and preparing in other ways for future operations. August 12th, the Associated Press telegram from the front was headed with what afterwards became a familiar expression: "All Quiet on the Potomac," or as one good old soul used to read it, "All quiet on the *Pot-o-mac*." There was some fighting in the West and South, but nothing of special interest to the people of Eastern Maine took place. Quite a number of officers came home on furloughs, some came home to stay, while many of our citizens made visits to the boys at the front. Thus it was that the soldiers were kept well acquainted with home affairs in which they took a lively interest.

If all was quiet on the Potomac, the same could not be said of the dwellers on the Penobscot. Other regiments were forming, and, in addition to this, men were being enlisted for the navy and for other branches of the service. The spirit of '76 seemed to be everywhere and every now and then a grand rally, or Union war meeting would be held. At midnight, Sept. 20th, the editor of "The Whig" penned the following:

"We have only time to say now, 12 o'clock, midnight, as the Union meeting is breaking up, that the meeting far outstripped all the glorious Union meetings which have been held in our city, since the war blood was sent coursing through our Northern veins, by the dastardly attack upon our glorious flag at Sumpter."

In September a National Fast Day was appointed by President Lincoln, and was generally observed throughout the North.

In this month, also, a call was made for regiments of Sharp Shooters, and, as was natural, the Government officials looked for material on the outskirts of the country, rather than in the cities and thickly populated districts. An advertisement issued at the time, will serve to show the kind of material needed.

SHARP SHOOTERS!—NOTICE!

"Those wishing to engage in the company of Sharp Shooters, now being formed in this State, will be examined by J. D. Fessenden, Esq., of Portland, J. J. Robinson, of Augusta, Jacob McClure, Rockland, or R. R. Park, of Bangor. The General Order has been so changed as to require but one examination. None but able bodied men need apply, and none who cannot, when shooting at rest at a distance of two hundred yards, put ten consecutive shots in a target, the average distance not to exceed five inches from the centre of the bull's eye to the centre of the ball, which is very easy to do with such rifles as are furnished for the test."

☞ "Office at C. V. Ramsdell's, No. 3 Harlow street, Bangor, Maine."

About this time Charles Hamlin, Esq., opened a recruiting office in Orland, and proceeded to recruit a company of cavalry.

A table, issued October 11th, made a showing in favor of Penobscot County and the City of Bangor, which was highly gratifying to the residents. Up to that time the County had furnished fifteen companies, as follows:

Second Regiment, 8 companies,
Sixth   "   2   "
Seventh   "   2   "
Eighth   "   2   "
Ninth   "   1   "

Bangor led all cities, having up to that time furnished nine companies.

October found Gen. Jameson in command of a brigade of four Pennsylvania regiments under Gen. Heintzelman, and located on the extreme left flank of the Army of the Potomac, and Gen. Roberts in command of Fort Corcoran, having been ordered there as follows:

HEADQUARTERS, PORTER'S DIVISION,
FORT CORCORAN.

Special Orders, No. 18.

For purpose of discipline and regularity, Col. C. W. Roberts, Second Maine Regiment, is assigned to the command of the post of Fort Corcoran."

"The post will comprise all within the limits of the breastworks of Fort Corcoran, also Forts DeKalb, Woodbury and Cass, redoubts 1, 2 and 3."

"The garrison of these forts, and forts Bennett, Haggerty and Corcoran, and the Ferry Guards, will look to Col. Roberts for instruction, and be governed by his orders. All requisitions, expenditures, etc., will be controlled by the Division and Brigade Commanders."

By command of
Brigadier Gen., F. J. PORTER,
JAMES F. McQUESTION, Lieutenant, A. D. C.,
COL. C. W. ROBERTS, Commanding Second Maine Regt.

In December, Monday the 30th, being the date, came the news of the suspension of specie payment, by the National banks of Boston and New York, and immediately on receipt of this, the officials of the Bangor banks adopted the following resolutions:

"Whereas, the condition of the country requires all the aid a patriotic people can render, and,

Whereas, the banks of New York and Boston have suspended specie payment, in order to aid the government and people by retaining the specie in the country in their time of trial.

Therefore, Resolved: That the banks of this city suspend specie payments, until otherwise ordered.

Resolved: That the banks throughout New England are in a sound condition, and able to redeem all their liabilities, on a specie basis; that the act and necessity of suspending specie payment, is to aid the Government and people in their efforts to put down a most wicked and unnatural rebellion in our sister Southern States."   SAMUEL VEAZIE, Chairman.

A. M. ROBERTS, Secretary.

The year 1861 was drawing to a close, and the army of the Potomac, like their friends at home, were in winter quarters. All those long winter months the two great armies, which, later on were to engage in some of the greatest battles known in the history of the world, lay opposite each other waiting for the warm months to come, when they should meet again. Little fighting was done, but many men lost their lives, some by disease, some by accident and many by the hand of the sharp shooter. When not engaged in military duty the men passed the time in card playing, reading, writing and at various games and feats of skill and strength, and so whiled away the dreary winter days.

Many are the stories told and many the jokes played among the men during there long season of inactivity.

A young Irishman, a member of a Bangor company in the Second regiment, is reported to have got off the following: While in camp in Washington he was giving an account of the fight at Bull Run, and on being asked "how he would like to see Bull Run again?" replied "Be jazes! that's just the kind of a Bull I don't want to see Run at all, at all." And he echoed the sentiments of the entire North, in these few but pithy words.

While the Tenth Regiment was in Portland, in October, '61, there was great trouble in keeping the men together, as is often the case, for it was but natural that men should look for all the enjoyment they could find in times like those, and it was necessary to keep a squad most of the time looking up stragglers. One of these parties came across a countryman, who, thinking to beautify himself, had put on a part of the uniform of the old First. He was immediately seized and dragged off, notwithstanding his protestations that he was not a soldier. He begged to be allowed to sell his load of wood and take care of his cattle, but no, his captors were inexorable. He must go. An officer took charge of his team, and the poor fellow was marched to camp, where we will hope he succeeded in convincing one officer that he did not "belong to the show."

During Gen. Butler's trip to Augusta, in '61, a large concourse of people collected at the depot, in Hallowell, to greet him as he passed through on the train. A resident by the name of Jefferson Davis was introduced as Mr. Jeff. Davis. Seizing him by the hand with an iron grasp, Gen. Butler said "You are the man I have been after for a long time; now I have got you." The amusement this incident excited at the time was immense.

A good story is told, at the expense of the neighboring town of Troy. One day, during the first year of the war, it was rumored that a gentleman, hitherto an ardent Union man and a loyal citizen, had raised a "secesh" flag on his house. Immediately all was excitement, and an immense crowd at once started for the house of the "vile copperhead," (as they supposed). On reaching the house there was the flag, as calmly floating in the breeze as if it had never caused war or bloodshed, but on closer inspection it proved to be a lady's balmoral skirt, that had been washed and hung from a window to dry. The husband avowed his determination to stand by *that* flag as long as he lived, and the effervescent crowd exploded and went away.

In the fall of '61, might have been seen opposite the Medical Hall in Great St. James Street, Montreal, above which is the office of the American Consul, a handsome tablet, on which was nicely painted the following: "*Erected in memory of the* SOLES (OF BOOTS) *who were left behind at the battle of* BULL RUN. MAY THEIR MEMORY NEVER WEAR OUT."

An anecdote is told of a down east Irishman, who was asked by another Maine man to assist him off the field. The good hearted son of Erin did so by enabling him to mount, strapping him to his horse and then riding on before. During the ride the head of the injured man was shot entirely away, unknown to Pat. Arriving at the doctor's quarters, Pat was asked what he wanted, "I brought this man to have his leg dressed." "Why," replied the doctor "his head is off!" "The bloody liar!" exclaimed Pat, looking behind him for the first time, "he told me he was only shot in the leg."

An amusing scene occured in the camp of a division that included many Maine soldiers early in the war. These troops were engaged in a brisk skirmish with the rebels, while on the other side of a small creek, was another division in camp and the paymaster counting out the gold, due to the troops for their services. Word was received of what was going on over the river, and the men sprang to their arms, expecting an order to march. The regiment among whom the money was being distributed turned their backs on the paymaster and his treasure, as if it were a matter of no account. One man was signing a receipt for the yellow heap then lying on the table, he dropped his pen, and rushed for the camp, leaving pen, paper and gold to take care of themselves. Another hastily shouted "hold on to mine till tomorrow," and darted from the tent. The paymaster was left alone with his gold with time to contemplate the curious incidents of war.

A squad of the Second Maine, out scouting, came across an old woman in a cabin, in the mountains. After the usual salutations, one of them asked her " Well, old lady, are you secesh?"

"No," was her answer.

" Are you Union ?"

"No."

"Well, what are you ?"

" *A Baptist, and al'ys have been.*"

The "log-roller from Maine" let down.

A member of one of the Bangor companies was seen soon after the battle of Bull Run, in Portland, and on being asked "how he came there," replied, " I got the order to *'fall back'* at Bull Run and hav'nt been ordered to ' *halt* ' yet, and shall fall back 'till I do, if it takes me clear to Bangor."

One of the Hampden men in the Virginia campaign, where the orders against foraging were very strict, killed a sheep and was enjoying the delicate tit-bit in company with his chums, when he was discovered and brought before his superior officers, and asked if "he did not know of the orders against borrowing food from the farmers." He replied that he did. "Then," said his captain " why did you kill that sheep ?" " Wal," answered the culprit, "yer see cap'n, there aint no darned sheep going to bite me and live." One can easily guess that he was let off without punishment.

One of our Maine soldiers was out on picket duty, early in the war, when the following incident occurred:

An F. F. V., with rather more than the usual superciliousness of his race, rode up in a carriage from the direction of Alexandria, driven by his "servant." The down-easter, of course, stepped into the road, holding his bayonet in such a way as to threaten horse, negro and white-man at one charge, and roared out "Tickets." Mr. V. turned up his lids, set down his brows, and by other gestures indicated his contempt of such "mud-sills" as the soldier before him, ending by handing his pass over to the darkey, and motioning him to get out and show it.

"All right" said the soldier, glancing at it, "move on," accompanying the remark with a jerk at the coat collar of the colored person, that sent him spinning down the road. "Now, sir, what do *you* want?" addressing the astonished white man.

White man had by this time recovered his tongue. "Want? I want to go on, of course, that was my pass." "Can't help it," was the reply; "it says pass the *bearer*, and the bearer is already passed. You can't pass two men through *this* picket on one man's pass."

Mr. V. reflected a moment, and glanced at the bayonet in front of him, and then called to the black man to come back. Sambo approached cautiously, but fell back in confusion when the "shooting iron" was brandished towards his own breast.

"Where's your pass, sirrh?" Asked the "Maniac."

"Here, massa," said the chattel, presenting the same one he had received from the gent in the carriage.

"Won't do," replied the holder of the bayonet. That passes you to Fairfax.—Can't let any one come *from* Fairfax on *that* ticket. MOVE ON." A stamp of the foot sent Sambo down the road, at a hand gallop.

"Now, sir, if you stay here any longer, I shall take you under arrest to headquarters," he continued.

Mr. V. grabbed up his lines, wheeled around, and went off at the best trot his horses could manage over the "sacred soil." Whether Sambo ever hunted up his master, is not known.

CHAPTER XIII.

The State Guards—A Company In Each Ward—One Or More In Each Town—The Officers—The Orders To Drill—The First American Boycott—A Great Rally—An Immense Crowd In Bangor—Gen. Howard Arrives—Serious Accident At Norombega Hall—The Platform Gives Way—Many Ladies Injured—The City Council Increases The Bounty—"Excursion" To Richmond.

Early in 1862 there was formed what was known as Ward Companies of Militia. Gen. Butler had received orders from Washington to form such companies, and he designated the Orderly Sergeants as follows:

Ward 1, Russell B. Shepard.
" 2, Theo. C. Johnson.
" 3, John A. Lancy.
" 4, Geo. W. Stevens.
" 5, Henry E. Sellers.
" 6, Edward P. Connors.
" 7, Joseph F. Snow.

WARD COMPANIES.

On Friday, July 11th, the Ward Three Company, 125 strong, met and made choice of the following officers:

John Gilman, Captain.
John F. McNamard, First Lieut.
Benj. C. Frost, Second Lieut.
Ezekiel Andrews, Third Lieut.
C. Edwin Smith, Fourth Lieut.

Ward Two elected as follows:

T. C. Johnson, Captain.
J. C. Thorndike, First Lieut.
Wm. Connors, Second Lieut.
N. G. Higgins, Third Lieut.
Roscoe F. Hersey, Fourth Lieut.

The Ward Six, a company of good size, chose:

L. J. Morse, Captain.
Levi Murch, First Lieut.
A. B. Marston, Second Lieut.
Wm. W. Seavey, Third Lieut.
Robert S. Graves, Fourth Lieut.

WARD FOUR.

James W. Williams, Captain.
Chas. L. Crane, First Lieut.
Warren G. Smith, Second Lieut.
Fred S. Davenport, Third Lieut.
F. W. Ring, Fourth Lieut.

WARD FIVE.

Benj. B. Thatcher, Captain.
Chas. I. Collimore, First Lieut.
Wm. F. Noyes, Second Lieut.
Sullivan D. Wiggin, Third Lieut.
Daniel C. Gould, Fourth Lieut.

WARD SEVEN.

CHRISTOPHER V. CROSSMAN, Captain.
JOSEPH F. SNOW, First Lieut.
ALBERT HASKELL, Second Lieut.
SETH E. DRINKWATER, Third Lieut.
CHARLES D. CLARK, Fourth Lieut.

MILFORD COMPANY.

ISAAC S. TWOMBLY, Captain.
JOHN STOCKMAN, First Lieut.
W. J. BUTTERFIELD, Second Lieut.
C. W. LENFEST, Third Lieut.
JOHN H. JACKSON, Fourth Lieut.

ORONO COMPANY.

JOHN W. ATWELL, Captian.
CHARLES W. ROSS, First Lieut.
E. W. BUTLER, Second Lieut.
CHARLES HOLT, Third Lieut.
JOHN E. BENNOCK, Fourth Lieut.

BREWER COMPANY.

A. H. BARNES, Captain.
E. C SWETT, First Lieut.
W. W. DOANE, Second Lieut.
M. H. PATTEN, Third Lieut.
A. WHITE, Fourth Lieut.

OLDTOWN COMPANIES.

COMPANY A.

DAVID N. ESTABROOKS, Captain.
BENJ. F. POOR, First Lieut.
JEROME W. SAWTELLE, Second Lieut.
J. A. SWAN, Third Lieut.
CHARLES NOYES, Fourth Lieut.

COMPANY B.

J. G. JAQUITH, Captain.
JESSE HARRIMAN, First Lieut.
CHAS. PURINGTON, Second Lieut.
SEWELL CHAPMAN, Third Lieut.
RICHARD MOORE, Fourth Lieut.

On Monday, August 4th, 1862, was inaugurated the famous Ward drills by the several companies. About nine hundred men turned out and when united in battalion made a fine appearance. Vice-President Hamlin turned out with Ward Three Company, and drilled the whole afternoon, and afterwards addressed his comrades. Nearly all the the stores were closed, but the few who did attempt to do business were dressed down in the Whig as follows: "The Times complains that a few parties kept their places of business open Monday afternoon, during the general drill."

* * * * * * * *

"Such parties will have no excuse in the future, and next Monday will show who thoughtlessly, and who knowingly violate the general rule, and we presume the loyal public will be slow to patronize those who are unwilling to give one half day in the week to their country."

These drills were thought at that time to be needed, so that all citizens would be prepared for emergencies. As may be supposed there was considerable fun, and the troops in their everyday dress presented anything but a soldierly appearance. Two companies only were armed with guns, and the others, in place of arms, carried laths gathered from the lumber yards. It is not now known whether Ward Three Company carried guns or not, but if they had laths, it must have been a pleasant sight to see our venerable ex-Vice-President, as he marched with his neighbors, and with military precision obeyed the orders to "Shoulder laths! Carry laths! Ground laths," etc.

The following order was issued soon after:

STATE OF MAINE.

HEADQUARTERS—FIRST DIVISION.
BANGOR, JULY 16TH, 1862.

Special Order No. 1.

The Commanding Officers of the several companies of Militia, in the city of Bangor, will call out their companies on Thursday, the 17th inst, at 6 o'clock P. M., for parade.

The line will be formed at 7 o'clock, precisely, on Main street, the right resting on Union street. The order of formation will be by Wards, from One to Seven—Right to left.

All the companies of Militia in the surrounding towns, who can make it convenient, are respectfully invited to be present, and will form on the left in the order of arriving.

By order of the Major General.

CHARLES E. DOLE, Orderly Aid-de-Camp.

The next evening was the one on which the grand rally was to be held, and promptly at the appointed hour the various commands assembled, with Major Gen. J. H. Butler in command, assisted by Col. I. B. Norcross and Major Thomas Hersey. They marched through several streets and then to Norombega Hall, where it was intended to hold the meeting.

Meanwhile an immense number of people had arrived from surrounding towns, among them being the Oldtown Militia and the Oldtown Band, a company and a band from Brewer, several bands and companies from along the line of the railroad and from down river. When the procession arrived at the hall it was found to be densely packed, and it was concluded to hold the meeting in the open air. In the twinkle of an eye after this announcement, Post-office Avenue and Central Bridge were filled with people, and it was then found the military organizations could not be placed within hearing distance of the speakers, and they were taken into the hall, and ladies admitted to the galleries. Outside of the hall a platform had been erected for Gen. Howard, who arrived by the evening train. So great was the crowd at this point, that the front approach to the hall gave way, and its human burden of men, women and children fell some twelve feet, to the foundation of the building. It was reported inside the hall that the bridge had given way, and a crowd rushed for the door, but, as the platform was gone they could not get out, and a panic ensued. The gas pipes leading to the hall were broken, and this added to the excitement. By the use of ladders the people were rescued from the pit, when it was found many were injured, the most serious being Mrs. Atkins, Mrs. Cobb, Mrs. Kenney, Mrs. McRuer, all of Bangor; and Mrs. Farrington, Mrs. Gregg and Mrs. Nealey, of Brewer.

The crowd now gathered at the Bangor House, and Hon. John A. Peters was made President. He addressed the people, and was followed by Gen. Howard, Vice-President Hamlin. Hon. S. H. Blake, Wm. H. McCrillis, Esq., and Hon. Lewis Barker.

Before the meeting closed there was an alarm of fire, and a great crowd rushed away, and the meeting closed at midnight.

Soon after this meeting the city council passed an order directing the city to offer the following bounty: $55.00 to every man joining an old regiment—this to be paid to residents of Bangor only, and being restricted to those who might enlist within 15 days—and put out the following inducements:

		Old Regt.	New Regt.
State Bounty,	- - -	$55.00	- - $45.00
City "	- - - -	65.00	- - 55.00
U. S. " ($100, ¼ in advance)		25.00	- - 25.00
1 Month's Advance Pay,	-	13.00	- - 13.00
Premium,	- - - -	2.00	- - 2.00
		$160.00	$140.00

In addition to this there was promised $75.00 at the close of the war, and 160 acres of land, if the soldier or his heirs should occupy it, and the address concludes:

"Here is a *cash bonus* to every volunteer of $202.00 in one case, and $222.00 in the other, besides the regular pay, rations and clothing of the soldier. Have more liberal rewards ever been given by any country, to those of her sons who came to her defence in the field, in the time of national peril?"

"Let the patriotic young men now rally to the flag! The Cause needs men *now!*"

The draft was hinted at again, and men were cautioned against entertaining the belief that if drafted they might then enlist and secure the above amounts of money.

Among the recruiting ads. at this time, was the following:

"*Grand Excursion to Richmond,* by Steamboat and Rail! Ticket entitles the bearer to passage to Richmond. Fare, food and clothes, gratis, and $160.00 given each one. Tickets free."

CHAPTER XIV.

History Of The Second Maine Regiment, From The Spring Of '62—They Leave Hall's Hill—Ordered To Yorktown—Siege Of Yorktown—They Receive The Thanks Of Gens. McClellan And Porter—Chickahominy—Battle Of Hanover Court House—Gaine's Mill—Malvern Hill—The Camp At Harrison's Landing—On To Fredricksburg—They Give Battle To The Enemy At Manassas—Picket Duty At Stone Bridge—The Battle Of Fredricksburg—Close Of The Year.

The Second Maine had, in the latter part of October, '61, been assigned to the First Brigade, Porter's Division, and went into camp for the winter at Hall's Hill.

Here they remained until March 1st, '62, when they received orders to march to Manassas, and one may readily believe that the gallant Second was only too glad to move after so long an idleness. The enemy, however, learned of the advance, and anticipated the arrival of our boys, and the Second was ordered to Alexandria where they remained for four days and then embarked for Fortress Monroe.

On their arrival they were put at picket duty on the road leading to Big Bethel. After nearly a week of this duty they received orders to go to Yorktown, where, with the Twenty-second Massachusetts, and Twenty-fifth New York Regiments, and Martin's Third Massachusetts Battery, they immediately engaged the enemy's right, who was found to be so strongly entrenched that the attempt was given up.

Through some oversight of the commanding officer the Second remained in the trenches in a cold rain storm for more than twenty-four hours. The enemy would make a sorte and "let blaze" in the direction of any slight sound that might be heard, then fall

BREVET BRIG.-GEN. GEORGE VARNEY.

back to their works and get warm again. But our poor boys could only lay quiet and shiver, and hope for orders.

One of the boys, (a tent-mate of Dr. Hanson of Bangor), was an inveterate smoker, and, cautiously getting on his knees managed to cut up a pipe full of tobacco and filled his pipe. He then proceeded to light a match, and with visions of a blissful smoke, put the flame to the tobacco; fatal act, for the rebs saw the flame and it made a fine target for them. Before our friend could draw a single cloud from the fragrant pipe a rebel slug was crashing through his leg. He crawled to Dr. Hanson, and, telling him that he was shot, asked what he should do. Our troops were then in a peach orchard, and the doctor directed him to follow the row of trees directly back of them, and he would come to an old cabin that had been established as a hospital. His left leg was useless, but dragging himself as best he could on his hands and one leg he finally gained the house. Here were a number of young surgeons, who thought they must cut off the leg to save the life, but even here they failed, as the poor man died soon after.

The regiments however, held their ground until the next day. During this spirited engagement the skirmishers of the Second, under Captains Foss and Wilson, Lieutenant Boynton and others, acted with great firmness, being under an extremely hot artillery fire over four hours. This attack was made long before the arrival of the main body of the Union Army. During the remainder of the seige of Yorktown, the Second was occupied in the trenches, in building bridges, doing picket duty, etc. The last ditch or trench before Yorktown was begun and completed by the Second, assisted by the Thirteenth New York Regiment. After finishing this work, (which must have been of great advantage to the Union Army in their operations, had the enemy not evacuated,) the Second, through Major Chaplin, received the thanks of both Generals McLellan and Porter.

Two days after the enemy's evacuation of Yorktown, the Second left for the Chickahominy, by the way of West Point. A march of several days brought them to Gaines' Station, where Porter's corps composed the right flank of the Army of the Potomac. On the night of May 26, the Second, with the greater portion of the corps, advanced on Hanover Court House, where they arrived the next forenoon, and immediately gave battle to the enemy. The Second was detailed, together with the Twenty-Second Massachusetts Regiment, to annoy the enemy's right, who only replied with one piece of artillery. Meanwhile they cut the telegraph wire running to Richmond, and also for some distance destroyed the railroad running in the same direction, about one mile from Hanover Court House, where the remainder of the corps had been ordered.

Moving on after the main body, the Second had not proceeded more than a mile before they were attacked by six Rebel regiments, who were posted in their rear, under cover of the woods.

The Second had only a portion each of the Forty-Fourth and Twenty-Fifth New York Regiments, and a section of the Third Massachusetts Battery, to assist them in resisting the attack. For one hour and a half they held their ground, saving the section of the battery, which the gunners were obliged to desert, and which decided the victory won on that day. In this encounter, the Second expended sixty rounds of ammunition, and had prepared for a charge, when they fortunately received re-inforcements, General Porter sending all his command to their relief. For their noble conduct on this occasion, Col. Roberts received personally for his command, the thanks of Gens. McLellan, Porter, Morell and Martindale. After remaining forty-eight hours, awaiting the arrival of McDowell's forces, which failed to appear, the Second was obliged to retrace their steps, making inside of fifty hours a forced march of over thirty miles, and entirely putting to flight a much superior force of the enemy. During this brilliant engagement their loss was slight, though the number of wounded was large.

During the month that followed, the Second was variously occupied in doing picket duty, building roads, etc. The last picket duty that was performed on the right bank of the Chickahominy, was by them, they leaving in season to particiapate in the battle of Gaine's Mill. Their conduct during this engagement was most gallant. For six hours they nobly stood their ground under a heavy fire, capturing the colors of the Fifth Alabama regiment, and totally routing the command to which they belonged.

This was the beginning of the grand retreat towards Harrison's Landing. During the seven day's retreat the Second were repeatedly under fire, and at the battle of Malvern Hill, successfully held a dangerous and conspicuous position during the day, and losing but few men.

At Harrison's Landing they remained several weeks, when finally, on its evacuation, they were ordered to join Gen. Pope, and Col. Roberts temporarily assumed command of the First Brigade, which included the Second Maine.

Marching across the Chickahominy near its mouth, or where it flows into the James river, thence across to Williamsburg, thence down the peninsular to Yorktown and Fortress Monroe, thence to Newport News, from whence they embarked for Acquia Creek, where they disembarked and marched to Fredricksburg, they at last encountered the enemy on August 30, at Manassas. In this terrible engagement the First Brigade made the attack. Each regiment charged simultaneously, but the enemy had chosen too strong a position, and for lack of proper support they were obliged to give way. Col. Roberts had his horse shot from under him. The Second retired in good order, in regular line of battle, led by Major

Sargent, who, although seriously wounded, refused to yield the command. The following morning, by order of Gen. Morell, they moved to Centreville, where Col. Roberts resumed command of the Second, thence to Chain Bridge, Hall's Hill and Alexandria, and finally camping on Arlington Heights, where, after remaining for three days, they received hasty orders to march into Maryland.

At Antietam the Second were under fire in the reserve. After the battle they were on picket at Stone Bridge, and their skirmishers were among the first to enter Sharpsburg after the enemy had left, and who were in possession of the town before the Union cavalry arrived. Shortly after this the Second, in attempting to ford the Potomac at Sheppardstown, were confronted by a superior force of the enemy, and under a galling fire were obliged to reford the river. Remaining at Sharpsburg nearly six weeks, they were ordered under General Hooker to Burnside's army at Falmouth.

At the battle of Fredericksburg the Second took part, and behaved with undaunted bravery. They suffered greatly among the commissioned officers, no less than ten being wounded. Col. Varney, who was in command was wounded. In addition to the severe engagement with the enemy, the regiment had to lie before the rebel breastworks twenty-six hours, exposed to the fire of their sharp shooters, being able to withdraw with safety only under cover of the darkness.

The Adjutant General's Report for 1862, says:

"The great success that has ever attended the Second, is, in a great measure, owing to the superiority of the officers. Since the regiment entered the service it has never received a word of censure."

"Among the most faithful, gallant and meritorious of all the volunteer officers in the war, was Col. Charles W. Roberts, of

Bangor, whose name has become a household word at every fireside in the State. Constant and unremitting service with his regiment, (which was the first at the seat of war from this State, and whose record is with the proudest in heroic deeds), so impaired his health, that in justice to himself he felt obliged to tender his resignation in the fall of '62, and at a time, when a Brigadier General's commission was being placed at his disposal."

"So reluctant was the War Department to part with his services, that the acceptance of his resignation was withheld until after he had renewed the expression of his unalterable determination to decline, not only further service as Colonel, but also the offered promotion to be Brigadier General, and it was only on the tenth of January, 1863, that he received an honorable discharge."

Col. Roberts was succeeded by Lieutenant Col. Varney, who is at this day, a member of the firm of Chas. Hayward & Co., the leading merchants in their line in Bangor.

The Second Maine was mustered out of the service, after the expiration of two years (its time of enlistment) at Bangor, June 4th and 9th, 1863, by Captain Thomas C. J. Baily, U. S. Infantry.

Of its record the Adjutant General's report for 1863, says:

"This regiment during its term of service was engaged in thirteen battles, and on every occasion invariably distinguished itself. During Gen. Hooker's operations at Fredericksburg and Chancellorsville, it formed a portion of his right wing.

At the last named battle it was mostly behind breastworks. When the regiment's time had expired in May, one hundred and twenty-five of the number who were sworn in for three years service, were transferred to the Twentieth Regiment. The regiment returned home with two hundred and seventy-five, including officers and men. It has a record second to none which has ever been in service, and officers and men of the command can look back with pride on the untarnished fame of the noble Second Maine."

CHAPTER XV.

History Of The Sixth Maine—Chain Bridge—On The March—Lewinsville—Fort Griffin—Col. Burnham—The New Officers—Much Fighting—A Singular Combat—The Axe Brigade—Sleeping On Their Arms—Much Fighting And Great Losses—Daring Deeds By Co. "D"—Col. Burnham Ordered To Maine—Lieut. Harris In Command—Rappahannock Station—Col. Harris Seriously Wounded And Maj. Fuller Takes Command—Defending Washington—Arrival At Portland—Mustered Out.

The Sixth regiment, after leaving Bangor, rendezvoused at Portland and reached Washington July 19th, '61. For the remainder of the year they located at the following places:

At Chain Bridge, July 20th to Sept. 3d.

At what is now Fort Ethan Allen, Virginia, from Sept. 3d to Sept. 28th.

On a line of march from Sept. 28th to Oct. 1st.

At Vanderberg's, Virginia, from Oct, 1st to Oct. 10th.

On a line of March from Oct. 10th to Oct. 12th.

At Lewinsville, Va., from Oct. 12th to Dec. 1st.

From December 1st to April 4th, '62, they occupied Fort Griffin, with occasional jaunts back and forth.

Col. Knowles having resigned in December, Lieut. Col. Burnham was promoted to his place, and Capt. Chas. H. Chandler, of Co. A, was promoted to fill his place. The roster of field and staff officers then stood:

Colonel, HIRAM BURNHAM, of Cherryfield.

Lieut. Col., CHAS. H. CHANDLER, Foxcroft.

Major, FRANK PIERCE, Bucksport.

Adjutant, JOHN D. MCFARLAND, Ellsworth.

Quartermaster, ADDISON P. BUCK. Foxcroft.

Brig.-Gen. HIRAM BURNHAM.

Surgeon, EUGENE F. SANGER, Bangor.
Assistant Surgeon, GEO. W. MARTIN, Houlton.
Chaplain, ZENAS THOMPSON, Portland.
The companies were commanded as follows:
Company A, Sewell C. Gray, Exeter.
Company B, Isaac Frazier, Ellsworth.
Company C, Benjamin F. Harris, Machias.
Company D, Joel A. Haycock, Calais.
Company E, Joseph Snowman, Bucksport.
Company F, William N. Lyser, Pembroke.
Company G, Ralph W. Young, Rockland.
Company H, George Fuller, Corinth.
Company I, William H. Stanchfield, Milo.
Company K, Theodore Carey, Eastport.

Up to this time there had resigned, Col. Abner Knowles, of Bangor, Quartermaster Isaac Strickland, of Bangor, Assistant Surgeon, John Baker, of East Machias, Capt. Moses Brown, Company A, Brownville, and Capt. Albert G. Burton, of Oldtown, of Company I.

Capt. Geo. Fuller, was sick at his home in Corinth.

At an early hour on the morning of April 5th, 1862, the Sixth Regiment left the camp at Warwick Creek and proceeded to reconnoitre the enemy's works in that vicinity. Four prisoners were captured, when the rebels commenced to shell the skirmishers of the Sixth, during which, several were wounded. The regiment however, held their position until the reconnoissance by Gen. Hancock and Lieut. Comstock of Gen. McClellan's staff, was completed. A second reconnoissance immediately followed, in the direction of Lee's Mills, and was attended with similar success. Another reconnoissance on the 7th, proved a considerable affair to to the Sixth, and which elicited from Gen. McClellan his thanks.

At the battle of Lee's Mills, on the 16th, the Sixth supported our artillery, and was exposed to a heavy fire.

On the 24th, another reconnoissance was performed successfully by the Sixth, in the direction of Warwick Creek, which was followed on the 28th by another to the same place, a brisk skirmish occurring on each occasion.

At the battle of Williamsburg, May 5th, the Sixth supported Kennedy's battery from 1 to 5 o'clock P. M., under a heavy fire from the enemy's artillery, until by order of Gen. Hancock, the four right companies of the regiment were placed in an earthwork in the centre of our lines, while the other companies were formed immediately on the left. Thus disposed, the regiment received the hottest of the enemy's fire, but not a man wavered. Our fire now became terrific, and the enemy was soon repulsed with great slaughter.

A charge was made by the Union forces and successfully executed. Two days after the battle Gen. McClellan made a complimentary address to the Sixth, for its services on this occasion.

The battle of Garnett's Farm took place June 27th. At an early hour of the morning of that day, the Sixth Regiment, which formed a portion of the first brigade under command of Gen. Hancock, was ordered to the front, where a working party was engaged in throwing up earthworks. On their arrival, Col. Burnham took a position a short distance in the rear of the earthworks, on the right, near a piece of woods, with orders to hold it at all hazards. In front of this earthwork was a large, level field, at the upper portion of which was planted the enemy's batteries, while at a short distance in Gen. Hancock's rear was a deep ravine, on the opposite side of which we had a masked battery of siege guns. About 9 a. m., the enemy appeared in force on the left, as if preparing for an attack. Upon this the working party with the force that supported it, withdrew across the ravine. At 10 o'clock the enemy opened with its artillery, directing his fire, principally at the woods where the Sixth lay, and at our own battery which had been unmasked, and which after an hour's rapid firing, silenced the enemy's guns, forcing the rebels to retire out of range.

During this duel, the Sixth had two men killed and one wounded. At sunset, the enemy again opened his batteries, but as before, he was shortly compelled to desist firing and retire. When it was quite dark in the woods a few shots from the enemy, instantly followed by a volley along our whole line, brought every man to his feet. The attack, though sudden, was not unexpected, and immediately the enemy's fire was returned, and with effect, as was afterwards ascertained when he advanced a short distance from the woods, and after nearly an hour's rapid exchange of shots, silently withdrew. This was a singular combat in many respects, as no enemy could be seen, and his presence was only manifested by the flash and crack of his guns, and by the whistling of his bullets over the heads of our men. During the engagement the Sixth had expended over fifty rounds of ammunition, on an average. Many of their guns were rendered useless by foulness, in consequence of which, as well as from want of ammunition, they, with the remainder of the brigade, were relieved by another brigade, and Col. Burnham was ordered to withdraw quietly with his regiment and return to camp, where he arrived shortly after 1 o'clock. During this engagement the casualties were, one man killed and twenty-three wounded. Three of the latter died shortly afterward.

At 4 o'clock, Col. Burnham received orders to prepare for a hasty move. Breakfast was quickly eaten, and the work of getting in readiness promptly commenced. It was evident that a movement towards James River was contemplated. Col. Burnham was ordered to report the whole of his command to Gen. Smith for fatigue duty, when the men were furnished with axes, and ordered to cut down the skirt of the forest, in which was located their camp. This was done in order to afford a range for our artillery, in case the enemy made an attack. On this being accomplished, the regiment was ordered to the left of the felled trees, with the rest of the First Brigade, when, as the order was being obeyed, a rebel battery opened a furious fire, which was silenced however, by one of our own batteries. The Sixth, however, succeeded in getting into position, with the loss of one man, who was seriously wounded. Another brief engagement shortly followed, ending in the rebels being repulsed with great slaughter, and no further fighting took place in that vicinity that day. Meanwhile the Sixth kept their original position, while the greater part of our forces made their retreat.

During the night they were bivouacked in line of battle, every man with his rifle at his side, ready to spring to his feet and give battle in case of attack. At last, only the division to which the Sixth belonged was left, and their position was evidently a critical one, for, notwithstanding, forces were within supporting distance, yet, it was plain that in case of attack they would have to stand the brunt of battle. But the enemy did not choose to attack. On the following Monday, (the 29th) their division began to fall back, leaving a proper force of cavalry and artillery behind, as a rear guard of the corps.

Falling back about three miles, they came to a large field, containing a strong force of our troops and a great number of baggage wagons. Positions were taken in line of battle, while a halt of about three hours was made, during which the retreat went on. Resuming the line of march, the division moved along slowly until they reached a field a short distance from Savage Station.

There another halt was made, and the division deployed in line of battle, and were stationed in the edge of a piece of woods, in which position they remained until about 2 o'clock, when, keeping up the line of battle, they passed through the woods to Savage Station, and halted a short way beyond. On resuming the march, they proceeded about a mile, when a rattling fire of musketry in the rear showed them that the enemy had attacked our forces at the station. Forthwith the division was marched rapidly to the scene of action, and when they arrived the battle was raging furiously. The Second Brigade of Gen. Brooks was hurled into the thickest of the fight, while the remainder of the division was stationed as a support. By the order of Gen. Hancock, the Sixth was marched half a mile through a piece of woods, and took a position on the right, in order to prevent the enemy from out-flanking. The position was an honorary as well as a dangerous one. Col. Burnham at once established communication with the rest of the Brigade, and awaited an attack on his right flank, which he doubted not would be made, as the enemy subsequently threatened.

After a sharp and bloody engagement, the rebels were repulsed. The Sixth did not actively engage in the battle, although they were under a heavy fire, and shared many of its perils. At 9 o'clock, the Division was again put in motion, leaving Heintzelman's forces to hold, for a time, the hard-earned field. The Sixth was put in the advance, and as it was expected that the enemy would, by their cavalry, make a dash for the road and attempt to cut them off, to lead the advance was surely an honorable position. The four right companies of the Sixth were detached, and thrown some distance ahead as an advance guard. Two squads, under non-commissioned officers, were thrown still farther ahead, to feel the way. In this order they marched until 3 o'clock on the morning of the 30th, when they crossed the White Oak Bridge, and took position on the heights beyond. Here a halt was ordered by Gen. Hancock, and the men, totally worn out by the severe labors of the past twenty-four hours, threw themselves on the ground, and were almost instantly asleep. At 10 o'clock, on the next morning, White Oak Bridge was blown up, and our troops were deployed in line of battle along the heights, where they could meet the enemy advantageously, in case he should approach. By order of Gen. Hancock, Col. Burnham posted his regiment on the extreme right of the line, near a creek, where it was thought the rebels would attempt to cross and turn our flank. He threw out pickets, and let his men rest in line of battle. The day was exceedingly hot and oppressive. The long hours passed slowly away, and up to noon there was' nothing which indicated the enemy's approach. Suddenly, without premonition, the enemy opened a spirited fire with twenty pieces of artillery from the opposite side of the creek. For a while the cannonading was terrific, an unceasing shower of shell raining upon a portion of our lines. In obedience to orders, the Sixth was marched from the right to the centre of our lines, taking a position in the rear of the batteries, within supporting distance. This position was maintained throughout the fight, which raged for three hours with awful fury, and during which the Sixth had two men seriously wounded. At 4 o'clock the enemy's guns were silenced, and they withdrew.

At 11 o'clock the Division was again put in motion, the Sixth still keeping the advance. Col. Burnham was instructed by Gen. Hancock, to use the utmost vigilance, as it was confidently expected that the enemy would make an attack with the intention of cutting him off. He therefore detached the four left companies of his regiment, and put them under the command of Major Harris. The night was spent in rapid marching, and the fortitude of the men, worn out as they were by the severe labors of the preceding three days, was taxed almost beyond endurance. It was exceedingly warm, and the men suffered terribly from scarcity of water, but with ranks well closed, the brave fellows kept pushing on steadily. Twice, during the night, Gen. Hancock sent orders for the advance guard to move with the utmost watchfulness and care, and be at all times prepared for the attack which was apprehended. At length, on the morning of July 1st, at a few minutes past 4 o'clock, they emerged from the swamps of the Chickahominy, in sight of the James River, at Turkey Bend. Here they remained until 11 o'clock, when their Brigade was put in motion, while they were stationed to guard a road, where it was thought the Rebel Cavalry might make its appearance. In this position they remained until 3 o'clock the following morning, when Col. Burnham was ordered to move with the rest of the Division down the river. Through a violent rain storm they marched until 2 o'clock in the afternoon, when they arrived at Harrison's Landing and encamped in a large wheat field. Here they remained until the next morning, when they were again put in motion, and marched about three miles from the James River, where they halted.

On September 11th, the Sixth formed the advance of our column, and in a skirmish with the enemy at the foot of Sugar Loaf Mountain, drove him back without loss. At the battle of Crampton's Pass, on the 14th, the Sixth participated, though they were not actively engaged. On the 15th, Col. Burnham took possession of a pass in South Mountain, after a sharp skirmish, during which he captured four prisoners. The position was held till night-fall, when his command returned to the brigade. At the battle of Antietam, on the 17th, the Sixth arrived on the field at ten o'clock, in the forenoon, and took position near the right of our line, where our forces had just fallen back, after a most desperate charge. The enemy opened fire on them but he was driven back. The Sixth participated in the battle of Fredricksburg. On the morning of December 12th they crossed the Rappahannock, at the lower bridge. At ten o'clock they moved up and took position under the entrenched batteries of the enemy, who shelled them severely all the day. The Sixth was in the center of the line of battle, and their position was an exposed one, as the rebel batteries on their right enfiladed them with ease and accuracy. This position was maintained three days, during which time the men acquitted themselves creditably. On January 3d, '63, the regiment was encamped near Bell Plain, Va. Here they remained until early on the morning of January 20th, when they left their camp and proceeded to Banks' Ford, where Gen. Burnside attempted crossing and giving battle to the enemy, but the mud being so deep, on account of a two day's rain, the movement was abandoned and the regiment returned to its former camp, arriving on the 23d.

Feb. 2d, the regiment being assigned to the "Light Division," proceeded to Potomac Creek and went into winter quarters.

On the forenoon of April 28th the regiment, under command of Lieut. Col. Harris, marched towards the Rappahannock, and that night was engaged in transporting and launching pontoons, preparatory to crossing the river. April 30th the regiment proceeded to Falmouth, and on the afternoon of May 1st went across the river and took position in the front line of battle. May 2d an advance of the entire line of battle was ordered, and the regiment went forward in line of battle, the skirmishers driving the enemy before them, until darkness put a stop to the advance. During the night the regiment was ordered to proceed to Fredericksburg, and soon after daylight it formed in line of battle, in front of the Heights of St. Marys. A few moments after 10 o'clock A. M., the order to charge was given, and the regiment advanced on the double-quick. In this battle, the Sixth won a reputation that will live with the history of the rebellion. The supporting regiments on the right and left, broke under the terrific fire, and the enemy turned his attention to the Sixth Maine and Fifth Wisconsin. The entire fire of the enemy swept through the devoted ranks of the two regiments, but with wild cheers the men rushed on to the fortifications, and the victory was won in four minutes from the beginning of the attack. The flag of the Sixth was the first to wave from the battlements of the enemy's works. The loss to the regiment in this terrible engagement was great, no less than one hundred and twenty-eight, officers and men, being killed and wounded. Major Joel Haycock, and Captains Young, Gray and Ballinger were instantly killed.

On the afternoon of the 3d of May, the regiment proceeded slowly up the plank road leading out of Fredricksburg, and supported our batteries, during the latter part of the battle of Salem Heights. May 4th, the regiment was not actively engaged with the enemy, but was moved from point to point of the line, in order to deceive the enemy as to our actual strength, and to support weak points. During the night the regiment, with the Light Division, covered the retreat of the Sixth corps (crossing the river), was attacked by the enemy, who had succeeded in cutting through the picket line, but escaped by a circuitous route, after handsomely repulsing the attack.

On the 11th of May, the "Light Division" was broken up, and the regiments composing it assigned to different brigades, in consequence of the discharge from the service of two years and nine months troops. The Sixth was assigned to the Third Brigade, First Division, Sixth Corps.

On the ninth day of June, the regiment having arrived at Kelley's Ford, in company with two other regiments of infantry, under command of Gen. Russell, dashed across the river, surprising and routing the enemy. The pursuit was continued until reaching Brandy Station, where joining Gen. Ames with a force of infantry and cavalry, the command retired to the north bank of the river, having accomplished the object of the expedition. which was the gaining of correct information about the movements of the enemy.

The regiment participated in the long and fatiguing marches of the Pennsylvania campaign, and arrived at Gettysburg, having marched thirty-six miles the same day. The Sixth was not actively engaged in that memorable battle, but occupied a responsible position on the extreme left flank of the army, until the last desperate charge of the enemy upon our left centre, when it was ordered to act as reserve. In the close pursuit of the enemy, July 5th, the Sixth regiment was in the front, skirmishing not unfrequently with the rear guard, and kept this exposed but honorable position until Lee succeeded in crossing into Virginia. July 12th the regiment being in line of battle near Turkstown, Md., supporting the skirmish line of the division, Captain Furlong, with his company (D), numbering twenty-five men only, went beyond the skirmishers and succeeded in surprising a portion of the enemy's pickets, killing and wounding about thirty and capturing thirty-two prisoners without losing a man. July 19th, the regiment crossed the Potomac on its way into the interior of Virginia. The day following, Col. Burnham was ordered to Maine, on duty connected with the Draft, and the command devolved upon Lieut. Col. Harris.

The regiment encamped near Warrenton, Va., during the month of August, until the first of September, when it proceeded to Culpepper C. H., Va., and was engaged in repairing the roads between Culpepper and Hazle River. After rendering the roads and ford passable, the regiment returned to Culpepper, and remained there until October 5th, when, with the corps it proceeded to the Rapidan, relieving the Second Corps October 10th, the regiment started on the return march with the army, and arrived at a point near Centreville and Chantilly, where a line of battle was formed, and the army remained there a number of days, awaiting the attack of the enemy. While there about fifty men of the Sixth, being on picket, were attacked by about five hundred of Stuart's Cavalry, but handsomely repulsed them after a spirited skirmish.

On the 19th, the regiment advanced to Warrenton, and at the battle of Rappahannock Station, was deployed as a double line of skirmishers, and with the Fifth Wisconsin, charged the enemy's works, which were carried at the point of the bayonet. The Sixth was ahead of the Wisconsin boys when it entered the fortifications, and had to resist the tremendous attack of the enemy until the arrival of the Fifth Wisconsin, rendered the victory ours.

The storming of the enemy's left by the Fifth Maine, and the One Hundred and Twenty-first New York completed the work, and the whole force, consisting of the very flower of the rebel army, was captured. Sixteen officers and one hundred and twenty-three men were killed and wounded. Lieut. Col. Harris was dangerously wounded in the early part of the battle, and the command devolved upon Maj. Fuller. Capt. Furlong and Lieuts. Wilkins and McKinley were killed. This frightful mortality, especially among the officers, (as the regiment went into the fight with only twenty-one officers and three hundred enlisted men), shows the desperation with which the fight was conducted.

On the 27th of October, the Sixth went to the support of the Third Corps, then engaged with the enemy at Locust Grove. The prompt arrival of the command turned the fortunes of the day, and the enemy promptly retired. The regiment returned with the army, and marched back to its former camp, near Wilbur Ford.

The Sixth remained in camp at Brandy Station, Va., from Jan. 1st, 1864, until the opening of Gen. Grant's campaign, May 4th, when two days afterwards they forming a part of the Sixth Corps, were engaged in the battle of the Wilderness, but not in that portion of the lines that suffered a heavy attack At the battle of Spottsylvania, on the 8th, they were engaged and lost a few men by the sharpshooters; also participated in the attack and capture of the enemy's works on the right, and being compelled to retreat, suffered a loss of one hundred and twenty-five men. On the 12th the regiment numbering only seventy men, was under fire eight hours, supporting Gen. Hancock's forces, and losing sixteen officers and men, killed and wounded. The regiment was engaged in several skirmishes, experiencing no casualties, until arriving at Cold Harbor, where for twelve days the men were engaged in building fortifications, skirmishing, etc.

On the 14th of June, the regiment started up the James River, reaching Gen. Butler's headquarters on the 17th, and Petersburg on the 20th, where it remained until the 10th of July, when, its term of service expiring on the 15th, they were ordered to Washington, arriving on the 12th. Here they volunteered to remain thirty days in defence of the city, and were marched to Fort Stevens. However, on the 13th they were relieved, and on the 17th left for Portland, where they arrived on the 22d, and were mustered out on the 15th of August. About two hundred and

CAMP TILDEN, MITCHELL'S STATION, VA.

thirty eight re-enlisted men and recruits whose term of service had not expired, were temporarily organized into a battalion, afterwards assigned to the First Regiment Maine Veteran Volunteers.

CHAPTER XVI.

The Eighteenth Maine—Organized At Bangor And Ordered To Washington—Changed To The First Maine Heavy Artillery—Twelve Months Of Idleness—They Join The Army Of The Potomac—The First Fight—The First Great Slaughter—They Are Mowed Down By Ranks—Placing The Blame—Death Of Col. Chaplin—His Last Words—His Military Career—Forty Days Under Fire—A Gallant Charge—The Winter Before Petersburg—At Amelia Springs—They Capture Artillery, Colors And Men—Back To Bangor.

On Tuesday, July 24th, 1862, a company from Lincoln arrived in Bangor, and was escorted through the several streets to quarters at the Arsenal camp grounds, by Ward Six Company, Capt. L. J. Morse. This was the first company of volunteers in camp for the new Eighteenth Regiment that was being formed by Col. Chaplin, and numbered ninety-seven men of the best stamp. They were commanded by Capt. Clark and Lieutenants Nute and Bunker. On August 4th, two large four horse teams arrived, bringing the Houlton Company, under command of Capt. Merriam. Shortly after this the camp of the Eighteenth was moved to the old racecourse on Union Street.

During the encampment at the Trotting Park the following "ad." appeared in the local papers:

OMNIBUS TO THE CAMP.

"I shall run an omnibus to Camp Chaplin, at the Trotting Park, until the troops leave the city. A fine chance is offered to parties wishing to see camp-life, at a very cheap rate."

J. H. ROBINSON.

The regiment quickly filled, and before the middle of August was complete, and companies begging to be allowed to enter.

While in camp the Eighteenth was presented with a beautiful flag, by the ladies of Bangor. The ceremony took place at East Market Square, where the regiment had been escorted by the citizens' military companies. Miss Mary E. Benson was introduced by Mayor Stetson, and on behalf of the ladies of Bangor, presented the flag in a very happy speech, to which Lieut. Col. Talbot, on behalf of Col. Chaplin, responded. Col. Chaplin, in a few remarks, presented the flag to the regiment, who received it with repeated cheers.

The Eighteenth Regiment was mustered into service of the United States on Thursday, August 21st, '62, by Capt. Bartlett of the Twelfth U. S. Infantry, and on Sunday the 24th they broke camp, at "Camp John Pope," and under escort of the Cavalry Company and the Independent Fusileers, marched to the depot where a train of twenty cars awaited them. This regiment was probably the largest that ever went into the service of the Government, and as they marched down the tree-lined streets of Bangor, that beautiful Sunday morning, the sight was indeed magnificent, and was well calculated to raise the enthusiasm of the multitude come to bid them "God speed." The weather was charming, and nearly 15,000 people, in Sunday attire, were out to see them depart. As the train moved away majestically, cheers, waving of handkerchiefs, mingled with the partings, and not a few sobs from near friends, rendered the occasion one of solemnity.

Little did the brave men think, that at the end of their term of service, so few would be left to tell of the glorious deeds performed by that command. Little did they dream of the awful death many would find in that first great action they would enter.

The following is a list of the Field and Staff officers, and a list of the companies of the Eighteenth Regiment, when mustered into the service:

Colonel, DANIEL CHAPLIN, Bangor.
Lieut. Col., T. H. TALBOT, Portland.
Major, CHARLES HAMLIN, Orland.
Adjutant, RUSSELL B. SHEPHERD, Bangor.
Surgeon, R. E. PAINE, Hampden.
Quartermaster, HORATIO PITCHER, Bangor.
Company A, Capt. Clark, Lincoln.
  " B, " Daggett, Bangor.
  " C, " Smith, Ellsworth.
  " D, " Crossman, Bangor.
  " E, " Clark, Sangerville.
  " F, " Hinkley, Hampden.
  " G, " Colby, Bucksport.
  " H, " Smith, Columbia.
  " I, " Atwell, Orono.
  " K, " Sabine, Eastport.

The non-commissioned staff were:
Sergeant Major, J. A. LANCEY, Bangor.
Commissary Sergeant, CHAS. DWINELL, Bangor.
Hospital Steward, B. C. FROST, Bangor.

The Eighteenth Regiment, on its arrival at Washington, crossed the Potomac, and at once occupied a position on the Virginia side. For nearly five months they performed garrison duty, when, by an order of the War Department, they were transferred to another branch of the service, and were then known as the First Maine Heavy Artillery. The arms of the regiment were rifles, as at first, together with both light and heavy ordinance, in forts and batteries. Eight companies were stationed at Fort Alexander under the immediate command of Col. Chaplin. Company E was at Batteries Vermont and Mattox, and Company K at Batteries Cameron and Parrott, on elevations not a great distance off.

Here they remained during the entire year of 1863, and in the month of March, the Third Battery was added to the regiment and classed as Company M. We may be very sure that the brave boys did not enjoy this inaction and many times they begged their commanding officers to petition the War Department to be sent to the front. During the winter of 1863, the regiment was stationed in the defence of Washington, north of the Potomac, with headquarters at Fort Sumner, Md., Col. Daniel Chaplin in command. The organization as a Heavy Artillery Regiment, with the maximum number required, (1,800), was completed in the month of February, 1864. On the fifteenth of May, in accordance with the orders of the Secretary of War, the regiment embarked at Washington on board transports, to join the army of the Potomac, debarking at Belle Plain Landing on the same evening. On the 19th sharp musketry being heard in the direction of their right and rear, near Fredericksburg Pike, their principal avenue of supply, the Brigade, consisting of the First Maine Heavy Artillery and the Seventh New York Heavy Artillery, was, in consequence of experienced troops not being at hand, ordered to the scene of conflict. At this crisis no other course remained. The enemy was upon them, having reached the pike and captured a train of supplies. The Brigade, being placed in line, this regiment formed the right. The skirmishers who had been deployed to the right and left, engaged those of the enemy and so quickly repulsed them, that they failed either to secure or destory the prize. The advanced line of the enemy, being hurled back and posted on the further side of a ravine and behind a temporary breastwork, the line was again regulated, and the artillery advanced until halted, half way down the declivity.

Here the action commenced in fearful earnest, and without faltering, the regiment maintained the position for two hours and a half, until night and despair of success caused the enemy to retire. The entire regiment suffered terribly, while the companies of the left wing, receiving the direct fire of the enemy's breastworks, lost more than one half of their number. In this battle the loss of the First Maine was: Commissioned officers killed, six; same wounded, six; enlisted men killed, seventy-six; enlisted men wounded, three hundred and eighty-eight; aggregate, four hundred and seventy-six—a number which might be greatly increased by adding those who died at Division Hospital.

On the morning of May 20th, the regiment was marched to Milford Station, and on the 23d from there to North Anna. The heavy artillery division being broken up there on the 24th, and distributed to the respective corps, the First Maine was ordered to report to Major Gen. Birney, commanding Third Division, Second Corps. Subsequently, it was assigned to the Second Brigade. On the 27th, the regiment marched towards the Pamunkey river, being ordered to report to Brig. Gen. Mott, of the Third Brigade; continuing its march, (forming a part of the force that successfully assaulted the enemy's works across the Ptolopotomy on the way), until it arrived at Cold Harbor on the 2d of June. The marches from the North Anna to Cold Harbor were exceedingly severe—rations being short, the weather hot, the movements being constant and rapid, and the regiment exposed to the incessant shelling of the enemy.

On June 3d, the regiment was held in reserve, and marched to different positions on the line; on the night of the 4th, marched to the left, and on the 5th, took position at Barker's Mills, remaining there until the 12th, when it took up the line of march toward the Chickahominy, and crossing it, arrived at the James River, which it crossed the following day. June 15th, they marched for Petersburg, halting at the Dunn House. On the 16th they rebuilt the works captured by the colored troops of the Eighteenth Corps. On the evening of the same day, the regiment, in common with the corps, assaulted the enemy's works, and under heavy fire, drove him back half a mile. On the 18th, they advanced on the enemy's works and carried two lines in the vicinity of the O'Haire House. On the afternoon of the same day, the command was massed with the Brigade, to assault that portion of the enemy's line that had been considered too strong to carry in the morning—the regiment, in three battalions, constituting the three front lines. Works had been constructed, extending from 600 to 700 yards in front of their position, and so arranged as to sweep by direct and enfilade fires, every foot of the intervening plain. Upon the word "Forward," the first lines, composed of the First Maine, moved promptly. The first battalion was swept away by the deadly fire of the enemy, before it had advanced one hundred yards,—whole companies reeling before the shock—yet the gallant few pressed forward, as if devoted to death. Unsupported, they rushed forward, a few getting within forty yards of the enemy's breastworks; when, more than two-thirds of the regiment being either killed or wounded, and not the barest possibility of success remaining, the order was given to "Fall Back."

The loss of the regiment, during the operations of the 16th, 17th and 18th of June, (nearly all of which occurred in this assault), was as follows: seven commissioned officers killed, and twenty-five wounded; one hundred and eight enlisted men killed and four hundred and sixty-four wounded.

That the fearful responsibility of this fatal assault, may not be charged to the gallant Col. Chaplin, it should in justice to him be known that he acted only under imperative orders, both as to his making the assault and to the disposition of the battalions of his own regiment in the front. The regiment remained in that vicinity until the 21st of June, when the brigade moved about three miles to the left. On the 22d, the brigade contributed a portion of the forces ordered to swing forward and establish a line to extend south of Petersburg, in order to menace the enemy's railroad communication. It was scarcely in position when the enemy made an impetuous attack, and our troops on the left giving way, an order was given to fall back. The regiment's aggregate loss was twenty men, chiefly prisoners.

On the 1st of July, the regiment was ordered to report to the Second Brigade, and being assigned a position in the first line, remained, doing picket duty, until July 11th. On the morning of the 12th, the artillery destroyed the works in their immediate front, and moved to the Jerusalem Plank Road, thence to the rear of the "Deserted House," remaining there until the 23d, when a movement was made to the right. On the 26th, they marched to Deep Bottom and crossed to the north side of the river. On the 28th, the regiment being ordered to report to Brig. Gen. de Trobiand, commanding the First Brigade, was assigned a position on the right flank. On the 29th, they arrived at the Bryant House, and moved forward to the works, relieving that portion of the line occupied by the Eighteenth Corps, in the vicinity of the O'Haire House, and they here remained until August 12th, when the column, composed of the whole corps, moved in the direction of City Point. On the 13th, they embarked on transports, and arrived on the north side of Deep Bottom, on the following day. On the 15th, the Brigade was marched to the front and right, where it deployed in line of battle. On the 16th, they relieved the picket in front and advanced the line, which they continued to occupy on the 17th and 18th.

On the morning of the latter day, Col. Chaplin, who commanded the line, was mortally wounded by a sharpshooter, and was borne bleeding from the field, cool, collected and heroic to the last. He left as a dying message to his command: "Tell the boys to obey orders, and never flinch."

Daniel Chaplin, of Bangor, was mustered into the service of the United States, May 28th, 1861, as Captain of Company F, Second Regiment Infantry, and on the 13th of September, the same year, was promoted to Major of the same regiment. While filling that position he was further promoted to the Colonelcy of the Eighteenth Regiment, his rank dating July 11th, 1862, and was in command when that regiment was organized into the First Maine Heavy Artillery.

At the battle of Hanover C. H., Gen. A. P. Martin, late Mayor of Boston, then in command of "Martin's Battery," lost his guns to the enemy. Major Chaplin seeing this started to recapture them, leading in person a portion of the Second in the charge. On the first advance the rebels opened a fierce fire, one ball striking and bending the scabbard hanging at the side of Chaplin, so that he was unable to draw his sword. Gen. Martin seeing this, immediately drew his own and handed it to Chaplin, who charged again, retaking the guns. Gen. Martin afterwards wrote a handsome letter of thanks to Col. Chaplin, refusing to take back his sword. Both the broken and Gen. Martin's blades are in the possession of Col. Chaplin's widow, residing in Bangor. As we have already seen, the Eighteenth Regiment was assigned to the defense of Washington. At this time, the strength of the sturdy sons of the Pine Tree State, was greatly needed in the work of fortifying the Capitol, and the men of the regiment were immediately detailed for the work at felling trees, in order to clear the country for the range of the many guns of the forts in that vicinity. By a rough estimate it is supposed that they thus cleared more than 3,500 acres of land.

The task of disciplining the regiment during the time it was thus stationed, devolved on Col. Chaplin, who performed the duty with consummate ability, and soon brought the men to a high degree of discipline. On the field of battle none were braver or more thoughtful of the men, than Col. Chaplin. His men loved him as a man, and honored him as a true and heroic patriot.

The Whig and Courier, under date of August 22d, 1864, says: "On Saturday the family of Col. Chaplin, of the First Maine Heavy Artillery, received the sad intelligence that, during a severe engagement on the James River, he had received a severe wound in the breast, and yesterday a second despatch was received that he died of his wounds. Thus is added another to the already long record of Bangor's brave and heroic dead. Col. Chaplin was one of the first to recruit a company for the gallant Second Maine, in which he was shortly promoted to the rank of Major, and from which he was discharged by promotion to the Colonelcy of the Eighteenth Maine, when that regiment was formed, in consequence of the reputation he had then acquired for efficiency and gallantry. His regiment soon learned not only to respect, but to love their commander. It made a record as brilliant and unfortunate withal, as that which has been made by any other regiment in the Union service. Under their gallant commander the First Heavy never faltered, never hesitated, never failed to obey orders from superior officers, no matter how apparently desperate the undertaking. Col. Chaplin has been in command of the brigade nearly all the time since joining the army of the Potomac, and after passing unharmed through scores of the fiercest and most sanguinary battles of the war, sleeps at last the final sleep of the brave and chivalrous soldier, perishing at the head of his command. He leaves a large circle of relatives and friends to mourn that so brave and effective a defender of the Union cause, is lost to its service in this supreme crisis of its fortunes."

The remains arrived on the steamer "Lady Lang," Thursday, Aug. 25th, and, under escort of Company B, State Guards, were conveyed to his family. On Saturday they were taken to the Universalist Church, where services were held, after which they were removed to Glenburn. Several of his old comrades, among them, officers of the Second Maine, acted as pall bearers.

The following letter, dated Aug. 18th, 10 P. M., 1864, written on the battlefield, described the fall of Col. Chaplin: It was written by Capt. F. E. Shaw.

"I have just left Col. Chaplin. He was wounded in the left breast, the bullet passing through the body. He was on the picket line examining the enemy's works with his glass, and was seen probably by the sharp-shooters. Two balls were fired at him. As the first one whizzed by, he said, "Ah, they see me!" and at that instant he was struck and fell, saying, "They have hit me this time." He was able to converse with me when I reached him, but was faint and bled freely. The wound is well up above the breast, I think, but we cannot now tell of its character. We all feel badly—the whole regiment is attached to him. Said he to me: "I'm sorry to leave the boys, but tell them to do their duty, and never make any feints,"—alluding to a brigade that refused to make a charge the day before, though they went forward as if

Col. DANIEL CHAPLIN.

to make it. It was the same one that refused to support our regiment in the charge on the 18th of June. We think the Colonel's wound is too high up to be fatal. He appeared strong for one wounded so severely. Dr. Lincoln has just seen him, says it is a bad wound, though some have recovered from such wounds. Major Shepard is with us.

While on the skirmish line, the regiment lost one man killed, and seven wounded.

On the 18th the regiment was relieved and marched to the vicinity of Fort Sedgwick, in front of Petersburg, where it remained until September 30th. The time the regiment remained here might be called, and aptly too, "forty days under fire." The loss in killed and wounded, however, did not amount to twenty. On the 1st of October, the division took the train to the terminus of the road, at the Yellow House, and on the 2d, massed for a reconnoissance. The First Brigade marched by the flank, on the Squirrel Level Road, where the skirmish line soon met the enemy, drove him from his works and advanced in the direction of the South Side Railroad. The regiment here remained, unprotected, under the enemy's fire, for several hours, lost seven men, and returned to the Preble's House, leaving there for Fort Sedgwick on the 6th. Under the incessant fire of the enemy, it was occupied with picket duty until withdrawn from the lines on the 24th. On the 26th, the division marched to the Gurley House, and on the 27th to the Vaughan Road; the course of march afterwards being changed to the Boydton Pike, on reaching which the regiment constituted a portion of the flank line. The Second Division of the corps had charged forward, two pieces of artillery having been placed some distance in advance.

Some troops of the enemy charged upon the artillery, drove back the support, captured the guns, and, from behind the brow of the hill, poured a fire into the Union rear line. The First Maine being ordered to charge, the regiment with terrific yells, pushed forward to the pike, and delivered a well directed volley to the scattering foe. The enemy, mistaking the number of our forces, threw down their arms, and about 200 were taken prisoners. Two pieces of artillery were yet 300 yards in advance, and the intervening field was swept by musketry from the cover of the woods. They were, however, recaptured by a part of the First, which, therefore, claimed the honor of capturing 200 prisoners, two pieces of artillery, and a stand of colors. During the sharp conflict of the same day, three commissioned officers were wounded, and twenty-nine enlisted men killed, wounded and missing.

On the 28th, the brigade marched back to the front of Petersburg, when the regiment was ordered to Cedar Level Station. On the 29th, four companies were ordered back to the lines before Petersburg, under command of Major Smith, while the other eight companies, commanded by Col. R. B. Shepherd, remained on duty until November 14th. Three of the latter companies were then ordered to the front, Col. Shepherd taking charge of that battalion, and Major Smith commanding the detachment at Cedar Level Station. On the 29th of November, the battalion before Petersburg moved out of the works and were joined at the left of the line by the detachment from Cedar Level Station. On the 2d of December, the brigade was ordered to Fort Siebert, and on the 7th, was massed outside of the rear line, near the Gurley House, proceeding on the next day to the Nottaway river, over which the whole division passed on pontoon bridges. The columns marched by Sussex Court House to Jarrett's Station, on the Weldon Railroad, the destruction of which it fully completed. On the 10th, the columns began to return to Petersburg, and the next day recrossed the Nottaway and bivouacked on the Jerusalem Plank Road, about fifteen miles from Petersburg, arriving within the lines on the afternoon of the 12th. The expedition was extremely fatiguing, the nights being cold and stormy, preventing sleep. In three days the men marched over ninety miles, on only half rations. On the 13th of December, the regiment moved to a position situated between the Halifax and Vaughan roads, in front of the works.

From January 1st to February 4th, 1865, the regiment was quietly encamped before Petersburg, doing the ordinary picket duty. On the morning of the fifth, the regiment moved, in connection with the First Brigade, Third Division, Second Corps, to extend the line on their left, near Hatcher's Run and attempted to turn the enemy's right flank. The Heavy Artillery, having the advance, met the enemy strongly posted on the opposite side of the Run, where, after skirmishing, was formed under cover of a hill, from whence it charged across the Run carrying the enemy's works, and capturing nearly fifty prisoners, without loss to the regiment. During this movement the lines were extended about two miles to the left, but the regiment was not again engaged, although fighting continued at various points until the 7th, when works were thrown up, for the permanent occupancy of the ground that had been acquired.

The regiment occupied a position on this new line, doing the usual picket duty until March 25th, when they made a general movement to test the strength of the enemy. After heavy skirmishing, with but little loss, while the First Brigade was forming in a deep ravine to charge the enemy's works, our line of battle was attacked and driven back. The First Brigade immediately deployed, the Heavy Artillery holding the extreme left. The deployment was scarcely finished, when the enemy made a vigorous attack on the new line. After fighting for more than an hour, he was repulsed with a loss of fifty prisoners, the regiment losing one commisioned officer killed and three enlisted men killed, seventeen wounded and six taken prisoners. The morning of March 29th, was assigned for a general movement, when the regiment with the First Brigade, being placed on the left and in the direction of the South Side Railroad, was engaged in skirmishing and manœvering until April 1st. Meanwhile, the enemy had been driven back to his main works along the entire line. The morning of the 2d was assigned for a general assault, and at daylight the regiment formed as a part of the charging column, with the left resting on the Boydton Plank Road. As soon as the outline of the enemy's works were visible the order was given to advance, when it was ascertained that during the previous night the enemy had abandoned his works and fallen back towards Petersburg. The regiment then moved up the South Side Railroad, to within twelve or fifteen hundred yards of the enemy's new line, where it remained inactive during the day. The rebels having evacuated Richmond and Petersburg during the night, the brigade commenced on the morning of the 3d to move rapidly along the south bend of the Appomattox river, in order to reach Burksville Junction in advance of them. On the evening of the 5th the regiment struck their advance guard, at Jettersville, where after a slight skirmish, they fell back towards their main body at Amelia Court House. The pursuit was continued on the morning of the 6th, when the enemy was reached and engaged near Amelia Springs, and driven in upon his line of battle. During the 6th the regiment charged and carried the rebel line seven different times, capturing prisoners, etc., on each occasion—in all, two stands of colors, three pieces of artillery, forty-seven wagons and three hundred and fifty prisoners, including several commissioned officers. The regiment lost four commissioned officers and twenty-one enlisted men wounded, and four enlisted men killed. The pursuit was again continued on the 7th, the regiment overtaking the enemy strongly entrenched at Farmville, on the morning of the following day, the whole of which was spent in skirmishing and manœuvering without loss or material advantage. On the 9th, having again fallen upon the rear of the rebel line near Appomattox Court House, our skirmishers were hardly engaged, when a flag of truce was brought in with the proposition of Gen. Lee to surrender, the terms of which were concluded at three o'clock P. M., and a formal announcement was made that the Army of Northern Virginia had lain down their arms.

The march towards Burksville Junction was commenced on the morning of the 11th, they arriving at that point on the evening of the 13th, and there remaining encamped until the 9th of May, when the regiment took up the line of march for Washington, arriving at Bailey's X Roads on the 16th. The First Maine Heavy Artillery participated in the Grand Review at Washington.

On the 27th of June, the regiment was transferred to the Department of Washington, and occupied the line of forts from Fort Washington on the Potomac, to Fort Mahon on the Anticosti, on the eastern branch, a distance of about fifteen miles. The regiment remained there, doing garrison duty until the 11th of September, when it was mustered out of service. Leaving Washington for Maine on the evening of the 12th of September, Bangor was reached on the 17th, where, on the 20th of the same month, the members of the First Maine Heavy Artillery were finally paid and discharged.

An account of the reception of the regiment on its return to Bangor, will be found in another part of this book.

CHARGE OF THE FIRST HEAVY ARTILLERY.

It has always been a disputed question as to who ordered the charge of the First Maine Heavy Artillery, on the 18th of June,

1864, when so many men from Bangor and vicinity lost their lives —there being left unhurt but 268 men out of the 900 who went into the fight. Following is a letter from Major-General Robert McAllister, which fully explains the matter, and fixes the responsibility of the order that sent so many brave men to their deaths. The letter was written to Major Low, of Bangor, and we append a copy:

ALLENTOWN, PENN., Jan. 14, 1871.

"Major FRED C. LOW :—

"Dear Sir :—In all my army experience no scene of carnage and suffering is so impressed on my mind as that fatal charge made by your regiment on the 18th of June, 1864. The history of that charge, as well as the one preceding it, is very familiar to me; I took part in the first.

"I was in command, temporarily, of the Second Brigade of our division for a few days. The commander of that brigade having been wounded while advancing on the enemy on the evening of the 16th, I was ordered by Gen. Birney to take command of it. On the morning of the 18th we moved forward on the enemy's works—carried the first line without much difficulty, as the enemy were about leaving this line for the stronger one in the rear of it. Arriving in front of that, we found it manned by a strong force of artillery and infantry. After delaying a little I was ordered to advance on the enemy's works. We went forward. They poured on my brigade a terrific storm of shot, shell and musketry, and my men fell like forest leaves under a hail storm.

"Seeing the utter impossibility of advancing further, we dropped down, planted our standard along the line and kept up the fire. I sent a report back to division headquarters, and asked what I was to do. Orders came to retire from my position. In doing this I lost heavily. On reporting to Gen. Mott for orders I was ordered to place my brigade on the reserve ready for action. I asked, "Where is my old brigade?" Gen. Mott replied, "Just going in where you come out." I exclaimed, "God help them!" He asked, "Why?" I answered, "They cannot advance on those works—they cannot live—the enfilade fire will cut them down." Just as I said this, an aid from headquarters rode up, and said to the General, "Order the advance at once." It was done.

"The brigade moved off—your fine regiment handsomely in the front. You went gallantly, not to meet success. That was impossible—you were a *forlorn hope*. In a few minutes, out of your regiment which advanced 900 strong, 632 lay low on the battlefield. Darkness soon overspread the field, and I was very anxious that my wounded men who had fallen in the previous charge, and lay between the enemy's line and ours, should be brought off, as well as those belonging to your brigade and regiment, some of whom had advanced still farther than mine. Expressing this anxiety, some of my command volunteered the hazardous undertaking; and that it might be done as quietly as possible, I sent only a few, with orders to move very quietly lest the enemy should discover them. With these orders, they went. It was necessary to go very close to the enemy's line, which they did. The enemy detected them—opened fire, and the opportunity was lost.

"All that night we could distinctly hear the groans of the wounded and their cries for help; but no succor could be sent them, on account of the constant fire. My brigade worked the whole night long to push our works forward, so that we might rescue them. That terrible night at last broke into another day, (the 19th); the battle continued with increased fury; the sun poured down on the dying and wounded, and amid the rattling of musketry and roaring cannon, we heard the cries of our comrades for "water!" "water!"

"When the long terrible day was over, and night again threw her dark mantle over the contending forces, and the fire slackened, I pushed my Brigade forward and built new breastworks, the line of which ran through where your men lay the thickest, and most of your dead and wounded, as well as mine, were brought off. That line was never pushed further, but remained as our advanced outpost until the end of that great and terrible struggle before Petersburg.

"Whether history will do you justice or not, permit me to say that no language can be too strong in its praise of your gallant regiment in that splendid, noble, heroic charge—when almost three-fourths of your number fell—fighting for their country; this, then, my dear Major, is why I regard the First Maine Heavy Artillery as a good regiment."

I am yours very truly,

ROBERT MCALLISTER,
Late Brevet Maj. Gen. U. S. A. Vols.

CHAPTER XVII.

Northern Politics—The Three Parties In Maine—Union Republicans, War Democrats And Breckenridge Democrats—The Last Also Called Copperheads—What They Did In 1861—A Thrilling Appeal For Volunteers—Politics In 1862—Eastern Maine "Locals."—Thousands Of Deserters North—McClellan's Address To The Press—Gloom And Despair Everywhere—Close Of The Year.

In 1862, as in the year previous, politics ran high in this State. A bitter feeling had existed since war commenced, which was heightened by the destruction of "The Democrat," and much hard talk and many personal encounters took place. Three parties were in the field in 1861, one headed by Israel Washburn, Jr., known as "Union Republicans," another having Col. Jameson for a standard bearer, and known as "War Democrats," and a third, led by Mr. Dana, termed "Breckenridge Democrats, or "Copperheads." Two editorials from the Whig and Courier will serve to show how each stood.

"EVERY REPUBLICAN TO THE POLLS."

Let every Republican throw his vote this day for *Washburn and the Union*, to sustain the administration and vindicate the Republican principles which he has professed. Let no personal disappointment or private prejudice induce any Republican to throw his vote against the Republican candidate. Every vote thus thrown will be a reproach against his own party, and virtually an admission that the Republican doctrines were wrong. Those who vote for Jameson vote for the Union, and are loyal men to the Government. Those who vote for Washburn vote for the Union, and for the constitutional principles of freedom upon which the Republican Administration was placed in power."

"LET EVERY MAN BE MARKED,"

"Who votes for a SECESSION CANIDATE. Register the names of the men, who by voting for John W. Dana, declare the defence of the Union to be an '*unholy war*.' Let us know who are the disloyal men. Let us know who are the men who are willing to destroy the *Government* for the sake of breaking down a Republican Administration."

The election resulted in a Republican victory, the city vote being: Washburn, one thousand three hundred and twenty-six; Jameson, six hundred and twenty-nine; Dana, thirty-one.

These thirty-one voters became from that time marked men, and in some instances were roughly treated and, in some cases being obliged to flee from the city to save their lives.

On one occasion some of them undertook to hold a convention in a private office. On learning the fact certain citizens brought out a hand engine, laid the hose, attached the pipe and manned the brakes, preparatory to throwing water into the window, when a motion to "adjourn" was carried unanimously, and the premises were evacuated. Another party put upon a piece of paper the names of several voters supposed to be disloyal, posting the same at one of the voting places. It is said also that a noose was here suspended, with a request that such of those whose names appeared upon the paper, who came to vote, be hanged. The paper is still preserved in this city, and it does not appear that any one was deterred from voting, on account of it or the hangman's circle.

At a Democratic county convention, August 30th '61, Mr. Wilson, of Orono, *said*: "So help me God, I will never support a man nominated on the Breckenridge Platform." "Why" said he, "they at their convention actually *hissed* the National Flag, and if I could have got hold of the man who did it, I would have dragged him out of the convention.

Mr. Geo. P. Sewall of Oldtown said, "We go for peace, but it is peace obtained by crushing out the Rebellion. I shall never consent to laying down our arms at the command of the rebels." "Whoever goes for Dana goes for aiding and comforting the enemy. Will you lay down and permit them to subjugate you? (loud cries of "no! never!") If we submit to a dishonored peace, we are all ruined and anarchy will surely come. I am glad that the Republican party has sustained us as well as they have in this war, and they have done well." (Loud applause).

Another call for short service men was made in '62, which brought out the following thrilling appeal:

AUGUSTA, MAY 26th, 1862.

"Another crisis is upon us, and the loyal States are again, and for the third time, called upon to save the capital of the nation from the beleaguering hosts of rebels that now threaten to lay waste and destroy the very seat of our National Government.

In answer to a request from the Secretary of War, to forward immediately the volunteers and militia of this state for the defence of Washington, and there being no organization of the militia, the Governor has determined, with the consent of the War Department, to raise *three months* volunteers for this emergency, and it is desirable that men enough to form several regiments, should at once organize themselves into companies, and report for duty as speedily as possible. All companies of able bodied men that may be raised under this call, including exempts, will be accepted if they report immediately.

Three regiments, at least, will be raised under this call. One will rendezvous at Bangor, one at Augusta, and one at Portland.

George W. Ricker will be the Colonel of the Augusta regiment.

Capt. David Bugbee, of Bangor, has been tendered the position of Lieutenant Colonel of the regiment to be raised at Bangor. Now is the time for the loyal, liberty loving men of the Dirigo State to show their faith by their works, and by their prompt response to the call of the President, manifest their willingness to *do something* that *shall* help to crush out this accursed rebellion. The sword that has hung so long must soon fall; the blow that has been impending must soon be struck, bringing liberty to toiling millions, a speedy end to the rebellion, and justice to the *infernal* traitors, who have brought all this trouble upon us."

Local companies continued to form in the surrounding towns. Company B, of Lincoln, elected H. G. Colburn as Captain, and M. B. Pinkham, A. J. Bodwell, H. I. Piper and Jonas Colburn as

Lieutenants. Dexter had two companies, with Geo. Hamilton and John B. Maxfield as captains, and B. F. Roberts. Daniel Plummer. Asa Moore, Sanford Oaks, E. B. Fifield, G. J. Shaw, H. S. Dole, John M. Hill, as Lieutenants. Ellsworth about this time sent in a bouncing company for the army, of one hundred and fifteen men, being one of two companies to come from Hancock county. The officers knew how to shoot, or ought to have known how to do so, for they had for some time been engaged in teaching the young. The captain was Z. A. Smith, formerly a teacher in the Ellsworth High School, First Lieutenant, W, T. Parker, once principal Boys High School, Bangor, while Geo. W. Grant was Second Lieutenant.

In May, Col. Rich, of the Ninth Regiment, was discharged from arrest.

Republican Convention nominated Abner Coburn for Governor, he having exactly enough votes, 330 out of 618.

Peoples State Convention, City Hall, Bangor, nominated C. D. Jameson, he having 166 out of 272.

Democratic State Convention, Portland, nominated Bion Bradbury, of Eastport, 278 out of 414 votes.

There were four so-called "Secesh" papers—Machias Union, North Anson Advocate, Eastern Argus and Maine Democrat. Four supported Jameson; the Augusta Age, Republican Journal, Bangor Times and Rockland Democrat.

Mattawamkeag raised a home company, with Thomas M. Blackmore, Captain; Lewis F. Stratton, First Lieutenant; F. P. Babcock, Second Lieutenant; Hannibal Thompson, Third Lieutenant, and D. W. Libby, Fourth Lieutenant.

In July Gen. McClellan caused the following to be issued to the daily press:

HARRISON'S LANDING,
July 10th, 1862.

"The shameful desertion of officers and men from the ranks of their regiments, which has been going on since the battle of Williamsburg, and which has more than decimated the army within the last fortnight, should receive notice at the hands of the press. The press can do no better service to the military interest of the Government of the Nation than in exposing men absent under pretence of sickness. Robust or slightly wounded men and officers are parading the streets of cities, or loitering at home, who are absent without leave, and who are needed here. *Make it detestable for any man able to do duty, to be away from the army. Hold him up to public view. Let him be shamed to his duty.* In the recent battles and movements, hordes of stragglers rushed to the hospital boats, and escaped from the army, while thousands who could not get on the boats, were only compelled to return to the ranks by provost guards and by hunger. Make a residence at home disgraceful to the deserters. The loyal police should arrest every man improperly absent from his regiment. The press can ascertain how far what is here said is true, by looking around and seeing the numbers of officers and men, who are in every street in every city, in every lane in every town and village of the North. If every officer and soldier fit for duty would emerge from his hiding-place and come to his regiment, the army would be strengthened, and the cause for which we struggle materially served."

The election resulted in a victory for the Republican party, Coburn having 44,870; Confederate Bradbury Democrats, as they were called, casting 32,371, while Jameson, the Union Democratic got 7,178. It will be seen that the Peace party was growing, almost one half the voters being against Coburn.

In September, too, the press began to cry out against McClellan. Maryland was invaded, and as the year drew to a close the clouds began to lower around the Union horizon, and gloomy forbodings possessed the souls of the faithful. *The Jeffersonian* put it as follows:

THE SITUATION.

"We have no heart to comment on the situation of affairs to-day. It thunders all around the sky. Another dreadful battle on the famous Bull Run ground has been fought, our loss being 8,000. The thunders of the cannon were heard by two hundred thousand federal troops. The enemy are reported near Chain Bridge. Kentucky is almost within the grasp of the Confederates, and doubt and despair reign in the hearts of the loyal people of other border States. To add to the gloom, the Indians of the Northwest, instigated by rebel agents, are rising and murdering white settlers by thousands, within thirty miles of Minneapolis, St. Anthony and St. Paul."

Bucksport Company choose J. C. Moses, Captain; T. W. Hawley, A. White, R. P. Patterson and S. West, as Lieutenants.

The Proclamation of Freedom was issued on the 22d, to take effect the following January.

The Army of the Potomac was placed under command of Gen. Burnside, who was repulsed at Fredericksburg.

The year closed with no bright rays of the sunshine of victory, which had been promised in the spring, and the army went into winter quarters, while the loyal people at home anxiously awaited the events of the new year, which were of great interest.

CHAPTER XVIII.

In 1863—Return Of The Second Maine—The Military Escort—The Speakers At Norombega—Vice-President Hamlin's Second Address To Them—Local Events.

The winter passed away about as did the previous one, many coming home on leave of absence, while such of our citizens as could do so, visited the army, always bearers of good things and letters and words of cheer. On Thursday, May 21st, the grand Second Maine, not now the dashing, gay, well clothed, well fed and light hearted body that had gone forth two years previous, but a war worn, battle scarred, haggard and ragged handful of men, left for home, arriving here May 26th. Notice had been given that they were due about that time, and a committee of the city council was appointed to take measures that the reception should be fitting, and on that committee were Aldermen Hatch, Strickland and O'Donohue, and Councilmen Dunning, Weed, Williams, Clark and Trickey.

The regiment left Alexandria in the steamer Expounder, Capt, Chas. Deering, an old Penobscot River steamboat captain, in command, on Thursday, May 21st, and without accident arrived at Newport, R. I., Sunday, where they took in coal. They left Newport Sunday night, for Bangor, experiencing some little uncomfortable weather, and at about four o'clock Tuesday morning, reached Bucksport, where they were met by Messrs. Strickland and Hatch, of the committee of reception, and by Col. Roberts, their old commander, who had in charge the old flags of the regiment. These flags, after having been borne defiantly, by this noble band of men, through eleven bloody battles, and which had been rent by traitorous shot and shell, torn and tattered by the fierce attacks, had been replaced by new ones, and were now left as silent mementoes of those bloody and terrible conflicts.

At ten o'clock, the booming cannon announced their arrival, and the crowd rushed pell-mell for the steamboat wharf, in a manner likely to terrify nervous people. Never had so much excitement been seen in Bangor. The police were powerless, and the strong fence at the steamboat wharf, needed the extra propping of several strong men to prevent its downfall, and to keep the multitude from rushing to embrace fathers, sons and brothers. Three ladies embraced one soldier at the same time, and nearly smothered the browned and happy veteran by their kisses and other demonstrations of joy. The wife of another soldier, seized his arm, and did not relinquish her grasp until he entered Norombega Hall.

The regiment was received on Front street, by an appointed escort, which was under the direction of Gen. J. H. Butler, and Col. James Dunning, and Major Thomas Hersey of his staff, and was formed as follows:

"A" Company Cavalry, Capt. Mansill; Bangor Drum Corps; Bangor Cornet Band, A. D. Harlow, Leader; Company A, State Guard, Capt. L. J. Morse; Company B, State Guard, Capt. D. Bugbee; Union Hose Company, Capt. Geo. A. Styles; Charleston Brass Band; Eagle Engine Company, No. Three, Capt. G. H. Chick; Tiger Engine Company, No. Six, Capt. W. H. H. Pitcher; Hook and Ladder Company, No. One, Capt. W. W. Taylor; St. Johns Commandery, Knights Templar, under command of Past M. E., Wm. H. Mills.

Following this escort came the "gallant Second."

A feature of the procession was the company of discharged soldiers of the regiment, who were placed in the rear of the Second, under command of Captains Emerson, Wilson and Bartlett. Some of these were minus arms, others were limping along with the aid of canes, fearfully telling the story of their trials and sufferings. Among the noticeable men in the procession were, Adjt. Gen. Hodsdon, and Col. Osgood of Gov. Coburn's Staff, and Col. Roberts, who rode with his former associate, Col. Varney. The regiment was received in military form and escorted to Broadway, where an immense throng had assembled, nearly filling the square. The processsion marched through Main, State and French streets, and all along the line, stores were closed and buildings hung gay with bunting. The most prominent decorations were from Wheelwright & Clark's block, which was completely covered with flags, one in particular having the names of the battles of the Second painted on it. After the military had taken position at the square, Alderman Hatch, Chairman of the Committee, presented Mayor Dale to Col. Varney and the regiment.

Mayor Dale then welcomed them in a very neat and appropriate speech, after which, Col. Varney briefly responded, thanking Mayor Dale and the citizens for their uniform kindness and attention to the regiment, and also for their generous and hearty welcome. A little daughter of J. S. Wheelwright, Esq., then advanced and presented Col. Varney with an elegant bouquet, which he gracefully received in behalf of his regiment. At the close, enthusiastic and deafening cheers were given for Col. Varney, the officers of the Second, and also for the regiment. The boys responded with three times three and a tiger, for Mayor Dale, the citizens and the ladies. The procession then marched to Norombega Hall, where a bounteous collation had been prepared. A blessing was asked by Rev. Mr. Gilman, after which the Second and the invited guests paid attention to unloading the tables, made heavy by the generous hand of "Murray." This portion of the programme being disposed of, Mayor Dale introduced Adj. Gen. Hodsdon, who was received with enthusiasm, and responded as follows:

"Col. Varney:

"It has become my high privilege, as well as my exalted duty, in the absence of Governor Coburn, (who would gladly have been present on this interesting and momentous occasion, had it been in his power), as Chief of Staff, to tender to you, and to your brave companions in arms, the *welcomes*, the *thanks* and the *profound homage* of the State, for the enduring honor you have conferred upon it, through all the numerous and varied scenes of peril and responsibility, which you have been called upon to pass.

Unreservedly, our hearts go out to you, and each of you, with love and gratitude for the toils and dangers you have braved and endured in the cause of your country.

The *first* regiment in the field from Maine, you are *second* to none in the annals of history, in your record of gallant heroism and faithfulness during every hour of your period of service.

With our laurels for your valiant living, and our tears for your glorious dead, the name and deeds of the Second Regiment of Maine Volunteers, will be enshrined among the most cherished and honored memories of patrotic heroism, held sacred by the State, and be linked with "Stone Bridge, Yorktown, Yorktown Siege, Hanover Court House, Gaine's Mills, the Seven Days Battles upon the Chickahominy, Malvern Hill, Bull Run, Antietam, Fredericksburg, and Chancellorsville, through all coming time."

A beautiful tribute to the Second Maine, written by a lady of Bangor, was then sung by a choir.

Ex-Governor Washburn was called upon, and his appearance was loudly cheered. He made quite extended remarks, thanking the regiment and applauding its valor and heroism. In conclusion he said:

"Hereafter, when the people of this Queen City, which sits beautiful as a bride, on the banks of the Penobscot and the Kenduskeag, and of the Empire county of the East, shall look over the record of their choicest possessions, they will discover none of which they will be more proud, than the fame of General Jameson and of the officers and the soldiers of the Second Maine Regiment."

"The Star Spangled Banner," was then rendered by the Bangor Cornet Band.

Vice-President Hamlin was called for, and received with enthusiasm.

As we have shown in an earlier chapter, Mr. Hamlin, at the time of the Second's departure from Bangor, for the field of war, delivered an eloquent address of farewell to the regiment, then made up of fresh, strong, able men, and one may easily guess the mingled feelings that leaped to his breast, on reviewing that remnant of a once large and active regiment. Instead of 800 earnest, loyal men, going out to do battle for their country, there were left but a fragment, with decimated ranks.

Mr. Hamlin said:

"He wished the Mayor had excused him. At such a time all hearts were beating, and the blood coursing so rapidly, there was no language adequate to the occasion. But in deep sympathy with the vast concourse of our people who had come to greet them, he was rejoiced to meet the returning veterans, officers and men of the gallant Second Regiment, who had returned with laurels won upon many a hard contested battle field. They had gone forth to battle for the integrity of our country, with a confidence in all true men, that they would do their whole duty bravely and gallantly, and well had that confidence been sustained. In all the duties of camp life, on picket duty, and in the stern strife of battle, there had come to those at home, whose care and prayers were for them, a uniform and uninterrupted account of their patriotic and soldierly bearing. But the tattered and stained ensigns that they bore with them spoke a language more eloquent than words. That once beautiful flag, donated by the ladies from Maine in California, and which was entrusted to me to designate the regiment to which it was to be presented, told the story of their valor and heroism. It tells us in its rents and stains, its own true story. No words could add to it. None but noble and gallant hearts could have borne it where it has been. All honor and praise to the brave Second Maine. To say that you have won our respect and praise is not enough. You have the homage of every true and loyal man, woman and child. But amid this greeting and rejoicing, this warm and heartfelt welcome, there will come the feeling of sadness at your decimated ranks. How many who went forth with gay and gallant tread to battle for an imperilled country, are slumbering in earth, and returned to their common mother? While we greet the living, we must pause to remember and do justice to the dead."

"How sleep the brave who sink to rest,"
"With all a country's honor blest."

"Another shade of sadness, too, intermingles with the occasion. It is because there are too many in our community, who have no friendly greeting, or sympathy in your heroic acts. Their faces are a perfect barometer of their feelings. They have mourned over your victories, and rejoiced at your defeats. But let them pass. Thank God, you have returned to your homes, your friends and all you hold dear, to rejoice with us at the glad tidings, that come from the heroic Grant in the West. Your acts shall be remembered in all time, by the true and the good, but upon all traitors shall be stamped, the undying seal of infamy, never to be effaced."

Lieut.-Col. and Brev.-Col. A. B. Farnham.

"Men of the Second Maine, we respect you as citizens, and we honor you for your heroic deeds, and your devotion to your country."

"Hail Columbia" was then played by the band.

David Barker, of Exeter, was called for and responded by reciting a beautiful poem, he had written for the occasion, with marked effect. He was followed by his brother, Hon. Lewis Barker, Esq., who, in a short speech, welcomed home the gallant regiment.

Hon. F. A. Pike, of Calais, was then called upon, and in glowing terms complimented the regiment on their bravery and valor. He was followed by the Rev. Dr. Harris.

Col. Roberts, formerly of the Second, was called for, and was loudly cheered by the soldiers.

Col. Roberts said, "He was unable to express his feelings on this memorable occasion. They had returned from their long, weary, tedious, but, thank God, faithful services. When he looked over their decimated ranks, a feeling of sadness stole over him, for those brave and gallant comrades, who had laid down their lives at the alter of their country. History would do justice to their memory. A marble shaft has been erected, upon which will be inscribed their names and deeds, which will be read and re-read in after years by their friends and relatives. He could only say, peace to their ashes—God bless them all. He had mingled with them in the camp and in the field, shared with them their sorrows and their pleasures, and time could never obliterate or efface those recollections. He now proposed three cheers for a man and patriot, one whose victorious troops had loved him, and who loved his troops, the brave and gallant Gen. Geo. B. McClellan."

The entire Second Maine gave rousing cheers.

The services closed with cheers for the Union and the Second Maine.

On the platform at the hall, were two field pieces, covered with flags and wreaths, and near them stood the old flags, the pride of the regiment, and the glory of the citizens. One was presented by the ladies of Bangor, the morning the regiment left the city. Another was presented by Maine citizens in New York, and still another, which was presented by the Maine ladies in California, and the last was a secesh flag, captured by the Second from an Alabama Regiment, at the hard fought battle of Gaine's Mill, and which will be treasured by our city, as an evidence of the prowess and valor of the regiment at that fearful struggle.

At the close of the services the boys were allowed the freedom of the city, and many went to their homes, while others who had no homes in the city, went to their quarters at City Hall, and at the Gymnasium.

The Second Regiment saw an amount of service, in their two years of war, that might put to blush many an old veteran. They were in eleven bloody conflicts, besides many skirmishes. During all their trials, tedious marches, and desperate battles, they never fainted or faltered, but steadily and steadfastly upheld the old flag, and were ready always to lay down their lives, that the glorious institutions of our free Republican Government might live.

The "*Whig*" in speaking of their return said:

"Bangor may justly feel proud of the heroic deeds of this gallant and noble regiment. Penobscot County may feel proud of them—yea, the whole State may look back at their regimental career, with pride and satisfaction, and future generations will rise to bless the living and revere the memory of the noble dead."

CHAPTER XIX.

The Draft—How It Was Avoided In '62—Patriotic Appeals And Odd Advertisements—Elijah Low Is Appointed Provost Marshal—What He Did—He Has A Row With The Maine Central—And Is Ordered To Take Possession And Run It At Government Expense—The Travel To Canada Becomes Large —A Patten Rebel Defies Uncle Sam—And Comes To Grief—Capt. Low Exposes A Defaulter—The Draft In Houlton—Bells Tolling For Lincoln And Clanging For Victory Over Lee—The Hunt In Maine For The Assassin Booth.

The first allusion made to the draft was in the Whig, when an Augusta correspondent predicted the State authorities would not be obliged to resort to a "compulsory draft." This was in 1862, and the article was called forth on account of the slowness with which men answered the President's call. To quicken them it was determined that Vice-President Hamlin should go through the State and address the people, urging them to their duty, and also that Gen. Howard attend meetings, having the same object in view.

The following address will serve to show how matters stood July 12th:

To The Citizens Of Bangor.

"The President of the United States calls for 300,000 men. Bangor's proportion is about two hundred men. Why should not this city emulate sister towns in old Massachusstts, in their patriotic efforts in furnishing volunteers, instead of allowing a detail under the law? Citizens of Bangor who are not liable to do military duty, and others, should at once come forward and raise a fund sufficient to give a *liberal bounty*, in addition to that allowed by the Government, and it should be so liberal as to at once bring into the service our two hundred men; and when this is done, ask the Governor to so modify his order as to allow the volunteers so raised to be attached to the gallant Maine Second, under the command of Col. Roberts."

"It is due to ourselves, and it is due to Col. Roberts and his fearless men, that his regiment be filled up. This two hundred men so raised and added to that brave Second Regiment, will be almost as effective under their brave young colonel as a new regiment that has seen no service. The writer will do his part.

BANGOR, JULY 11th.

Another communication speaks for itself;
MESSRS. WHEELER & LYNDE,

Gentlemen—"My age and health forbids my entering the service of my country, and I have no son old enough. You will please say in your paper, that I will pay to the first able-bodied man belonging in Bangor, who will volunteer and enlist in the service of our country, twenty-five dollars as a gratuity."

HOOPER CHASE.

The patriotism of the people seemed to grow more and more intense, as the English across the water and the secessionists in the North sought, by every way possible to prolong the war. The following call for a meeting at Norombega Hall is worthy of close inspection.

GRAND PATRIOTIC RALLY!
OF THE MEN OF PENOBSCOT!

FOR THE COUNTRY!

"The President of the United States has called upon the *Nation* for *Troops* to defend the *Flag*. From every part of this great nation the voice of the loyal heart is heard; The Union! The

Nation must be preserved! and the glorious *Stars* and *Stripes* shall never trail in the dust!"

"The despots of the old world and the traitors at home are trembling at the response of the people."

FREEMEN OF PENOBSCOT!

"Shall we refuse to listen to the call of duty and patriotism? Shall we be behind our *Sister States* in coming up to the great work of redemption of our country, and the preservation of our free government?

"All the people of Penobscot are invited to assemble at

NOROMBEGA HALL,

THURSDAY, JULY 17th, at 7 o'clock."

We have elsewhere given an account of this meeting. The results of it, combined with the liberal action of the City Council, induced great numbers to enlist. Those who did so, could not have been induced by the prospect of money alone, for it was, now well understood that the greatest rebellion, yes, one of the greatest wars known to either ancient or modern times, was inaugurated at Sumpter, and that the struggle was to be a long and bloody one. Men came in freely, however, and quarters were assigned them at the old race course on Union street. The camp was known as "Camp John Pope." Here was formed the Eighteenth, and other bodies of men, and the scenes familiar to those of the old Essex street camp were re-enacted.

About this time long advertisements appeared in the papers of the day, announcing the quota of each city, town and plantation, and men were eagerly sought for to fill this demand, and thus avoid a draft. Men in good circumstances contributed from their private purses, money to be added to the several bounties offered. Agents were now sent over the line, to induce "Blue Noses" to come over and enlist, while others looked after men who were residents of Bangor, and who had entered the army or navy from other States, and whenever they could do so had them credited to their native place.

On Tuesday, July 29th, there appeared in the Whig the following, and it speaks volumes for the fighting qualities of the Second Maine. Although it was made up of "home boys," yet recruits were offered more money to enter this regiment than any other:

INCREASE BANGOR BOUNTY.

At a special session of the City Council a resolve was passed offering a city bounty of one hundred dollars to volunteers in any new regiment, one hundred and twenty dollars to volunteers in any old regiment *except the Second*, and one hundred and forty dollars to volunteers for the Second."

Early in August the Government determined upon a Draft, the men to serve nine months. Up to this time the North had sent as volunteers, over one million of men, a spectacle never before seen, and which caused the monarchs of the old world to look on with wonder and surprise, but more men were needed, and the Draft was the quickest and cheapest way to get them.

Here is a warning put out by Capt. Garnsey, now a popular purser on the Boston and Bangor steamship line:

"We Are Coming Father Abraham,
300,0000 More."
"Fill up the Gallant Second Maine.

Last Chance! A Draft is Coming! Rally boys, and volunteer and receive the Bounties. No drafted men receive bounties.

FRANK A. GARNSEY,
Capt. Company H, Second Maine.

Early in May, 1863, the mail brought to one of Bangor's most patriotic and capable citizens, Elijah Low, the following:

WAR DEPARTMENT.

WASHINGTON, APRIL 30th, 1863.

Sir:

You are hereby informed that the President of the United States has appointed you Provost Marshal, for the Fourth Congressional District of the State of Maine, with the rank of Captain of Cavalry in the service of the United States, to rank as such from the Thirtieth day of April, 1863.

Immediately on receipt hereof, please to communicate to the Department, through the Provost Marshal General of the United States, your acceptance, or non-acceptance; and with your letter of acceptance, return the *oath* herein enclosed, properly filled up, *subscribed* and *attested*, and report your age, birthplace and the State of which you are a permanent resident. You will immediately report by letter to the Provost Marshal General, and will proceed without delay to establish your headquarters at Bangor, Maine, and enter upon your duties in accordance with such special instructions as you may receive from the Provost Marshal General.

EDWIN M. STANTON,
Secretary of War.

With this came special instructions, and, after looking them over, Mr. Low accepted, and at once entered upon the duties of the office. It will be seen that his was an important position; that Capt. Low was an official in the *regular* army, and transacted business independent of State authorities. He had charge of Aroostook, Piscataquis and Penobscot counties, and his word was almost law. The Maine Central Railroad, and Mattawamkeag Stage Company did not realize this at first, but as will be seen, their eyes were opened and their senses quickened.

The first move was to appoint enrolling officers, and divide the territory into sub-districts, then *every* man, between the ages of twenty and forty-five was enrolled. This included the lame, blind and halt, and a man with one eye or one leg was, at first, liable to a draft. Again, a man, when drafted, *was from that moment a soldier in service of the United States*, and failing to report, *was a deserter*, subject to all the penalties. This fact was not generally understood, and men who committed crimes against the Government, got free at time of trial, through ignorance, in one case at least, as will be seen, of the U. S. Attorney.

All male citizens being enrolled, next came the apportioning, that is: finding out just what each town, city, or plantation should furnish as their quota. The office where this work was done was over the office of D. M. Howard, Esq., but later, when the draft came, quarters were secured in Granite Block, where men were clothed, fed and lodged. As Capt. Low was obliged to assume the duties of Commissary and Quartermaster, it will be seen that he had a great deal to do, and this may account for his not becoming a president, board of directors and superintendent of the Maine Central, as he at one time was requested to by the Government. The story as related by Mr. Low is as follows:

"When men began to come in, their numbers would be reported to headquarters, and at short intervals requisitions would be made on me for a certain number, these orders coming by mail or telegraph at night. In the morning I would march them to the station, and the officials there, thinking I ought to have ordered cars in advance, growled at the inconvenience to which I subjected them, and which I could not prevent. One day there arrived seventy-five thousand dollars worth of supplies, and when I sent for them, I was informed the freight bill must be paid in advance. As I was not a disbursing officer I at once wired the authorities at Washington."

"Maine Central refuse delivery supplies until freight bills are paid."

Soon the answer came:

"Take posession Maine Central Railroad, and run it at Government expense."

"Of course," said Mr. Low, "I didn't want to do that, so I wired the superintendant at Waterville, and when he answered, I got my supplies quick, and after that I had no trouble about cars."

Soon came orders for a draft, which were carried out. The next step was to inform such as had drawn "a ticket," of that fact, and order them to Bangor for an examination.

"How did they respond to this, Mr. Low?"

"From towns along the line," was the answer, "they skedaddled awfully, but from the other places nearly all came in."

Then examinations were held, and many thrown out, and went home rejoicing. Those who were taken had two chances; pay three hundred dollars down, which exempted them for two years, or provide a substitute. Many who had the cash paid it out, but there were those who could not do this and who, not wishing to enter the army, searched about for some one to represent them at the front. Thus it was that substitute brokers became important factors, and many of them reaped bountiful harvests while engaged in their traffic in human flesh.

Those who had made up their minds to go, as well as the substitutes and bounty jumpers who had been hired, were provided with clothing, etc., and then drafted men were given a few days leave of absence, in order that they might go home and close up their affairs, take leave of friends, etc.; but the hired ones were not given such privilege, and, in order to keep them until turned over to the Government, their money and advance pay was retained by Capt. Low. When a squad of these men went forward their money was sent along also, being turned over with the men. It is related that on one occasion an officer in Portland embezzled $300,000 of such money, and he was tried by a court martial. At the trial Capt. Low, who took receipts always, showed that he had turned $150,000 over to the accused, and on this testimony he was convicted.

Reference has been made to the flight across "The Line." In the town of Patten resided a man named Leslie, well known as "Jim" Leslie. He was a rank "secesh," had often cursed the Government and Lincoln, and had defied the officers to come to Patten, and take him through the town of Benedicta. The Government required of the provost marshals that they should send, from time to time, copies of all disloyal sheets, which was done. Some of these contained utterances of Leslie, and at last Capt. Low was ordered to arrest the man on the first proof of any disloyal act. Soon it was discovered that Leslie was helping men over "The Line," and two officers were sent to Patten after him, arriving there about dark. Going to the house of Leslie, they called him out and at once handcuffed him, bringing him the next day to Bangor. Here Capt. Low was met by a delegation of Leslie's friends, in sympathy with him in his utterances and acts, and offered bail to any amount. Capt. Low said "No," and the gentleman from Patten was sent to Portland. His crime was *aiding deserters*; drafted men, as I have said, being really in the service, and could become free only upon being rejected by the surgeons, *and given discharge papers.* Of the fact this U. S. Attorney was in ignorance and Leslie got clear, but did not again conspire to defeat the law's intent.

The working force of the Provost Marshal's office consisted of, Elijah Low, Provost Marshal; Dr. S. A. Porter, of Monson, Sur-

Capt. ELIJAH LOW,
Late Provost-Marshal 4th Dist. Me.

geon; Col. C. H. Chandler, late Lieut. Col. Sixth Maine, Commissioner. They being styled the board of enrollment.

Wm. Arnold, Deputy Marshal; Geo. R. Smith, clerk of the board; Eben Woodbury, Deputy Marshal for Houlton; Dr. S. D. Morrison, Asst. Surgeon; Dr. E. H. Thompson, of Dover, Asst. Surgeon; Dr. E. N. Mayo, of Orono, Asst. Surgeon for Holton; J. S. Patten, G. W. Stevens, Horatio N. Hatch, I. E. Leighton and Wilder H. Taylor, Special Agents. John C. Flint, First Clerk; Wm. H. S. Lawrence, Second clerk; and Chas. Lowell, C. P. Wiggin and Frank Averill, Clerks.

Early in May, '63, the office was opened, and for over two years was run " day and night."

Col. Chandler was obliged to resign early in the season, by reason of ill health, and John E. Godfrey was appointed in his place.

When a man was drafted, a notice was sent to the enrolling officer of his town, who served the paper on the man, if he could find him, and if not, left it at the last known place of residence.

At one time so much money belonging to soldiers, had accumulated at the office in this city, that fears were entertained for its safety, and as rumors had been afloat to the end that the Copperheads had planned an attack on the office, measures were taken to protect it by a guard, and the money was turned over to Aaron A. Wing, Collector of Internal Revenue, for safe keeping.

At this time there was upwards of three hundred thousand dollars of money belonging to soldiers, in the keeping of the Provost Marshal.

As may be supposed many ludicrous, and many sad scenes were witnessed. In fact the same may be said of all enlistments. Sometimes a careless, ignorant lout would come along, enlist, get a suit from Uncle Sam, together with a good supply of money—often more than he had ever seen before—

and then start out to see the sights, treat everybody who would drink, patronize the photographer, and have a good time generally, until the provost guard gathered him in, and sent him South on more serious business. Then would come along a poor man, who, perchance, had started a home for his wife and little ones in some back clearing. Anxiously the fond wife awaited the decision of the surgeons, and tears of anguish would roll down her cheek, as she learned that her husband had been accepted and must go to the war. All about the city at this time were recruiting offices, many being on the Custom House approach, and the shrill tones of the fife, the rattling of the drums and the shouts of the runners for the various booths—all calling the attention of the would-be-soldiers—served to keep well before the people the fact that war, grim war, with all its horrors and bloody scenes was then, and was likely, for some time to come, to be the fate of the nation.

The Draft In Aroostook.

When the Civil War broke out, the good people of Aroostook knew little about scenes of death and carnage. They, like our early settlers, had gone into a wilderness, and were rapidly converting it into a garden, and the peaceful scenes of "seed time and harvest," of flocks and herds, of peace and plenty, of prosperity and good will, had been their lot. It is true there had been a so-called "Aroostook War," but it had not been prolific of deeds of daring, and days and nights of slaughter. Armed men were upon Aroostook soil—armed men from Bangor too—but it does not appear that they went there with harmful intent, because on the approach of the enemy they fled towards the Penobscot, and one poet records the fact in song, that that flight was one of marvelous swiftness.

Save this bloodless invasion, Aroostook knew nothing of war, but she was not one inch behind her sister counties, and early and often her stalwart sons came in and joined the swelling ranks that were marching to the tune of the Union in 1861. The women too, were filled with patriotism, and by their steady work and zeal did much to help along the cause. As the boys went away, the scenes so novel and sad, yet so common then all over the country, were daily enacted. Mothers said "Good Bye" to husbands and sons, sisters to brothers, fathers, and sweethearts, while the younger lads, not quite old enough to take an active part, looked on with jealous eyes, which gave out at the same time admiring glances, as their brothers and fathers looking so gay in their new uniforms, marched away.

The time came, however, when volunteers could not be had, and in common with the rest of the loyal North, Aroostook stood the Draft. The result of it was such as to cause the northern and eastern parts of Maine, to become a highway for about all the copperheads and cowards of the North, who were drafted, and I suppose Aroostook county has had within her borders, more deserters than any other section of country in either this or the old world. The stage lines, as well as many individuals who owned teams, did a thriving business, while the sale of intoxicating liquors was immense. Of course many men came in and entered the army, or gained exemption in a legal way, and so filled the various quotas, but so many failed to report from "along the line," that orders were issued to hold a Draft at Houlton, and thither Capt. Low repaired in person.

In order that the younger portion may understand the situation, let us glance back a moment at the condition of Aroostook at that time. Houlton was quite a town, but had no railway or telegraphic communication, while the country round about was thinly settled, with but few good roads. While the inhabitants were not poor —in one sense—yet there were few families who could spare the men, even for a few months. Imagine a family, consisting of husband, wife and two or three small children, living in a clearing, and having a partly completed dwelling and a few head of stock. Perhaps their nearest neighbor was a mile away, and equally poor. Then think of the news of the drafting of the husband, who was to go down to Southern soil, where one of the bloodiest wars known to history was in progress! Imagine the helplessness of the mother, and you can imagine what a draft was to Aroostook! While the cities and towns had relief corps and aid societies—Aroostook had none—and her people, when the support of the strong arm of the husband and father was withdrawn, were left helpless.

Capt. Low plead for this section of the district over which he was placed, and begged the Government to spare it, but no, the army needed men, and just such stalwart men as Aroostook could produce, and the draft must go on. Capt. Low occupied the Court House, being seated in the judge's chair, while his officers were within the bar. As fast as the men were drawn they were notified, but, much to the surprise of the officials, few responded.

It appears that enemies of the Government had circulated a story to the effect that there were twenty-five hundred pairs of handcuffs secreted in Houlton, and as fast as the men came in they would be secured with these, and sent forward, without the privilege of making a visit home. Thereupon Capt. Low informed them that all would be given five days leave of absence, and many came in for examination. Among them were two brothers from Presque Isle. The oldest, who was married and had a family, had been drawn, while the younger one, named Fred, was single and had escaped the draft. While at the Court House Capt. Low overheard the following conversation between them :

"I tell you what it is," said Fred, "you can't leave your family. I am bound to go in your place."

"I can't allow that," was the response; "you stay at home and run my farm, and I will pay you well. I am stronger, and the one to go."

Considerable of an argument ensued, but finally Fred won, was examined and accepted. He was then given a little blue ticket, which entitled him to the five days leave of absence and he returned to visit his parents at Presque Isle, and bid them "good bye." Capt. Low, however, who was struck with the noble offer, wrote them that he would retain the son on his guard, which he did, and Fred finally returned home without having been south.

Not all were as loyal as Fred, and these fled over the line, when they found they had been drawn, and here they remained until after the war. An order was issued stating that all who desired a pardon must come to Augusta, which many did, and after being registered on the roll of dishonor, were dismissed. One of these fellows had the nerve to ask for a pension for disability, caused by sickness while at the State House, and even went so far as to ask Capt. Low to sign his petition. Said Capt. Low:

"Go home. If I were as big a coward as you, I should not dare look a pine tree in the face."

Of course many sad scenes and many joyful ones were witnessed during the Draft, but perhaps the most peculiar day—one of mingled joy and sadness—which Houlton ever experienced, was when the news came of the surrender of Lee; that Lincoln had been assasinated, and that orders had been issued to stop the Draft.

As I have said, there were no telegraphic or rail road communications in those days, the mail coming over from Woodstock or was brought up the "old military road." By some chance the stages had been delayed several days, and when they did arrive they brought one week's mail containing information about all of the above important facts. Capt. Low hardly knew what to do, but after a moments thought he ordered the bells tolled for Lincoln, then rung with a will for Lee's surrender, while mounted couriers were dispatched through the county telling of the news, and informing drafted men that they were not needed. The Government had also sent a portrait of Booth, and Capt. Low at once established a guard along the line to watch for him, but later learned of his capture, and returned to Bangor.

In connection with the Draft many curious items were printed, among them being the following: "Those drafted persons who have knocked out their front teeth to procure exemption, are informed that they will be accepted in the Cavalry, where front teeth are not needed to bite off cartridges." Here is another: "At a second meeting in Northport called to vote three hundred dollars to each conscript to stay at home, the Copperheads were out-voted more than two to one, and some thorough Union resolutions passed."

There was the usual bitter political campaign in 1863, — the Draft being used by the opposition as the subject of many speeches, but they "availed not," and Cony, the republican candidate, was elected by about 20,000 majority. Nearly all of the Northern States fell into line, victories multiplied and the cause of humanity and the Union brightened day by day. Thus closed the year of 1863.

CHAPTER XX.

In 1864—Another Call For Troops—And Another Draft Ordered—The "Soldiers Rest"—The Big Sanitary Fair—The Elections—The Close Of The Year—Gold And Merchandise—Its Rise And Fall—How Fortunes Were Made—How Some Lost Them—The Boom In Groceries, Cotton And Woolen Goods—Boots, Shoes And Clothing At War Prices—Something About Hardware—Fools And Their Folly—A. T. Stewart & Co. Are Caught—Sliding Down And Sliding Out—Making Change With Veazie And Hersey Scrip.

In February, 1864, the President issued an order calling for 500,000 more troops, to be raised by a Draft, beginning March 10th, and preparations at once commenced to carry that order into effect. There was a general opinion that the following summer would see the close of the war, hence there was a lack of uneasiness which had characterized the people on the receipt of the first order.

Early in the year it was determined to establish a "Soldiers Rest," for wounded and sick veterans, the place selected being the "Gymnasium," on Columbia street. To secure money it was decided to have a dress ball. The whole matter was carried to a most successful completion, and one thousand one hundred dollars was realized. This money was used to fit up the place, and on June 20th there were forty arrivals, nearly as many more coming in before the end of the month. During the summer over three hundred additional veterans were received. Liberal appropriations were made by the citizens, and many devoted a great deal of time to the nursing of the sick and wounded men. Dr. Morrison was always present, and rendered valuable aid. In December of this year a monster fair was held, the proceeds—fifteen thousand dollars —being used for the benefit of the institution, and it speaks volumes for the loyalty and generosity of Bangor that she freely gave this magnificent sum. On September 7th, Company A, State Guards, returned from sixty days' duty at Kittery. People often laugh at the occupation of the fort there, unmindful of the fact that by going there as State Guards, the men of Bangor released a New Hampshire company of volunteers, who entered the Union Army.

Politics ran high this year, as usual, but the Republicans headed by Lincoln and Johnson, carried twenty-three Northen States, while the Democrats, under the leadership of McClellan and Pendleton, were obliged to be content with victories in Delaware, Kentucky and New Jersey. The second Draft was held this year, additional troops were sent to the front, the Union forces were victorious in most of the battles, and little by little the Confederates were driven back, and the year closed with bright prospects of the speedy suppression of the rebel element.

GOLD AND MERCHANDISE.

Elsewhere has been mentioned the fact that late in 1861, the National banks suspended specie payment, giving as a reason their desire to aid the Government by keeping specie in our country. Although the seventy-five thousand volunteers known as the "three months men," had not succeeded in suppressing the rebellion, no one doubted but that the great army then forming at Washington and in the military camps of the North, would swoop down during 1862 and annihilate every vestige of secession, and it did not alarm the people therefore when the great financial institutions of the land withdrew specie from circulation.

On New Year's Day, 1862, gold became in this country, no longer money, (in the sense which we are accustomed to speak of money), but merchandise, and subject to fluctuations identical with groceries, grain, iron, etc. On that day gold opened at $1.03\frac{1}{2}$ and although it dropped somewhat during the month, it remained the same on the closing of the last day. No great change took place until the following June, when it advanced, and was quoted June 30th, 1.08⅜. The last of July saw it at 1.14½, September 30th, 1.24; October, 1.29; December, 1.33⅝. This was an advance of 30 per cent. in twelve months. The precious metal was on the jump the first month of 1863, going a little higher each day, and advancing in thirty days to 1.60. This was pretty big interest, and every one who had gold began to sell, while those who had already sold caught the fever and bought again. The last of February it stood 1.72, and then dropping, ranged along the 40's until the latter part of the year, when quotations stood 1.51⅝. In February, 1864, he who wanted the "yellow boys" had to "climb the golden stairs" to the tune of 1.59; in March, 1.64; April, 1.79½; May, 1.90; June, 2.50; this being an advance of 60 cents in thirty days. Monday, July 12th, saw gold open at 2.76 and close at 2.85, this being the highest point reached. From that time it began to recede, although at times there would be a temporary advance, until at last it touched par in New York, December 17th, 1878, having been at a premuim sixteen years, eleven months and four days.

During this time gigantic fortunes were made. Many bought and sold, until gold got well above 200, when they, having great confidence in the Government, put their winnings into bonds paying large interest and free from taxation. Sometimes they lost. Mr. P. M. Blake, a leading broker of Bangor, bought one thousand dollars, of Col. Norcross, paying him $2.750. This was within ten per cent. of Boston quotations. When the gold arrived in Boston the next day, quotations were but 2.40, and at that figure it was sold, and Mr. Blake lost three hundred and fifty dollars by the transaction. During this time the now much despised "dollars of of our daddies" and the half dollars then put out of the mint, were eagerly sought for and commanded, at one time 2.50.

As might be supposed this advance exerted a great influence on the prices of dry goods, groceries, and in fact every merchantable commodity. Those articles which came wholly or in part from foreign lands, varied in price with gold. The new money issued by the Government was not taken for duties and therefore, when the importer took his goods out of bond, he was obliged to buy the gold to do it with. If the merchant paid 2.75 for gold one day and then paid his duty, and the next day his competitor bought gold for 2.40, of course the latter could undersell the former, although the goods were bought abroad at the same price. Here at home prices ran high, and seemed strange, even to many who paid them then. Mr. M. S. Jackson kept a grocery store here through the war, and has preserved his day books, then in use. In 1861 he retailed butter eighteen cents; eggs twelve cents; nails four cents; oats forty-two cents; kerosene forty-two cents; sugar eleven cents; starch ten cents; saleratus eight cents; best tea seventy-five cents; flour five dollars, etc.

In 1864, sugar sold for thirty-four cents; cream tartar, sixty cents; butter, fifty cents; nails, twelve cents; potatoes, two dollars; eggs, thirty-five cents; brown sugar, twenty-nine cents; kerosene, one dollar and ten cents per gallon; tea, one dollar and forty cents; Castile soap, twenty-five cents; crackers, twenty-five cents; salt, thirty-five cents per box; molasses, one dollar and twenty cents per gallon; flour, twelve dollars per barrel; lard, twenty-five cents; while in one case Mr. J. T. Budge paid forty-nine dollars for one barrel of Boston pork. In many instances prices ran higher, and the author well remembers being sent all over Belfast in search of a pound of butter. Some of the officers of the U. S. man of war "Rhode Island" were coming to dine, and butter must be had. At last a pound was found, and sixty-five cents was paid. The sailor boys of this same steamer, then just off a long cruise with the blockade squadron, gladly paid my chum and I, who had the exclusive privilege of running a "bum" boat alongside, as she lay in Belfast bay, one dollar a pound for butter; twenty cents a sheet for gingerbread; seventy-five cents a dozen for eggs; two dollars a peck for greens; twenty cents a piece for cigars, and a proportionate price for other luxuries. Spices were very high, ginger being at one time sixty cents, and cassia eighty cents per pound. Nutmegs retailed for sixteen cents an ounce, or two dollars and fifty-six cents per pound. Oats at one time commanded one dollar and ten cents per bushel, and corn meal two dollars and ten cents. Miss Wyer, on December 2d, 1864, paid for a barrel of "Buchanan" flour, fourteen dollars and seventy-five cents, and some fancy brands commanded eighteen dollars.

Dry goods, especially cottons, went up with a rush. Southern cotton was, of course, out of the market. One day a farmer came into Bangor to purchase sheeting. He found what he thought was a bargain, and took three pieces. These he took away with him easily, but he left in payment a hundred dollar bill. The same goods to-day would sell for about seven dollars and fifty cents. Warp before the war cost ninety cents, but in 1865 it took just twelve dollars to purchase a bunch. Cassimeres advanced about three hundred per cent. One merchant purchased five bales of sheeting, not a great order, yet the bill footed up strong three thousand dollars. Some of this was retailed at seventy-five cents, but a decline soon brought the price down to thirty-five.

When the war commenced, this country produced from one half to five eights of all the wool we used. Farmers began to increase their flocks, and this kept wool from rapid and frequent advances. When the war was over, we were producing fifty per cent. more wool than ever before in our history.

A pair of first class hand-sewed boots cost eighteen dollars; a good pair from twelve to fourteen dollars, while a low crown dress hat, sold for six dollars. Fifty dollars was often paid for a good suit of clothes, made to order, and ready-made goods and underwear were in proportion.

Hardware doubled every now and then, and fortunes were made quickly in this branch of trade.

No one was in distress, however, consequent on these high prices. More than one million sturdy men had ceased to be producers, and had become consumers, yes, and huge destroyers as well. Labor commanded large wages. Money went where it had never gone before, and has never been since. Poverty stricken men took bounties, the purchasing power of which they thought inexhaustible, spreading it with a liberal hand, buying without regard to their needs. Everything was in demand, and these possessors of sudden wealth, like children, bought whatever caught their fancy. Later on they realized the truth of the old saying:

"A fool and his money are soon parted."

When victory was assured to the Union armies, things took "a drop," and everyone made haste to unload, and the "mark downs" of those days would discount anything now put out to attract the public eye. Mr. J. C. White, after the war, bought of his brother, then connected with A. T. Stewart, of New York, several pieces of cassimere, paying one dollar and sixty-two cents per yard. For those same goods Stewart was paying two dollars and fifty cents per yard, he having made a contract the previous year, to take all the product of a certain mill at that price. To men who remained in trade, it was like walking up a hill, then sliding down again. In the beginning and at the end they were at the foot. Some, however, went to the top and, instead of sliding down, slid out—of trade—and are now passing their latter days in ease, free from the vexations and care of business.

The advance in gold and silver influenced the cheaper metal, copper, and the old-fashioned cents disappeared. The Government sent out first the little Indian head, then the eagle cents, and followed these with the three cent piece, the three, five, ten, fifteen, twenty-five and fifty cent scrip, and the much abused greenback. For a long time, however, great trouble was experienced in making change, and thus it was that postage stamps became current. As these *would* stick, it was the custom to enclose a certain number of threes and ones in an envelope and seal this, marking the amount upon the outside. This was passed without inspection at its "face value," until worn threadbare, and the last receiver, on examination, would find the whole mass stuck firmly together, and discolored by perspiration, tobacco, etc.

Gen. Veazie and Major Thomas Hersey issued scrip, which were to all intents, their notes, in denominations mentioned above, and these were often purchased in packages by the merchants. Much was lost or destroyed, more was carried away, but all that was presented was afterwards redeemed. Many of our citizens have preserved specimens, and the sight of them often starts a train of humorous anecdotes of the days when "change was mighty skace."

CHAPTER XXI.

In 1865—The Draft Continues—Glorious News From The Army Of The Potomac—Victory All Along The Line—Twelve Thousand Prisoners In Three Days—Surrender Of Lee And His Army—Great Rejoicing At Home—What The People Did—A Great Day For Maine—Interesting Accounts From An Old Journal—A Procession Forms In Bangor And Many Calls Made—What Was Said And Done.

In March, 1865, Provost Marshal Low resumed the Draft, and the usual scenes were re-enacted. In April came the news of a succession of Union victories, the following being the head lines of the dispatches:

"GLORIOUS NEWS FROM THE ARMY OF POTOMAC!"

"DISPATCHES RELIABLE. FROM LINCOLN AND GRANT.

THREE DAYS FIGHTING.

TWELVE THOUSAND PRISONERS TAKEN."

On Monday, April 10th, came the news of Lee's surrender, and great was the rejoicing thereat. The following head lines were displayed in the papers of that, and the following day:

"VICTORY!"

"GLORY TO GOD!"

"FINAL TRIUMPH OF FREEDOM!"

"SURRENDER OF LEE!"

"UNION AND FREEDOM TRIUMPHING!"

Nearly four years had passed since the war began. Those four years had been long ones, freighted with much sorrow, anxiety and doubt. Widows mourned for their husbands or sons, or perhaps both; mothers of stalwart boys had seen them go forth,

APPOMATTOX C. H.; PLACE OF LEE'S SURRENDER.

strong in their manhood, and only knew that their bodies lay in some unknown trench or hastily made grave, on Southern soil. Fathers shed tears in secret, as they dwelt on the happy days ere their sons had gone to the war. The cheek of many a maiden had grown thin and white, as she sat in her Northern home, thinking of her dead lover, and felt that life before her had no bright days. The whole land was in mourning, and it was therefore with glad hearts, that they heard that the fighting was drawing to a close. All felt a burden had been lifted, and that war was not to longer add to their cup of sorrow, already so full.

The following account of the doings of the day, was written over twenty-two years ago, and was intended only for the eyes of the sons and daughters of the author, and their intimate friends. It is in fact a part of a journal, containing accounts of important events, transpiring during his life time, and therefore is undoubtedly correct. The narrative is as follows:

"Sunday night, at eleven o'clock, April 9th, 1865, the news on the previous page was telegraphed to the Bangor Daily Whig and Courier, and at three o'clock on Monday morning, the sky being clear, although threatening rain, owing to a damp air and south wind; boom! boom! went cannon from Court street heights, and the principal church and the court house bells were rung, announcing something of importance. Having taken a long walk about the fields on Sunday, P. M., I slept the first part of the night quite soundly, but waked perhaps at a quarter to three, and was wide awake when the sudden salute was given. Knowing something of importance had transpired, I out of bed and dressed, and told my wife I believed Lee had surrendered, and I made my way down town, coming in view of various bonfires blazing, and many houses illuminated, principally with gas. All the time cannons were booming from Court street, until one hundred rounds had been discharged. I found the Custom House, George Stetson's, Rufus Dwinel's, George W. Merrill's, as well as several stores illuminated. Geo. W. Merrill's house, in the night, situated on the corner of Prospect and French streets, behind numerous fir trees, presented through them, one of the handsomest sights I ever witnessed in illumination. The scene, as I passed down Park street, resembled in every respect, all but the bonfires, the scene during the freshet, March 29th, 1846, which I have described in my family history, under that date. Men running to and fro, no head to any point. I went to the Post Office, and through on to Kenduskeag Bridge, and up to City Hall, but could not gain admittance. While going up Hammond street, I was grabbed by Mr.——who *hurrahed* for the Union, stating that Lee's whole army had surrendered. By this time men were gathering dry goods boxes and barrels, left on Main street, to show samples of dry goods, and carried them to the centre of the square, and made a bonfire. About half past three I made my way to the Whig and Courier office, and a dense crowd was in and out the office. I pushed my way through and purchased a copy at five cents, containing the portion of news I have preserved on the previous page.

As my paper would not reach my house until after six o'clock, I cleared myself from the crowd to go home. At that moment Willard B. Heath, with a tenor drum, and Z. L. Bragdon, with a bass drum, marched across the lower Kenduskeag Bridge, calling aloud, "Fall in," and a company of, say one hundred men and some boys were already marching in time with the drummers. I fell in and marched up Hammond and back, up Main and back, down Broad, and back to the bonfire in the square, where the company halted with the music still playing. I waited a short time, when

I felt anxious for my wife and children to hear the news, and started for home. I came a short distance, when my soul burned within me to persuade the crowd to go to Marcellus Emery's boarding house, and call him out and inform him that the Rebellion had gone up. I went back, and my first impulse was to offer the music ten dollars to follow me an hour. Then I thought I might be doing too much for my part, and I started for home again, and again came to a halt, thinking I would go back, and do as I was about to do at first, but it occured to me to go home and read the news, get a cup of tea, and return immediately. So I kept on, and when I reached ——street, I met Mr. Nath'l Harlow, walking down in the middle of the street. and he turned about and went to my house with me, and, after I built a fire in the dining room stove, I read the news to him, my wife and children coming down stairs while I was reading.

A singular thing happened as Mr. Harlow and I passed through my gate. A bird—having been aroused by the cannon probably—sang a beautiful shrill and clear song—this being long before daylight—she sitting on a tall fir tree, and Mr. Harlow and I stopped and listened until she had finished her song.

When we were marching down Hammond street, some were laughing, some hurrahing, and instead of passing the time of day when they met, men grabbed each other by the hands, and often kissed each other. An acquaintance said to me, that although many were laughing, he could but cry, at which tears gushed from my eyes in a moment, and we both shed tears of joy at the same instant. The scenes in these dead hours of the night were sublime. Take those drummers for instance: I I knew them both well. They appeared to have got out of bed one minute, seized their drums the next, and were beating glad tidings. The Stars and Stripes floated from many a dwelling, and a man was parading the streets with an ensign, and hundreds following its folds.

While I was at home and it was growing daylight, a company of men, loyal ones of course, secured the music and a flag, and marched to Gorham L. Boynton's premises, to compel him to hang out the Stars and Stripes, but on their arrival at his house on Court street, they found he was down in the city. They then marched to the Bangor Democrat office, and were about to enter by violence, when the Mayor, Samuel H. Dale, requested them not to damage property so early in the day, but if the inmates of the office did not put out the American flag, to put it out for them, whereupon, a number as a committee, entered and requested the flag to be run out, to which they demurred. The committee then ran the flag out for them, and made them promise to let it remain for the day.

At half-past seven I joined a procession of two hundred citizens, who were visiting stores and offices with a committee in lead, who, when the procession arrived in front, entered the stores, etc., and requested the Stars and Stripes be hung out from doors or windows. We marched until noon, and were commanded by Col. Israel Norcross, supported by Llewellyn J. Morse, Mr. Adams and other good men.

First to Daniel Dakin's, where they run out a flag; then down Water street, to Shaw & Tyler's, where they promised to do the same; then up Broad, to Amos Patten's, in Strickland's new block, and E. W. Elder's, in the Pendleton & Russ store adjoining. The procession, when we reached this location, had increased to about four hundred in the ranks, and from three or four hundred on the sidewalks. The committee entered Mr. E. W. Elder's sail loft and requested him to put out a flag, at which he demurred, and remonstrated, and swore he would not, and a long contest arose, he saying at first that he had no flag, and did not consider himself under obligations to get one, at which the committee agreed to get one, and an old flag was sent for and brought into his loft on a long pole, and he was requested to run it out of the window, and he was so loath that they compelled him to take hold of the pole, and with a Union man hold of the end to steady it, he ran it out of the window, and pushed the window down and agreed to let it remain during the day.

The next step was to wait on Isaac W. and Amos Patten, in Strickland's new block, where they kept a ship store. Amos was out, and his father, Isaac W. locked the door, and he and Amos' clerk remained inside, and refused to let the committee in, whereupon a portion of the front ranks left the street and collected around the door, and demanded admittance, which the old veteran denied, and swore until he was as pale as a ghost, and, about this time, Edwin B. Patten came to the rescue, to defend the outside of the premises. Mr. Wheeler, the editor of the Bangor Daily Whig, Llewellyn Morse, Mr. Duckworth, Israel Norcross and J. S. Wheelwright's clerk, demanded of "Ed" that he nail up the Stars and Stripes, at which he wormed around, and tried to argue and expostulate, and pretended that they were immediately going to put out a large flag, etc., and he kept the procession waiting in the mud for over half an hour, when various voices ejaculated, mine among the rest, "Nail up the flag," "Nail it up yourself," and other like commands. A flag was put into a boy's hand, to hold up in front of the door, and shortly Edwin snatched it out of his hands, at which the line of people began to grow determined, and called loud and long: "*Make him nail it up*," "*Make him give three cheers for it*," etc., and the crowd increased so the streets were jammed, and difficulty was experienced to keep some soldiers dressed in blue, from rushing through the windows, the panes of glass being very large, and, in rushing to and fro, those standing back to the lights in the doors had their elbows pushed through, by which time old Isaac became so infuriated that he looked more like a ghost than a citizen. At this point, John A. Peters, the world renowned speaker and lawyer, standing in the ranks, the third section in the rear of my section, called out:

"*Nail up the flag, or by the Eternal God, it will be nailed up for you!*" and then made his way through the crowd to the door, and seized the flag, formerly held by the boy, and some one gave him a hatchet and a nail, and he drove in one nail, and then he and some others told Edwin what must be done, at which Edwin stepped up one step higher, and said to the whole crowd thus:

"MEN OF BANGOR,"

"There is no man in Bangor who thinks more of that very same flag than I do."

With a new hammer in his hand, he drove in one more nail, and then took off his hat and gave two faint cheers, not three, as he was requested to do. This infuriated his father so that he had a branding tin, such as he describes the various qualities of shingles with, laying on the show case, and he picked it up and sent it through the window, demolishing a ten dollar pane of glass, at the crowd. Edwin agreed to let the flag remain up all day and all night, when the line moved to Geo. W. Ladd's, and he hung out a flag and cheered it with a laugh, bare headed.

The line then moved a short distance and requested Jacob C. Smith, and A. M. Campbell to put out a flag, and Jacob Smith nailed one on his door with his own hands, and we then marched to J. S. Ingraham's, corner of Hammond and Central, and requested him the same, and he *demurred*, and had a long contention, but finally yielded, although in a very feeble manner. He afterwards told, that, had it not been for his wife and children, he would have died before he would surrender.

The next came John S. Ricker, cashier of the Mercantile Bank, who nailed up his flag in a gentlemanly maner, but gave no cheers. The "secesh" reading room was thenext, and here they ran out two flags, one at each window. From here we went to the Franklin House, and Henry McLaughlin appeared on the balcony, and stuck up a little mean flag, just big enough to pacify the procession. We now went down Harlow and Exchange streets, and on the march Doct. Ambrose C. Warren hung out two small flags, which saved "Fort Warren," so called. We made some calls on Exchange street, and closed a rum hole, and then marched down Broad street, to see if Patten had taken down his flag. It was all right, and in the next story they had suspended a large one.

We now went towards the ferry, then up Union and High, to Calvin Seavey's house. Calvin was my friend as a physician, but was a leader and sympathizer in rebellion. He was in Westbrook, and, as we were at a dwelling house, we made no demonstration. We then went to Silas Drew's, and (here a name is omitted by request), and found flags out. Drew was one of the men who advocated the resistance to the draft. On going over Kenduskeag Bridge, we halted at the store of Wm. H. Flagg, and were detained a long time, in bringing about what we had accomplished with equally as hard nuts, but, after some half hour of parley, speaking. etc., with reluctance he mounted a shoe-box, cheered the flag, and stuck up a small one, in a pair of boots hanging as a show at his door. The next, overhead, in the same block, Jones the barber, a strong "secesh," who knocked down John Wyman, in the beginning of the war, was called for, when his wife came to the window and shook a hood, in place of the flag, he demurring, and said he had no flag, but on a loud call from a hundred voices, "*Run out your flag, Jones.*" "*Do it with your own hands,*" he sent out, after a parley, and purchased two, and run one out of each window, but did not cheer them. I left the procession in front of "Ed" Flagg's office, and went to dinner, having marched over four hours in the mud. My soul was full of glory, and my fellow citizens in the ranks being the same, as we went marching along.

While I was at breakfast I lost one sight, which would have done my inmost soul good. The first company in the morning marched to the Franklin House, where Marcellus Emery boarded, and called him out on the balcony, and asked him to make a speech, and he, thinking no doubt that tar and feathers might be near by, complied, and said he had blundered some, had been mistaken in many of his editorials, etc., in the "Bangor Democrat," and then withdrew. The crowd were not satisfied, and demanded him a second time, and made him take the flag and cheer it. This was a rare show, and every one present enjoyed it to their own full satisfaction. The procession after breakfast purchased a number of small flags, and they were carried in the ranks, and, when a "secesh" man objected to raising one on account of not having it at hand, the procession furnished him one free of cost.

THE FLAG DISHONORED.

After dinner the flag was dishonored. Amos Patten, on going to his store, took down the flag raised by Edwin, and burned it, whereupon a crowd went down, and by either he or them another was put up, which they requested to remain. A mob was now feared, and the Mayor tried to still them. Lewis Reynolds and others were furious to enter the premises, but were persuaded to desist, and as I learned afterwards, a rope was carried there by some men, in case Amos could be found they might have a use for it. Amos Patten left town, and was last seen crossing to Brewer. Diligent search was made for him, and fifty men were placed at different points to watch for him, but during the day and night no trace of him could be found. In the afternoon the invalid soldiers, from the "Soldier's Rest," being the Gymnasium on Columbia street were taken in carriages, and, with a band of music, and the old tattered, battle worn flags of the Second and Eighteenth Regiments, were driven all about the city. Then these flags were marched about town by an independent company, and a band who for a short time escorted our column in the forenoon. In the evening the city was illuminated in a wonderful manner. At Norombega there was an immense meeting, where Prof. Harris, Rev. Mr. Battles, John A. Peters and Hannibal Hamlin made speeches.

After retiring that night, I reviewed the various transactions of the twenty-four hours. Of all the days of my long life this was the best. First, the cause of the celebration. Second, to see the men who had labored for years against us, run out the Stars and Stripes, and cheer them, and I record again, this was my great day.

A SINGULAR AND MAJESTIC SIGHT.

During the forenoon, some one in Brewer made a large kite, twelve feet long, and on the cord, some twenty feet long below the kite, made fast a flag, and sent up the whole, two thousand feet into the air. Looking at it from this side, the cord did not show, owing to the distance, and it appeared as though the beautiful flag, doubly dear and precious now, was supported by unseen hands in the Heavens."

TUESDAY, APRIL 11th, 1865.

"People are resting, and congratulating on the proceedings of yesterday. Every one feels the fatigue of the past thirty-six hours, and are speculating on the future movements of rebellion.

Fifty men still looking for Amos Patten, and do not find him. A meeting was held in City Hall and a committee of twenty-three men, the best we have, chosen to attend to Patten and others."

WEDNESDAY MORNING, APRIL 12th.

From Bangor Daily "Whig and Courier."

"CITIZENS MEETING."—A large and influential number of our citizens met at City Hall, yesterday afternoon, and organized by the choice of Wm. P. Wingate, Esq., as Chairman, and John Wyman, Esq., as Secretary. The object of the meeting as stated by the chairman, was to take into consideration certain treasonable practices of some of our citizens. A large committee, consisting of the following gentlemen, was appointed to investigate the circumstances, viz:

Rufus Dwinel, J. B. Foster, B. B. Farnsworth, John Bacon, S. P. Bradbury, L. J. Morse, John Wyman, Jas. Littlefield, F. H. Dillingham, Geo. Stetson, John A. Peters, F. A. Wilson, James Dunning, Chas. E. Dole, F. Muzzy, Wm. A. Smith, Chas. B. Lord, J. S. Wheelwright, Wm. P. Wingate, Robert O. Davis, R. K. Hardy, E. G. Thurston, Chas. P. Stetson, Chas. Haywood, Jas. Adams, Hooper Chase.

After which the meeting adjourned to meet at same place this evening, at half past seven, to hear the Committee report."

"During the night of the 11th, a piece of crape was fastened to Wm. P. Wingate's door—he being now the Custom House Collector—with a letter, stating that if any harsh means were used on Amos Patten, that he, Wingate, might have use for the crape."

"The citizens were in a fever heat, and on the next morning fired one hundred guns, thirty-six at noon, and one hundred more at night. Samuel H. Dale, the Mayor, rode about the city that day, cautioning the people to refrain from acts of violence, and doing all in his power to preserve the peace of the city."

"At seven and one-half o'clock, Wednesday, the citizens again met in City Hall, to hear the report of their committee appointed on Tuesday."

"The committee reported that in pursuance of their instructions they had waited upon Mr. Amos Patten, to request of him an explanation of his conduct in tearing down the American flag with expressions of insult and contempt, on the occasion of the rejoicing of our national victories, on Monday last; and that he had furnished them with the following apology."

"In destroying a flag on Monday last, I intended no disrespect to the American flag, but was excited by what I deemed, and still deem, an unwarrantable interference in my affairs. I regret the affair as much as any one, A. PATTEN.

Bangor, April 12th, 1865.

"And the committee report that in their opinion, said apology and explanation should be acceptable to the citizens of Bangor, and they accordingly recommend its acceptance.

"It was voted to accept the report of the committee, and that the doings of the meeting be published in the city papers."

"After three times three for the flag of our Union, voted to adjourn."

WM. P. WINGATE, Chairman.

JOHN WYMAN, Secretary.

These are the facts:—

The great multitude were for lynching Patten, if he could be found, and expected, after the meeting to prosecute a vigorous search for him. Hardly a man would say a word for Patten, until that sterling citizen, A. G. Wakefield, rose up in his behalf.

Mr. Wakefield pictured the young man as he was; a strong-headed passionate fellow, subject to paroxisms of rage, and at such times entirely beyond control; and then drew a picture of a Bangor mob hunting him down. Heated, as his hearers were, they did not take kindly to these utterances, nor did they do so to the committee report. They clamored for vengeance. Long search was made for Patten, but he could not be found, and finally the matter was dropped, but Patten was never forgotten nor forgiven for his act.

CHAPTER XXII.

The Nation In Mourning—Another Great Crime Of The Slave Power—President Lincoln Assassinated—A Nation In Tears—Terrible News—The President's Case Hopeless—Almost Miraculous Escape Of Grant.

The above head lines are taken from the papers issued soon after the news of the assassination of President Lincoln, which of course, cast the whole community into a gulf of gloom and sorrow. The wild hilarious joy which had pervaded, since the news of Lee's surrender, gave way to feelings of grief for the stricken man and his family. Then came feelings of anger and a loud call for revenge, and with eager eyes and quickened ears the loyal men sought the company of the sympathizers with rebellion, ready and willing to hang the first man who uttered one word against the Union, or the "Martyred President." The absorbing grief of the people, great though it was, left room for deeper indignation that arose against the authors of the monstrous deed, which took from the nation its father and its friend. It was there, down deep in the heart of every loyal man. Our whole city was draped in mourning,—some of the crape hanging before the doors of those who were in sympathy with the South, being so placed by the demands of the loyal men— business was suspended, flags craped and at half mast, all the church bells tolled, and minute guns fired from noon till four o'clock.

At ten o'clock in the morning, by order of the Mayor, the bell on City Hall was rung, and soon after the hall was filled to overflowing by the citizens. Judge Appleton was called to the chair, and he appointed J. Bartlett, Secretary. After a prayer by Rev. Dr. Pond, Hon. Hannibal Hamlin was called upon, but that gentleman, who knew Lincoln so well; who had been so intimate with him through the dark days of the war; said he could not trust his feelings to speak. By his suggestion a committee of two from each ward was appointed, to determine what measures should be adopted to express the feelings of the community, and the following gentlemen were named: Josiah S. Ricker, R. D. Manson, Charles Hayward, Thomas Mason, W. H. Mills, Enoch Pond, S. H. Blake, A. W. Paine, Charles Stetson, Hastings Strickland, S. P. Strickland, Thomas Trickey, D. Bugbee and J. H Bowler. Again that loyal body, termed by Emery, "the mob element," came forth on that day, and highly enraged crowds marched about the city, seeking certain persons, who had been heard to rejoice over the death of Lincoln. In one instance a large crowd surged up Main street to a dry goods store, where a fool-hardy clerk was employed, who had said he was "glad the Old Rail Splitter had been killed." Advised of their approach, he fled from the rear of the premises, and sought the seclusion of the jail for safety. Others were arrested and confined at the same place, in order that their precious (?) necks might retain their usual length..

COMING HOME.

On June 11th, there arrived a portion of the First Maine Heavy Artillery, who, of course, received a cordial greeting at the hands of Bangor. They arrived by special train, at three-thirty in the morning, yet the citizens were ready to receive them, and, as the train rolled into the station, the veterans heard the familiar sound of the booming of cannon, sending out, not iron messages of death but peaceful and joyful welcome. They heard too. another sound, not so familiar, yet one they all knew well, the clanging of church bells, which, with busy tongues and varied voices, sent down from the high belfries, a glad reception home. It must have been a spectacle, carrying food to the thoughtful mind. Those thin, bronzed, weary looking men, clad in old clothing which had been rent and torn in many a conflict, were but a handful of what had constituted the regiment that had "marched away, so glad and gay," a few months before. While relations rejoiced to see their loved ones back again, did not many an eye grow dim, and many a cheek turn pale, as they viewed the decimated ranks, and noted many vacant places along the line where once the embattled soldiers stood? Yes, there was ever present, even in the "coming home," that dark cloud which overhangs a land of war, and the insinuating shadows linger to-day, and will linger, for many days to come.

The men were escorted to City Hall, where a collation had been prepared, and after this had been disposed off, eloquent and thrilling words of welcome were said by Ex-Vice-President Hamlin. The officers in command were Lieut. Col. Smith, Quartermaster Horatio Pitcher, Captains, G. E. Fernald, B. T. Atherton, Lieutenants, Geo Pote, J. J. Dunham, F. E. Robinson. It would seem as though the citizens could not see enough of these men, for the next day they pursuaded then to parade, crowds being in attendance. The following day Gov. Cony arrived, and again the boys came out, this time for a "dress parade," after which they waited on His Excellency, and gave him a salute. The day after, the men were paid off and departed to their homes, to again take up the peaceful pursuits which they had forsaken at their country's call.

On July 4th, of this year, Bangor had a big celebration, in which all, save a few disappointed ones, participated. Never before, and never since, have the people enjoyed themselves so well as on that occasion. They had much to be thankful for, much to rejoice over, and from early morn till late at night there was one continual round of festivities.

Early in July, the Thirty-first Regiment, Col. Daniel White, commanding, and seven hundred strong, arrived. They were met by companies A and B, State Guards, and escorted to Abbott Square, where a generous meal had been provided. This regiment was raised in Eastern Maine, in February, 1864, and left Augusta April 18th, nine hundred strong. Without time to perfect its organization or acquire proficiency in drill, it was sent into active service at a very critical period of the campaign. Notwithstanding all this, however, the regiment acquitted itself most nobly. Many of its men and officers, it is proper to add, had seen service in the Second Maine and other regiments. On the 6th of May, just ten days after its departure from Augusta, at the Wilderness, the regiment saw its first fight. It lost fearfully in killed and wounded, but sustained itself equally well with older organizations. On the 12th and 18th of May it fought at Spottsylvania. It was in all the subsequent engagements of the army of the Potomac, at Cold Harbor, Bethesda Church, Petersburg, June 17th, and July 30th; the latter, the terrible charge made after the explosion of the mine; at Poplar Spring

Church, September 30th, Hatcher's Run, at Petersburg, in the final charge and capture of those formidable works.

At one time, after an engagement, the regiment had less than fifty men present for duty. In October it was re-enforced by two full companies of recruits. In December, 1864, the Thirty-Second Maine, five hundred strong, was merged into the Thirty-First. The Thirty Second was originally nine hundred strong, and was from the western section of the State. The regiment lost seventeen officers, killed in battle or died from wounds, this being one half the number with which it entered the field one year before. Before the boys were paid off, they indulged in a torch light procession, calling on the leading citizens.

In September, the remaining portion of the First Heavy came home, and gradually, all having returned that were alive, the press of the day ceased the printing of the war news, and devoted its space, as now, to items regarding trade, society and fashion.

We close this last chapter, dealing directly with the local affairs of Bangor, with a reference to Fort Sumpter, taken from the "Whig and Courier," printed April 15th, 1865:

"OUR FLAG IS THERE."

"Yesterday, the 14th, was the fourth anniversary of that disgraceful day, when the flag of our Union was ruthlessly torn from Fort Sumpter by rebel hands, after the fort with its little garrison had been reduced by the fire of hundreds of rebel cannon. That flag was proudly restored yesterday by the hands of loyal and patriotic men, after the great rebellion had been effectually and forever suppressed by the power of a free people. The occasion was noticed here by a national salute at noon, by a general display of flags from public and private buildings, and by raising of the stars and stripes more than a thousand feet above the city, by means of a monster kite bearing in huge capitals the name of the Lieutenant General of all our armies, "U. S. Grant." The flag was raised from Thomas's Hill, by Capt. Nickerson, Col. Dunning, and others, and floated over the city to the admiring gaze of thousands. The flag thus raised was fifteen feet long and eight wide.

CHAPTER XXIII.

The First War Meeting In Rockland—Flag Raisings—Rockland Votes To Raise Ten Thousand Dollars For Aid Of Soldier's Families—Elijah Walker Opens A Recruiting Office—Arrival Of The Companies For The Fourth Regiment—The Work Of The Ladies—The Departure Of The Fourth Regiment—Meeting At Camden—The News From Bull Run—The Ward Companies—The Draft.

Knox County was not behind the rest of the State, in her response to the call of the country. On the 18th of April, 1861, a monster war meeting was held in Rockland, by call of Mayor Wiggin. That night Atlantic Hall was completely filled with patriotic citizens. T. K. Osgood was called to the chair, and the following Vice-Presidents elected: John Gregory, C. L. Allen, Chas. Crocker, A. Stanley, Wm. McLoon, Elk. Spear, G. J. Burns, J. W. Hunt, Samuel Bryant, S. Whitney, A. C. Spaulding, E. S. Smith, Wm. Thompson and T. Williams.

The following gentlemen acted as secretaries: Edw. Sprague, Z. Pope Vose, N. C. Woodard and O. G. Hall.

Committee on Resolutions: J. K. Kimball, Alden Sprague, A. D. Nichols, C. A. Miller, Wm. A. Banks and M. Sumner.

Speeches filled with intense patriotism were made by Hon. N.

A. Farwell, Gen. Davis Tillson, Dr. J. Rouse, Joseph Farwell, J. C. Cobb, Gen. Wm. S. Cochran, Josiah Getchell, John Ham and many others.

Among the resolutions adopted, was the following:

"*Resolved*, That it is the duty of every American citizen, in the present crisis of the American Union, to give a patriotic support to the Government, and that the State of Maine, and the City of Rockland, will respond to the extent of their ability, both in men and money, to maintain the liberty of the country and the Union of all the States, as we believe the time is now come when the whole power of the General Government, and the patriotic people of the several States, should be at once exerted, to crush the rebels who are attempting to destroy it."

The Gazette of that week in an editorial said: "Rockland will not haul down the stars and stripes, until the honor of our flag has been fully vindicated, and will be found ready to furnish her quota of men and means to defend it."

The day before the meeting, a flag was raised over the City Council Rooms, and patriotic airs were played by the Rockland Band. On the 19th, flags were raised from the top of Crockett Block, from Rankin Block, from the residence of O. H. Perry, on Lime Rock street, and from many of the blocks in the business part of the city. At Spear Block a flag was thrown to the April breeze, and speeches were made by T. K. Osgood and others.

On the 23d, another grand meeting was held, and the city asked to vote ten thousand dollars for the aid of soldiers' families. Capt. C. F. Hodgdon, offered twenty dollars to the first man to enlist, and S. H. Chapman at once came forward, enlisted and drew the prize. Curiously enough, the very first man to fall in battle was this same S. H. Chapman. He was a brave man, and universally loved by his comrades and friends.

During the meeting Elijah Walker came forward, and offered the services of twenty-five men of Dirigo Engine Company, (of which he was at that time captain). Resolutions were offered, denouncing the rebel sympathizers in the North, and amid great enthusiasm the meeting adjourned. On the next day, Elijah Walker opened a recruiting office at No. 7 Kimball Block, and by the vigorous use of fife and drum, obtained over eighty volunteers the first day.

All this time flag raisings were going on in the towns about, and in Camden a grand war meeting was held near the Orthodox church, over which Dr. J. H. Estabrooks presided, and which was addressed by Hon. A. P. Gould.

Among the noble-hearted women, who gave up home, and oftentimes much more, and enlisted as nurses, were Miss Ruth S. Mayhew, Miss O. A. Packard and Miss Jennie Grafton, all of Rockland. Miss Mayhew was a teacher in the public school at this time, and for several years after the war, was in charge of the Soldiers Orphans' Home at Bath. Miss Packard was a compositor in the Gazette office.

On the 26th of April, the enlistments had become so large, that it was decided to form three companies and elect officers. This was done with the following result:

FIRST COMPANY.

ELIJAH WALKER, Captain.
O. P. MITCHELL, First Lieutenant.
J. B. LITCHFIELD, Second Lieutenant.

SECOND COMPANY.

O. J. CONANT, Captain.
WM. FESSENDEN, First Lieutenant.
CHAS. A. ROLLINS, Second Lieutenant.

On the 27th, the Third Company elected:

L. D. CARVER, Captain.
T. B. GLOVER, First Lieutenant.
C. L. STRICKLAND, Second Lieutenant.

On Sunday, the 28th, the companies marched out on Lime Rock street, where an open air sermon was delivered to them by the Rev. Mr. Mariner.

On May 6th, another company was formed, and elected the following officers:

GEO. J. BURNS, Captain.
JOHN C. COBB, First Lieutenant.
B. BRACKLEY, Second Lieutenant.

From this time on the companies had a street drill every day, and many were the envious glances cast on the soldiers, by the ever-present small boy. The election of officers, for the Fourth Regiment occurred on May 15th, and on the 20th the out-of-town companies began to arrive. They were encamped on Tillson's Hill, and excited much enthusiasm as they marched through the streets, on their way to the camp. Mr. G. O. Kuhn, while firing a salute, on the arrival of the Damariscotta Company, was instantly killed by the bursting of the gun. He was given a military funeral, at which the Damariscotta Band furnished the music. The regiment remained quietly in camp, and on May 23d were marched to the Kimball Block, where uniforms were distributed. On June 1st, a grand parade of the regiment through the city was given, and many were the compliments bestowed upon the soldiers.

Previous to this time, a call was made on the ladies, to meet at Pillsbury Hall, to prepare clothing. Some idea of the amount of work done by them can be arrived at, when it is known that they made up to June 17th, one thousand and fifty shirts, two thousand towels, fifty-two bed sacks and four hundred havelocks, besides furnishing each man with a "catch-all," (or as a sailor would say "diddy-bag"), to hold pins, needles, etc.

A very bitter feeling against the "*Free-Press and Democrat,*" was manifest in the city. This paper shaped its tone and style from the "Bangor Democrat," and that class of reading did not suit the patriotic "Sons of Knox." No violence was offered the paper, and after a little persuasion the journal dropped its advocacy of "State's Rights," and has ever since been a strong Union organ.

On the 15th of June the Fourth Regiment was mustered into service, by Capt. Thomas Hight, U. S. A., and on the 17th, left for Portland, on its way to Washington, by the steamer Daniel Webster. All was excitement in the city that day, for were not the brothers, fathers and sweethearts of many going to war, perhaps never to return, or perchance to come home cripples for life? Many were the sad scenes both at the camp and on the wharf that day.

The regiment was accompanied on their way, as far as Washington, by the Rockland Band. As they marched down from the camp and through the streets, crowded with people, and gay with bunting, they presented a truly glorious appearance, and were received with cheers on every hand. They carried a large banner on which was inscribed "From the home of Knox." At the wharf a small flag was presented to the regiment by Gen. Titcomb, and received in an appropriate speech by Col. Berry Gen. Titcomb accompanied the regiment as far as New York.

On reaching Portland, the regiment left the boat and took the cars for Boston.

Just before leaving Rockland, the commissioned officers were presented with elegant swords, by Mr. T. K. Osgood, on behalf of the citizens, and they were received in a few well chosen words, by Elijah Walker, for the officers.

On the arrival of the regiment in Boston, they were met by the Cadets, headed by the Brigade Band, and escorted to the temporary camp. They left for New York, by the Fall River Line, and on their arrival there went to the Park Barracks. At City Hall they were received by the "Sons and Daughters of Maine," and were presented with flags. While there they also received a beautiful banner from the hands of the " Daughters of Maine in Brooklyn." From here the regiment went to Washington by rail, and soon was in the thickest of the fight and carnage. The history of the Fourth, from this time forward will be found in another part of the book.

Just before the Fourth Regiment left Rockland, Capt. Chas. Mink, while visiting the drill-room of Capt. Jones' Co., tripped and fell, the length of the stairs, and was instantly killed.

When the news from Bull Run arrived in Rockland, it caused great consternation, as it was soon learned that many of the brave boys, who had so recently left there, had fallen, and that many more were wounded and missing. As we have before said, the first to fall was Mr. S. H. Chapman. A store was now opened for supplies to be forwarded to the soldiers, and many were the packages left there to be sent to friends, brothers, fathers, sons and sweethearts.

On August 24th, an immense meeting was held in Camden, and speeches were made by Wm. H. McCrillis and others. About this time John D. Rust, of Rockport, was raising the Eighth Regiment, and was assisted in Camden, by Hon. T. R. Simonton. On August 26th, a grand war meeting was held in

Rockland and among the speakers were, D. A. Boody, Geo. A. Starr, and E. K. Smart, of Camden. Owing to the great loss in the Fourth Regiment, it was decided to recruit the regiment at Rockland, and an office was opened at the old recruiting office of Elijah Walker, and the number required promptly applied.

About this time talk was made regarding a Cavalry Regiment, from that vicinity, and soon after J. P. Cilley opened an office for cavalry enlistments. September 7th, the first company of Home Guards was formed with the following officers: William Farrow, Jr., Captain; David Pratt, First Lieutenant; N. C. Woodward, Second Lieutenant, with one hundred and nine names on the roll. After the first few meetings it got to be a thing of the past, and little interest was manifested in the organization for a long time. On the 5th of October, the gunboat "Kennebec," was launched at Thomaston, and on December 14th, she left for Boston, where her armament was ready and waiting for her. About this time, a report of the resignation of Col Berry, came to Rockland and excited much surprise, but was immediately denied by the gallant officer, on its reaching his ears.

During the latter part of the year, Gen. Tillson began to raise his battery of mounted artillery, and found many recruits in Rockland, Thomaston and that vicinity.

Many of the men of Rockland enlisted in the Navy, among them being Acting Masters, Geo. Cables and Joshua Rowe, who were on the sloop of war "St. Louis;" Acting Ensign Fred Furbush, (who died of yellow fever at New Orleans); Lieut. John F. Harden, who at one time was in command of the U. S. Steamer "Antona;" Acting Ensign Chas. W. Snow, and many were with the fleet when it passed New Orleans, while the city was represented in the fleets of both Porter and Dahlgren. In all, Rockland had some one hundred and two men in that branch of the service.

During all this time the neighboring towns had not been idle. Thomaston had raised one thousand three hundred dollars, for the care of soldiers' families, and had formed a company of flying artillery, on the departure of which every member was presented with a revolver. Camden also was doing good work both with money and men, and at the close of 1861 had sent far more than her share of men to the front.

In March, '62, the steamer "Rockland" was chartered by the Government, at a price of one hundred and fifty dollars per day. Things went quietly along that spring, and in the week of July 17th, the ward companies were formed and officered as follows:

WARD ONE.

M. A. ACHORN, Captain.
R. H. HAVENER, First Lieutenant.
J. T. SHERER, Second Lieutenant.
LEONARD GREEN, Third Lieutenant.
JOEL THOMAS, Fourth Lieutenant.

WARD TWO.

B. B. BEAN, Captain.
J. H. ELWELL, First Lieutenant.
A. E. HEWETT, Second Lieutenant.
J. G. FARNHAM, Third Lieutenant.
C. M. DAVIS, Fourth Lieutenant.

WARD THREE.

C. S. CROCKETT, Captain.
C. N. BEAN, First Lieutenant.
T. E. SIMONTON, Second Lieutenant.
E. GRAY, Third Lieutenant.
A G. HUNT, Fourth Lieutenant.

WARD FOUR.

WM. ADAMS, Captain.
H. M. BROWN, First Lieutenant.
NATH'L JONES, Second Lieutenant.
E. E. WORTMAN, Third Lieutenant.
WALTER TOLMAN, Fourth Lieutenant.

WARD FIVE.

T. K. OSGOOD, Captain.
J. R. RICHARDSON, First Lieutenant.
GEO. W. BERRY, Second Lieutenant.
A. W. PERRY, Third Lieutenant.
O. G. HALL, Fourth Lieutenant.

WARD SIX.

JOHN T. BERRY, Captain.
A. SAYWARD, First Lieutenant.
J. N. INGRAHAM, Second Lieutenant.
HENRY FLINT, Third Lieutenant.
E. P. HALL, Fourth Lieutenant.

WARD SEVEN.

JOHN BIRD, JR., Captain.
O. P. TOLMAN, First Lieutenant.
C. C. LOVEJOY, Second Lieutenant.
E. P. WITHAM, Third Lieutenant.
C. HANRAHAN, Fourth Lieutenant.

On August 2d, the city voted to raise the city bounty from fifty-five to one hundred and twenty-five dollars, in order to induce men to volunteer, and so escape having a draft. During the month of August, notices were posted in various parts of the city, denouncing the war as "unholy," etc. The press of the day, asked that a sharp lookout be kept for the authors, and that if found "they should be marked with the brand of infamy."

The fear of a draft in the early part of '62, was unfounded, as the quota was at once filled, and in the draft of September 10th, the men drafted found no trouble in filling their places, if they so wished, with volunteers, as the nine months' men received a city bounty of two hundred dollars. Towards the close of the year, among the enlistments, we find the name of Gen. W. S. Cochran, who enlisted as a private, and about the same time, or rather a little later, Company E, of the Twenty-ninth Regiment, elected the following officers: A. Thompson, Rockland, Captain; Isaac Murch, Vinalhaven, First Lieutenant; John F. Perry, South Thomaston, Second Lieutenant.

The ward companies, formed the same year at Thomaston, elected:

COMPANY A.

A. A. AUSTIN, Captain.
R. H. COUNCE, First Lieutenant.
E. K O'BRIEN, Second Lieutenant.
G. G. NANSON, Third Lieutenant.
W. E. CRAWFORD, Fourth Lieutenant.

COMPANY B.

E. B. HINCKLEY, Captain.
BENJ. AYER, First Lieutenant.
W. K. BICKFORD, Second Lieutenant.
T. S. ANDREWS, Third Lieutenant.
ALVIN A. REED, Fourth Lieutenant.

In Camden the officers were:

COMPANY A.

G. C. ESTABROOK, Captain.
A. E. CLARK, First Lieutenant.
H. E. ALDEN, Second Lieutenant.
R. PHILBROOK, Third Leiutenant.
W. E. NORWOOD, Fourth Lieutenant.

COMPANY B.

W. H. WASHBURN, Captain.
GEO. SIDELINGER, First Lieutenant.
G. W. STUDLEY, Second Lieutenant.
C. A. PAYSON, Third Lieutenant.
J. F. SUMNER, Fourth Lieutenant.

COMPANY C.

E. VINAL, Captain.
C. H. CUTLER, First Lieutenant.
R. S. HOWARD, Second Lieutenant.
R. S. THORNDIKE, Third Lieutenant.
G. A. MILLER, Fourth Lieutenant.

During the year there had been grand meetings in Thomaston, Rockport, and in fact all the towns in that vicinity, and every one was seized with the war fever.

CHAPTER XXIV.

Presentation Of Silver Service To Gen. Berry By His Officers—Rockland Ships Seized By The "Alabama"—Funeral Of Gen. Berry—Vice-President Hamlin's Opinion Of The Man—The Harbor Batteries—Return Of The Fourth Regiment—Rockland Raises Thirty Thousand Dollars To Fill The Quota—Capture Of The "Rouen"—The Coast Guards—The Fall Of Richmond—Death Of Lincoln—Close Of The War—Return Of The Soldiers.

Early in 1863, there arrived in Rockland the elegant silver service, presented to Gen. Berry by his officers. This was one of the finest specimens of the silversmith's art ever gotten out in this country. About this time, T. K. Osgood was appointed paymaster in the army. He had charge of the High school, and was alderman from ward five, and resigned these positions and went to the front.

Many of the ships owned in Rockland and adjoining towns, were seized by the "Alabama," and other confederate cruisers, among them being ship "Bertha Thayer," owned by Wm. McLoon, which was released on a bond of forty thousand dollars; the "Louisa Hatch," the "C. A. Farwell," valued at forty thousand; "Ocean Eagle," valued at twelve thousand, besides the cargo of lime; the "Joseph," valued with cargo at forty-four thousand, and many more. Early in '63 the ladies held a grand "Soldiers Levee," to raise money to aid the Sanitary Commission, and by that means raised a very neat sum.

On the 3d of May, Maj. Gen. Hiram G. Berry was shot and killed, at the battle of Chancellorsville, Va.

Upon the arrival of the remains in Washington, from the bloody field of Chancellorsville, the wish was expressed by President Lincoln and General Halleck, that funeral ceremonies should be performed in that city; but his friends determined that his obsequies should be held in Rockland.

On Monday, the day following his death, the citizens of Rockland received intelligence of the lamentable event. In the evening the City Council met, and chose a committee of arrangements to make preparations for the reception of the body, and take the necessary measures for giving the honored dead such a burial as his rank, distinguished services, and heroic end, merited. On the ensuing Saturday, the body,—accompanied by a detachment of the Maine Seventh Regiment, as a Guard of Honor, and a delegation of Rockland citizens appointed to receive it in Portland and escort it to Rockland—arrived in the latter place by steamer. Minute guns were fired on the shore, from the time the steamer rounded

Maj.-Gen. HIRAM G. BERRY.

Owl's Head, until she touched the wharf, in Rockland harbor. All the bells in the city were tolled, the stores, offices, and public buildings were closed, and the Supreme Court, which was in session, adjourned. The buildings on the principal streets were generally draped in mourning, and all the flags on the shipping, and throughout the city, were set at half-mast. On the wharf was a procession of citizens, composed of the Mayor, City Council, Committee of Arrangements, and Masons, while the adjacent ground was covered by a large and silent concourse of people, as though the inmates of every house had come forth to honor the sad occasion. The coffin was removed from the steamer to the wharf by bearers selected from the ex-members of the Rockland City Guards, —the first military organization commanded by General Berry. Joseph Farwell, Esq., Chairman of the Committee, which had escorted the remains from Portland, then stepped forward, and in brief and appropriate remarks committed them to the City authorities, who, through Hon. S. C. Fessenden, fittingly responded in acceptance of the charge. This ceremony over, the coffin was placed in the hearse, and followed by mourning friends, and preceded by the Masons, City Council, Committee of Arrangements, and the Guard of Honor, with arms reversed, the solemn cortege took its way through the crowded streets to the late residence of the General. There the remains were left, where they lay in state until the following Thursday. During the time which elapsed before burial, they were visited by thousands; those who saw them will never forget the manly figure, in full Major General's dress, the wreath around the right shoulder and body which President Lincoln presented in Washington, and the Kearney badge—symbol of valor—upon the breast.

On Thursday morning, the day of the burial, the air was shaken by the thunder of cannon, served by a squad of the Wiscasset

Company of Artillery of Coast Guards, detailed by Governor Coburn for ordnance duty through the day. Although the weather was inclement, and the heavens covered with gloom, as though sympathizing with the mournful scene beneath, the streets were filled at an early hour, and the buildings began to put on their drapery of woe. On the evening before, Governor Coburn and Staff arrived, who had spared no pains to discharge faithfully the duties of the State, in the preliminaries, and at last came in person to attend the final ceremonies. The attentions of Adjutant General Hodsdon were unremitting from the first to the closing act. Hon. Lot M. Morrill and Ex-Governor Washburn came to pay their tribute to the brave deceased. In the course of the forenoon, arrived from Bangor, Company A, State Guards, Capt. Morse, with whom came Hon. Hannibal Hamlin, Vice President of the United States. Major General J. H. Butler and Staff also arrived at the same time. The attendance of Masons was very large—many Lodges from abroad having sent in delegations. At one o'clock P. M. an irregular procession was formed on Main street, by Major General Wm. H. Titcomb and Aids, and marched to the residence, where the religous services were to be held. These were performed upon a stand erected in front of the house, but the thousands that crowded almost every spot near—streets—fields—chambers —and even roofs of houses—were, only in small part, enabled to see and hear the speakers. The services were opened with the reading of portions of the Sacred Scriptures by Rev. H. A Hart, of Rockland.

Rev. Nathaniel Butler, of Auburn, then offered a fervent prayer to the Throne of Grace, after which he pronounced the eloquent "discourse," a just tribute to General Berry, and a fair summary of his glorious career. Rev. Joseph Hallock, of Rockland, uttered a benediction, the Rockland Band played a dirge, and immediately the procession began to form. It was formed as it appears in the following order of exercises for the day.

Fifteen Minute Guns at Sunrise.
Half-hour Guns until 12 M.
15 Minute Guns. Ceased firing until the Procession moved, when Minute Guns were fired until the Procession arrived at the Grave.
Half-hour Guns until sunset, then 15 Minute Guns.
Flags set at half-mast at sunrise.
Bells tolled from 7 to 8 A. M.
Buildings Draped in Mourning at 10 A. M.

ORDER OF PROCESSION.
Maj. Gen. Wm. H. Titcomb, Marshal of the Day.
Assistant Marshals,—Col. John S. Case, Col. S. H. Allen, Maj. Charles A. Miller, Maj. E. W. Stetson, Maj. G. W. Kimball, Jr.,
Bangor Cornet Band and Drum Corps.
Masons.
Military Escort.
Rockland Band.
Maj. Gen. Butler and Staff.
Adj. Gen Hodsdon, Col. Harding and Lieutenant Col. Osgood of the Governor's Staff.
Guard of Honor.
Bearers.
Hearse, drawn by Four Horses, led by Grooms.
The General's War Horses, led by Grooms.
Family and Relatives in Carriages.
General's Military Staff.
Governor, Ex-Governor, and Members of Congress.
Justices of Supreme Court.
Members of Legislature.
Officiating Clergymen.
Disabled Soldiers.
Invited Guests.
Mayor and City Council of the City of Rockland.
Committee of Arrangements.
Citizens and Strangers.

The long cortege was an interesting spectacle. The Masons in their rich regalia, the State Guards in their showy uniform, the Major Generals and Aids in complete military array and handsomely mounted, the bands, the decorated car drawn by four white horses led by grooms, the riderless horse of the deceased General, equipped just as he was at the battle of Chancellorsville, and the extended procession of mourners and citizens, made an imposing demonstration. Arriving at the cemetery, the coffin was lowered into the grave, and the impressive rites of Masonry were then performed. Governor Coburn and Ex-Governor Washburn stood with uncovered heads, near the brink of the grave, through these ceremonies. This finished, the military advanced, and with three volleys from the State Guards over the inanimate body, Major Gen'l Berry's mortal remains were left to their repose.

Vice-President Hamlin's action in marching in the ranks, that day, gave rise to some talk, by people who pretended not to know the feeling that actuated him in so doing, but far from any disrespect, was it, but quite the contrary. Those who know Mr. Hamlin, know that his natural modesty made him, at all times, wish to keep himself not in the foreground but back with the masses, and he then wished to do honor to Gen. Berry, in his capacity as a *citizen*. In an interview, but a few weeks ago, Mr. Hamlin said of Gen. Berry:

"General Berry was one of the grandest men I ever knew. I was more intimate with him than with any other Maine officer, and came to have a high regard for him as a man and a soldier. He was a true patriot and went into the service for *results*, and his work proved it. Of all officers I knew in command of regiments, I knew no Colonel who remained so continuously and devotedly as Berry. I don't remember that he ever asked for a furlough. One of nature's noblemen was Berry; self-reliant and valiant, nothing could so disturb him as to cause him to swerve from the path of duty. He saved our army at Chancellorsville, and, said Secretary of War Stanton, to me after that fight: 'Mr. Hamlin, *we owe our safety to Berry.* Disastrous as it was, it would have been infinitely worse but for him. I believe, had he been in command, defeat would have been turned into victory. He is fitted to head our armies, and Mr. Hamlin, I can't tell you how long it will be before we shall see him there.'"

On the 28th of July, Dr. James Rouse and Mr. Cornelius Hanrahan met in the shop of Geo. C. Lovejoy, and in the course of conversation brought up the matter of the "Democratic Club." Both got rather excited in the discussion, and Rouse, on going out, called Hanrahan a "liar" and said something about shooting. Soon after, Hanrahan left the shop, and when in front of Robbin's drug store encountered Rouse, who drew a pistol. They grappled, and during the scuffle the pistol, (then in Rouse's hand) went off, the ball taking effect in Hanrahan's hip. Dr. Rouse was secured, and by the court, bound over in the sum of $3,000. He left town at once and is now supposed to be living in Nevada. Mr. Hanrahan recovered and is now a prominent citizen of Rockland.

On the 19th of August, '63, Company G, Twenty-Eigthth Regiment, arrived home, but no public reception was given them. About this time a paper said: "The State Guards fear that they are a little behind the army sharp shooters, and have purchased a target, with which they have considerable sport, but do not damage to any great extent."

The last of October, cavalry enlistments go on in Rockland, and for the last call for troops for 1863 the volunteers come in rapidly.

On the 11th of December, the gunboat "Agawam" called in at Rockland for coal, she being in pursuit of the Cheseapeake.

The year '63 must have been a hard one on newspapers, as the following from the "Gazette" will show:

"Wanted at this office,—Two or three barrels of apples, several pounds of dried apples, three or four bushels of nice, clean wheat, and a few cords of wood. Will some of our country subscribers, who are in arrears, supply us with the above."

In the year '63, there had been fears all along the Maine coast of invasion by the rebels or their friends across the line. In Rockland the fears were so strong that earthworks were erected guarding the harbor. These were finished and a salute fired from them on Jan. 21st, '64. Meanwhile, in the towns about, there was also alarm, as the rebel sympathizers had, in the case of Camden, threatened to burn the whole town. In Rockport the alarm was so great, at one time, that a government schooner was sent for, and was laid off the harbor, with guns trained on the buildings of the "supposed" rebels.

In the spring of '64 a draft was ordered, and after learning the quota for Rockland, the citizens went at work in earnest, and in three weeks raised the desired number, and had a surplus of sixty men to apply to next draft.

On the 11th of May the State Guards were inspected at Phoenix Hall.

On the 28th of May, 1864, the U. S. gunboat Pontoosuc, arrived in Rockland harbor. She was on recruiting service and secured several volunteers for the Navy, during her stay of three days. On the 16th of June, Company C, Coast Guards, of Eastport, thirty-three men, including lieutenant and non-commissioned officers, arrived and immediately garrisoned the forts of the harbor.

On the 25th of June, the remnant of the "Old Fourth" arrived in Rockland. Two hundred and seventeen men of the regiment had been transferred to the Nineteenth Regiment, and the remainder, one hundred and thirty-two privates and thirteen officers were ordered home. On the morning of their arrival all was gay, and flags were flying, and bells ringing. As the steamer which brought them slowed up towards the wharf, they were greeted by the booming of cannon, and the cheers of the excited people.

A procession was in waiting to receive them, consisting of the Common Council, State Guards and Fire Companies, headed by the band, and all under command of Gen. Titcomb. As the Fourth formed on the wharf, the band played "Home sweet Home," and "When Johnny comes marching home again." They marched through the main streets of the city, and in their midst were carried the torn and battle-stained flags. At the conclusion of the parade they were marched into Atlantic Hall, where a grand repast had been provided for them, by the ladies of the city. After disposing of the tempting viands, as only hungry soldiers could, they were addressed by Hon. N. A. Farwell, who in a few words of welcome, complimented both the officers and men on their grand record at the front. At the conclusion of his remarks, an order was read, disbanding the regiment, and ordering all the men to report on the 19th of July, when they would be mustered out of service.

The officers who returned were: Col. Elijah Walker, Adjutant Chas. F. Sawtelle, Surgeons Cobb and Hunkin, Quartermaster Rankin and Captains Libby, of Company A; Conant of Company C; Carlisle, of Company E, and Abbott, of Company I.

On July 11th, the funeral of Capt. Keene, of the Twentieth Regiment, who was killed at the front, occurred at Thomaston, and was attended by the State Guards from Rockland. On August 6th a grand meeting was held in Rockland, at which it was voted to form an association to raise thirty thousand dollars, to fill the city's quota. Each member of the association agreed to pay twenty-five dollars on joining, and to to pay as the first dues, another sum of twenty-five dollars if it was needed.

About this time, it was reported that the rebel cruiser "Tallahassee," was off the coast, and soon after it was learned that she had destroyed the schooners "Pearl" and "Magnolia," of Friendship. At the time it was said that she lay behind Monhegan, waiting to destroy the "Katahdin," but no attack on the steamer was made.

On the 18th of August, a grand Union war meeting was held at Camden, and speeches full of intense loyalty were made by Hon. N. A. Farwell, of Rockland, and T. R. Simonton of Camden. On the 29th of August, the U. S. gunboat "Merrimac," which had been laying in Rockland harbor for several days, steamed outside and captured the steamer "Rouen." The "Rouen" had been a blockade-runner, and was captured and sold, as was customary, at auction. Her owners, at this time claimed that she was bound for St. John, but as she was not on her course for that port, she was brought to Rockland and examined, after which she was allowed to depart.

In the month of September, Col. Jacob McClure raised a company of sharp-shooters, and they left the State on the 10th of November. Before this there had been enlistments from Rockland in the Berdan sharp-shooters, who left in September, '61, about ten men going from that town, and through the whole war not one of the men in that command, from Rockland, was killed. During the fall of '64 there was considerable activity in military circles, and finally Company B, of the Coast Guards filled their ranks to the maximum, and began to drill in Beal's Hall. Captain C. H. Conant was elected Captain of Company F, down the American flag. This he refused to do, and being again ordered, broke down and cried like a child, but continued to refuse, even after threats were made. He was presented with a gold medal afterwards, by the Maine citizens of San Francisco, through the hand of Commander Sherbrook. He died November 30, '65, and was buried with naval honors, no less than four commanders following his remains to the grave.

CHAPTER XXV.

Belfast And Surrounding Towns During The Rebellion—The Early War Meetings—The First Enlistments—Stealing The Flag From The Custom House—Searsport Responds—Militia Attend Church—News From Bull Run—Building The Gunboat—Something From "Old Troy"—The Draft In 1863—Names Of Those Drawing Tickets—The Searsport Unfortunates.

Twenty-six years ago Belfast was a thriving, growing city. Along the shores of the beautiful bay, as well as up the stream and above the ancient toll-bridge, the sounds of the hammer, the ring of the axe and the calking irons were familiar and frequent. Gradually each year there rose in her ship yards huge frames, which, later on would be covered in, and rigged out and sent to distant lands, where they became famous as specimens of advanced naval architecture. In those days, too, the country round about came to Belfast for a market. Early in the morning, in the winter and in the summer alike, long lines of country teams came in over "Wilson's Hill," "Johnson's Hill," up the "Northport Road," and from "over the river," filling the streets and squares, and finding a ready market for the products of the farm, which they bore. These, later on, found their way down to the various wharves, always then in good repair, where the "coasters" were in waiting to take them away. Peace and prosperity reigned on every hand, the law breakers were few, no frowning policeman, with comical Kaizer helmets, paraded the streets, and such was the general character of the citizens, that they and their home might well have furnished the poet a fit subject for an Acadian song.

To this happy community, there came one April morning, in the year 1861, the echoes of rebel cannon, as they opened fire on Sumpter, and, as might have been expected, the community was thrown into a state of great excitement. One man only fully understood the magnitude of the rebellion thus inaugurated, and that man was the Hon. A. G. Jewett. On the 19th after President Lincoln had issued a call for troops, a large and enthusiastic meeting was held in Pierce's Hall, where addresses were made by Hon. A. G. Jewett, Hon. W. G. Crosby, J. G. Dickerson, T. H. Marshall, Hon. N. Abbott, Wm. M. Rust and Wm. H. Weeks. It was resolved that all party differences were to be ignored, and that Republicans, Democrats, Bell and Everett men, one and all, should stand upon the common ground of the Constitution, the Union, and the protection of the Government.

As in other towns, the loyal people of Belfast began the practice of displaying the colors of the Union, an example being set them by Collector Dickerson, who raised the Stars and Stripes on the Custom House. Immediately the people gathered and began to cheer it, and, as was customary then, speech-making began early and lasted long.

On April 23d, Capt. H. W. Cunningham opened an office for recruits, and immediately several men signed, while others circulated a paper which was well received, in which it was agreed that all men who enlisted should be paid twenty dollars per month so long as they were in service. Over in Searsport they did even better. Twenty men enlisted at once, and at a special town meeting it was voted to pledge the credit of the town in the sum of ten thousand dollars, for the support of the families of those who might enlist, and one patriotic farmer, Mr. Larrabee, agreed to devote one-half the product of his farm for this purpose. About this time Joseph S. Noyes Esq., of Belfast, placed two hundred dollars in the Bank of Commerce, to aid the families of volunteers, and the City Government took steps to make an appropriation for the same purpose; also to purchase the additional equipments of a revolver and bowie knife for each volunteer.

The "Progressive Age," of May 2d, said:

"The "City Greys," Capt. Marshall, have full ranks—sixty-four privates, besides their non-commissioned officers, and their commander has notified the Governor that he is ready to march at any moment. This company has heretofore numbered about forty-five men with about forty uniforms. Some ten are now absent. Of the remaining thirty-six about twenty-five have enlisted. We have not heard of so large a proportion, according to the number of old members, enlisting in any of the volunteer companies in the State. This company is made up wholly from this city, and is composed of our best young men. Many leave at a great sacrifice of pecuniary interests, but they let nothing stand in the way of their country's call at this hour. There is no fear but they will do honor to themselves and their city."

"Capt. H. W. Cunningham, has closed his quarters, having enlisted nearly ninety men. The company was fully organized on Saturday, by the choice of Geo. Gunn, Esq, of Searsmont, as First Lieutenant, and Richard S. Ayer, of Montville, Second Lieutenant, both excelent men, and will make excellent officers. The company paraded for the first time in Custom House Square, on Saturday, and were addressed by several of our citizens. It is a tip-top company. There is scarcely one among them we judge that does not weigh over one hundred and fifty pounds, and they are all tough, hardy men, who will not turn their backs upon Jeff Davis's Southern powder and Southern steel. They are now drilling and will probably leave the last of this week."

"Who comes next with enlisting orders? A full company can be enlisted here every ten days."

Searsport had one company organized at this time, with F. S. Nickerson Captain, John B. Wiswell, First Lieutenant, and E. E. Bergen, Second Lieutenant.

The "copperhead" element, present at Belfast as elsewhere, came to the front early, as will be seen by the following notice issued May 9th.

VILLAINY.

"The *dastardly puppy* who stole the Flag, which was suspended from the Court House, on Saturday evening, April 27th, had better return the same *forthwith*. His *character* is well known in this community. The citizens have taken the matter in hand, and the body of the THIEF may dangle in the place of the flag."

On Thursday evening, May 2d, Capt. Cunningham's company assembled in Pierce's Hall, which was filled to overflowing, on the occasion of a presentation of a set of revolvers to each of the officers. Miss Caro Williamson presented a set to Capt. Cunningham, in behalf of the Belfast ladies; Miss May E. Moore those to Lieutenant Gunn, in behalf of the ladies of Searsmont; and Miss Arbella Johnson, the set to Lieutenant Ayer, in behalf of the ladies of Liberty and Montville.

On the 8th Capt. Marshall was elected Major of the Fourth

Regiment, and then followed an election of officers for the "City Greys," which resulted as follows: Silas M. Fuller, Captain; Alden D. Chase, First Lieutenant; Horatio H. Carter, Second Lieutenant.

On Sunday the 12th, the companies in the city attended, in a body, the services at Rev. Dr. Palfry's church, the services throughout being solemn and impressive. The text was from Ephesians, VI-13—"Take unto you the whole armor of God, that ye may be able to stand in the evil day, and having done all, to stand."

During the delivery of the sermon the attention of the large congregation was intensely fixed upon the speaker, and "The Age" said that at the close, "the heavy measured tread of the soldiers as they passed through the aisles, forcibly reminded us that the days of our revolutionary fathers, who worshipped God on the Sabbath, in the church, with their arms beside them, were indeed again upon us. The occasion will be long remembered by our citizens."

The little village of Unity raised a company about this time, and the town quartered them at "Chandler's Hotel," where the time was spent in drilling. For Captain they had C. H. Robinson, with A. S. Moore, and Hall C. Myrick, as Lieutenants. Monday night, July 22d, was a sleepless one to many in this community. The day had been one of gloom, for at that time had come the vague news of the battle of Bull Run, and reports that Maine regiments had been cut to pieces. Another dispatch stated twenty-seven were missing from the City Greys, but gave no names. Gradually, however, the news assumed a more favorable appearance, and the intense excitement gradually subsided.

In the fall of 1861, Messrs. C. P. Carter & Co., constructed a six hundred ton gun boat for the Government, which was named the "Penobscot." She was a fine craft and reflected great credit on her builders. This vessel was pierced for twelve guns, and also carried two pivot guns on deck. She was towed into the bay January 13th, 1862, as the harbor had began to freeze over.

All the towns round about were patriotic, and the action of Troy, July 22d, '62, was referred to by a correspondent as follows:

"Raised fifteen hundred dollars to encourage enlistments. Surely old Troy will not be found skulking from her duty while our beloved country is in danger."

In 1863, in common with other portions of the State, Belfast stood a Draft, Capt. A. D. Bean being Provost Marshal. The scenes and incidents conected with this, were identical with those of Bangor, which are described in her military matters, save that scenes of bloodshed were enacted consequent upon the proceedings at Belfast. These took place in Washington and Waldo counties, and will be found in another portion of this book. The following men drew tickets.

J. Welman, Geo. A. Russ, Jos. E. Stevens, H. M. McDonald, Wm. M. Wooster, W. H. Scobles, Geo. W. Burgess, C. M. Havener, Wm. H. Hall, D. P. Gilmore, G. S. Berry, H. C. Gray, John Kellock, Daniel Pillsbury, M. Robbins, Jas. Furbush, W. C. Huntley, Andrew Stevens, Horace Banks, John Dunnells, Augustus Philbrook, Wm. Mathews, Edmund Stevens, Jr., F. J. Durham, Hiram Darby, W. H. H. Sweetser, Benj. K. Shaw, Thos. Clark, James W. Frederick, Chas. A. Bean, A. H. Kennison, John D. Smart, C. W. Sweetser, Peltiah Shaw, Geo. H. Johnson, Augustus Clark, Isaac Darby, Oscar W. Pitcher, Thos. H. McFarland, Moses Trussell, John Thomas, Geo. N. White, Wm. H. Simpson, Hugh J. Anderson, Jr., Noah Bailey, M. Gannan, Albert E. Cunningham, A. V. Sawtell, Robt. F. Russ, Horatio Spicer, Wm. Crosby, Jas. E. Dodge, F. S. Coombs, Q. M. Henderson, S. B. Herrick, Alonzo Shute, John A. Wheeler, S. A. Payson, Thomas Owens, Geo. F. Brier, H. L. Killgore, J. A. Keller, C. W. Mears, Wm. Flanders, Andrew Patterson, Geo. P. Ames, J. P. Maddocks, W. C. Emery, Edwin Sides, W. P. Morrill, E. V. Nickerson, Eben P. Blake, Geo. W. Cottrell, C. C. Gregg, Samuel Michaels, Horace Park, James Lewis, F. A. Ellis, T. J. Burgess, H. H. Parker, Geo. B. Furgerson, A. H. Gray, Saml. Dutch, J. Philbrick, Edmund Cross, C. R. Piper, George Crosby, J. P. Wight, Moses W. Rich, Chas. Kimball, W. H. Reeves, C. Crammer, C. A. Banks, J. M. Clark, Frances V. Patterson, Geo. T. Quimby, Ambrose Thombs Isaac Sides, Levi Rogers, E. D. Burd, James B. Miller, John B. Mason, T. H. Shaw, C. T. Cottrell, John L. Page, Otis Maddocks, Geo. W. Warren, Andrew Bates, Thomas Crowell, Joseph H. Bean, Edward Smart, Edwin Salmon, O. G. White, T. O. Havener, M. H. Gray, J. C. Howard, Horace Anderson, Geo. H. Brier, Thos. W. Pitcher, Boynton Barton, J. B. Littlefield, A. A. Pitcher, H. H. Haws, Wm. Glover, J. C. Lewis, B. B. Whitaker, C. B. Stepherson, A. Gammon, A. K. Simpson, Otis Whitmore, D. P. Perkins, E. W. Baker, J. H. Emery, J. E. Trask, C. P. Brown, J. C. Cates, Jr., Moses W. Emerson.

The following Searsport men were drawn:

S. Blake, C. F. Fowler, James Ford, A. B. West, W. H. Blanchard, John Dow, D. Y. Mitchell, C. B. Ellis, E. W. Seavey, L. Lampher, A. J. Nichols, P. Nichols, Z. Berry, A. S. Carver, A. C. Kenney, J. S. Johnson, F. Shute, H. Whitcomb, F. R. Averill, Geo. E. Merrill, D. Treat, R. T. Waterhouse, L. P. Small, B. C. Smith, E. Mathews, Geo. Mathews, Wm. Ford, A. Fowler, E. N. Bassick, D. Lufkin, D. A. Dow, Geo. W. Bowen, Chas. Field, E. Blanchard, H. B. Hart, C. F. Beckmore, Geo. H. Smith, A. P. Colcord, J. L. Nichols, P. Gilkey, J. B. Nichols, A. Ford, A. Warren, G. C. Small, J. S. Colcord, J. H. Nichols, T. C. Pendleton, B. Carver, 2d,

W. G. Nichols. A. Closson, J. B. Wiswell, Nichols Parks, A. T. Gilmore, Atwood Gilmore, J. S. Fowler, H. H. Houslon, E. L. Griffin, A. W. Carter, B. L. Colcord, A. Havener, P. J. Beale, E. W. Mossman, Ferdinand Dodge, Wm. Rice.

CHAPTER XXVI.

Building Belfast Batteries—Excitement In Mercantile Circles—Dixie Prices—A Landlady Buys Largely—An Editor Arrested—The Killing Of a Waldo Sheriff In Wesley—A "Hard Gang" Resist The Belfast Officers—Deserters Stealing Horses—They Are Pursued—They Shoot Chief Of Police Charles McKenney—Additional Men Join In The Pursuit—One Of Them Shot Through The Heart—They Are Finally Captured—And Are Beaten To Death—News Of Lee's Surrender—Belfast Celebrates And Burns A Building—Men Blown From A Cannon's Mouth—The People Nearly Hang An Innocent Man—Copperheads Go Fishing—The Death Of Lincoln—Belfast Of To-Day.

Although the people were patriotic, as a whole, there were in every community men who, to use an old quotation, "kept an eye open for the main chance," and many of them accumulated dollars faster than honest ways and honest intentions would permit. Those having local influence, who remained at home, were constantly scheming to get money from the Government, either through fat contracts for furnishing supplies, or selling men, who deserted at the first opportunity, only to re-enlist and "divide up" again with the sharpers. There was also a constant attack upon the officials in power, urging upon them the necessity of fortifying the coast of Maine, to the end that resistance might be successfully made against supposed enemies, lurking over the and after the arrival of Company E from Augusta, (the company being nearly all Rockland men), was ordered to Belfast, on Jan. 21st, '65.

At the beginning of the draft in Belfast, on March 1st, Rockland lacked only twenty men of her quota, and these at once volunteered.

On the 4th of March, a grand celebration took place. A monster meeting was held in the First Baptist Church, and speeches made by Rev. C. F. Cutler, L. W. Howes, A. Sprague, O. G. Hall and others. During the day, guns were fired, flags set, bells rung, and a general good time enjoyed. Two schooners in the harbor set their flags "union down," at which a volunteer delegation visited them and asked the cause in a rather threatening manner. The now thoroughly frightened skippers replied that it was "only for a joke," but they decided it was not so smart a one when the Collector of the Port visited them and demanded their papers.

When the news of the fall of Charleston reached Rockland it was received with great joy. Many of the far-sighted ones seeing in this "the beginning of the end" of the Southern Confederacy. On that day, Capt. Bunker woke the echoes, by firing a salute of twenty-six guns.

When the news of the fall of Richmond, reached the city, the entire population turned out and began a real, old time, Rockland celebration. No pen can describe the events of that day, no imagination can depict the scenes; sufficient is it to say that such a celebration was never before seen in the city, and probably never will be again. The people were fairly wild with joy, and nothing was too great or seemingly impossible for them to attempt.— Processions were formed, and amid the booming of cannon, the blazing of bonfires and fireworks, the ringing of bells, and the cheers of the people, paraded the streets from long before daylight till the small hours of the next morning.

The order to stop enlisting came on April 15th.

The news of Lincoln's assassination, threw the people of this section into the profoundest grief, and had the men who had said they wished for such an event, been found, they would have probably ornamented lamp posts at short notice. But these rebels fled the city on hearing the first news, nor did they dare to return until long after. The town was draped in mourning, and flags hung at half-mast everywhere. As in other cities, exercises appropriate were held, and the people truly felt they had lost a friend and leader, and a noble man.

From this time on the story of Rockland is that of every Nothern city. The troops, or rather what was left of the noble bands of men who had gone away with such a gay appearance, came back, some without arms or legs, and some with health ruined by the climate of the South; but many never returned. Their bodies are laying on Southern soil, but their memory will ever live in the hearts and minds of the loyal North, for whose sake they fought and died.

Camden, in all, furnished four hundred and fifty-eight men, to the army and navy. In bounties she paid $90,129.51. Seventeen of her men were killed in battle, and thirteen died of disease. Among her noble soldiers was Geo. S. Cobb, who was a sergeant in Company I, Nineteenth Regiment. He was killed by the bursting of a shell, on October 17th, '64, while in front of Petersburg.

In the navy, she had many brave men, and of them perhaps the most noted was Wm. S. Conway. He entered the navy when but seventeen years of age, in 1825. and served under Hull. He was promoted to quartermaster in 1861, and while stationed at Pensicola navy yard at the breaking out of the war, was ordered by Lieutenant Renshan, who had captured the yard, to haul border. In this way they finally secured the privilege of erecting alleged batteries along the coast, for which large sums were paid. Old soldiers know that better ones have been erected in a night, by a single regiment, and old sailors know that they would have been powerless, had a second or third rate war vessel chosen to enter the ports where they were erected. However they were built, Belfast Bay having two, though it does not appear that they were ever used, save for the purpose of firing an occasional salute, and as channels leading from the greenback printing-rooms, through which the dollars flowed to the pockets of the projectors.

In Belfast, as elsewhere, merchandise rose rapidly in value after the second year of the war, keeping pace with gold, and the prices in the Bangor markets which appear under the head of "Gold and Merchandise," will recall to many a good house-wife the time when "keeping house" was expensive. Down south things were even worse, as the following, taken from a Richmond paper, will show;

RICHMOND MARKETS.

APRIL 18th, 1864.

"There is considerable activity in the markets, though supplies are not coming in as largely as they were some days ago. Transactions are now slightly in favor of the new issue, but owing to the scarcity of that medium, five dollar notes are more generally in use. We give quotations in the new issue.

Flour—Demand still brisk. Superfine $240; extra superfine $255, a $260.; family $275. Supply of all grades light.

Wheat—None offering.

Tobacco—No change in the market. Lugs, common, $16.00 a $20.00; good lugs $20.00 a $28.00; bright and suitable for smoking, $30.00 a $40.00; common leaf, $50.00 a $80.00; extra fine, $90.00 a $110. Manufactured holds about the same as at last report, but with a better feeling in the market. Fine brights,. lbs. old, may be quoted at $350. a $450.; medium do $175. a $275.

Apples—$150. a $200. per barrel.

Bacon—$6.50 a $7.00 per pound.

Butter—Firm at $8.00 a $10.00 per pound.

Beef—Fresh beef, $3.00 a $4.00 per pound; wholesale.

Beeswax—$5.00 a $5.50 per pound.

Beans—$35.00 a $45.00 per bushel for white.

Candles—$5.25 a $5.50 per pound.

Cheese—Imported $8.00 a $10.00 per pound; country $4.00 a $6.00.

Coffee—$12.50 per pound.

Corn—$37.50 per bushel, and scarce.

Corn Meal—$40.00 a $45.00 per bushel.

Hay—Scarce. $20.00 a $25.00 per cwt.

Onions—$30.00 a $35.00 per bushel.

Peas—$25.00 a $40.00 per bushel, all kinds.

Potatoes—Irish, $12.00 a $20.00 per bushel, latter very fine.

Leather—Little on the market. Sole $10.00 a $11.00; last sales of upper $12.00.

Lime—$20.00 a $25.00 per barrel.

Lard—$7.50 a $8.00 per pound.

Liquors—Whiskey, $60.00 a $80.00 per gallon; apple brandy, $50.00 a 75.00; peach brandy, $80.00 a $90.00; rum, $80.00 a $90.

Molasses—$50.00 a $60.00 per gallon; Sorghum, $35.00 a $40.00.

Nails—$110. a $130. per keg; factory price $85.00; but orders cannot be filled, owing to the scarcity of iron.

Sugar—Brown, $7.25 a $8.00 per pound; Crushed, $9.00 a $11.00 per pound.

Pork—$4.00 a $5.00 per pound.

Pepper—$12.00 a $15.00 per pound.

Rice—$1.00 a $1.25 per pound.
Salt—40 cents per pound last sales.
Soap—$3.00 a $3.50.
Tar—$40.00 per barrel.
Turnips—$5.00 a $7.00 per bushel.
Venison—Dry $4.00 a $4.50 per pound.
Vinegar—$5.00 a $6.00 per gallon.

FINANCIAL.

Gold $21.00 a $21.25 for $1.00. Silver $19.00 a 19.50. Virginia Treasury notes $1.28; coupons of 15 million, fifty cents premium. Sterling $20.25; Virginia bank notes $3.00 for $1.00."

On one occasion the Belfast folks got an idea that there was to be a "boom," as we say now-a-days, and every one who could do so, began to lay in a good supply of the necessary articles. Mrs. H. N. Lancaster, on one occasion bought two thousand dollars' worth of tea, sugar etc., and it was considered that she had, as the "Age" puts it, "done a handsome thing."

Editor Simpson, of the "Rebublican Journal" seems to have printed a sheet, in which appeared sentiments, that the loyal men and women could not brook, and accordingly, on complaint, he was arrested, an indictment being found against him, in the U. S. Court at Bangor, for using treasonable language, tending to discouraging enlistments, and inciting resistance to the draft.

For a while the paper was suspended, but later re-appeared, and has since been one of the regular publications of the place. The time of suspension was in December, 1864.

In October, of this same year, Mr. David W. Edwards, a Waldo County deputy, lost his life, while in the performance of his duties, as a special agent of the Provost Marshal's office. Previous to this a draft had been held in Belfast, for a portion of Washington County, and the names of the men so drafted, had been given to a

Mr. Perry, a deputy of Washington County, with instructions to serve the usual notices. Arriving at Wesley, he called at the house of one Day, a hard character, having several brothers, and was about to proceed to business, when such threats and suspicious actions were advanced, as to cause him to withdraw without having fulfilled his mission. In fact pistols were drawn at the time, and only a quick retreat saved Perry. On the following Wednesday, officers Edwards and Burrows were sent with Perry, to arrest Day, the ringleader. Arriving at the house, the following day, just after twelve, they found it locked. Day was inside, however, and, raising the window, blandly inquired what was wanted. On learning the nature of the errand, he gave a whoop, evidently a pre-arranged signal, which was answered from various directions; from behind stumps, trees and from the woods beyond, and a shot was fired, the slug grazing an officer, and burying itself in the woodwork of the house. This was returned. Thereupon a volley from the thicket was fired, a slug entering the forehead of Edwards, killing him. The defeated and saddened officers returned without Day, bringing the body of their late comrade, which was interred at Liberty. At this time, or soon after, Capt. Bean was removed from his position, for not taking prompt action looking to the arrest of Day, and was succeeded by Capt. Sanford.

There was enacted, also, another tragedy, which grew out of the war, and which caused great excitement in Belfast, and all through Waldo County. Charles Knowles, a member of the Seventh, and Isaac Grant, of Palmyra, a member of a Massachusetts regiment, deserted, and came down into the vicinity of their homes, Knowles being a native of Troy. They first stole a horse and wagon, of Eben Whitcomb, of Waldo, the wagon being afterwards discovered at the home of Knowles' father, in Troy. Later they stole a horse and wagon, from one Bearce, in Dover, which they brought to Belfast, where they sold the horse, leaving the wagon and harness with John Mahoney, who resided in the lower part of the city. They remained about some days, finally selling the wagon to Mr. Mahoney. Later, the true owner came and identified his property, whereupon Mahoney got out a warrant. putting the same into the hands of the plucky Chief of Police, Charles O. McKenney, who with Mahoney for a companion, started in pursuit. This was Saturday. On Sunday evening, the good people who were in attendance at the usual prayer meeting, at the Methodist church, were startled by the hasty entrance of a messenger, who inquired for Sheriff Tucker. He brought the information that McKenney had been shot, and probably could not live. It was soon learned that the unfortunate man, together with Mahoney, had gone up river from Belfast, and soon got track of the deserters. They learned that Grant and Knowles, after their departure, had stolen two other horses, one owned by the Rev. N. W. Miller, of North Searsport, and the other by John Neally, of South Monroe. The officers searched in vain along the Bangor road, and, while returning, heard of the men having been at a house in Monroe the day before, and, also, that they had been detained there awhile, and then allowed to depart. About this time Constable Prescott, of Troy, appeared and joined in the pursuit, the party being in two wagons, Prescott and Mahoney ahead, with McKenney and a young man following. About five o'clock Sunday afternoon, the forward party overtook Knowles and Grant, they walking along the road, separating, to allow the wagon to pass as it drove up. Prescott and Mahoney jumped as they arrived opposite the men, Prescott giving Knowles a blow over the head, which stunned him, and Mahoney throwing Grant, but Grant succeeded in turning him, and getting the pistol which

Mahoney held. At this moment McKenney drove up, jumping from his wagon while it was in motion, and being turned part way round by the momentum, and partly bent down. At this instant Grant fired at him with too true aim, the ball entering the back of McKenney, passing upward along the spine, and out through the shoulder on the right, disabling the cords of the arm on that side. Shifting his pistol to his left hand, with uncertain aim McKenney fired at Grant, the proximity of Mahoney making it dangerous for him to do so however. Three shots were exchanged, when another ball entered the forearm of McKenney, and at this time he fell. Taking the pistol of McKenney, Grant ordered the release of Knowles, and both started for the woods. After going a few rods, Grant, who seemed crazy with rage, again turned on McKenney, exclaming: "G—d d—n you, I'll finish you before I go," and fired three times, one ball passing through the clothing, just above the hip, and another grazing the head and breaking the skin of the hapless McKenney. In company with Knowles he then disappeared in the woods.

As might be supposed this news caused great excitement in Belfast, and volunteers freely offered to go with Sheriff Tucker, who took ten men well armed, and started for the scene of the fight. Word was also sent to Troy, the home of Knowles, and many who had been his school mates turned out with guns and searched the woods in the vicinity of his house. Sheriff Tucker and his men tracked them along the bloody trail into the woods where all trace was lost. The search was continued however until the party became exhausted, and, meeting three men, Jenkins, Myrick and Hurd, he engaged them to keep up the search for the trail while his men slept. McKenney was in the meantime removed to Belfast.

The new posse entered upon their work with vigor, searching along the muddy low lands of the Sebasticook for foot prints, when suddenly Grant and Knowles rose from the reeds directly in front of them and opened fire. Jenkins and his companions carried cocked guns, and responded instantly. A ball from Jenkins' rifle passed through the lobe of one ear of Grant—through the head also—cutting off the lobe of the other ear, yet, strange to say, touching no vital part. At the same instant a ball from Grant's pistol was plowing its way through the breast and heart of Jenkins, who fell dead. Myrick got a ball in the leg from the pistol of Knowles, while the latter got two balls—one from each of his opponents rifles—in his body. Hurd was the only man of the five who had not been hit, and he, clubing his gun, rained blow after blow upon Knowles, crushing his skull and beating him to the ground. Myrick, wounded as he was, had crawled to the dazed Grant and secured him with a rope, but later on, Grant promising to refrain from violence, and reminding his captors that they had been friends as boys, and that he was near death's door, secured his release. Instantly on being set free, he clubed his pistol and set upon Myrick, but Hurd coming to the rescue, Grant was clubed until he was dead. Knowles died the next day. His body was taken to Troy, and buried there. The guns were afterwards brought to Belfast. They were all broken at the breech, the barrels bent and covered with hair and blood. McKenney lay for some time in a critical condition, and, although he lived for years, never fully regained his health.

NEWS OF LEE'S SURRENDER.

In common with the other patriots, nearly all the citizens of Belfast rejoiced greatly at the news of the surrender of Lee.

Exhilaration began early, and the people hardly knew what to do. They thronged the streets, while many joined a procession carrying a long rope and dragging a pair of wheels. They repaired to the lower part of the town, and, securing an old building, hauled it to Custom House Square where preparations were made for a bonfire. In the meantime the bells were clanging wildly; not rung in the usual way by rope, but by men and boys in the belfries, whose whole ambition seemed to be to "turn them over boys," until they flew from their bearings. The guns of the batteries, as well as those of the U. S. Steamer "Rhode Island," then laying in the harbor, belched forth congratulations and were answered from Searsport, where the good citizens were making merry over the joyful event. Searsport in turn could hear the guns from up river, while flags were flying from every staff. The Belfast citizens also got out their field pieces, and while working these a sad accident occurred. John S. and Lewellyn Maddocks, two brothers, were blown from the mouth of one cannon by a premature discharge. Other citizens had business out of town that day, but they were not of the Union sort, but constituted the class who holding party fealty above their country's salvation, had labored hard to block the wheels of progress, which, under Lincoln and his party, were sweeping away the fanaticism and bigotry of the South, and planting upon her soil the ensign of freedom and right.

A week later came the sad news of the Assassination of Lincoln, and joy gave way to sorrow. Some citizens who had thought it well to take a fishing trip on the receipt of the news of Lee's surrender, had returned, and gave expressions of satisfaction at the sorrowful news. This aroused the indignation of the patriots, and quick flight only saved the disloyal ones. By some misapprehension of facts, the crowd became convinced that one disloyal man who had uttered obnoxious sentiments, was secreted on board a certain schooner at one of the wharves, and, procuring a rope made their way there. A man was found on board, taken ashore and preparations made to hang him, when he succeeded in getting the attention of some of the excited throng, and convinced them

CAMP LEAVITT.

he was not the man they wanted. As a merchant afterwards put it: "It was a narrow squeak for the sailor chap."

Belfast was truly glad when the war was over, having during all the struggle bravely borne her part, and ever evinced her loyalty to the Union. For some years after, her vessels sailed to all quarters of the world, many came to her markets, and prosperity was on her right hand and on her left. In an evil hour she caught the railroad fever, and, after giving her money freely, was betrayed and given over to her enemies. Later she met with another misfortune, when she was handed over to that great monoply—the Me. Central Railroad—which, winding its serpentine trail through our state, crushes everything and everybody not in full accord with its own selfish interests. The iron horse has been her ruin, and to-day her ship building is a thing of the past; her customers, or most of them, have sought other markets, her wharves are tumbling and decaying, and compared with Belfast of twenty years ago, she seems like a city stricken with palsy.

CHAPTER XXVII.

The First Cavalry—They Were Never "Rattled"—The Organization—The Officers From Eastern Maine—"Dashing" Spurling—Why Col. Goddard Resigned—How The Band Got Even—Leaving For The Front—Scenes Of Inactivity—Douty Gains Command—Raiding And Skirmishing—They Save The Army Of Banks—The Gallant Fight At Brandy Station—Another At Aldie—The Fall Of Douty—The History Of The Regiment To The Close Of The War—Coming Home.

The First Maine Cavalry was raised from all sections of the State, and it is no discredit to other regiments, to say that, as a body, it took high rank, both in intelligence and fighting qualities. It is a remarkable fact that this regiment, although like the others originally made up of raw recruits, was never "rattled" or put to wild, dis-organized retreat, as was the case with many new regiments. Its record shows that its men and officers had confidence in each other, had a mutual high regard, and through thick and thin, in camp life, hospital life, and on the field of strife, stood shoulder to shoulder, always ready to aid each other in every way; and their record, like that of the Second, Sixth, First Heavy, and other regiments, is something of which the State of Maine may well be proud. Eastern Maine was well represented, nineteen of the fifty-one officers being from that section.

The regiment was mustered in at Augusta, the thirty-first of October, 1861, under the following organization:

JOHN GODDARD, Colonel, Cape Elizabeth.
THOMAS HIGHT, Lieutenant Colonel, U. S. Army.
SAMUEL H. ALLEN, Major, Thomaston.
DAVID P. STOWELL, Major, Canton.

Calvin S. Douty, Major, Dover.
Benj. F. Tucker, Adjutant, U. S. Army.
Edward M. Patten, Quartermaster, Portland.
George W. Colby, Surgeon, Richmond.
Geo. W. Haley, Assistant Surgeon, Eastport.
Benj. F. Teft, Chaplain, Bangor.
A. P. Russell, Sergeant Major, Houlton.
E. C. Bigelow, Quartermaster Sergeant, Portland.
Charles S. Crosby, Commissary, Bangor.
Samuel C. Lovejoy, Hospital Steward, Rockland.
A. D. Bickford, Principal Musician, Houlton.

Of Eastern Maine men, Company A had Sidney W. Thaxter, First Lieutenant; Company B, J. P. Cilley, Thomaston, Captain; Wm. P. Coleman, of Lincolnville, and Frank L. Cutter, Union, Lieutenants; Company D, Chas. H. Smith, Eastport, Captain, with Andrew B. Spurling and Wm. Montgomery of Orland, Lieutenants; Company E, Black Hawk Putman, Houlton, Captain, and O. A. Ellis, of Lincoln, Second Lieutenant; Company K. George Cary, Houlton, First Lieutenant; Company, M, Geo. M. Brown, Bangor, Captain, with John C. C. Bowen, Bangor, and Evans S. Pillsbury, Guilford, Lieutenants.

Spurling was a dashing officer, and the following story is told regarding his enlistment. Early in the war, Gen. Chas. Hamlin occupied an office in Orland, and one day Spurling entered it and said: "I don't suppose, Mr. Hamlin, that the Abolition party would take me, would they?"

Mr. Hamlin informed him that he knew of no reason why Spurling could not enlist, and told him so, whereupon Spurling unfolded his plan. There was to be a regiment of sharp-shooters raised, and he, (Spurling), had a number of men ready to enlist, provided Gov. Washburn would commission him to raise a company.

Mr. Hamlin immediately went to Augusta, saw the Governor, got the required papers, and brought them home, and Spurling at once set about raising the men. Matters progressed well for awhile, when Spurling again made his appearance at Mr. Hamlin's office.

"Say," ejaculated he, "my men don't care about this sharp shooting business. The cavalry is the thing that hits us! Can't you get this commission changed?"

Later Mr. Hamlin got it "changed" to suit; the company was made up, entered the branch of service "that hits us," and made a grand record. Spurling won his way up, and was finally promoted to the regular army.

The regiment remained at Augusta during the winter. Early in March Col. Goddard resigned. He was an arbitrary, haughty man, ruling his officers and men as he had been accustomed to rule his back-woodsmen and river drivers. When the time came for the regiment to go to the front, about forty of the officers waited on the Governor, and informed him that they could stand no more of the Goddard rule, and should resign. Of course this was not to be thought of, and the Colonel was asked to hand in his resignation which he did. One incident will serve to show how the men regarded him. For some slight breach of military decorum, he at one time placed the entire band in the guard house. They determined on revenge. The next Sunday the regiment was ordered out for church. On these occasions Goddard made a great spread. He had secured a hall in the city, and every Sabbath day, Dr. Teft held services. The men had fine overcoats, new uniforms with top boots, having accross the front the words "First Maine Cavalry;" gloves, etc. It was the order of Goddard that the band play while marching by the State House, and again when approaching the hall. On this occasion the first part of the order was carried out, and then the band allowed their brass instruments to *freeze up.*

When the time came to play again no sound was heard, at which Goddard became wroth, and sent an orderly forward to learn the cause of the silence. The band orderly informed the messenger that the band was frozen up, and the same was reported to Goddard. He swore as only troopers are supposed to swear, and when the hall was reached and the soldiers and the large audience seated, he ordered the band to go to the stove, thaw out their instruments and "*play that tune,*" which they did, while Dr. Teft, with sober face, and the audience with merry countenances, looked on in silence. Later, during the war, Goddard visited the regiment, and the band tendered him a serenade, playing two tunes, after which the former colonel addressed them, saying among other pleasant things, that in his opinion, "the climate hereabouts is evidently much better for your business than that of Augusta, as I observe you can play two tunes without freezing up." The boys gave three cheers at this, while the band answered with the new tune: "Right you are old man!"

Maj. Allen was promoted to the position vacated by Goddard and a few days later the regiment embarked for the front. Companies A, D, E and F, under Col. Allen, March 14th, '62, arriving in Washington the 19th, when thirty men under Capt. Smith, were sent to Upton's Hill, Va., to guard property.

On the 20th, Companies B, I, H and M, left Augusta, under Major Douty, arriving in Washington on the 24th, and were four days later joined by Companies C, G, K and L, under Major Stowell.

On the 30th, Companies A, B, E, H and M, under command of Major Douty, marched to Harper's Ferry, where they joined Mill's brigade. Here they remained guarding railroads, etc., until May 11th, when they joined Gen. Banks, and were attached to Gen. Hatch's Cavalry Brigade. Just before this, Major Douty was promoted to Lieutenant Colonel, *vice* Lieutenant Colonel Hight, resigned. In the meantime, the seven companies, under Major Stowell, on April 5th, joined Gen. Abercrombie's brigade at Warrenton Junction. On the 12th, six companies, under Major Stowell, went towards Culpepper C. H., and discovered about one hundred rebels, drove them, and captured eight prisoners. This was done by Lieutenant Taylor, and a squad of only fifteen men. On the 20th, Lieutenant Colonel Douty, with three companies had a skirmish with the enemy at Woodstock, and captured the place. On the 23d, Col. Douty made a charge with his command, against two thousand rebel infantry and six guns. It was a terrible and daring charge, one that caused great loss to the regiment, and was the result of an unauthorized order to "charge." The loss of horse was one hundred and seventy-six. After the engagement, Col. Douty and his command covered the retreat of Gen. Banks to Williamsport.

On the 28th the regiment, under Col. Allen, joined Gen. McDowell at Manassas Junction. Two companies under Col. Douty, were selected for the very dangerous work of opening communication between McDowell, at Fort Royal, and Banks, at Williamsburg, and on the afternoon of July 2d, under Maj. Whitney, they started. This perilous trip was successfully carried out, and the return made July 5th.

On August 9th, the whole regiment, under Col. Allen, took part in the battle of Cedar Mountain. They were attached to Bayard's Brigade. On the 20th, they engaged the enemy's advance near Brandy Station, from eight thirty A. M., to two P. M., when they fell back across the river. On Sept. 3d, they marched to Fairfax C. H., reported to Gen. Reno, and joining his column, moving to Union Mills. On the 14th, Company G was in the battle of South Mountain, acting as body guard to Gen. Reno. On the 17th, Companies M and H were in the battle of Antietam, under Gen. Fitz John Porter.

The total number of horses lost by the regiment, from March to the close of the year, was nearly seven hundred.

The opening of the year 1863, found the Cavalry in winter quarters, at Camp Bayard, near Belle Plain. On the 16th of January, the regiment was furnished with Sharps' Carbines, and on the 21st, an attempt to advance was made, but given up on account of the mud. On the 20th of February, Gen. Gregg was assigned to the command of the Third Division, Cavalry Corps, and this regiment assigned to the First Brigade of that division, under Col. Kilpatrick.

Col. Allen had resigned on account of ill health, and Lieut. Col. Douty was now in command.

On the 13th of April, the regiment broke camp and marched to Deep Run, where the night was spent, and the next day they advanced to Rappahannock Station. On the 16th of April they moved to a point in the woods near Warrenton Junction, where they had been encamped the November before. Soon after they joined in Gen. Stoneman's raid, and made many marches, and had numerous skirmishes up to the first of May. Early in the morning of the 2d, the regiment arrived near Louisa C. H. The railroad was destroyed and the cavalry marched into the town, greatly alarming the natives, who at first mistook them for Stuart's Cavelry. Here the object of the raid, i. e. the cutting off of the enemy's means of communication, was explained to the officers. After doing their work, and doing it well, on the 4th the return march was begun. For seventy-two consecutive hours they marched, and at last arrived at Bealton Station.

With a force of less than five thousand men, Stoneman had cut loose from his own base, and for nine days moved wherever he pleased. In the raid he destroyed twenty-two bridges, seven culverts, five ferries, one hundred and twenty-two wagons, three trains of cars, besides many store houses, etc.

The regiment remained at Bealton, with the exception of several short skirmishes, until June 8th. On the 9th the regiment started for Brandy Station, and on its arrival, after a detour through the woods, attacked the enemy in the gallant charge, so well known in history. Col. Douty's words, "I can drive the rebels," will go down to the end of time. By some oversight the gallant First were completely surrounded, but, by a quick movement by Col. Douty, the regiment turned and cut their way out in safety. In this terrible charge the command had thirty men missing, and captured seventy-six prisoners, a battle-flag and two pieces of artillery. The regiment then crossed the river, and camped the next night at Warrenton Junction. Here the brigade was re-organized, and Col. Gregg placed in command.

On the morning of the 17th the regiment left for Union Mills, and reached Aldie while the battle was in progress. They arrived at a critical moment, as the official report shows.

In that report Col. Smith says:

"Having reported to the Brig. Gen., Col. Douty was ordered to proceed to a position to the left of the town, but before arriving there, he was ordered to return *in haste*. The regiment returned at a "gallop," left in front, and ascended the hill on the right of the town, near the battery, just in time to meet and resist the impetuous attack of the enemy, upon our exhausted forces. A portion of the regiment, led by Col. Douty, charged, turned the enemy, and drove him from the hill, and his stronghold among the stone walls."

"The regiment gained the position, secured our wounded, collected the trophies of the field, and were burying the dead, when relieved just before dark."

Here the brave Col. Douty fell.

Having led his regiment that day a long and exhausting march, he had reached the field at a moment when victory seemed on the point of deciding for the enemy. Without a moments rest, he had been ordered to support the exhausted forces of the First Brigade. At the order to advance, the cheers that arose from those bold, tough men of Maine, attested their willingness to follow their brave commander. In the first charge, the gallant Douty fell, at the head of his command, but his fall did not check the ardor of his men.

The regiment on the 19th met the enemy again, and again drove him.

On the 21st the regiment advanced towards Upperville, and again gave battle to the enemy, and again defeated him, capturing seventy-five prisoners. The day after the fight at Upperville, the regiment returned to Middleburg, and on the 26th marched to Leesburg, and on the next day on to Monocacy Junction. The column reached Frederick at noon, on the 29th. On they went, until they halted at a point within two miles of Gettysburg.

On the 3d of July, the regiment took part in a severe engagement, and on the 4th was engaged in reconnoitering. From here, by short marches, the regiment went to Halltown, where they arrived on the 15th. Here they engaged the enemy, silenced him, and continued the march. When near Shepardstown they met the enemy again. After severe action, they were relieved by the Sixteenth Pennsylvania Cavalry, but on seeing that the Sixteenth was being hard pressed, Col. Smith ordered the First back again, and they shared the fortunes of the rest of the day.

From Shepardstown the regiment marched to Harper's Ferry,

from there through Leesburg and on to Bristow Station, arriving there on July 22d. On the 29th they marched to Waterloo and Gaines' roads, where they remained till August 7th. In the next few days they marched to White Plains, through the Thoroughfare Gap, and returned to near Haymarket. On the 24th of August, they went to Sulphur Springs, and here remained till the 13th of September. On the morning of the 13th, they advanced toward Culpepper, and drove the enemy beyond to a point near Cedar Mountain. They then went to Thoroughfare Mountain, and on being relieved, returned to camp at Cedar Mountain. On the 24th the march was taken up to Rappahannock Station and here they remained till the end of the month. On the 2d of October, the regiment moved to Bealton, where it remained on picket duty till the 10th. On that day they marched to Fox Mountain, and then on to Sulphur Springs, skirmishing with the enemy part of the way. On the 12th, a reconnoissance was made in the direction of Thompson's Gap. Returning they found the corps of A. P. Hill in front, and made a rapid retreat and finally reached our lines on the morning of the 13th, near New Baltimore, having marched over one hundred miles in twenty-six hours.

The whole army was now falling back to cover Washington, and the regiment retreating with it, arrived at Bull Run on the 14th, and the same day marched to Fairfax Station. On the 24th a brisk skirmish took place at Beverly Ford, and the enemy was driven across the river. Sunday, November 1st, found the regiment in camp near Fayetteville, and here they remained till the 5th. On the 7th a brilliant charge gave them the enemy's works at Rappahannock Station. From this time till the 23d, the time was put in on picket duty and like work. On the 23d, the march was taken up via White Chapel, across the Rapidan to White Hall, to Robinson's Tavern. Here considerable fighting was done, and much picket duty performed till December 16th, when the regiment was relieved, and began to build winter quarters near Bealton Station. On the 21st, the regiment left on an expedition to Luray, where they destroyed everything possible, and returned in time for Christmas, well supplied with tobacco.

On the 1st of January, 1864, the regiment was in temporary camp at Bealton, Sta., but on that day began the march on an expedition under Col. Taylor, of the First Penn. Cavalry. Capt. Taylor, with one hundred and fifteen men, was sent in advance and met a force of Moseby's men near Salem, and with slight loss drove him. During that day twenty prisoners and twenty-five horses were captured.

On the 4th, march was continued, and on the 6th they reached Turkey Run Station, and there went into winter quarters, having marched eighty-one miles. On the 27th of February, three hundred men and officers reported to Gen. Kilpatrick, for duty in an expedition to Richmond, and were assigned to the Second Brigade, Third Division, Cavalry Corps, under Gen. Davis. They crossed the Rapidan at Ely Ford, and continued to Spottsylvania C. H. On arriving before Richmond, one hundred and fifty men, half from the First Maine Cavalry, were selected to form a part of the storming party. They did not succeed, owing to superior force of the enemy. On the 2d of March, the march was resumed, and a squad from Companys A and E, under Capt. Cole and Lieutenant Hussey, charged on the enemy at Old Church Road, inflicting a much larger loss than they themselves sustained. The column then moved to Tunstall's Station, having lost in the raid, forty-nine, killed, wounded and missing. On the 3d, being joined by the main force of Col. Dahlgren's command, they left for Williamsburg, where they were met by a brigade under Col. Spear, and, on the 4th the whole command left for Gloucester.

In the charge on Richmond, Company F charged with marked vigor, and lost nearly half of its men. After pressing the enemy back to their works, a retreat was ordered, and Col. Dahlgren and a few of his men, being separated from the command, entire charge fell upon Capt. Mitchell. They finally took refuge in a swamp, and the next day re-joined Col. Kilpatrick, having lost forty-four men, in killed, wounded and missing. On the 12th of March, the regiment went into camp at Alexandria, and there remained until the 17th of April, when it went to Sulphur Springs, on a reconnoissance. On the 24th and 27th, also, detachments went on same duty, to Warrenton. On the 27th, the regiment went into camp at Paoli Hills. On the 7th of May the regiment had an all-day fight, at Pine Run Church. Soon after that, the regiment began the march to Richmond, and saw more or less of fighting every day. At a slight skirmish at Ground Squirrel Bridge, Lieutenant Col. Boothby was mortally wounded. The regiment finally went into camp at Pole Cat River, where the first "Sheridan Raid" ended, and where the command was joined by Major Cilley.

On June 1st, they marched on the Cold Harbor Road, met the enemy, repulsed him, but with some loss. Chaplain Bartlett was here killed by a solid shot. On the 24th a general engagement took place at St. Mary's Church, and the brigade was forced back to Prince George C. H. On July 4th the regiment was in camp near Light House Point, and remained near here until the 26th, when it moved towards Lee's Mills. During the march several slight engagements took place. During the month of August the regiment's work was mostly picket duty and marching. Skirmishes were had at Charles City Road, where, after hard fighting, the enemy was driven back three miles. At Dinwiddie C. H., on the 23d, was a slight skirmish, followed by a severe engagement on the 24th, near Ream's Station, the First, though in the thick of the fight, suffering but little. During the month of September little was done.

On the 20th of October the regiment met the enemy at Gravelly Creek. They were driven by a charge of the First Maine, and Sixth Ohio, dismounted. The month of November was taken up in picket duty. On December 1st, six companies under Lieut. Col. Cilley, marched to Stony Creek Station, and assisted in its destruction, and, on the 7th, five other companies assisted in burning the Weldon Railroad Bridge, and tearing up the track. On the ninth, the command guarded the infantry in their work of destruction, and on the 10th destroyed the bridge at Janell's Station. From this time to the end of the month the regiment was employed in picketing and scouting.

From this time to February 5th, 1865, the regiment remained quietly in winter quarters, and, on the morning of the 5th, they advanced, by way of Dinwiddie C. H., to Hatcher's Run. Here the enemy was found and driven back. At day light on the morning of the 7th, the whole regiment went on a reconnoissance to Halifax Road and Ream's Station. The next day the regiment again returned to camp. As a result, our lines were extended nearly five miles on the left. On the 20th, the whole regiment was ordered on picket duty on the old line, and beyond this constant duty, nothing of special interest occured until March 29th. On that day the regiment moved to Dinwiddie C. H., remaining there in the rain and mud till the 31st. On that day they again advanced until within twelve miles of Petersburg, near Stony Creek. Here the First Cavalry had one of the hardest, if not the hardest fight of the whole war. Owing to a much larger force of the rebels, and the want of ammunition, they were forced to withdraw. In this action they lost fifteen killed, and eighty-two wounded.

On April 1st, the regiment relieved the First Vermont Cavalry from picket duty, and that night bivouacked on the Vaughan Road.

On the 2d they acted as rear guard for the brigade train, and halted near Sutherland Station. On the morning of the 4th, the march was taken up, and continued until reaching Jettersville. On the 5th, after a short engagement, routed the enemy. On the 6th they attacked a supply train of the enemy, and captured no less than seven rebel officers. On the 7th they moved to Briery Creek, then to Appomattox Station, and threw up breastworks on the hill, near the Court House. Here they participated in the last great battle of the war, and as ever, proved themselves to be brave soldiers, and noble men.

After the surrender of Lee, the regiment returned to Petersburg, and camped about two miles west of the town. On the morning of April 10th, they advanced to San Marino P. O., where a halt for the night was ordered. The march was continued until on the night of the 26th, they arrived at Boydtown. On they went, and at South Boston, in Halifax County, the glorious news was received that Johnston had surrendered.

The return march was without anything of great interest, and the regiment arrived at Ettrick, where they remained until ordered into Chesterfield County, to protect the freedmen, and here they remained until August 1st, doing provost guard duty. On that day the regiment was mustered out of the service, by Lieutenant L. H. Bowen, A. C. M.

Leaving Petersburg on the 2d, they arrived at Augusta on the 9th, where the men were finally paid and discharged.

Col. CALVIN S. DOUTY.

In the biographical sketch of Col. Douty, will be found the details of the charges at Brandy Station.

CHAPTER XXVIII.

CALVIN S. DOUTY.

When the rebellion broke out, Calvin Sanger Douty resided in the quiet village of Dover, and his standing there will be at once understood when it is known that he was then serving his third term as sheriff, to which office he was elected by a large vote. Soon after the battle of Bull Run, he notified the State authorities of his desire to resign his position and enter the army.

On October 24th, he was commissioned Major of the First Maine Cavalry, and devoted himself with his accustomed energy, to the enlistment and equipment of that superb corps.

On the 20th of March, 1862, Major Douty left Augusta for the seat of war, in command of a detachment of four hundred men, and repaired to Harper's Ferry, acting as a guard to the Baltimore and Ohio Railroad. On the 9th of May he received a commission as Lieutenant Colonel of the regiment. Soon after General Banks, a man who seemed to take delight in heaping insults upon Maine officers, got caught in a trap at Winchester, and, but for a ruse of Douty's, and the gallant fighting of his men, he would have been overpowered. The cavalry that day held two thousand infantry, and a battery of six guns, four hours, during which the retreat was secured. The rebel Gen. Ashby says that Col. Douty's cavalry saved Bank's army. Says the Maine Adjutant General's report:

"Byron has somewhere defined glory as 'dying on the battlefield, and having your name spelt wrong in the Gazette.' Strangely enough, the First Maine Cavalry were not singled out for honorable mention in General Bank's report of his eventful retreat. Col. Douty scorned puffery, but had a true soldier's pride in laurels, nobly earned. He made no complaint, however, but when, sometime after, he proposed to the General that his detachment should join their regiment, at Frederick, Gen. Banks replied: 'I cannot spare any of my cavalry, Colonel, least of all the Maine Cavalry, which is the best in my corps.' Col. Douty, who had a vein of quiet humor in his composition, answered, 'Why, General, I read your report, and I did not learn from it that you had any Maine Cavalry with you at the time of your retreat.'

Gen. Banks made the *amende* with soldierly frankness, regretting the omission, and explaining he had written his report, from minutes made by his Adjutant. 'But,' said he, 'I fully appreciate the great service you did me, and if you will prepare a report of the part you took in that campaign, I will forward it to the War Department, with a satisfactory endorsement.' Such a report *was written* and forwarded to Banks, but the Colonel *never heard from it afterwards.*"

Col. Douty made a brief visit to Dover, in March, 1863, and at that time took his last leave of family, friends and home, and at the expiration of fifteen day's furlough, returned to the army

Mention has been made of the inactivity of the First Regiment Cavalry for one year or more after entering the service. To tell the truth about the matter, the army officers did not know how to fight them, being unused to mounted troops, and, rather than acknowledge this, made light of them, and often declared they could not be used on the battle fields, unless there were large, open and level places. So for over a year the impetuous Douty was obliged to assist with the other officers, in such play as escorting scouts, guarding supply trains, etc. At last he was placed in command of the regiment, and at once determined to show the regular army men that volunteer cavalry could fight. He had for a long time chafed under the restraint, and, when he read in the Maine papers which came to headquarters, long accounts of the gallant conduct of the Second, Fourth, Sixth, and other bodies of Eastern Maine men, he could at times hardly contain himself. While wrought up on one of these occasions, he did what might have brought a less valuable man into difficulty. He wrote a letter, a personal one, to Secretary of War Stanton, direct, stating that he and his men were disgusted with there enforced idleness, and virtually insisted on being given a chance to show their mettle. "Give me back my companies now dancing attendance on wagons, and I will show you one of the best regiments of cavalry that ever mounted horse." Military men can well understand the character of Douty. He had ignored all his superior officers in writing to Stanton, but that gentlemen liked him for it, and soon sent him back his men. Douty now began to scheme to get to the front. He was in a measure successful, being ordered to support a battery in one engagement. Over he went and drew horse just in the rear of the guns. The artillery men laughed at the idea of cavalry men staying there, but stay they did, and Douty returned only when an orderly appeared with imperative orders for him to do so.

But it was at the battle of Brandy Station that Douty made a record for himself, and for the First Maine Cavalry, that will be as enduring as the fame of the army itself, for on that day the hitherto despised cavalry saved the brigade under Kilpatrick, and, when the fight was over, dismounted with the consciousness of knowing that they were the admiration of friend and foe alike.

Fifty miles southwest of Washington, the Orange and Alexandria Railroad crosses the Rappahanock river, and on this road, one-half way from the bridge to Culpeper, about five miles, is Brandy Station. About one-half mile from the railroad, stood an old-fashioned mansion, surrounded by a beautiful lawn, and back of this, a line of woods. This house was the headquarters of the rebel General Stuart, and around it was a heavy force of artillery, cavalry and infantry. The whole sloping field, many acres in extent, formed of undulating, smooth ground, was as fine a place for a cavalry fight as could be found on Southern soil. When it was learned that there was to be a fight, Douty ordered an inspection, made sure that everything was in first class shape, and even went so far as to have the sabres ground. The horses had had a week's rest, and were in high mettle.

Early in the morning, the First Maine crossed the river, at Kelly's Ford, and heard at that early hour the artillery, which was already engaged. For awhile they remained in idleness, but, later, the battle seeming to go against the Union arms, they were hurried forward at a trot, none more eager, and none more earnestly wishing for a chance to enter the conflict, than Douty. As the Maine boys swung from the woods, into the broad and beautiful field, the aspect was one tending to dishearten the men, but they seemed to be *oblivious* to everything, save the movements of their colonel Men were fleeing on every hand, and all evidence pointed to a terrible defeat, when Kilpatrick, seeing the First Maine advancing, hurried up to Douty, and called:

"Colonel Douty, for God's sake, tell me what you can do with your regiment. Can you save me?"

Glancing proudly back to the six hundred grim and silent horsemen, Douty raised himself in his saddle and said:

"I can drive those fellows to hell."

He got the great desire of his courageous heart—an order to engage the enemy—and a moment later there rang out, clear and loud above the din of battle, the bugle sound to charge. Away went that gallant body, and as they rode, men shoulder to shoulder, and horses flank to flank, they saw before them a picture which no artist could paint, and no human brain comprehend save by eye sight. That wide, undulating plain was filled with fleeing Union men and pursuing Confederates; horses, now riderless, dashed madly to and fro, or gave out wild cries of pain as their quivering flesh was plowed with lead; dead men were there on every hand; others were taking their last glassy look at their comrades and their flag; shrieks of the wounded filled the air, and were heard above the resounding tread of the horses of the flying cavalrymen, while "the thunder of artillery, the heavy thug of solid shot, the strange scream of shells, the rattle and roar of musketry, the clashing of steel, and the fierce shouts of eager combats," filled the air.

Soon the scene changed. On went the daring riders. Up the hill and along the brow they went, driving the enemy before them and dashing at the battery, which they captured, cutting down such of the gunners as remained. There was a sharp clashing of sabres, an incessant crack of revolvers and carbines; but on went the regiment, seemingly mad with the excitment of their first battle.

Here Douty made a mistake. Some of the men wanted to carry off the battery, but their colonel, with the enemy before him, failed to realize the danger of leaving it, and, still at the head of his men, urged them forward, first planting a Union flag at the guns. Sweeping forward after the retreating foe, Douty left the guns unmanned, and from the woods, upon the side of the plain, came other rebels, who regained them, and, when Douty turned, he saw, not only the guns turned against him, but quite a force of the enemy in position. Not a moment was lost. Again rang out the bugle notes, and again the battery was charged, and through, and over and around it they went. Again the excited horses were wheeled, and for the third time Douty's men rode straight at those guns, scattering the enemy in every direction. Gallant work was that, and every man who could see it, knew then, if he had not known it before, that the Maine Cavalry men were equal to any body of men in the service.

Says the history of the First Maine Cavalry:

" The last charge brought them to a point, in the valley between two hills, west of the battery, and directly under its guns. At this critical moment, it was discovered that they were completely surrounded, and cut off from all support, whilst the rebels were literally swarming on every side. The gunners on the hill were waiting to pour death through their devoted ranks."

" Lieutenant Colonel Smith, was now in command, as Douty and some of the officers had been separated from the regiment, during the hand to hand fight at the battery, and he saw only one avenue of escape. The men were formed and moved directly towards the battery, as if inviting attack. For a moment they dashed on, and when it was seen that the guns had been sighted, and were about to be discharged, the order was given to swing to the right. In an instant after came the cannon's roar, but not a man or horse fell. The grape and canister tore along the left flank, plowing the ground, vacated but an instant before." Just here bayonets were seen glistening along the woods, and, to an orderly hurrying across the field, the question was put:

"What troops are those along the woods?"

"'Tis the Sixth Maine," was the answer.

For an instant all was quiet, and then rang out a glad shout. They were safe! They knew the Sixth; probably the grandest regiment of infantry that ever carried the colors of the Union. Indeed, there stood there too, perhaps, the best regiment of cavalry that entered the Union army, and if any State ever had reason to be proud of her representatives, Maine had a right to be proud of her sons who stood together after the fierce conflict at Brandy Station.

On the 17th of June, Colonel Douty fell, while leading his men in another charge. This was in the action at Aldie. Again he turned the enemy, and greatly contributed to the success of the day. Isaac H. Bailey, of New York, in the Northern Monthly says:

"But the shouts of triumph, which heralded the substantial success at Aldie, were soon hushed, as in the presence of a great sorrow, for the intrepid Colonel had fallen dead in the *extreme front*. He had covered himself with glory, but, alas! he had sealed his devotion to his country with his blood, he had exchanged the laurel for the cypress. The praises which echoed through the ranks of his comrades, as they saw him dash with impetuous bravery against the foe, were lost to him.

He had won his star, but it was not destined to glitter on his shoulder. Yet the radiance of his fame will endure when the insignia of rank shall have faded away. The witnesses of his valor, will remember him as one of the truest and bravest patriots who ever unsheathed a sword in defense of his country's honor. It was a noble life, crowned by a glorious death."

Before this battle, Douty and some of his officers, were talking of the rapid promotions in some New York regiments, made on account of resignations. Turning around, Douty said: "If you gentlemen get promoted, it will be by fighting. If I am killed and you survive, you'll have a chance."

Saturday, June 28th, 1863, the remains of Col. Calvin S. Douty were laid away in the churchyard, in Dover. Soon after dinner, on that day, all the roads leading to the village were thronged with teams, loaded with people, all anxious to testify their respect to his memory. Hundreds of teams were in the streets, and about four thousand people were in the town. The services at the house consisted of singing, reading a passage of the scripture, by Rev. Mr. Darling, of the Congregational church, and a prayer by Rev. Mr. Herring, of the Baptist church.

The procession previously formed, then received the remains, marching to the cemetery in the following order:

Colonel Geo. Varney, Second Maine, Marshal.
Captain Jefferds and Lieutenant Kittredge, Assistants.
Hale's Brass Band.
Company C, State Guards, Capt. Harlow.
Mosaic Lodge, F. and A. M. Joined by members of neighboring Lodges, to the number of one hundred.
Pall Bearers. Hearse drawn by two black horses, led by grooms. Pall Bearers.
Family and relatives in carriages.
Returned officers and soldiers.
Clergymen and speakers.
Committee of Arrangements, Messrs. A. G. Lebrook, R. Dearborn, C. E. Kimball, S. P. Brown, G. W. Sawyer, Colonel Silas Paul and C. Chamberlin.
Muncipal officers of Dover and Foxcroft.
Dover and Foxcroft Union Leagues.
Citizens and Strangers.

The services at the grave were singing, followed by a prayer by Rev. Mr. Abbott, and an address by Hon. John Rice, after which David Barker, Esq., recited an original poem written for the occasion. Remarks were then made by Mr. Hayden and Mr. George Pickering, of Bangor.

Masonic ceremonies were then performed, after which, benediction by Rev. Mr. Godfry, of the Methodist church, and a dirge by the band closed the services at the grave. They were solemn and impressive, and made a lasting impression on all in attendance.

CHAPTER XXIX.

War Matters In Dexter—A Strong Union Sentiment—And A Large "Secesh" Element—Local Matters—The Great Peace Conventions—Fifteen Thousand People Gather—"Seven Barrels Of Doughnuts"—A Monster Procession—Sentiments Hostile To The Union—The Dexter Band "Play It" On The Democrats—Interviews With Men Who Participated—Scenes At Barton's Grove—Treasonable Talk—The Dinner Cooked On The Vice-President's Stove.

Dexter, the largest town in Penobscot County, was the home of some strong Union men, when the war broke out in 1861, and she had, also, within her borders, some whose whole sympathy was with those who were trying to destroy the Union of the States, and, under the plea of being "States Rights Men," and "Peace Men," said, and did all in their power, to block the wheels of the Federal Government. The Union men early responded to their country's call, and freely enlisted at the office, which had been opened by Mr. N. Dustin. Indeed, eighty men, a full company, enrolled themselves there, but owing to orders, which are mentioned in the history of the local events of Bangor, were disbanded, but later on were re-enlisted and entered the army, going to the front as a portion of the Sixth Regiment.

As in other places, war meetings were held, and the people gathered, were addressed by such men as the Hon. Lewis Barker, and others. From time to time the required quotas were filled, the town always showing a spirit of liberality, although opposed at every step by the opposition, many of whom were large tax payers. At one time the town had a standing offer of one hundred dollars bounty, in addition to all other bounties, for any man who would enlist and be credited to Dexter. When the proposition was first made to pay this sum, the "secesh" element raised the point that the town could not legally give it, that it would require some change in the then existing laws,—but, not disturbed by this, Mr. Dustin raised the necessary funds on his own notes, having full faith that his townsmen at the right time, and in the right place, would make the amount good to him, which they did.

When the Draft came there was the same anxiety, and the same scenes enacted as in other towns, although it would seem that there was not the same spirit of patriotism abroad there as was seen elsewhere. Out of thirty-five men drafted at one time, no less than thirteen fled the county, and in some cases the country too.

The "secesh" element began operations early, forming what they were pleased to term a "Democratic Club," which was composed of the men who dared to place themselves on record as against the Government. Although using a party name, this club was not a democratic gathering, doing great dishonor to the loyal men who enrolled themselves under the banner of Jameson. The democratic party was for war, and it was the opposition to this sentiment that gathered and adopted a motto of "Peace among Brethren." Early in 1863, this party began to "talk up" the matter of having a grand open air meeting, it being suggested that

Independence day would be the proper time to declare their sentiments, and to discourage what Emery termed an "Unholy War." Finally an executive committee was chosen, letters and circulars freely sent out among the faithful, many of whom lived in the adjoining towns, and particularly in Charleston; advertisements were inserted in such papers as would advertise their gathering, and finally they made Mr. A. L. Barton chairman, with full power to "proceed with the proceedings," as one of the members put the motion.

Mr. Barton lived then as now, on the Garland Road, about three miles from town. In the rear of his house stood a twenty acre wood lot, or grove, of hard wood, containing only two soft wood trees. It is a beautiful spot, and a fit place for a much better gathering than the one which proposed to meet there. At first Mr. Barton was instructed to give an estimate on the probable cost of a first class dinner, but, later on was told to "go ahead" and get up just the biggest kind of a "feed" he could. He now raised a flag across the road in front of his house, and by the middle of June was hard at work, perfecting the arrangements for the "Convention." In speaking to the author about it, Mr. Barton said:

"The first thing I did was to buy a cow, to be roasted whole, and she weighed nigh onto twenty-two hundred, and I paid one hundred and seventy-five dollars for her. Then I went to Bangor to buy other supplies. I bought a barrel of corned-beef, six barrels of flour, and two barrels of sugar, of R. S. Morrison.

Then I bought seven barrels of tumblers, and a big lot of knives and forks, the folks agreeing that I could return what was left. I went to see my friend, Henry A. Wood, who, though he did not agree with me in politics, yet was always a good friend. I wanted to hire a stove suitable to cook on, with all the fixings, and he took me up stairs and showed me a nice, big stove, and asked me if it would do. I told him I thought it would, and he then told me it was a stove that belonged to Hannibal Hamlin, but that it was stored there, and that he had the letting of it. I asked him if Mr. Hamlin would allow it to be used by me, to cook a peace dinner on, and he told me that it would be "all right." I took it home, and on that stove all the food was cooked. We cooked piles of stuff, and my wife did all of it, except what the neighbor's girls helped. Amongst other food, she cooked up seven barrels of fried-cakes, or what you call doughnuts. In the grove we had eight tables, each nearly one hundred feet long, and they were full of people twice. I got fifty cents for each dinner, and took in all, nearly eight hundred dollars, though some didn't pay. When I got all fixed up, all the help paid, and their receipts taken, I found there was eighty-four dollars left over. That I gave to the Club, but they voted to give it to me for my trouble. I think we had ten thousand people on the grounds that day, and the procession reached from my house to Dexter, nigh onto three miles. I tell you it was a big time."

Undoubtedly there were fifteen thousand people, in and about Dexter that day, and it is said to be a fact, as Mr. Barton states, that the procession reached from the town to the grove. As the head of it marched away, escorting the distinguished guests and speakers, the loyal men secured the Dexter Band, which, on being stationed near by the line, struck up the tune "John Brown's Body," while others held out hats and boxes for contributions. The marching "Peace Men" and their families, thinking it a part of the regular show, "chipped in," quite liberally, and applauded the tune, which was the only one the band would play. Quite a sum was realized, and quite a time was enjoyed with it, by the Union youngsters, and as may be supposed, the deluded people were mad when they learned of the neat trick, which had been played upon them.

At the grove, the multitude was addressed by the Hon. Moses McDonald, of Portland; Abraham Sanborn, Esq., of Bangor; Hon. Adams Treat, of Frankfort, and Henry Hudson, Esq., of Guilford. For music they employed the Guilford and Corinth Bands. One of these bands had forgotten some of its earlier expressions, as they once voted "confusion to all rebels," and also volunteered to "play free at any Union flag raising this side of New Orleans."

In 1864, there was held another of these "Peace Meetings," at the same grove, and from "The Democrat," which had been re-established, we take the following account, printed July 12th, 1864. A perusal of the utterances will at once show that the speakers were either the most deluded of men, or were villains of the deepest dye, bent on misrepresenting existing facts, and striving in every way to injure the Government.

THE GREAT PEACE MEETING.

"The Great Peace Meeting of the Democracy of Eastern Maine, at Barton's Grove, in Dexter, on the Fourth of July, was the grandest political demonstration that has ever taken place in this State. The day was most auspicious. The fine rain of Saturday afternoon and night had satisfied the thirsty earth and completely laid the dust, and the air was clear, cool and fragrant. The sun had hardly risen before the people began to assemble. They came in long lines from the valleys of the Penobscot, the Piscataquis, and the Kennebec, and from Union river, and even far off Aroostook was represented there. As the morning hours rolled on, the roads from every quarter centering at the grove became black with carriages as far as the eye could reach. By ten o'clock the great grove was densely thronged with thousands of men, women and children, and yet the great procession had not appeared. At length the inspiring strains of music were heard, and the head of the procession was seen coming over the hill towards Dexter Village, escorted by the East Corinth Band, and under the chief marshalship of Jesse Nutting, Esq., of Parkman. Far away towards the rear, in the midst of the long line was also the Hartland Band. It was half-past eleven o'clock before the procession had wound its long length through the grove. The meeting was immediately called to order by Stephen D. Jennings, Esq., of Garland, and organized by the choice of officers. The immense audience was then entertained by excellent music from the two bands in attendance. The meeting was opened by a fervent and ardent prayer for the country and the restoration of Peace, by the chaplin of the day, the Rev. Mr. Lyford, of Dexter. After prayer, the Declaration of Independence was recited in a earnest and effective manner, by Master J. Wesley Jones, of Dexter, and the President then in happy language introduced the orator of the day, the Hon. C. Chauncy Burr, of New York. As Mr. Burr stepped forward the immense throng arose to their feet, and received him with loud and prolonged cheers. The speech of Mr. Burr will be found on the outside of the paper to-day. It is a masterly piece of eloquence and power; but to have been appreciated it should have been heard as it fell from his lips. No language of ours can give any idea of its effect upon the audience. *The seed has been sown; may it bear its fruit!*"

After Mr. Burr's speech, the throng made its way to the dinner park, which had been enclosed in a delightful part of the grove, where the Committee of Arrangements had spread eight tables, each one of which was nearly two hundred feet long. They were covered with clean, white cotton cloth, through the munificence of S. S. Drew, Esq., of this city. In an inconceivable short space of time, these tables were filled with twenty-five hundred people, of both sexes; and yet, again and again, were they spread and re-spread, and filled and re-filled, during the afternoon.

On the assembling of the multitude, after dinner, the President introduced S. S. Drew, Esq., of Bangor. Mr. Drew made a brief and happy speech. He paid a glowing tribute to the great speech of Mr. Burr, and to the thousands of ladies in attendance. He said that Judge Kent, at the late inauguration of the Soldier's Monument, in Bangor, had declared that the ladies would not permit this war to end, even if the men were inclined to close it. He said that the vast audience of ladies before him, who had, with true womanly sympathy, so unmistakably expressed their approbation of the Peace sentiments, so eloquently uttered by the orator of the day, gave the lie to Judge Kent's slander and libel on the character of the women of Maine. Mr. Drew dwelt with great force upon the importance of adhering to the great doctrine of the Sovereignty of the States, as the sheet anchor of our liberties. His remarks were received with great favor and applause.

The President next introduced *Marcellus Emery*, of Bangor. Mr. Emery said: That he had hoped to be excused from speaking to-day, but that he dared not disobey the commands of the President, who was then a man in authority, having, on that day, an immense Democratic army at his back, and he 'had but to say to this man, go, and he goeth, and to this man come, and he cometh.' He had, however, no heart to address them on this occasion. The same pall of darkness, that settled down upon their souls, oppressed his own. He would not deceive them if he could, he could not if he would. They were standing to-day amidst the wreck and ruins of the most glorious Republic that ever adorned the earth, and over the graves of buried liberties. The gentle summer breeze, which was sighing so mournfully through that grand old forest, seemed to him to be playing a requiem of the Union, buried beyond the hope of resurrection.

Four years ago, he had seen the very flag that floated from yonder liberty pole, unfurled for the first time in the city of Bangor. There was then upon it, in the language of Governor Seymour, 'a star for every State, and a State for every star.' As he looked upon that banner now, he felt that the cluster of stars only remained there now a mocking emblem of a glory, and a joy which once existed, but are now gone forever. He almost felt that he could reach forth his hand, and pluck from that mocking constellation, the bright star, that glitters in the name of Maine, but he would leave the stripes behind, as a fitting emblem of her present degradation. He came before them to repeat his old story. He came to exhort them to put an end to the unholy strife. Sixteen months ago he addressed them in their town hall, at the village. *He then told them of the impossibility of conquering the South.* He had foretold there, how army after army would be called for and swept away, if the war should be continued. There were some, on that occasion, who regarded his words, but in the rear of the hall, there were many young men, who seemed to mock at his warnings. Where are those young men to-day? How many of them may not be sleeping their last sleep, on the bloody fields that stretch from the Rapidan, away beyond the banks of the James.

He would not appeal to Democrats to exert their power and influence to end the war. Their hearts were already in the work; but he would appeal to Republicans, to all who had hitherto given their support to the war in the vain hope that it would be productive of fruit meet for the sacrifice made, to lay aside all passion, all party associations, and in the awful presence of the appalling events of the past sixty days, to unite with all good men and put an end to this accursed war. There were men, however, that we could not hope to reach or move by any appeal. He meant the President, his Cabinet, and his Congress.

There is a poetical legend that when the midnight storm rages, and the wild waves of the ocean lash the rock bound shores of St. Helena, as they did on the eventful night when the spirit of the great Napoleon took its departure from earth, the shades of a drummer-boy appears upon the island and beats the roll-call upon his spectral drum. The shades of the soldiers of the great chieftain throughout Europe and Egypt respond to that call, and over the ocean they come from the fields of Austerlitz, Lutzen, Borodino and from the base of the pyramids, all arrayed in spectral armor. The ghostly line is formed—long interminable lines—and then Napoleon himself appears upon his spectral charger, and reviews that ghostly army until the morning light scatters the mists and myths away.

The speaker would have such a legend for this unhappy country too. He would have the President, his Cabinet and his Congress gathered on the dome of the Capitol; he would have the shade of of some drummer boy appear upon the scene, and beat his ghostly roll call. Then let the shades of the myriads who have fallen in this ungodly strife come forth from their graves. Let the ghostly columns come from Gettysburg, from Shiloh, from Fredericksburg, Chancellorsville, and from those hundreds of other battle fields that stain the land from the Potomac to the Rio Grande; let them wind through and fill the streets of Washington; let them cover the hills and valleys around; then let that President, that Cabinet, and that Congress look upon the work of their hands. What family, what man, what woman in this vast audience, would not find a representative of their homes in that innumerable throng of shades? If such a sight would not move our rulers to Peace, 'twere vain to hope for peace from them. In concluding, Mr. Emery said there was an arm contending against us stronger than any arm of flesh—it was the omnipotent arm of the God of Liberty."

In the forenoon Chauncey Burr said: "Looking over the plain of my country what do I see? A battlefield and a graveyard. I see at one end of this plain a people fighting for their liberties; and at the other end, a people trying to throw them down faster than a mountebank tyrant can pick them up. I see every fourth woman in mourning, and every little child an orphan.

Where there were fruitful fields, I see a gulf of blood. I see brutal butcher's shambles in the church where stood the altars of religion.

I see judges, forgetful of their oath of office, yielding to the scandalous delusion of the hour, allow the courts of sovereign and independent States to be made null by act of Congress.

I see generals and provost marshals sitting in the seats of judges, and military commissions, in the place of jurors. I see virtuous and unoffending citizens dragged to the Bastiles, not only without law, but in violation of both the organic and statute laws of the land.

I see a debt amounting to more than one half the value of the property of the North.

I see a corpse in every family, and want scowling at every man's door.

I see the rich madly crowding along on the road to poverty, and the poor approaching the brink of beggary.

And I see the Goddess of Liberty, like Caesar, writhing in the midst of our Senate, covering herself with her mantle as she receives thrice times three and twenty wounds, and breathing out her last with an *et tu quoque mi fili.*"

There were of course some local disturbances in Dexter, on account of this "secesh" element. One Southern sympathizer was given a ride, "straddle-bug fashion," on a razor-like rail, and the older inhabitants tell with much glee of the discomfiture which came to a party of young bloods, who undertook to punish one of the women who denounced, on every occasion, the Union boys, and always seemingly rejoiced at the news of Union defeats. At last—so the story goes—it was concluded to punish her, and the occasion of the news of the death of Lincoln, was thought to be one on which she would utter some treasonable sentiment. A large hayrack was procured in which to bring her to town, and quite a party started for her home. Arriving at a hollow near her residence, a halt was made, while two men proceeded to the door of her house, just over the hill, to relate the news of the assassination, when it was expected she would rejoice and commit herself. Now the old lady happened to be in her buttery, saw the party as they approached, and "smelt a mice," as the saying is. She kept cool however, and, when a few moments later a knock came on her door, appeared with her sleeves rolled up and arms covered with flour, as was also her apron.

"Good morning!" said the spokesman.

"Good day, gentlemen!" was the answer.

"We have come up, Aunt ———, to tell you some bad news."

"For the Lord's sake, you don't tell! What on arth is the matter?"

"Well Aunt, President Lincoln has been shot."

For a second only, there was a bright gleam in the old lady's eye, and then she hesitated, but not long. Reaching her ample arms down under her equally ample apron she brought it up, covering her face and head, and cried.

"Oh dear! Don't, don't tell me that! Has our dear, good President really gone?"

For a moment the man looked at her thunderstruck, and then, seeing that the old lady had them, shook his fist in her face, and said:

"You d—d old she devil, we'll pay you for this," and then departed. It was some time before they were allowed to forget the hayrack trip to the suburbs.

CHAPTER XXX.

The History Of The Twenty-Second Regiment—To Fortress Monroe—Newport News—New Orleans—Up The Mississippi—Baton Rouge—Disease And Death—Donaldson—Irish Bend—Quelling Negro Insurrections—A Gallant Charge—Port Hudson—Jerrard In Command—He Is Placed Under Arrest—Banks Again Displays His Dislike Of Maine Officers—Capture Of Port Hudson—Return Of The Regiment—The Twenty-Sixth—An Extensive Tour—A Little Fighting—Some Guard Duty—Returning Home—The Third Battery—The Twenty-Eighth—Account Of The Formation—Sleeping In Beecher's Church—To The Front—Regimental History.

The Twenty-Second Regiment left Camp John Pope, Bangor, October 21st, 1862, and arrived at Washington on the 24th. On the following day it was ordered to Arlington Heights, and placed temporarily in the Third Brigade, Casey's Division, Reserved Army Corps, commanded by Colonel Fessenden, of the Twenty-fifth Maine. Here they remained until November 3d, employed principally in drilling. On that day they received orders to proceed to Fortress Monroe. November 5th, they embarked in the "S. R. Spaulding," and moved down the Potomac, reaching their destination on the 7th. It was the first regiment of the famous Banks expediton, to rendezvous at Fortress Monroe. Not being premitted to land at the fort, the regiment proceeded to Newport News, where comfortable barracks were provided. Remaining here until the 2d of December, the regiment embarked for New Orleans, arriving there on the 15th. On the 16th they moved up the river, reaching Baton Rouge at daylight in the morning, where they landed without opposition, being the first regiment to land and occupy the works. Here they suffered much from sickness and death; and it was only after the regiment entered more active service that the prevalence of disease abated. Here died, among others, First Lieutenant W. Prince Hersey.

On the 26th of March, the regiment, together with the rest of Grover's Division, boarded river steamers, went to Donaldson, thence marched to Prashear City, reaching that place April 11th. Previous to leaving, Col. Jerrard was taken ill and the command devolved upon Lieut. Col. Putnam. The object of this movement was to get possession of Western Louisiana, then held by the rebel forces.

On the 13th, a portion of the Division, including seven companies of the Twenty-Second, proceeded to Irish Bend in the rear of Franklin, and encamped for the night. Early on the next morning the force was moved towards Franklin, the Third Brigade to the front, followed by the First. A fight took place in an extensive cane field, in which the enemy were repulsed and driven.

From this time until June 9th, the Twenty-Second were moved from point to point, doing guard duty, suppressing negro insurrections, etc. On that day Col. Jerrard was informed that in one hour Grover's Division would make an assault. This was at Port Hudson. Col. Jerrard was ordered to advance on the works in front of the batteries, and if possible to carry them. The skirmish line was called in, and at the appointed hour the regiment was moving forward. The ground over which the charge was to be made was naturally rough, and to further impede the progress of the assailing forces the "rebs" had covered it with fallen timber.

The Ninetieth and One Hundred Thirty-first New York regiments were on the right and left respectively, and these, becoming engaged, so attracted the attention of the enemy that the Twenty-Second was enabled to work forward unmolested, and apparently unobserved, until the skirmish line had nearly reached the outer works. A portion of the advance, being separated from their comrades, entered the works, driving the enemy, but, being unsupported failed to maintain their position. Capt. Gilman and Lieuts. Anson and Knowles were in command, Anson being taken prisoner. At this time the New York regiments were repulsed, the enemy immediately turning their attention to the Twenty-Second, driving them back to their former position. In this attack Capt. Henry Crosby fell mortally wounded.

Still bent on reducing Port Hudson, the commanding officer appointed June 14th as the day for another, and the third assault, which, like the previous ones, resulted in defeat. Col. Halcom was shot dead while attempting to rally his brigade, and the command devolved upon Col. Jerrard.

In this fight, after Jerrard had assumed command, he attempted to arouse the skulking One Hundred Thirty-First New York, and persuaded them to charge, but the men refused duty, and the only available troops were the few remaining officers and men of the Twenty-Second, who stood bravely by their commander. Knowing that any attempt to carry the works with this handful of men was useless, and believing that neither duty to country nor to the men required of him any further attempts in that line, Jerrard withdrew. The next day, on representations made against him by Col. Morgan, Col. Jerrard was placed under arrest, but no charges were preferred. On the 22d an order from Gen. Banks was received, dismissing him from the service, on the charge "of using discouraging and insubordinate language in the presence of a number of officers and men while forming the Brigade for the charge." July 8th Port Hudson surrendered, and on the 24th the regiment left for Bangor, where it was mustered out August 16th.

The Twenty-sixth Maine left Bangor October 23d, 1862, for Washington, thence to Alexandria, Fortress Monroe, Newport News, New Orleans, where they quarantined on account of the small-pox; thence to Port Hudson, where they participated in the same battles as did the Twenty-Second, and after the capture of that place were employed on guard duty. They were not afforded such opportunities as were given Maine regiments in Virginia, to distinguish themselves, but did such duty as was put upon them, well. They returned to Bangor August 9th, and were mustered out on the 17th.

The Third Battery, Captain James G. Swett, left Augusta, March 19th, 1862, for Portland, where they remained in barracks at Island Park until April 1st, when they left for Washington, arriving there on the 3d. They remained in camp on Capitol Hill until the fourteenth, when they were ordered under General McDowell, to act as Pontooniers. On November 7th the pontoon trains were ordered to the Engineer's Department, and went to Fort Lincoln, where they engaged in building "Battery Maine."

March 28th '63, the Third battery was transferred to the First Heavy, and with them remained in defence of Washington. Captain Swett was discharged May 14th, and First Lieutenant E. R. Mayo promoted to the captaincy. From this time to the disbandment of the Heavy Artillery, the history of the battery is identical with that of the First Heavy. After December 11th, '63, the original members were eligible for re-enlistment as veteran volunteers, and by the 5d of January, '64, seventy-two men had re-enlisted as veterans. The battery then being a veteran organization, was entitled to furlough.

On January 18th, '64, Captain Mayo, with two officers and the re-enlisted men, left Fort Sumner for Augusta, Maine, for veteran furlough and re-organization. A detachment of twenty-four men, not veterans, remained at Fort Sumner, under command of Lieutenant S. J. Oaks. On February 22d, Captain Mayo (then at Augusta), received a telegram from Washington, ordering the Third battery to be detatched from the regiment, and to report at Camp Barry, D. C., as light artillery. They reached Camp Barry on the 28th, and were joined by the detatchment left at Fort Sumner, and by some recruits. Owing to some delay, the equipments did not arrive till the last of April. They consisted of six three-inch rifles, and the usual small arms, etc. On the 5th of July, the battery left Washington for City Point, from there to the front of Petersburg, arriving July 9th, and were then assigned to the Third Division, Ninth army corps, and took up a position before the rebel works on Cemetery Hill. Here they remained till August 19th, being engaged almost daily. On the 22d, the battery went into position in Fort Rice. The Third division, Ninth corps, having been consolidated with the First division, the battery was transferred to the Artillery Reserve, Army of the Potomac, August 30th, but still retained its position in Fort Rice. On the 25th of October they were withdrawn from Fort Rice, and sent to the defences of City Point. Here they remained till May 3d, '65, when they took up the march to Washington, and went into camp near Fairfax Seminary, where they remained until the 2d of June, when the start for Augusta was made. The battery was mustered out at Augusta on the 17th of June, and finally paid on the 22d. Owing to its position at City Point, the battery was not actively engaged at the final operations about Petersburg, but during the campaign performed as arduous duty as any, and by its vigilant and watchful work earned the highest praise from the Chief of Artillery.

The Twenty-Eighth Regiment, nine months men, was recruited from various parts of the State, three companies coming from Washington, one from Lincoln, one from Knox, and one from Hancock Counties. Four of the companies were made up at Camp John Pope, Bangor, the balance at Augusta. They left the latter place October 26th, 1862, the first of the nine months men to leave the State, although the last mustered in, proceeding by rail and boat to New York. On reaching Jersey City, the regiment was ordered to occupy Fort Schuyler, New York bay. Here they exchanged their Austin guns for new Enfield rifles, and on November 26th they were ordered to East New York, a suburb of Brooklyn, on Long Island. As they landed at the ferry in Brooklyn, they were met by Rev. Henry Ward Beecher, who chatted with the officers and men, remarking at one time on the neat, clean appearance of the men. Later on he invited them into the church, to pass the night. As the men approached the entrance, each one, without orders, took off his muddy boots at the door, and the most critical examination in the morning failed to find a book disturbed or a particle of dirt upon the rich carpets and cushions. Mr. Beecher congratulated them on their manliness, and, at his request, some wealthy members of the church cared for some sick men then with the regiment.

In January, the 17th being the day the regiment sailed for New Orleans via Fortress Monroe, which place they reached January 29th. Here they were moved from point to point by the much over-rated Banks, and like the other Maine regiments under the command of that politician, were required to do much hard work that was useless, and were needlessly subjected to exposure and disease. Companies were detached from the regiment from time to time and did, whenever they were given an opportunity, good service, and were equal in every way to the Maine men in Virginia, who, under able leaders, distinguished themselves.

After much service and hard work, the regiment proceeded up the Mississippi river to Cairo, Ill., and thence by cars via the N. Y. Central Railroad, etc., to Augusta, having made a complete circuit of the Confederate States, save Texas. August 31st they were mustered out, after having served nearly one year.

CHAPTER XXXI.

The Eighth Regiment—Its Organization—The Capture Of Hilton Head—Colonel Strickland Resigns—Capture Of Fort Pulaski—The First Emancipation Proclamation—Capture Of Jacksonville, Fla.—The Furlough—Presentation To Colonel Rust—Again At The Front—Drury's Bluff—Cold Harbor—In Front Of Petersburg—Bermuda Hundred—Forts Gregg and Baldwin—Appomattox C. H.—Killed And Wounded—Return Of The Regiment.

The organization of the Eighth Regiment was as follows:

Company A, Captain WOODMAN, Wilton.
Company B, Captain TWITCHELL, Patten.
Company C, Captain STRICKLAND, Livermore.
Company D, Captain BOYNTON, Detroit.
Company E, Captain HUTCHINGS, New Portland.
Company F, Captain HEMINGWAY, Sanford.
Company G, Captain RICE, Ellsworth.
Company H, Captain RUST, Camden.
Company I, Captain MCARTHUR, Limmington.
Company K, Captain CONANT, Oldtown.

The Field officers, were elected by ballot from the Line officers, and were commissioned by the Governor. The regiment was

BREVET BRIG.-GEN. J. D. RUST.

mustered into the U. S. service, at Augusta, on September 7th, 1861, by Captain Thomas Hight, U. S. A.

The original roll of Field and Staff officers, at the organization of the regiment, was as following:

Colonel, LEE STRICKLAND, Livermore.

Lieut. Col., JOHN D. RUST, Camden.

Major, JOS. S. RICE, Ellsworth.

Adjutant, JAMES DINGLEY, JR., Auburn.

Quartermaster, A. H. STRICKLAND, Livermore.

Surgeon, PAUL M. FISHER, Corinna.

Asst. Surgeon, JNO. S. HOUGHTON, Solon.

Chaplain, HENRY C. HENRIES, Lincoln.

Sergeant Major, EDGAR G. PERRY, Rockland.

Quartermaster Sergt., JOHN M. ROBBINS, Greene.

Commissary Sergt., FRANKLIN GRAY, Skowhegan.

Hospital Steward, W. W. WEST, Waterville.

The regiment had barely time to select their clothing, after being mustered into service, and left on the ninth of September for Washington. They reported to Gen. Egbert L. Viele, of the U. S. Army, at Hampstead, Long Island, and were merged into his brigade, and immediately moved to Washington.

From Washington they reported at Fortress Monroe, and then rendezvoused at Annapolis, from which place they left on the steamer 'Ariel,' for Hilton Head, S. C. After a voyage of twenty-two days, encountering heavy gales and storms, they reached the place of destination. Soon after, the bombardment commenced, resulting in the capture of Hilton Head and Port Royal. The "Wabash," of the navy, and smaller naval vessels, all opened upon the defences of Hilton Head. Much credit is due the "Wabash," and her brave officers, as well as the other gunboats engaged in the bombardment. The "Wabash," notwithstanding being a wooden vessel, encountered the batteries on the shore, and opened on them with terrific effect, and at times, doing great execution, and nearly silencing the fort, until at last it was believed that the infantry could capture the enemy's works. They landed under the protection of the fleet, and immediately took possession of the works.

The Eighth Maine was one of the first regiments to set foot on Southern soil. They were armed with flint-lock guns, re-vamped over, and right well did they use them, until finally they were furnished with arms of a more modern pattern.

The 8th of November, 1861, finds Col. Rust with his command at Hilton Head, S. C., Col. Strickland having resigned on account of ill health, being unable to withstand the malaria of the Southern climate, from which disease he suffered until his death. The vacancies caused by Col. Rust's promotion were filled by Capts. Woodman, Twitchell, and Hemingway.

Col. Rust's regiment was for months constantly engaged in throwing up breast-works, and erecting needed fortifications, for the extraordinary exigencies of the service; still remaining in the Brigade of Gen. Viele, at Hilton Head.

General Viele, was from New York State, from the regular army, and one of the finest officers and best drilled disciplinarians in the service. He published a "Hand Book," for the use of the army, which was adopted by Congress, and very generally used for the government of the army in the field, in the Department of the South.

The Eighth Maine took a prominent part in the capture of Fort Pulaski, Georgia, on the Savannah river. It was found necessary, in order to reduce Fort Pulaski, to cut off the retreat and capture the garrison, to erect batteries on Jones' Island, at the edge of the Savannah river, between Savannah and Fort Pulaski. In order to accomplish this work, a road was built for a long distance with sand bags. These were carried by soldiers and at the end near the river, a mound high enough to protect the batteries from the rising of the water, was built. At low water the guns were taken along this road and mounted on the elevation of earth made by sand bags. If the soldiers were overtaken by the tide, they were forced to climb trees, and remain aloft until the tide ebbed. This battery proved to be a valuable ally in the reduction of Fort Pulaski.

On Tybee Island were numerous batteries, planted behind natural earth-works of sand, thrown up, perhaps, centuries ago, with breaches in them at occasional intervals. Behind these elevations of sand, the Union batteries were erected at night, and in short range of the fort, unknown to the garrison. A corduroy road from Tybee Island, most of the way to these works, was built. This was made of small trees, inverted and bound together with withes and laid upon the marsh. The batteries and mortars were transported over this road to localities where they were mounted. One heavy mortar slipped off the carriage on which it was being moved, and fell outside the road into the marsh, and sunk so rapidly that it was impossible to extricate it. When all preparations were ready for the reduction of the fort, the batteries were opened and Col. Rust placed in command of the forces. Several detachments of the Eighth were detailed to man the guns, and several companies of the same regiment were intrenched near the river, to be ready in case of attack in the rear. The second day it was discovered that a breach had been made in the fort, and the fire was concentrated on this point, until the aperture was sufficiently large to permit soldiers to enter. Preparations were made to storm the fort that night, but before the sun had gone down a white flag was raised on the fort, and in obedience to it, Col. Rust and Gen. Gilmore went to the fort and received the formal surrender. Gen'ls. Hunter and Benham decided that the flag of the Eighth Maine should be raised on the walls of Fort Pulaski, in token of the gallantry of Col. Rust and his regiment.

Maj. Gen. Hunter, who commanded the Department of the South, was of the regular army. He served with distinction in the Mexican War, and was a most gallant soldier. He issued the first Emancipation Proclamation in the South, he seeing the results of the momentous crisis, which demanded the freedom of the bondsmen; notwithstanding, the President deemed the order premature, and caused it to be rescinded. It will, however, be remembered that the President, within a few months, issued a similar order, which was greeted with joy and thanksgiving throughout the North.

After the surrender, Colonel Rust was placed in command of the post at Tybee, but owing to the bad health of the men, they returned to Hilton Head. Much credit is due to Captain McArthur and the officers of Company I, and Captain True and the officers of Company H, for the bravery of themselves and of their commands, in working the batteries during the bombardment; as well as to all the other officers and soldiers of the Eighth Maine.

The regiment remained at Hilton Head, until the spring of 1863. They were employed in guard duty both at that place and at Beaufort, S. C., Colonel Rust being in command of the post. On the 19th of March, they were ordered to Jacksonville, Fla. They landed under the fire of the enemy, and the gun boats "Norwich" and "John Adams," were ordered to open fire in support of the troops. The enemy soon retired, and Colonel Rust, with his command occupied the city, with Colonel Rust in command of the force, and Captain Henry Boynton, Acting Provost Marshal. On the 25th, Colonel Rust ordered a reconnoissance in force, with the Eighth

Maine on the right, and drove the enemy's pickets, being under a hot fire all the while. The lines being satisfactorily established, on ground previously occupied by the rebels, Colonel Rust's command retired, with trifling loss.

March 29th, Colonel Rust received peremptory orders from General Hunter, to evacuate Jacksonville, and proceed to Beaufort with his command, to make preparations to assist in the contemplated attack on Charleston. They embarked for Stone River, where they lay on transports during the bombardment of Fort Sumpter, after which they returned to Beaufort. Subsequently they received orders to proceed to Charleston, but owing to a severe gale and storm, this attempt was abandoned, and they were obliged to return to Hilton Head, where they were engaged in doing guard and picket duty. While here the regiment re-enlisted for three years, and the veterans returned to Augusta. While in Augusta they presented Colonel Rust with a colonel's uniform, complete, including an elegant gold mounted sword, spurs and a very elaborate horse equipage, as a token of their high esteem of their commander. During their furlough, Colonel Rust made a successful application, through the Governor, for his regiment's transfer from the Department of the South, to the Army of the Potomac; the regiment having suffered intensely from sickness and debility, and being much reduced in vitality.

The soldiers who composed the Department of the South, had, not only the enemy to contend with, but also the yellow fever, small pox, swamp fever, malaria and other life destroying agencies, which reduced the ranks more speedily and effectively than did the Southern Confederacy. Gen. Mitchell, who was sent to take command of this department, died of the yellow-fever soon after his arrival, and his case was but one of the many. Gen. Mitchell was a very fine officer, and his death was greatly regretted by the entire command.

On the 17th of April, 1864, the regiment was ordered to Washington, and then to Alexandria, where Col. Rust was placed in command of the Second Provisional Brigade, Third Division. On the 25th of April, Col. Rust was ordered, by Maj. Gen. Casey, to report to Maj. Gen. Butler, at Fortress Monroe, and subsequently to Gen. Ames, at Bermuda Hundred. On the 30th, Col. Rust was placed in command of the Second Division of the Army of the James.

The remainder of the regiment continued at Beaufort, until April 13th, 1864, when they were ordered to join the regiment in the Army of the James, at Bermuda Hundred, where they took part in all the active operations of that body. On the 16th of May, they participated in the engagement at Drury's Bluff, losing three men killed, sixty-four wounded, and twenty-nine taken prisoners. On the 27th of May, they proceeded to White House Landing, and from thence, on the 31st, to Cold Harbor. In the meantime they had been assigned to the Second Brigade, Second Division, Eighteenth Corps.

On the morning of June 3d, they took part in the assault of the enemy's lines, losing during the day, ten men killed, fifty-three wounded and sixteen taken prisoners. On June 12th, they marched to White House Landing, and from there to Petersburg, where on the 15th, 16th and 17th, they were engaged with the enemy. On the 18th, they made a successful attack, and carried a portion of the enemy's lines, losing eleven men killed, and thirty-nine wounded. From this time until August 25th, they remained in the trenches, in front of Petersburg, under constant fire, and engaged on duties of the most exhaustive character. On that day, they moved to the opposite side of the Appomattox, going into works before Bermuda Hundred. On the night of September 28th, they crossed to the north side of the James river, with the Eighteenth and Tenth Corps, and were engaged in the successful assault of the following morning, on the enemy's works, near Chapin's Farm. October 27th, they took part in the assault on the enemy's line, near the old battle-field of Fair Oaks, and here the regiment lost heavily. The next day they returned to the trenches near Chapin's Farm.

On December 5th, upon the re-organization of the Tenth and Eighteenth Corps, this regiment was assigned to the Fourth Brigade, First Division, Twenty-Fourth Corps, and moved to near Deep Bottom, taking position in the fort at Spring Hill.

On the 16th of December, they lost five men killed, and six wounded, in a reconnoisance made by the enemy, on the right of the Union lines, in the vicinity of Spring Hill. They remained near Spring Hill until the 27th of March, 1865, when they proceeded towards Hatcher's Run, where they arrived on the next day, and remained doing picket duty until the 2d of April. On that day they participated in the assault and capture of Forts Bragg and Baldwin, and on the 3d proceeded towards Barkersville, which place they reached on the 5th. On the 6th, they bore an honorable part in the engagement at Rice's Station, and on the 9th, in that at Appomattox C. H. After the surrender of Lee, they, with the rest of the troops of the Twenty-Fourth corps, proceeded to Richmond, where they were camped till August. They were then sent to Manchester, and remained there until ordered to Fortress Monroe, in November, at which place they remained until the 18th of January, 1886. On that day they were mustered out of service by Lieutenant Wm. Harper, Asst. Commissary of Musters, and then proceeded to Augusta, Maine, where they were finally paid and discharged.

The following officers of the regiment were killed in action or died of their wounds, during the war: Henry E. Tozier, Waterville, Captain; Charles F. Monroe, Livermore, First Lieutenant; Albert F. Kyes, Jay, Second Lieutenant; Lorenzo Warren, Patten, Second Lieutenant; John Stevens, Morrill, Second Lieutenant; Charles C. Carr, Belfast, Second Lieutenant; Warren H. Hill, Exeter, Second Lieutenant.

The Regiment bore a most efficient and prominent part in the following engagements: Destruction of Richmond and Petersburg Railroad; Swift Creek; Chester Station; Drury's Bluff; Port Harrison; Chapin's Farm; Laurel Hill; Cold Harbor; Rice's Station; Petersburg; Forts Gregg and Baldwin, and Appomattox C. H.

CHAPTER XXXII.

The Eleventh Regiment—Its Organization And Officers—To The Front—Siege Of Yorktown—The Battle Of Seven Pines—In The Rifle Pits—Honorable And Dangerous Duty—The Best Axe-Men Of The Army—The Mathews County Invasion Destruction Of The Salt Works—Twenty-One Days Afloat—Presentation To Colonel Plaisted—At Morris Island---The Florida Trip---On To Richmond—Death Of Lieutenant Colonel Spofford---To New York---Clover Hill---Patrol Duty---Return Of The Eleventh.

The Eleventh Regiment was the first raised in the State at the direct expense of the general Government.

The organization was as follows:

JOHN C. CALDWELL, Colonel.
H. M. PLAISTED, Lieutenant Colonel.
WILLIAM H. SHAW, Major.
Company A, Captain PENNELL, of Portland.
Company B, Captain KIMBALL, of Augusta.
Company C, Captain CAMPBELL, of Cherryfield.
Company D, Captain HARVEY, of Weston.
Company E, Captain STRAW, of Bangor.
Company F, Captain DAVIS, of Gardiner.
Company G, Captain SPOFFORD, of Dedham.
Company H, Captain NASH, of Gray.
Company I. Captain POMEROY, of Bancroft.
Company K, Captain HILL, of Stetson.

The regiment left Augusta, Nov. 13th, 1861, and proceeded to Washington, where it went into camp on Meridian Hill. Here they arrived on the 16th, and on January 1st, they went into winter quarters, and there remained inactive till March 28th, 1862, when they with their division (Casey's), moved for the Peninsula via. Alexandria. They encamped at Newport News, till April 6th. On the 17th, they advanced to before Yorktown, and on the 29th, were sharply engaged with the enemy. On May 4th, the enemy gave battle and the Eleventh was the first to plant our flag on the rebel works, after the enemy had vacated. On the following day the battle of Williamsburg took place, and this regiment bore a distinguished part. On the 13th, Colonel Caldwell was made a Brigadier General, for personal valor and soldierly conduct, and Lieutenant Colonel Plaisted was promoted to the command of the Eleventh. On the 23d, the regiment moved to Seven Pines, where they gave battle to the enemy on the 31st. During the advance the Eleventh was detailed to fell trees, build bridges, etc. In the battle of Seven Pines the regiment did honorable and gallant work.

Colonel Plaisted, with three companies charged the enemy, but was finally driven back. Of the ninty-three men led by Colonel Plaisted, fifty-two were killed or wounded.

After the battle, the Eleventh occupied the rifle pits of the rear defences until June 4th, when they moved to Bottom's Bridge, and afterwards to the high bluff near the railroad. They participated in the battles of Beaver Dam and Gaines' Mill, and at the latter, the Eleventh destroyed the bridge, thereby making safe the Army of the Potomac. It was a hazardous undertaking, and could only have been done by trained axe-men. For the next few days the Eleventh was almost continually in action, and on the 30th, took part in that bloody fight at White Oak Swamp. For five hours they were under the heaviest of the fire. During the retreat that followed, the Eleventh was the rear guard of the whole column, and so faithfully did their duty that not a man or even a knapsack was missing when they reached the James River. On July 1st, the regiment was in the reserve at the battle of Malvern Hill, and that night were again made rear guard of the retreating column. On the 2d, they arrived at Harrison's Landing, where they remained till August 16th, when they left for Yorktown, at which place they were engaged in the reconstruction of the fortifications until the latter part of November. While here the regiment suffered terribly from the severity of the labor and the general insalubrity of the climate—losing thirty-four men by death, and eighty by discharge on account of disability. During the latter part of the month, the regiment made an expedition into Mathews County, for the purpose of destroying salt works, upon which the rebel capitol depended in a great measure for its supply. The expedition was wholly successful and on their return, the commanding General ordered that "Mathews County," be inscribed upon the banners of the regiment. The regiment lost one commissioned officer, and one enlisted man, both taken prisoners. On December 11th, the regiment in company with three others, under command of General Nagle, penetrated the country to within a few miles of the Rappahannock, operating as an important diversion in rear of the Rebel army during the battle of Fredericksburg, and clearing five counties of rebels.

On the 26th of December, the regiment, with Nagle's Brigade, embarked for North Carolina, where it arrived, and landed at Morehead City, on the 1st of January, 1863, after a stormy passage, and went into camp at Carolina City. On the 20th of January, they again embarked, and arrived at Port Royal, on January 31st, but did not land till February 10th. During the twenty-one day's trip, seven men were lost by ship fever. While at St. Helena, a beautiful flag was presented to Colonel Plaisted, by the officers of the regiment. A few day's before leaving, the regiment received their four month's pay, in all some thirty thousand dollars. After a stay of about seven weeks, the regiment, on the 4th of April, embarked for Charleston, and on the 5th entered North Edisto Inlet. Here the regiment remained five days without landing, and the attack on Charleston having failed, left for Beaufort, S. C., where they arrived on the 11th. The Eleventh remained here until June 4th, when, on the arrival of General Gilmore, detatchments were sent as artillerists to Morris Island, where they served with great credit, during the siege of Forts Wagner and Sumpter. They were afterwards assigned by General Gilmore, to the "Swamp Angel" battery, and had the honor of firing the first shells into Charleston. From here they went to Fernandina, Fla., where besides doing heavy fatigue duty, they built a fortification for the town, requiring two thousand five hundred day's labor. The regiment left Florida October 6th, having been ordered to Morris Island, where it arrived on the 7th.

The regiment remained at Morris Island during the fall and winter of 1863, and did excellent service in the seige of Charleston. A large portion of the regiment was detached by General Gilmore, to work the large guns in Forts Gregg, Chatfield, and Wagner. In April, 1864, the Tenth corps was reorganized, and a large portion transported to Gloucester Point, Va., joining General Butler's command. The Eleventh was assigned to the Third Brigade, First Division, under command of Colonel Plaisted. On the 4th of May, they left for Weir Bottom, where they arrived on the 6th. On the 7th of May, a battle was fought at Port Walthall Junction, in which this brigade had an important part. On the 12th, nearly the entire army moved out and advanced upon Richmond. On the 16th, the enemy under Beauregard drove the Union forces back to the lines at Bermuda Hundred. The loss to the Eleventh, in this action was, twenty-four men killed and wounded. On the 17th, the regiment attacked Beauregard's train, had a fierce fight, and lost twenty-six killed and wounded. On June 2d, the regiment stood the brunt of the battle at Bermuda Hundred, and repulsed the enemy at every attack. The loss to the regiment during the day was forty-one killed and wounded, including five commissioned officers. Among the number mortally wounded was Lieutenant Colonel Spofford. From this time till August 14th, the regiment remained at or near Bermuda Hundred, and Deep Bottom, with companies H and A, detatched as a garrison on the bluff, a mile below Deep Bottom. The regiment engaged in numerous skirmishes and repulsed many attacks of the enemy during this time. On August 14th, the regiment entered the Seven Day's campaign, taking a conspicuous and honorable part. The amount of work they did may be judged from the loss, which was five commissioned officers, two field officers, three company commanders and one hundred and forty-four men, only four of whom were taken prisoners. On the morning of the 21st, they returned to Deep Bottom. On the 26th, the regiment, with its brigade moved to Petersburg, remaining to take its full share of work in the operations before that city until September 28th. They were in the trenches before the city for thirty days, performing heavy fatigue duty under fire, losing five men killed, besides many wounded. On the 28th, they left Petersburg and returned to Deep Bottom, and on the 29th, assisted in the attack on Spring Hill. The regiment, on the 30th, took up a position to the south of the New Market Road, after having made an advance on the Darbytown road, to within two miles of Richmond. Here they remained till the 7th of October. Several skirmishes took place near here and the Eleventh did their share of the work. On the 7th, a battle was fought on the New Market Road, in which the regiment took a most important part, and but for their bravery in holding their ground against the Alabama brigade, the result might have been vastly different. As it was the Union forces won, but at considerable loss to themselves. On the 13th, the regiment was under fire for ten hours, and captured the only prisoners of the day.

On the 27th, they again advanced on Richmond, drove the enemy into his main lines, and then retired. On the 29th, the Eleventh, with the brigade advanced on the enemy's lines, and by a daring charge, by this regiment, captured his works, and drove him in disorder. Although the time of many of the men had expired, they gladly volunteered for this fight, and acted with great bravery. On the 2d of November, one hundred of the men, whose time had expired, left for Maine, and the remainder, numbering in all four hundred and ninety, were left in charge of Lieutenant Maxfield. On the 3d, the regiment left for New York, being one of the number selected to accompany General

Butler, to assist in keeping the peace of the city, at the Presidential election. Only two hundred men could be mustered at this time, the remainder being in the hospital. Major Baldwin joined the regiment while at New York, and assumed command. On the 18th, the regiment returned to the front. On the 12th of November, the regiment lost, by reason of term of enlistment expiring, twelve commissioned officers, and one hundred and thirty men. None of the original members of the regiment were ever court-martialed, or subjected to any degrading punishment, during their term of service, which is truly a record that can be looked back to with pride. Among the officers killed during the year, were Lieutenant Colonel Spofford, Captain Sabine, Captain Lawrence and Lieutenant Brannon.

The original regiment was mustered out of service on November 18th, by Captain C. Macmichael, Ninth U. S. Infantry. A large number of re-enlisted men and the recruits, whose term of service had not expired, together with sufficient number of volunteers, substitutes and drafted men, assigned and forwarded from Camp Berry, Portland, Maine, enabled Colonel Harris M. Plaisted to re-organize the regiment.

During the first three months of 1865, the regiment was stationed near the New Market Road, about ten miles from Richmond, and formed a part of the Third Brigade, First Division, Twenty-Fourth Corps. On the 27th of March, they with the division, moved across the James and Appomattox rivers, and to the vicinity of Hatcher's Run, where on the 31st, they engaged the enemy, and remained exposed to the fire until the 2d of April, losing several men, killed, wounded and taken prisoners. On the 2d, they participated in the assault and capture of Forts Gregg and Baldwin, losing during the day, twenty-five men, killed and wounded. On the 9th, they engaged the enemy at Clover Hill, losing six men killed, and thirty-one wounded. From the 25th of April, to the 24th of November, they were encamped near Richmond, and on duty in that city the greater part of the time. On the 26th they moved to Fredericksburg, and remained, doing patrol duty, until the middle of January, 1866, when they were ordered to City Point, for the purpose of being mustered out. On the 2d of February, they were mustered out of the U. S. service, by Capt. J. Remmington, Assistant Commissary of Musters, Department of Virginia, and the regiment left for home on the 3d, arriving at Augusta soon after, and were paid, and finally discharged.

CHAPTER XXXIII.

Ellsworth And Hancock County---The First Meeting---Ringing Resolutions---Money For Soldiers Aid---The First Flag Raising---Jesse Dutton Opens Recuiting Office---The Hancock Giants---Rebels Cut Down The Liberty Pole At Blue Hill---The Rifle Company---The Noble Work Of The Ladies-- Ellsworth Men In The Navy ---Return Of Wounded Soldiers---Death Of Lieutenant Rice---The Ward Companies---The Ellsworth Band---Recruiting Continues---The Dirigo Club---Lee's Surrender---Close Of The War.

Hancock County was as large in patriotism as any of her sisters, and at once on hearing the awful news from Sumpter, a meeting was called at Ellsworth, an account of which is given elsewhere in this book. Strong resolutions were adopted upholding the Government, and declaring that the " Government should be sustained, in this crisis, at any cost." At the close of the meeting the band called on Colonel James S. Rice, at his hotel and tendered him a serenade.

Steps were at once taken to raise money for the support of soldiers' families, and the large hearted and patriotic citizens responded liberally; twelve hundred dollars being raised the first day. To Mr. Tucker, then landlord of the Ellsworth House, seems to belong the honor of raising the first flag, as no account of a prior flag-raising can be found; but his neighbors were not far behind him, for in a very few days the sky was alive with bunting.

The first recruiting office was opened by Mr. Jesse Dutton, and the patriots of Ellsworth kept him right busy, as they enlisted with great rapidity; no less than fourteen names being put on the roll in the first hour. On the 25th of April, the good citizens of Bluehill had a grand meeting, and on this occasion threw out a large flag. In the first part of this book will be found the list of officers of the first company raised in Ellsworth. The entire company were large men, nearly one half being over six feet tall. At Ellsworth Falls, the two parties put out the flags that were left over from the fall election, on one pole, thus showing to the world that *parties* were a secondary consideration to them, and that they were as *one man*, for the good of the country. A strange sight might have been witnessed on a bright May morning that year. It was a two-horse team bearing eight sturdy fellows, while aloft over their heads, flew the "Stars and Stripes." They had driven all the way from Amherst, that they might enlist in their country's cause.

On the 29th of April, the town voted to raise twenty-five hundred dollars, for soldiers' aid.

Recruiting continued all through the month of May, and flag raisings were frequent. A strong "secesh" element existed in several of the towns, and culminated in the cutting down of the liberty-pole, at North Blue Hill. Among the first prisoners captured by the rebels, was H. M. Blaisdell, of Company H, Second Regiment, who had enlisted at Ellsworth.

The men of Hancock County did not need urging, and were ever ready to enlist for the cause, but for some reason, that part of the State was not given the chance to show what it could do in that line, so in order that the Governor might see the patriotic feeling thereabouts, a company was raised, and its services tendered to the Government, *without expense to the State.* The agents for the purchase of cavalry horses, did not take much stock in that part of the State, seeming, as a paper of the day said, " to think that the State line was on the east bank of the Penobscot," as they bought but three horses at Ellsworth, though nearly two hundred fine animals were presented for sale. During the last part of the summer, a rifle company was recruited, by P W. Perry, and chose for its officers, W. P. Spofford, Captain, Chas. E. Illsley, First Lieutenant, and John E. Dodge, Second Lieutenant. They filled their ranks to ninety men, and left for the front on October 19th. All this time troops from surrounding towns had been passing through Ellsworth, and hardly a day passed, that did not see soldiers parade the hitherto quiet streets of the city. The ladies had not been idle, but under the leadership of Mrs. Seth Tisdale, worked from out the crude cloth, sheets, pillow-cases, shirts, and many a piece of clothing, that was destined to cover the dead and mangled remains, of what was once a brave and noble man. Could the work for the Union, that was done by the loyal, generous-hearted women of our country, be estimated, it would be found to be as much in value, as that done by our army and navy, combined.

Late in the year, Lieutenant O. W. Kent returned from the front, bringing nearly four thousand dollars, of soldier's money with him, which had been sent to the loved ones at home, by the brave boys.

Hancock County had representatives in the navy, as well as in the land force, and among them were, Jos. A. Smith, who was a paymaster on the Kearsage; Gilbert M. Small, of Gouldsboro, and Byron Pettingill, and S. D. Joy, of Hancock, who were acting masters; Geo. Grant, of Ellsworth, who was on board the "Cumberland," when she was sunk by the "Merrimac;" and Captains Alvin and Geo. Lord, who were acting ensigns.

During the spring of '62, things moved along quietly, people having begun to get over the novelty of a Civil War. The only thing of great interest, being the return of the invalid soldiers from the front. Among these was Mr. Henry B. Denaco, Company G, Eleventh Regiment. We may be sure that these returned veterans did not suffer, and if their heads were not turned, by the attentions lavished upon them, it was because of the strong head, and not from any lack of cause.

In June, recruiting for three months' men was begun, and the company had been nearly filled, when orders were received to stop. About this time, it was reported that the officers of Company B, Sixth Me., were not with the company at Williamsburg. As the company was raised in Ellsworth, this news made a great sensation, which, however, was soon over on the receipt of an indignant denial of the charge, from Captain Frazier.

Lieutenant W. H. H. Rice, of Ellsworth, was wounded at Richmond, on the 31st of May, and died at hospital, on June 18th. He was a heroic soldier and a noble young man. On the reception of his body, a public funeral was given at his home in Ellsworth.

A sketch of Lieutenant Rice, will be found in the back part of this book.

Enlistments continued during the summer, and in the month of July, Ward Companies were formed, as related elsewhere in this volume. Up to the first of August, Ellsworth had sent two hundred and seventy men to the front, and must have been intending to send, if necessary, the whole male population, as nearly all the citizens might have been seen, on one day of every week, drilling in the streets, armed and equipped, if not "as the law directs," yet with murderous, and wicked sticks, canes, etc.

During the fall of '62, there was great fear of a draft, and the loyal citizens, feeling that it would be a dishonor to the city, to be obliged to submit to such a means of raising men, contributed liberally to avoid it. Up to this time the Ellsworth Band, had furnished eight of its members to the army. On the 25th, of November, Mr. P. W. Perry, received twelve hundred dollars, being the allotment of Company I, Thirteenth Regiment. There had been some "hitch" in paying the regiment at first, but that had been fixed, and so the money was forwarded. Soon after this, Company C, Twenty-Sixth Regiment, received their allotment, amounting to thirteen hundred and ninty-seven dollars.

The spring of '63 found the city crowded, and at that time every store was occupied, and calls for many more. Recruiting still continued, one office being kept open by Captain H. C. Snow, of the Seventh Regiment. About this time, the ministers of the city called a meeting, to devise ways and means for more aid to soldiers, and immediately the Dirigo Club subscribed thirty-two dollars, to be forwarded to the sanitary commission. Tea parties were held by the ladies, all through the spring, and considerable money raised for the same purpose.

Men came in fast during 1863, but fast as they might come, even faster, did that gigantic demon, War, destroy them, and then call for more. On the 20th of November, Mr. P. W. Perry, who had done so much in raising the companies, was appointed recruiting officer for the city. Through the fall and winter, the ladies worked on in their glorious mission, and many a weary heart. under Southern skies, was made glad by their handiwork.

The wild charges of the First Heavy, brought sorrow to many a home in Ellsworth and her sister towns, for many of the bravest soldiers in that noble regiment, were from Hancock County. But the people were not frightened by a few of their friends being killed. In one family, of four boys, one was on the "Cumberland," when she went down; one was killed at the Wilderness; one wounded at Port Hudson, and the last hired and sent a volunteer in his place. The season of 1864, was really the quietest of any during the war, in Ellsworth. In the spring of '65, the town began to feel the heavy pull, that the war had made on her finances, and at a town meeting, it was decided to pay the bounty to volunteers, in town notes, bearing interest. So high was the credit of the town, notwithstanding the lack of ready money, that the notes were easily disposed off at face value. After this, it was decided to pay four hundred dollars bounty, to all men who would volunteer before the draft was made. As may be supposed, many took advantage of the liberal offer, and enrolled their names. A committee was appointed to recruit, and on that committee were Captain Isaac Frazier, Mr. P. W. Perry and Eugene Hale, (now U. S. Senator).

When the news of the fall of Richmond was received, the towns people evinced great joy; in fact, they were so happy that they could express their joy in no way except by extravagant celebration. Bells were rung, and old men were seen dancing about in front of stores, and in like manner showing how pleased they were with the glorious news.

The news of Lee's surrender, was brought from Bangor by

Albert Smith, of that city, who, at once, on learning of it, set out with his team, to spread the good word. During the day a procession was formed, and headed by the band, marched all about the town.

When the awful news of the death of Lincoln reached the city, it caused the profoundest sorrow. Measures were at once taken that a fitting ceremony should take place, and it was decided that exercises should be held in Rev. Dr. Tenny's church. This was done, and on that day, not a store was open in the city. Houses and business buildings alike were draped, and flags hung at half-mast throughout the entire city.

Soon the soldiers began to come home, and scenes of joy, (as friend once more met friend), and of the sorrow and anguish of the mother, wife or sweetheart, (when she saw comrades of her loved one arrive, and knew that her hearts-love could never come), cannot be told by living pen. In this respect the story of one city, is the story of all, and sad and bitter enough was it at the time, so that at this late day we need not seek to tell it over. We only know that if any are entitled to a "home beyond," these noble patriots, who freely gave up their lives that their fellow-men might live in freedom, surely shall fill the very highest places in that "Haven of Rest."

CHAPTER XXXIV.

The Second Cavalry—Its Formation—The First Detachment At New Orleans—Its Battles—Arrival Of The Main Regiment—To Florida—Raids And Skirmishes—Return To Augusta—The Thirty-First Regiment—Its Organization—Its Battles—Tolopotomoy Creek—Cold Harbor—Bethesda Church—Weldon Railroad—In Front of Petersburg—Arrival Home.

THE SECOND MAINE CAVALRY.

This regiment was organized at Augusta, from November 30th, 1863, to January 2d, 1864; and January 11th, having been assigned to the Department of the Gulf, commenced leaving Augusta for Portland, for the purpose of embarking on transports, for New Orleans, La. Companies A and D, and about half of G, being the only portion of the regiment which had arrived at New Orleans, were, on the 16th of April, ordered to proceed to Alexandria, La., where they arrived on the morning of the 21st, and being assigned to duty with the Third Cavalry Brigade, participated in the engagements at Cherryville Cross Roads, Marksville, Avoyelle's Prairie and Yellow Bayou, and rejoined the regiment at Thibodeaux, June 1st.

The main body of the regiment arrived at New Orleans, in detachments on the 18th, 19th, 22d and 23d of April. On the 9th of August the regiment embarked at New Orleans, for Pensacola, Fla., arrived on the 11th, and encamped near Barrancas, being employed in fatigue duty, besides taking part in quite a number of raids, to Marianna, in September, and to Pollard, Ala., in December.

During the year, the regiment lost by death, one officer, and two hundred and seventy-eight enlisted men. On the 23d of February, 1865, Lieutenant Colonel Spurling, with three hundred men, attacked the enemy in considerable force, at Milton, Fla., and after a sharp encounter, completely routed them. On the 19th of March, the regiment joined General Steele's command, concentrated at Pensacola, preparatory to the movement which resulted in the capture of Mobile, and the opening of the State of Alabama, to the advance of the Federal troops. During the whole campaign, the regiment rendered efficient service, had several encounters with the enemy, destroyed a large amount of railroad, and other property, besides opening communication with General Canby, besieging Spanish Fort. and capturing a large number of the enemy.

After the fall of Mobile, a detatchment of the regiment was assigned to the Sixteenth Army Corps, being the only Cavalry with that body of thirty thousand men. The detatchment did efficient duty during a long march of nearly two hundred miles, to the city of Montgomery, Ala. In August the detatchment was ordered to return to Florida, and rejoined the regiment at Barrancas. The regiment was then broken up and small detatchments were stationed at various points, throughout Western Florida, to preserve harmony and suppress any insurrectionary movements that might take place. By the 1st of December, the entire regiment was concentrated at Barrancas, and mustered out of the U. S. Service, on the 6th, by Lieutenant Schryver, Assistant Commissary of Musters. Twenty-five commissioned officers, and about one-hundred and sixteen enlisted men were mustered out in Florida, to become residents of the South, making oath of their intention to remain there, and receiving from the Government mileage in lieu of transportation. The remainder of the regiment, comprising fourteen officers, and five-hundred enlisted men, embarked on the 8th, for Augusta, Maine, where they were paid and finally discharged, on the 21st.

The Thirty-First Regiment.

This regiment was organized in Augusta, Maine, in March and April, 1864, to serve three years, and left April 18th, for Washington, D. C. Upon their arrival at Alexandria, Va., they were assigned to the Second Brigade, Second Division, Ninth Army Corps, and immediately marched to Bristow Station, Va., where they remained a few days.

On the morning of May 4th, they broke camp and on the 6th participated in the battle of the Wilderness, in which they lost heavily in killed and wounded. On the 12th, they were engaged with the enemy at Spottsylvania Court House, losing in the engagment twelve killed, seventy-five wounded and one hundred and eight missing. On the 24th, they crossed the North Anna River, under a heavy fire from the enemy. During the night of the 26th, they recrossed the North Anna River, and in two days reached the Pamunkey River, where they skirmished with the enemy on the 29th and 30th.

On the 31st of May, and 1st of June, they were engaged with the enemy at Tolopotomoy Creek, and on the 3d, participated in the engagement at Bethesda Church, losing fifteen killed, and thirty-nine wounded. On the 4th, they marched to Cold Harbor, and remained under fire in frequent skirmishes, until the 12th, suffering greatly from the shelling and sharpshooters of the enemy. On the 12th, they commenced a long, weary march across the Chickahominy and the James rivers, and on the 16th, skirmished with the enemy in front of Petersburg. On the 17th, they participated in the assault and capture of the enemy's works, and from that date until the great battle of July 30th, they remained constantly under fire, losing largely in officers and men.

In the battle of July 30th, celebrated by the explosion of the rebel fort, they were assigned to an important position, and were the first to enter the rebel's works. They lost, on that day, ten killed, thirty-one wounded, and forty-seven prisoners From this time until the battle of Weldon Road, August 18th, they remained under fire before Petersburg, doing picket duty. On August 18th, they went to the support of the Fifth Corps, in taking the Weldon Railroad, remaining in the front lines until September 14th, when they were relieved and allowed a few days of comparative rest. On September 30th, in the battle of Popular Spring Church, they rendered most effective services, and lost on that day, five killed, fifteen wounded, and sixteen taken prisoners. From the 1st until the 27th of October, they were engaged mainly in drilling, and on picket duty. At the grand onward movement on the 27th of October, they were ordered to Fort Fisher, which they occupied and garrisoned, until the 29th of November, being meanwhile strengthened by the Fourth and Sixth companies of unassigned infantry, organized at Augusta, Me., on the 4th and 18th of October, 1864, to serve one year, and which were assigned as companies L and M, respectively.

On the 29th of November, the Ninth corps was ordered to releive the Second corps, and the regiment was assigned to garrison Fort Davis, on the Jerusalem Plank Road, in front of Petersburg. During the month of December, the regiment received an accession of fifteen officers and four hundred and seventy enlisted men, by the consolidation with it of the Thirty-Second Maine Volunteers. They remained at Fort Davis until February 11th, 1865, when they were ordered to the left, and encamped near Parke

Station, on the Army Line and City Point Railroad, where they remained until the 2d of April, on which day they were engaged in the assault upon the enemy's works, and suffered severely. On the 3d of April, they marched through Petersburg on the South Side Railroad, in pursuit of the enemy, arriving at Nottaway Court House, on the 6th. On the 8th, they proceeded with a detachment of prisoners to Ford's Station, where they arrived on the 11th, delivered up their charge and at once returned to Burksville Junction. On the 20th of April, they proceeded to City Point, and there embarked for Alexandria, Va., arriving at that city on the 27th. On the 15th of July, the regiment was mustered out of the U. S. Service, near Alexandria, Va., by Lieutenant E Rose, A. C. M., and arrived on the 19th, at Bangor, where the men were paid, and finally discharged on the 27th.

BIOGRAPHICAL SKETCHES.

Major Gen. Hiram G. Berry,

was born in East Thomaston, now Rockland, August 27, 1824. On reaching manhood, he was regarded as one of the most useful and enterprising citizens in that section, and was honored by being sent to the Legislature to represent his native place. After Rockland became a city, he was elected its second Mayor. While engaged in pursuing the peaceful callings of civil life, his attention was turned to matters of a military nature, in which he displayed ability of a high order, from the outset. His efforts originated the Rockland Guards, which he commanded for several years. On the breaking out of the Rebellion, he was among the first to offer his services in his country's defence. Enlisting with his company in the Fourth Regiment, he was commissioned Colonel of that corps, which, while under his command, was considered one of the best disciplined and most efficient regiments in the army; a reputation it has ever since maintained.

At the first battle of Bull Run, he developed a military genius, which gave evidence of a brilliant career, and made him a marked man. He was the first to discover the retreat of the enemy, which fact he immediately caused to be telegraphed to President Lincoln.

In March, 1862, he was promoted to the rank of Brigadier General, and assigned to the Third Brigade, First Division, Third Corps. He entered at once upon the discharge of his duties with his characteristic energy, and at the Siege of Yorktown, which shortly followed, he distinguished himself both in the trenches and in the field. At the battle of Williamsburg, he was awarded the honor of having saved the day. By a rapid movement, on that occasion, he hastened to Hooker's relief in the front, during a pelting rain storm, and by his skillful manœuvring, drove the foe to his rifle-pits, and ended the fight by driving him thence, capturing a large number of prisoners, and retaking all our artillery that had been lost. By his timely arrival with his command, Gen. Heintzleman acknowledged that Hooker's division was saved from defeat, and the battle turned in our favor. At the battle of Fair Oaks, May 31st, he hurled back the enemy, who had repulsed Casey's and Couch's divisions, retaking all the ground that had been lost, and holding his position until reinforced. When moving to support the front, pressing on with his brigade through the mass of defeated Federal troops, who were flying in all directions, he was met by Gen. Kearney, who asked him if he "was not afraid to take his men through such a rabble," when he quickly replied: "No sir, not if I march at their head." This gallant reply was characteristic of the man. He never demanded of his men the performance of a duty, that he was not willing to undertake, even at the hazard of his life. The next day when the enemy was routed one of the regiments of his brigade, Third Michigan, drove four rebel brigades in succession from the woods.

General Berry was foremost in the fight, having three of his Staff killed, and his own hat and clothes pierced with shot. In a report of the battle, Prince de Joinville, who was an eye witness, states: "As at Williamsburg, Kearney arrives in good time to reestablish the fight. Berry's brigade of this division, composed of Michigan regiments and an Irish battalion, advances as firm as a wall into the midst of the discordant mass, which wander over the battle field, and does more by its example than the most powerful reinforcements." Generals McClellan, Hooker, Kearney and Heintzleman, also complimented him for his skill and undaunted bravery. The latter officer in his report, speaking of his troops says: "They most gallantly kept their position on the rebels right flank and kept up such a deadly fire that no effort the enemy made could dislodge them. He remained until dark, firing away sixty rounds of ammunition to each man, and then supplying themselves with cartridges from the dead and wounded. Their fire completely commanded the open space in their front, and not a mounted man succeeded in passing under their fire." After this battle he was ordered to erect fortifications, and to establish a picket-line, the right resting on Hooker's left, and running below White Oak Swamp, connecting with the Second corps, a distance of about five miles. The position of this picket line being in the advance, was an exposed one. For nearly a month there was picket fighting almost every day, besides three severe engagments which occured. The line was however, maintained at all hazards according to his orders, his men fighting immediately under his eye. Faithful to his trust notwithstanding his life was at one time briefly threatened by disease occasioned by his arduous labors, care and exposure, he remained at his post.

The battle of Gaines' Mill, resulted in our army being driven, and all communications with White House Landing, our base of operations, cut. A new base having been decided upon, Gen. Berry, after being consulted in regard to the crossing of White Oak Swamp, was ordered to build roads immediately for the passage of the army; which work he accomplished in twenty-four hours. The army then commenced its movement toward the James river, Gen. Berry covering the retreat, skirmishing with the enemy on the way. Two days afterward, was fought the battle of Glen Dale. While the battle was raging, Gen. Kearney being unwell, the command of his division was turned over to Gen. Berry, his brigade remaining in the reserve. The attack of the enemy, in full force, caused a portion of the reserve to abandon his position, whereupon, Gen. Berry immediately filled up the gap by placing his brigade in the opening, and sending for reinforcements. For three hours the battle raged fearfully, our army losing heavily. Every assault of the enemy was repulsed. During the battle Gen. Berry was slightly wounded by a musket ball, which cut into his sword belt. The battle of Malvern Hill followed, which was fought on our side mostly by artillery. His brigade was on the right of the line, engaged in supporting batteries in an exposed position, until the enemy was repulsed, and left us at night masters of the field. On the arrival of the army at Harrison's Landing, his brigade was assigned a position on the center of the front line. In consequence of its great loss in men and officers, and the large amount of service it had performed during the retrograde movement, it was excused from performing any fatigue duty The hardships and privations of the Peninsula Campaign, together with a severe cold, caught on his arrival at Harrison's Landing, so affected Gen. Berry's health, that he returned, for the first time since his departure, to his home. During the brief period he remained at Rockland, the most lavish ovations were paid him by his fellow townsmen, as a token of their appreciation of his noble and gallant conduct. Notwithstanding his health was not fully restored, his convictions of duty were such that he felt he could be absent no longer, and before three weeks had expired he returned to his command.

During the Maryland campaign he was assigned to duty in the fortifications at Upton's Hill. At the battle of Fredericksburg, Dec. 13th, after crossing the Rappahannock, and moving down the plain under a terrible fire, he supported with his brigade four batteries of artillery. On the repulse of General Franklin, the enemy pursued that officer's command through Gen. Berry's lines, when the latter opened on the enemy with grape and musketry, driving him back with heavy loss. It is related that Gen. A. P. Hill, the Confederate general commanding the division opposed to Gen. Berry, took occasion, under a flag of truce, to compliment him for his generalship; the only instance of the kind, we believe, that occurred during the war. In March, 1863, the rank of Major General was conferred on Gen. Berry, and he was assigned to the command of the Second Division, Third Corps, which had been so long under the command of Gen. Hooker, and was acknowledged to be one of the best in the Army of the Potomac. At the battle of Chancellorsville, the heroic Berry gave his life to his country and mankind When Gen. Hooker commenced operations, Gen. Berry was ordered with his division down the river, as a feint, to cover the real move intended upon the right. As soon, however, as Gen. Hooker had got well across the river above Fredericksburg, Gen. Berry was ordered to rejoin his corps at Chancellorsville, which he did with his usual promptness. A correspondent states that when the Eleventh Corps commenced coming, panic stricken, down the road toward headquarters, it was a critical situation, and brought out the superb resources of Gen. Hooker. Whom, of all others, should he send in at this fearfully critical moment but the darling child of his own creation, his own corps, now commanded by Gen. Berry. "General," shouted the commander, "throw your men into the breach; receive the enemy on your bayonets; don't fire a shot; they can't see you."

At the double quick that glorious band rushed to the rescue, pressing up in their horrid array of glittering steel, the enemy's advance was quickly checked, and he had to withdraw to the line of breastworks just vacated by the Eleventh Corps. In an account of this last and greatest success of Gen. Berry's, Gen. Howard, in a letter to Adj. Gen. Hodsdon, says: "I met him, (Gen. Berry), close by his line of battle, on Saturday, May 2d, near the plank road, south of Chancellorsville. He had drawn up his division of veteran troops perpendicular to, and on both sides of the road, to cover the retreat of the Twelfth Corps, and check any further advance of the enemy in that direction. He met me with great cordiality, consulted as to where the line would be hardest pressed, and in answer to my suggestion that the chief difficulty would be upon his right, said, 'well General, if you will take care of the left here, I will go to the right,' and he went in that direction. Upon this he put himself at the head of his brave men, and with an irresistible charge, they drove back the rebels, and retook the ground which the latter had won."

The next morning General Berry fell. The circumstances attending his death are related by Captain J. B. Greenhalgh, a member of his staff, as follows: Turning to Captain G., General Berry directed him to ride to General Hooker's headquarters, and inquire for orders as to whether he should hold his position or not. Captain G. at once started, and General Berry, and the remainder of his staff dismounted, General Berry saying that he would walk across the plank road—only a few rods—and communicate with General Mott, the senior officer of his division. One of his aids remonstrated against his going, and offered to go in his stead, but the General replied that he himself would go. He started, went across the road, saw General Mott, gave him his orders, turned and was coming back, and when but a short distance from the spot where the members of his staff stood, a minnie rifle ball struck him in the arm close to the shoulder, passed downward through his vitals, and lodged in his hip, killing him almost immediately. His aids saw him fall, and instantly started for him. Lieutenant Freeman knelt by his side. "I am dying," said the General, "carry me to the rear." The Lieutenant asked him if he had any wish to express. By a feeble shake of the head he indicated that he had none, and the next moment his spirit had gone forever. The body was at once raised and carried to the Chancellor House, where General Hooker stood. When it was laid before him he burst into tears and kneeling down kissed the cold forehead, and then exclaimed, " My God, Berry, why was this to happen? Why was the man on whom I relied so much, to be taken away in this manner "

After General Hooker had paid this tribute to the lifeless form of General Berry, he ordered it to be carried to the rear at once, where it rested Sunday night in the same room which the General had occupied previous to the late move of the army. While on the way, a squad of the Fourth Maine Regiment, learning that the body of their former commander was being carried by, desired to have it laid down, and each one of the brave fellows came forward and kissed the cold brow of the man they loved, and had just followed into the battle-field, and then silently and tearfully took their places in the ranks.

In making a record of Gen. Berry's character. one who had been an intimate friend during the two last years of his life, says: "Gen. Berry was a man of marked ability, which distinguished him in every position he filled. Under the guidance of a benignant Providence he was the architect of his own fortune. His own ability and industry raised him from the more humble condition of his early life, to the eminence he reached. In all the important issues of his life, it may be truly said he never failed. He surprised men by what he accomplished; he never disappointed them by his failure. Although he enjoyed no advantages for literary culture, beyond those which are possessed by nearly every young man in the State, yet he acquired a degree of culture that could fairly characterize him as an educated man; and those who have a right to judge, affirm that his official reports and correspondence were rarely excelled in perspicuity and accuracy, by any of our public men. He never spent a day in a Military School, and yet he was thoroughly versed in the art of war. He knew his own strength, and was confident in it, and knew how to use it. He quietly formed his own plans, and depending on himself, entered upon their performance; but men knew little of them till their completion announced them. He was a man of untiring energy. During the latter years of his life, he maintained an almost ceaseless struggle with disease, and yet his record is what could be expected only of a man of iron frame and perfect health. While in the army he often issued his orders from a sick bed, or rose from that sick bed to lead his soldiers. When his friends and superior officers urged him to suspend his active labors, he remained at his post, performing the duties of camp and field, when he seemed more properly a subject for the surgeon's care. His whole military career attests the great resources, the strength of will, and the power of execution, which were never measured by what other men could do. He was faithful to the trust committed to him by his country. He held the performance of his duty a sacred obligation. He never refused to do all that his duty demanded, even those details which are felt to be irksome or repulsive. While other officers sought the comforts and luxuries of the metropolis; from the day he left the State with his regiment, till his last battle was fought, he shared the camp, the watch, the painful march, and the deadly struggle with his men. His life was a sacrifice to his fidelity. To those who knew him little, his conduct in the battle in which he lost his life may seem like rashness, but he would not commit to another what he felt could be done better by himself. His soldiers fought immediately under his eye and by his side. By his personal presence, he held his men to their position.

He was a leader and a favorite in the political party which opposed the administration that governed the country at the begining of the war; but when he had girded on his sword in his country's cause, he buried all party prejudices, sectional ties, and political preferences, and knew first and only, his country. He loved the flag of his country, and followed with all who loved it wherever it led. He fought beneath it, and, though it were tattered and rent by the storms of a hundred battles, he clung to it still; clung to it until death. He was a noble and brave officer. We know not but his daring courage amounted to an utter disregard of his own life. He was never more calm than when the storm of battle raged around him. He served in some of the bloodiest battles of the war, and more than once his command was the last to leave the field. Men fell around him like autumn leaves, officers of his staff fell dead by his side, and the iron hail pierced the uniform he wore. For two years he was as familiar with death as with an associate, and met him often face to face, but never trembled or grew pale in his presence; nor was his an animal courage, that was fearless because insensible. With the lion's heart, he joined the utmost gentleness and considerateness He would never ask a soldier to go where he feared himself to go. He could weep over a fallen comrade, but his eagle eye never quailed before the foe. And thus it was to the closing scene. A weaker nature might have been living to-day. But his was one that would not accept life at the price of falling back one step from his post. His brave and gentle nature made him the object, not only of admiration, but of the warm affection of his associates in arms. His soldiers loved him, therefore followed unhesitatingly wherever he led, and stood in their position so long as his commanding form was with them. Blessings shall be upon his memory, and the nation's song shall perpetuate his fame."

Major Whiting S. Clark,

Left the senior class of Colby University, in June, 1862, for the purpose of raising a company for the Eighteenth Maine Infantry Volunteers. This he speedily accomplished, and was commissioned captain in that regiment. In November, of that year, he was assigned, with his company to the charge of batteries Vermont and Kemble, in the defences of Washington. He remained there till June, 1863, when he rejoined his regiment at Fort Sumner, D. C.

On the 19th of May, 1864, when Ewell's Corps attempted to cut off our supply trains, Captain Clark, was first actively engaged. With what spirit the enemy was encountered, may be inferred from the fact that he lost two lieutenants, and seventy men, in killed and wounded, being a greater loss than that of any other company in the regiment. After the battle he advanced with the remnant that he had left, and captured a rebel captain and about twenty men.

He participated in the battles of North Anna, Hanovertown, Cold Harbor, and the other engagments that occurred in the advance on Petersburg. At Petersburg he distinguished himself by taking the third battalion, (which he commanded), to an advanced position beyond the entrenchments, capturing a number of rebel skirmishers, and holding his position under a heavy fire and alone, for nearly an hour, before communication was established with the troops on his right and left.

On the evening of the same day, while leading the battalion to the desperate encounter in which the regiment lost two thirds of its numbers, he was himself shot down and carried from the field, in what was thought to be a dying condition, having received no less than three bad wounds. Shortly after this action, he received a Major's commission, but did not recover from his injuries in season to rejoin his regiment.

Major Clark was one of four brothers, who held commissions in Maine regiments during the war. All of them were severely wounded, one of them dying of his injuries. Like the Horatii of antiquity, these brothers united their efforts against the foes of their country; and though they may not hope, like their prototypes, to become heroes of classic tradition, yet in a peculiar degree are entitled to the gratitude and appreciative remembrance of their fellow-citizens.

Captain Benj. F. Hunter,

Of Hodgdon, entered the service in 1861, as a private in Company A, Seventh Maine Volunteers. Conspicuous for his bravery in every battle, and several times wounded, a late promotion found him serving as First Sergeant in the First Maine Veterans, in the Shenandoah Valley, in the fall of 1864. On the first engagement in the ensuing and last campaign of the war, he was killed in the abattis of the enemy's works, in the extreme advance of a charge made by Col. Hyde's Brigade, on the Squirrel Level Road. The warrant for his first promotion bore the words, "for especial gallantry at Antietam."

Brig. Gen. Thomas W. Hyde.

We need say nothing of the bravery and gallantry of Gen. Hyde, as that is so well known throughout the entire State, that no words of ours could add to its brightness.

Every school-boy knows of the glorious deeds performed by Gen. Hyde, and his name is in every household. We can only say that no braver soldier ever went out to do battle for any country, and the people of this State truly understand his real merit and worth.

Lieut. Wm. R. Newenham,

Was born in Cherryfield, and spent the earlier years of his life in that town, usually engaged in the lumber business. For three or four years prior to entering the service, he had given his whole attention to hunting in the extensive forests of that portion of the State, often spending whole weeks alone. He entered the service in the latter part of July, 1862, as Second Lieutenant, in Company H, Eighteenth Maine Volunteers, afterwards First Heavy Artillery.

When the regiment was reorganized as Heavy Artillery, he was promoted First Lieutenant. After the regiment joined the Army of the Potomac, he participated in the battles of Spottsylvania, North Anna, Tolopotomoy, Cold Harbor, and at Petersburg the 16th and 17th of June, and was mortally wounded on the 18th, in that fatal charge, when so many of the regiment were sacrificed. He died at Portsmouth Grove Hospital, July 9th, 1864, aged thirty-four years.

He was a brave, intelligent and trustworthy officer. His earlier life had fitted him for a soldier. As an officer, he readily acquainted himself with his duties, and was classed among the best soldiers of the regiment.

BREVET BRIG. GEN. LLEWELLYN G. ESTES,

Of Oldtown, entered the First Maine Cavalry, as a private, September 21st, '61, and was made Orderly Sergeant September 30th, and served as such until May, 1862, when he was promoted to be First Lieutenant. He was taken prisoner at Warrentown, Va., in August following, and returned to Bell Plain after being exchanged. He was immediately detailed as Aid-de-Camp, on the Staff of Gen. Kilpatrick, and took part in the Stoneman raid around the rebel army. During this raid he was dispatched with ten men to go through the rebel lines from Richmond, and communicate with Gen. Hooker, then fighting the battle of Chancellorsville. On the route he captured an officer and sixteen men. Lieut. Estes was himself afterward taken prisoner, and started for Richmond, but in turn captured the party that had him in charge, and conveyed them within our lines; a feat full of romance, and worthy of the best days of chivalry. In March, 1864, he was promoted to be Captain of Company A, First Cavalry, and at the same time, Captain and Assistant Adjutant General; when he resigned his position in the regiment, and was assigned to duty as A. A. G., Third Cavalry Division, Army of the Potomac, Gen. Kilpatrick commanding. In April, he was relieved from duty in the Army of the Potomac, at the request of Gen. Kilpatrick, and assigned to duty as Adjutant General of Cavalry, Military Division of the Mississippi, and as such, served through all of the Georgia and Carolina campaigns. He was promoted to be Major, in September, 1861, and Lieutenant Colonel and Colonel, by brevet, in March, 1865. From March to September 30th, 1865, he was Adjutant General of Western North Carolina, comprising forty-one counties. He was further promoted to be Brigadier General, by brevet, September 30th, when he resigned his position in the army. He also received the very strong recommendation of Generals Sherman and Kilpatrick, for a full Brigadier Generalship, in March, 1865, which he would have received but for the discontinuance of the war. Gen. Kilpatrick, on whose Staff he was during most of his career, and who appreciated his manly character and heroic deeds, wrote of him: "To Major Estes, my Adjutant General, I am greatly indebted for my success in the raid around Atlanta, and in the campaigns through Georgia and the Carolinas. He deserves, and should be made a Brigadier General;" and Gen. Sherman added as his testimony: "This officer I recommend for great gallantry and skill in battle." The career of Gen. Estes was indeed remarkable. In the short space of less than three years, through his own skill and bravery, without the aid of powerful, political friends, he advanced from the position of a private in the ranks to that of a Brigadier General, before he had reached the twenty-fourth year of his age.. He was made prisoner three times, wounded, and participated in no less than one hundred and twenty-one engagements.

LIEUTENANT COLONEL GEORGE FULLER.

This officer enlisted as a private on the 24th of April, 1861, in a company raised in Corinth, of which he was elected Second Lieutenant, and which became Company H, Sixth Regiment. He was subsequently elected Captain, and was mustered in with his regiment, July 15th, 1861. The command soon after proceeded to Washington and joined the Army of the Potomac, in which the regiment served until mustered out, August 15th, 1864.

The record of Lieut. Col. Fuller is identified with that of the regiment with which he was always on duty. He therefore participated in the battles of Warwick Creek, Lee's Mills, Williamsburg, Garnett's Farm, Savage's Station, White Oak Swamp, Crampton

Pass, Anteitam, First Fredericksburg, St. Mary's Heights, or Second Fredericksburg, Bank's Ford, Kelly's Ford, Gettysburg, Rappahannock Station, Locust Grove, the Wilderness and Spottsylvania Court House. In the four last of these he was in command of the regiment, after the fall of Lieut. Col. Harris.

On the 22d of May, 1863, Captain Fuller, was commissioned Major of the regiment, and on April 24th, 1864, was further promoted Lieutenant Colonel.

Lieutenant Colonel Fuller did not pass through the war without experiencing some of its most painful vicissitudes. In the battle of Garnett's Farm he was struck in the breast by a spent ball. At Rappahannock Station, his horse was killed under him, his sword shot off and his clothes pierced; and at the battle of Spottsylvania Court House, when of the two hundred men of the regiment who went into the charge on May 10th, 1864, one hundred and sixty were killed and wounded, Colonel Fuller was also shot and carried off the field. On the 1st of July, he rejoined his regiment, at Washington, then on its way to Maine, to be mustered out, but was retained by General Russell, commanding the division. Subsequent to the consolidation of a remnant of the regiment with the First Veterans, Colonel Fuller tendered his resignation, and was honorably mustered out, July 28th, 1864, having been in the service thirty-nine months, and earned for himself a soldierly reputation of which he may well be proud.

BREVET BRIGADIER GENERAL JOHN D. RUST.

Brevet Brigadier General John D. Rust, late Colonel of the Eighth Maine Regiment, war of 1861–'66, commenced his military career in 1858, as Aid-de-Camp, upon Governor Lot M. Morrill's staff, with the rank of colonel. He was one of the reviewing officers, at the Brigade Review at Belfast, Maine, in which Hon. Jefferson Davis, late President of the Southern Confederacy, was present, and reviewed the troops. It is said that Mr. Davis, at that time, made the remark in the hearing of Colonel Rust, that one Southern soldier could successfully cope with half a dozen Yankees, to which Colonel Rust took vigorous exceptions.

At the commencement of hostilities in 1861, the lamented Governor Washburn had sufficient confidence in Colonel Rust, as in many others, to confer with him upon matters pertaining to the raising of troops, for the suppression of the rebellion.

At this time, Colonel Rust made strong endeavors, which were successful, to harmonize the two prominent political parties, in his section, and in that behalf, succeeded in securing the nominations of Hon. E. K. Smart, of Camden, and N. A. Farwell, of Rockland, as State Senators, on the Union ticket, the former a Democrat, and the latter a Republican, both being triumphantly elected. The result of this election, did much towards harmonizing the two political parties. Soon after this, Governor Washburn sent to Colonel Rust, through Adjutant General Hodsdon, the requisite papers for enlisting a company of infantry for the Eighth Maine. Colonel Rust immediately enlisted Company H., and enrolled his name as a private therein, and later was elected and commissioned Captain, and subsequently, thereat, was made Lieutenant Colonel of the regiment. He soon became Colonel, by the resignation of Colonel Lee Strickland. The record of this gallant commander, and of his brave and patriotic troops, in active service from September 3d, 1861, constitutes a bright page in the annals of our Civil war. Colonel Rust's patriotism was of that practical and unselfish character, which rendered him not only willing, but eager to serve his country in any military capacity, in which our Government was pleased to place him. His military history exhibits him commissioned as Captain, Lieutenant Colonel, Colonel and also Brigadier General by Brevet, by the President; an honorable rank, worthily bestowed.

In an interview with General John L. Hodsdon, ex-officio Adjutant General, Quartermaster General and Paymaster General of Maine, relative to General Rust's service, he said:

"I had the pleasure of meeting Colonel J. D. Rust, at Belfast, in 1858, he being on Governor Morrill's staff, and I in command of the Bangor Light Infantry. I have been intimately acquainted with General Rust since, and know he served with gallantry and great credit in the war of '61–'66, in suppressing the rebellion in which his bearing and skill as an officer was most apparent and distinguished. Colonel Rust was ever laboring for the good of the service and his regiment, and when he was at home on sick leave of absence, he was always striving for the good of the service, enlisting men for his own, or other commands. His great desire was to put down the rebellion at the earliest possible moment and save the Union from division and destruction."

Ex-Governor Washburn, writing to Secretary of War, Stanton, said: "When at home, a year ago, such was Colonel Rust's interest in his regiment and the service, that he gave every hour, that the condition of his health would permit, to the work of raising recruits, and such was his success, owing in good part to his earnestness and capacity, that when he returned he had procured an addition to his numbers, of between two and three hundred men. In the State House, at Augusta, is the flag of the Eighth Regiment, which was raised upon the walls of Fort Pulaski, by order of the Commanding General, after the surrender, in token of the gallantry of Colonel Rust and his regiment, on that occasion."

The following letter from Representative to Congress, Egbert L. Viele, will be appreciated, when it is known that General Rust does a large business, shipping ice and lumber to the South. He writes to General Rust as follows:

NEW YORK, SEPTEMBER 1st, 1886.

"My Dear Colonel:

I was very glad indeed, to receive your kind letter, and to hear from one of my old soldiers. I remember you with a great deal of pleasure, as one of the most earnest and zealous of my command. I remember the evening your regiment reported to me at Hempstead, Long Island. They were all unused to war, but all of them true, and earnest men. I was in Portland a year ago last summer, at the Grand Army encampment, and I hoped to meet some of the 'Old Eighth,' but was not so fortunate.

They were worked to death without any necessity, on Port Royal Island, at that absurd stockade of Gilmore's. If we had gone direct to Charleston and Savannah, there would have been less sickness, and fewer lives lost. But the war is all over, and I am glad to see by your business card that you are engaged in active business. You are literally sending *cold comfort* to the South, but they are more grateful for it than for what they received in '61. You have an excellent delegation of men from Maine in Congress, although of course I should not object if more of them were Democrats. You have my best wishes, and warm remembrances of your manly and soldierly qualities."

Yours with regards,
EGBERT L. VIELE.

The original of the following is in the War Department at Washington.

[Extract of letter from General W. H. Benham.]

HEADQUARTERS ENGINEER BRIGADE, }
CITY POINT, VA., SEPTEMBER, 2d, 1863. }

Lieut. Maj. Gen. U. S. Grant, Commander U. S. Army:

General:—I called yesterday to present to you Colonel J. D. Rust, of the Eighth Maine Volunteers. I would desire to say in favor of Col. Rust, that he had a most excellent regiment when I had command of the division, which is now the Department of the South. That I knew him well, to be faithful, honest and a good duty soldier, anxious always to do his every duty to the best of his ability.

Most respectfully and truly your obedient servant,

(Signed) W. H. BENHAM.

The following was written in 1863, the original being in possession of the author.

BEAUFORT, S. C., APRIL 16th, 1863.

Major General D. Hunter. Commanding Dep't of the South:

General:—In parting with Colonel Rust, Eighth Maine, it gives me great pleasure to state that my relations with him have been of the most friendly character. He has ever performed, in good faith any duty which I have required of him, and I consider his regiment one of the best I have seen in the service. I am, General, with great respect, your obedient servant,

RUFUS SAXTON,

Brigadier General and Military Governor.

The author, also, has possession of the original of the following letter:

WASHINGTON, SEPTEMBER 30th, 1864.

Colonel John D. Rust, commanding the Eighth Regiment of Maine Volunteer Infantry, served under my immediate orders at the capture of Fort Pulaski, Georgia, and during the whole of my service in the Department of the South, to my entire satisfaction. I always considered him a first rate officer.

D. HUNTER, Major General.

Colonel Rust, re-enlisted at the end of two years, and, after a furlough, succeeded in getting his regiment transferred to the Army of the Potomac. Later he was promoted to the command of the Second Provisional Brigade, and later, reporting to General Butler at Fortress Monroe, was placed in command of the Second Division of the Army of the James. On August 19th, 1864, he resigned, and was honorably discharged for physical disability. General Rust is now a leading citizen and successful business man in Rockport, Maine.

CAPTAIN JOHN H. BALLINGER.

Captain John H. Ballinger entered the service of his country in the early days of the rebellion, having enlisted as a private in the first company formed at Machias, where he resided, as early as the middle of April, 1861. On the organization of his company, he was First Lieutenant. The company was assigned to the Sixth Maine Volunteers, as Company C, and with the regiment left the State for the seat of the war, about the middle of July.

Lieutenant Ballinger was a most useful man to the regiment, as he had served several years in the English army. In March, '62, on the very day that the Army of the Potomac broke camp to commence active operations against the enemy, Lieutenant Ballinger was promoted to the command of his company. With it, he landed at Old Point Comfort, the latter part of the month, and marched up the Peninsula. He fought during the siege of Yorktown, and participated in the battles of Lee's Mills and Williamsburg, leading his company, with ability and gallantry. He led it up the Peninsula, in the advance on Richmond, took part in the principal operations of the army, in that vicinity, and during the "seven days battles," fought with it at Garnett's Farm, Savage's Station, and White Oak Swamp. When the tide of war surged into Maryland, Captain Ballinger fought at the head of his company at Sugar Loaf Mountain, Crampton's Pass and Antietam. Late in the autumn, he again marched into Virginia, and fought with his men at Fredericksburg. In the spring of 1863, Captain Ballinger, with his men, took part in the preliminary operations about Fredericksburg, being on the skirmish line, and hotly engaged with the enemy, near Franklin's Crossing, May 2d. He led his company in the assault upon the Heights of St. Mary, cheering them with unusual gallantry. When half way up the heights, however, and just as he entered the first rifle pit, a minnie ball crashed through his brain, instantly terminating his patriotic and heroic career. After the enemy was routed and the works captured, his comrades buried him where he had fallen, on the slope made sacred by his blood, and that of many of his brave followers. The memory of his heroic deeds will be gratefully cherished, by the loyal hearts of a redeemed nation.

Surgeon John Benson.

Dr. Benson, of Newport, was first commissioned as Surgeon in the Eighth Regiment, but declined. He was subsequently, January 23d, 1863, commissioned as Surgeon in the Twentieth Regiment, and occupied that position until August 27th, 1863, when, owing to ill health, he was obliged to resign. That he fulfilled his severe and arduous duties promptly and efficiently, is unequivocally declared in the testimonials of the surgeons in chief, under whom he served. Lieut. Col. Gilmore, said of him: "His kindness and discrimination, and the unusual assiduity with which he applied himself to his duties, rendered him exceedingly useful and popular with the regiment, while his marked ability, gave him at once a high reputation among the other surgeons of the army."

ASSISTANT SURGEON WILLIAM R. BENSON.

Dr. William Roscoe Benson, of Bangor, was commissioned as Assistant Surgeon in the Fourth Maine Infantry, May 14th, 1862, but being soon afterwards attacked with camp-fever, he returned to his home and resigned. His sickness was protracted and severe. On his recovery, however, desiring to re-enter the service, he was, April 13th, 1863, appointed to the Second Regiment, filling his position as Assistant Surgeon, until mustered out, June 9th, 1863.

On the 15th of August, he was appointed to the Eighth Regiment, where he remained until within two months of his decease, having been discharged for disability, January 4th, 1865. He died, aged twenty-six years, at Newport, at the residence of his father, Dr. John Benson. The lamented deceased was greatly loved by the medical staff with which he was connected, all bearing testimony to his amiable qualities and his skill as an operator. He was also universally popular with the men of his regiment, the survivors of which will never fail to remember his kindly care and professional aid.

CAPTAIN BILLINGS BRASTOW.

Billings Brastow, of Brewer, enlisted into the U. S. Service, as Second Lieutenant, of Company I, Ninth Infantry, and was subsequently promoted First Lieutenant, and then Captain, of the same command. When his regiment was in General Gilmore's department, his name was often rendered conspicuous for valor, and especially for the gallantry of his command in the charges, and capture of battle flags, at Fort Wagner. Whilst a lieutenant, he was for a large part of the time, acting adjutant and captain, and whilst captain, acting colonel. He participated in every battle, in which his regiment was engaged, excepting one —making, in all, nearly thirty actions. Captain Brastow was in command of the regiment, at the taking of St. Mary's, and at Morris Island; with one hundred and twenty-five men, he attacked the Twenty-First South Carolinia Regiment, numbering six hundred men, driving them from their rifle-pits, and taking some thirty prisoners, and two stands of colors. At the battle of Deep Bottom, his regiment was out-flanked, on the right and left, but by a bold and rapid movement, he pierced the enemy's lines, and in the midst of a most deadly fire, carried his command to the Union lines, with the loss of thirty-nine men, and all the officers then on duty, who were either killed, wounded, or otherwise disabled. He also led the attack on the enemy, at the time that General Weitzel was in danger of losing his right, and driving the enemy nearly a mile over almost impassable barriers. Captain Brastow never asked his men to go where he was not in readiness to lead them in person. After the fatal attack on Battery Gilmore, the command of the regiment again devolved upon Captain Brastow, when, leading his men against the enemy, at Laurel Hill Church, September 29th, 1864, he was instantly killed. He was a noble young man; none braver ever drew a sword.

Colonel Charles W. Roberts,

A member of the Bangor Light Infantry, was commissioned Lieutenant Colonel of the Second Maine Infantry, at its organization, and upon the promotion of the lamented Jameson, became colonel. At the period of his promotion, his regiment was stationed at Fort

Corcoran. He participated in the siege of Yorktown, in a brilliant engagement at Gaines' Station, and in June following, in the battle of Gaines' Mill or Chickahominy, in the latter of which, Col. Roberts, was in the thickest of the fight, but escaped unharmed. He was also at the battle of Malvern Hill, and again in the battle of Groveton, or Manassas, better known as the Second Bull Run, August 30th, 1862. Here the colonel, who had temporarily assumed command of the brigade, had his horse shot under him, but again escaped without personal injury. In each of these, and several other engagements and skirmishes, Colonel Roberts proved himself to be eminently fitted for his post of command.

In the fall of 1862, Colonel Roberts tendered his resignation, on account of impaired health, the result of unremitting service in the field. He had never left his command for a single day. After much demur, on the part of the Government, and a proffer of a position as Brigadier General, his resignation was finally accepted, and he was honorably discharged, January 10th, 1863.

Captain C. A. Boutelle.

After a brief period at the School of Instruction, at the Charlestown navy yard, he was ordered to report to Rear Admiral S. F. Dupont, commanding the South Atlantic Blockading Squadron, and was by him assigned to duty, on board the United States steamer Paul Jones, a side wheel double-ender, armed with a heavy battery. On this vessel, Mr. Boutelle participated in the blockade of Charleston, South Carolina, in the disastrous Pocataligo expedition, in several engagements with rebel batteries, on Morris Island, and an exchange of rifled compliments with the rebel ironclad Chicoia, across Charleston Bar. Also, in the combined naval and military operations, against the ten-gun battery, on St. John Bluff, near the mouth of the St. John

HON. C. A. BOUTELLE,
LATE U. S. NAVY.

River, Florida, at the capture of which he commanded a battery of navy howitzers, landed and served by United States marines. At the subsequent occupation of Jacksonville, he also landed with howitzer battery, to check the offensive demonstrations of the enemy. The Paul Jones was actively engaged in expeditions and blockading, all along the South Carolina and Georgia coast, and the Atlantic coast of Florida.

In the fall of 1863, Mr. Boutellé was ordered to the United States steamer Sassacus, one of the new double-enders, then fitting out at Boston. On this fine vessel, he was navigator and ordinance officer, and during her first week of service, on the off shore blockade, near Wilmington, North Carolina, two valuable blockade-runners were chased ashore, and destroyed by a boarding crew, from the Sassacus, under Acting Master Boutelle. In the spring of 1864, his vessel was ordered to Albemarle Sound, North Carolina, where the rebel ram, Albemarle, (similar to the Merrimac), had created havoc with our little fleet. May 5th, 1864, a desperate engagement took place, between the ironclad Albemarle and two steam consorts, and the Union wooden fleet, led by the double-enders, Mallabessett, Sassacus, and Wyalusing. In this fight the Sassacus sought to sink the Albemarle, by ramming her at full speed, and very nearly sent her to the bottom. For some twelve or fifteen minutes, the two vessels were engaged in a death grapple, when a hundred pound, solid rifle shot from the ironclad, crashed through the boiler of the Sassacus, killing, and fearfully scalding a number of the latter's crew, and temporarily disabling her, but not until a solid shot, from the one hundred pounder, Parrott gun, of the Sassacus, had entered the Albemarle's port, and inflicted very serious damage.

The rebel iron-clad rapidly retreated to Plymouth River, and remained there moored under the guns of a land battery, until blown up by Lieutenant Commander Cushing, of the navy, with his torpedo launch, some months later. In the early part of the action, the rebel steamer Bombshell, surrendered to the Sassacus. In his report of this engagement, Lieutenant Commander F. A. Roe, of the Sassacus, said : "I take great pleasure in testifying to the fine conduct of Acting Masters A. W. Muldaur, and C. A. Boutelle. These officers were as cool and fearless as if at a general exercise. I respectfully recommend each for promotion to the grade of lieutenant. Deserved for good behavior and ability before the enemy in battle."

Under date of May 24th following, Secretary Wells promptly bestowed upon Mr. Boutelle a commission, declaring : "In consideration of your gallant conduct in the action with the rebel ram Albemarle, on the 5th inst., the department hereby promotes you to the grade of Acting Volunteer Lieutenant in the Navy of the United States."

This was the highest rank then attainable by any volunteer officer of the navy, and there were but few instances of its being conferred in so complimentary a manner. Lieutenant Boutelle after serving temporarily as Executive officer of the United States steamer Eutaw, on the James River, and convoying the ill-fated monitor, Tecumseh, from Norfolk to Pensacola, was ordered in the autumn of 1864, to command the light-draught gun boat Nyanza, stationed at Berwick's Bay, Louisiana. In the winter of 1864-65, he succeeded in obtaining the transfer of his vessel, to participate in the operations against Mobile, Alabama. He volunteered his vessel to pilot the proposed ironclad assault, and his was the first naval vessel that passed through the obstructions to that city. He was immediately dispatched by Admiral Thatcher, to follow the retreating rebel fleet up the Tombigbee River, and captured a boat's crew from Admiral Buchanan's flag ship, Nashville, and a rebel commissary steamer, laden with cotton. A few days later, he made a trip nearly five hundred miles, up the Alabama River, through the heart of the rebel country, bearing dispatches to our army commanders at Selma and Montgomery, terminating the Sherman-Johnson armistice, and ordering a renewal of hostilities. Lieutenant Boutelle, with his vessel, participated at the surrender of the rebel naval fleet at Nannahuffa Bluff, by Confederate Commodore Eben Farrand, May 10th, 1865, and was afterwards ordered to the command of naval forces in Mississippi Sound, the district extending from New Orleans, *via* Lake Ponchartrain to Mobile Bay, with headquarters station at Pascagoula. This closed his active service, and at his own request, Lieutenant Boutelle was honorably discharged from the United States Navy, January 14th, 1866.

During his naval service, he received the highest encomiums of all his superior officers, in their official reports, now on file in the Navy Department. Captain (now retired Rear Admiral), Steedman writes the Secretary, that Mr. Boutelle "performed his duties in a manner to merit my approbation." Commander, (now Commodore) A. C. Rhind, the heroic commander of the Keokuk, in the famous assault on Sumpter, states, officially to the Department: "I regard him, (Mr. Boutelle), as one of the best of the volunteer appointments. Officer-like in his bearing, intelligent, and exhibiting interest in his professional improvement, gunnery and small arms, unusual in one not bred to the service."

Since the war Capt. Boutelle has been engaged in the publishing of a newspaper, and at present ably represents the Fourth District of Maine in Congress, where he has made a national reputation.

Brigadier General Hiram Burnham.

General Burnham commenced his military career as captain of an independent company, at Cherryfield, which he soon made famous for its precision of drill and perfect discipline, and when, in 1839, a war with England, in relation to the north-eastern boundary question, appeared to be impending, and troops were called for to defend the border, Captain Burnham, and his fine company, immediately came forward and offered their services. The command was marched to Calais, where they remained until the threatening cloud of war had happily passed over. Although Captain Burnham saw no actual service at that time, his prompt response to his country's call, and the admirable discipline of his small command, secured for him the high commendation of those in authority, and he was soon promoted to a higher grade in the militia. When the rebellion began, in the spring of 1861, he was offered a command in one of the first regiments raised in Massachusetts, this, however, he declined, in order to assist his own State, in furnishing promptly, her full quota, on the first call of the President. Although no longer a young man, the weight of nearly fifty years being upon him, and his thin locks well sprinkled with gray, and although surrounded by a family of children, whose mother had but recently been removed by death, he did not hesitate as to his duty, when the old flag was fired upon by the hands of traitors. The brave, strong men in the swamps, and on the drive, heard his clarion voice, calling upon them to go with him to the defence and rescue of his imperiled country. He believed in the patriotism and fidelity of the men, and it therefore required but a few days to raise a company in the town of his residence, for the Sixth Regiment, then being organized in that part of the State, and of which he was elected Lieutenant Colonel. In that capacity he was mustered into the U. S. Service, July 15th, 1861. The Sixth Regiment was at once ordered to Washington, where it arrived on the 19th of July. The disastrous battle of Bull Run was fought before this regiment could be incorporated into the main army, but stationed at the Chain Bridge, a few miles above Washington, for several days, during the panic that succeeded the defeat of McDowell, it was the only force defending that important approach to the national capitol.

When the Army of the Potomac was formed, the Sixth was assigned to the brigade of Col. W. F. Smith. Col. Smith being immediately promoted to the command of the division, Brig. Gen. W. S. Hancock was assigned to the command of the brigade. Thus it was Colonel Burnham's good fortune to see his first active service in the war, under these two brave and capable commanders. The drill and discipline of his regiment, from the very first, devolved upon Lieut. Col. Burnham, and he more than verified the promise of military capacity which he had given in his younger days. On the 11th of December, 1861, he was promoted to the Colonelcy of his regiment. While the Army of the Potomac remained inactive in front of Washington, from October, 1861, to March, 1862, Col. Burnham made good use of the time in drilling and disciplining his regiment, and when at last a movement was made by the way of the Peninsula, he had the reputation of commanding one of the most efficient organizations of the army. When the army was organized in corps, his regiment was assigned to the Fourth Corps, Maj. Gen. E. D. Keyes, commanding. With this corps, Col. Burnham participated in the Siege of Yorktown, and during the first week of operations in front of the enemy's lines, his command received the thanks of Gen. McClellan, for a successful and brilliant affair with the enemy, in which no other troops were engaged. He was also in the battle of Lee's Mill. At Williamsburg he distinguished himself in Hancock's brilliant charge on the right of the lines, which virtually decided the battle. So sensible was Gen. McClellan, of Col. Burnham's services on this occasion, that he personally addressed the regiment, a few days after the battle, thanking them for their gallantry and good behavior. In front of Richmond, Col. Burnham participated in all of the operations of the army; his regiment meanwhile having been transferred to the Sixth, A. C., Maj. Gen. Franklin, commanding, but still under its former brigade and division commanders.

In the seven day's battles, he again bore a conspicuous part, his command being engaged with the enemy at Golding's Farm, Savage's Station, White Oak Bridge, White Oak Swamp, and Malvern Hill. His uniform gallantry and efficiency, in all these contests did not escape the observation of his superior officers, and on arriving at Harrison's Bar, Generals Hancock, Smith and Franklin united in recommending him for promotion.

In the action at Crampton's Pass, September 14th, and the battle of Antietam, September 17th, Col. Burnham displayed his usual coolness and bravery. He also bore an honorable part in the unfortunate battle of Fredericksburg, which closed up the operations of the Army of the Potomac for 1862.

In the winter of 1862 and '63, General Smith, commanding the Sixth Corps, organized a Light Division, composed of the picked men of his corps, in which Col. Burnham was assigned to duty, when, Gen. Pratt having tendered his resignation, a few days before the battle of Chancellorsville, the command of that division devolved on Col. Burnham. The famous charge of the Light Division, on the 3d of May, 1863, through the "Slaughter Pen," over the old stone wall, and up the heights of St. Mary, carrrying the enemy's strong works, and capturing seven guns, with many prisoners, again added to the laurels of this officer.

Gen. Sedgwick, who had witnessed this desperate and successful assault, and the cool valor of Col. Burnham, as he led his men on to victory, rode forward to the captured works, and while the battle yet raged fiercely, thanked him for his glorious achievement, and assured him that his services should be rewarded with promotion, at an early day. When Gen. Sedgwick deemed it necessary to withdraw his command to the left bank of the Rappahannock, to Col. Burnham was assigned the important duty of covering the withdrawal of the corps, a perilous duty, which he performed to the full satisfaction of the general in command.

The reduced state of the army rendered it necessary, not long after this, to break up the Light Division, and Gen. Sedgwick, in general orders, expressed his regret at the necessity which compelled the step, saying, "that its services fairly entitled it to be a permanent organization, and its gallant leader, Col. Burnham, to its permanent command."

In the fall of 1863, Col. Burnham's health being completely shattered by his long, arduous and exhausting labors, he was detailed to superintend the recruiting service for his regiment, in Maine, on which duty he remained until February, 1864. During most of that time he was also president of a general court martial, convened at Portland.

On returning to active service, Col. Burnham was assigned to the command of the brigade in which his regiment was serving, and so continued till he was promoted to the rank of Brigadier General, April 15th, 1864. About this time, Gen. Smith, his old commander, was organizing a force at Yorktown, to operate on the south side of the James River, and at his request, Gen. Burnham was ordered to report for service in this force, and was assigned to the command of the Second Brigade, First Division, Eighteenth A. C., on the 22d of April. With the army of the James, he participated in the movement up the James River, and in the subsequent operations at Bermuda Hundred. He was also engaged in the successful attempt to cut the South Side Railroad, May 7th; his command doing the severe fighting on that occasion, driving the enemy from the road, and holding them at bay for several hours, while other forces destroyed the track. He also participated in the demonstration against Petersburg, May 9th and 10th, in which several miles of the South Side Road were destroyed. His command was constantly engaged with the enemy, during these operations, and his gallantry and efficiency were never more conspicuous and serviceable.

During the unfortunate battle near Drury's Bluff, May 16th, he is reported as performing prodigies of valor. Holding his position for hours after our lines were beaten back at other points, he repulsed continuous and determined attacks of the enemy, and captured numerous prisoners. Although two horses were shot under him, during this hotly contested engagement, he miraculously escaped uninjured.

On the 31st of May, he joined the Army of the Potomac, and on the 1st of June, engaged the enemy at Cold Harbor, his command handsomely driving the foe and gaining important advantages. He also fought in the great battle at that place June 3d, and in the subsequent operations in that vicinity up to June 11th, adding to his already glorious record, and winning new commendations from his superior officers.

In the attack upon Petersburg, June 15th, he stormed and carried the enemy's works with his skirmishers, capturing five pieces of artillery, and a considerable number of prisoners. Of this affair an eye witness says: "The success which he achieved placed Petersburg in the grasp of our Union forces, and had there remained two hours of daylight, the terrible struggle which was subsequently waged around the "Cockade City," would never have taken place. Gen. Burnham commanded the First Division of the Eighteenth Corps, on the 30th of July, at the Burnside Mine, holding, with his command, the fortifications of the Ninth Corps, while the attack was made upon the enemy's lines.

About the middle of August, his reduced health rendered rest and a change of climate imperatively necessary. He accordingly proceeded north, and having recruited himself somewhat, by a few weeks with his family, he returned to the field, and again assumed command of his brigade, September 27th. At the time of his return, preparations were being made for a movement of the Army of the James, to the north bank of the James River, and an attack upon the enemy's fortifications at Chapin's Farm. Within twenty-four hours of his arrival in camp, he marshalled his men for a last endeavor against the enemies of his country. During the night of September 28th, a pontoon bridge was thrown across the James, at Aiken's Landing, over which the Eighteenth Corps crossed to the north bank, and with the first gleam of light on the morning of the 29th, the attack upon the rebels commenced. As at Petersburg, on the 15th of June, Gen. Burnham was selected to lead the attacking column. At a short distance from the point of crossing the river, he came upon the enemy's skirmishers strongly intrenched. They were routed and pushed back toward their fortifications, a running fire ensued, the rebels being driven rapidly.

At a distance of about two miles from the river, Gen. Burnham came upon the enemy's work, at Chapin's Farm, and commenced the assault. The struggle was desperate and bloody, but the enemy's resistance was in vain. Gen. Burnham carried their works, triumphantly capturing all of their artillery, and hundreds of prisoners. Still the enemy clung to a portion of the line, and from the right, poured down a destructive fire upon our victorious forces. Gen. Burnham, who had dismounted, in order to enter the captured fort, now rallied such of his forces as he could assemble, and was making a detour, to the rear of these troublesome rebels, in order to attack and secure their capture. As he cheered his men on to the execution of this movement, a minnie ball pierced his abdomen, and he fell. Sorely wounded though he was, and in the agonies of death, he retained all of his mental faculties, and saw his approaching dissolution with a composure and resignation which well became so distinguished a soldier, so eminent a patriot, and so true a man. With shortening breath, he spoke of his family, and then as his long and unselfish services for his country, seemed to flit through his mind, he said: "I have tried to do my duty," when he died without a struggle, as he was being carried from the field, he had so nobly won.

In honor of his memory, the fort, which his stern valor won from the enemy, was called "Fort Burnham."

His remains were embalmed at City Point, and conveyed to his quiet New England home, by a member of his staff, where his obsequies were celebrated.

The funeral of Gen. Burnham occurred at his late home at Cherryfield, on October 6th, 1864.

A committee of the town's people had been elected, and on them devolved the solemn duty of arranging for the last sad honors to the departed hero. By daybreak, the roads running into the town were full of teams, and at the time the exercises were begun, it was estimated that fully three thousand strangers had assembled to do homage to the dead.

The exercises were held at the Baptist Church, and consisted of:

Music by the Ellsworth Band.
Invocation.
Anthem, by the Choir.
Reading of the Scriptures.
Hymn, by the Choir.
Prayer, by Rev. H. F. Harding, of Machias.
Voluntary, by the Choir.
Remarks, by the Rev. Mr. Harding.
Brief address, by Mr. Wm. Freeman.

After the conclusion of the services at the church, a procession was formed in the following order:

Ellsworth Band.
Committee of Arrangements.
Pall Bearers.   Hearse.   Pall Bearers.
Col. Burnham's horse, saddled and booted.
Carriages.

Long lines of citizens followed all that remained of the once noble, gallant patriot, to his last resting place, and lingered even after the good minister had consigned, "dust to dust, and ashes to ashes," to tell, with tearful eye, of the brave deeds and noble traits of character of the dead.

CAPT. SAMUEL W. DAGGETT,

Was commissioned on the first day of August, 1862, as Captain of Company B, First Maine Heavy Artillery, which regiment left the State on the 24th day of August, 1862, under Col. Daniel Chaplin, as the Eighteenth Maine Infantry. The First Maine Heavy Artillery joined the Army of the Potomac, very soon after that army crossed the Rapidan, southward, in the commencement of the summer campaign of 1864, Maj. Gen. Meade commanding, and accompanied in person by Lieut. Gen. U. S. Grant. With full ranks, (eighteen hundred strong), this regiment had its first encounter, with the army commanded by Gen. Lee, in which the casualties were four hundred and fifty killed, wounded and missing.

The regiment thus sadly reduced in numbers, but not in courage and patriotic enthusiasm for the cause of the Union, was in several other engagements in the triumphant progress of the gallant army toward Richmond and Petersburg, in all of which Capt. Daggett, and his gallant Company B, participated, until that in which he, while leading on his brave comrades, received the wound which resulted in his death. In the engagement of June 18th, while very near the enemy's lines, and in the midst of continuous musketry, Capt. Daggett received a wound in the knee, at the moment of drawing his pistol. Being unable to walk, he crawled toward the rear. Encumbered by his rubber coat, he threw that aside, and in the moment of doing this, he received a severe wound in the face. In his further progress toward the rear, the enemy pressing on in squads, he heard a rebel officer give an order to shoot him, when he received another wound in the knee. But faint at times, almost to unconsciousness, for loss of blood and over exertion, he was obliged at last to cast away his sword. He soon reached a gully where he lay concealed, until under the cover of darkness, he found himself among some of his comrades. A corporal bore him on his shoulder to the rear, where he was cared for, for a time, in the field hospital.

He was at length conveyed to David's Island Hospital, in New York, where he died on the first day of July, 1864, at the age of 23 years and 7 months. He bore his sufferings with remarkable fortitude. His widowed mother and one of his sisters were with him in his last hours, and witnessed the peaceful death of a devoted, affectionate, Christian son and brother, one of the worthiest and bravest of the gallant young officers in our Federal Army, who had volunteered their services, and at last their lives, in the glorious cause of Union and Liberty.

CAPT. WILLIAM R. CURRIER,

Of Brewer, responded to the call of his country, in April, 1861, and with others from the same town, joined Company C, Second Regiment Infantry. He was immediately made First Sergeant, and leaving Bangor in May, was in the first battle of Bull Run. August 30th, he was promoted First Lieutenant of the same company. He was in most of the engagements of the Army of the Potomac, and was wounded in action in Virginia. He continued with his regiment until they were mustered out in Bangor, in 1863, having, in the meantime, been promoted Captain. Captain Currier again entered the service, March 15th, 1864, and was mustered in as Captain of Company F, Thirty-First Regiment. He was subsequently promoted Major, but not mustered, having been wounded in battle, which caused his death, August 25th, 1864. He bore the reputation of having been an excellent officer, a strict disciplinarian, and fearless and brave in all the numerous engagements, in which he took any part.

CAPT. HENRY CROSBY.

At the time of his entering the army, Mr. Crosby was part owner, and superintendent, of a paper mill in Hampden, the place of his birth. From the commencement he took a strong interest in everything pertaining to the war, and his first impulse was to enlist among the foremost men who entered the service. But being prevented by private duties, of paramount importance, he gave his immediate attention to aid in raising the quotas of his town. When, however, in 1862, the call for troops for nine months, was made, he obtained the necessary recruiting papers, and in a few days enlisted the town's quota, of about sixty men, who with others from neighboring towns, were organized into a company, of which he was unanimously elected Captain. This company being the first organized, to report at the muster in, of the Twenty-Second Regiment, at Bangor, became Company A. From the time he was mustered in at Bangor, until his death, before Port Hudson, he remained with his company. His brief career in the army, is, therefore, comprised in the history of the Twenty-Second Regiment. Though not favored by the fortunes of the war, with many opportunities for the display of courage and bravery in battle, there were not wanting daily opportunities for the exhibition of virtues more rare. Accepting the command of his company, as a position imposing responsibilities, rather than as conferring privileges, he considered it to be his duty to relieve his men, as far as possible, of the hardships and privations, incident to camp life. Capt. Crosby was struck by a musket ball in the side, early in the morning of June 11th, 1863, while leading his company, in a reconnoissance before Port Hudson. He lived until the next morning, and dying, left as a legacy to his mourning comrades, his last words: "It is a glorious cause to die for."

Dr. Lincoln, chaplain of the regiment, in writing of the deceased to the Bangor Whig, paid a well merited tribute of respect to his memory, when he said: " In the death of Capt. Crosby, we lost one of our best officers, and one of the noblest of men." He was frank, large hearted, and true, like a father in his company, and universally beloved. He had won the confidence of his superiors, as a military man, and only the day before he was wounded, Gen. Banks had offered him the command of a colored regiment. But he had borne his part, and his work was done. Brave and faithful to the last, he fell at the head of his company, leading forward his men. His remains were entombed in New Orleans, but were finally brought home, and found their final resting place in his native town.

Dr. A. C. Hamlin,

Of Bangor, commenced his military career by enlisting at his own sole expense, in Company H, Second Regiment Infantry. He entered the service as Assistant Surgeon, in April, 1861, and served with the above named regiment in the first Bull Run campaign. In April, 1862, he was appointed Brigade Surgeon, and served with the Army of the Potomac, in the Campaign of the Peninsula, up to the battle of Williamsburg, after the fall of Yorktown. He was then transferred to Fremont's Army, in North Virginia, and assigned as Chief Surgeon of the advance guard, and served in all the actions of the campaign, which ended with the battle of Cross Keys. Subsequently, he was chief of the flying hospital of the Army of Virginia, serving in all the actions commencing with the battle of Cedar Mountain, and closing with the battle of Bull Run. He was next assigned a Medical Director of the Eleventh Corps, and retained that position until the battle of Fredericksburg, when he was appointed Medical Inspector of the regular army, and assigned, in the spring of 1863, to the charge of the hospital at Washington. In June following, Dr. Hamlin became Inspector of the Army of the South, operating against Charleston, and participated in the assault against Fort Wagner. In November, he was assigned to the Inspection of the Department of Washington, and served in that capacity until November, 1864, when he was appointed Medical Inspector to the army of Major General Thomas, commanding the Military Division of the Mississippi, in which position he remained until mustered out of service, November, 1865. Dr. Hamlin served in the several campaigns of Generals McDowell, McClellan, Fremont, Siegel, Pope, Burnside, Hooker, in Virginia; Gilmore in the South; and Thomas in the South-west. His record proves him to have been an active and invaluable officer.

LIEUT. GEORGE W. GRANT,

Of Ellsworth, was in the navy at the commencement of the war, and was on board of the "Cumberland," when she sank, barely escaping with his life. He was afterwards mustered into the U. S. Service, August 21st, 1862, as Second Lieutenant of Company C, Eighteenth Regiment Infantry, afterwards First Maine Heavy Artillery, in which he was promoted to be First Lieutenant. He fell, mortally wounded, in the engagement which his regiment and others had, with General Ewell's Corps, in Virginia, May 19th, and died May 27th, 1864. Lieut. Grant was a gallant officer, and one of the bravest of men. His remains were taken to Ellsworth for interment.

BREV. BRIG. GEN. CHARLES D. GILMORE.

This eminent officer, a resident of Bangor, enlisted in the ranks August 10th, 1861, and was commissioned and mustered Captain of Company C, Seventh Regiment, August 21st, 1861. He served with that regiment in the Army of the Potomac, until the 9th day of August, 1862, when he was promoted to Major of the Twentieth Regiment. He was further promoted to Lieut. Col., May 20th, 1862, and to Colonel of the same regiment, June 18th, 1862. He was, also, breveted Brigadier General, to rank from February 6th, 1865, for long and meritorious service, and for gallant conduct in the battle of Hatcher's Run. While Captain in the Seventh Regiment, he was severely wounded by a shell, at the battle of Lee's Mills, April 16th, 1862.

At the battle of Hatcher's Run, February 6th, 1865, the advanced line was forced back, and Col. Gilmore was captured by the enemy. A new line of battle having been formed, which stopped a further advance of the enemy, the Colonel made his escape, by running from the enemy's lines to his own brigade, under a severe fire of the contending armies. On the 7th of December, 1863, Col. Gilmore was detailed by the War Department, as a member of a general court martial, convened in Washington, of which Gen. Robert B. Mitchell was President. He was retained on this duty until October, 1864, when, being relieved, he joined his command in front of Petersburg. On the 22d of February, 1865, he was ordered by the Secretary of War, to report in person to the Adjutant General, at Washington, when he was detailed, as a member of the military commission, of which Col. N. P. Chipman, was Judge Advocate. From his record in the War Department, it appears that Col. Gilmore participated with the Army of the Potomac, in nineteen battles, and that he served with a high degree of fidelity, and with great credit to himself and State. By his own request, after nearly four years' service, and the war having terminated, he was honorably mustered out of the service, May 29th, 1865.

LIEUT. ISRAEL H. WASHBURN,

Of Orono, was one of the young men of Maine, who, from a conviction of duty, when enlistments did not keep pace with the requirements of the service, came forward and encouraged patriotic action, by enlisting in the Sixteenth Regiment. He was appointed Second Lieutenant, and afterward promoted to First Lieutenant. The first battle of his regiment was at Fredericksburg, in December, 1862, and his gallant behavior on that occasion coming to the notice of Maj. Gen. Berry, that lamented officer gave him a position on his staff. Resigning the service in June, 1863, he was subsequently appointed Lieutenant, in the U. S. Marine Corps, and was ordered to report on the U. S. Steamer Rhode Island, the Flag Ship of the West India Squadron.

Col. George Varney.

This officer was mustered into service at Willett's Point, Long Island, N. Y., as Major of the Second Regiment, Maine Volunteers, on the 28th of May, 1861, having previously served in the regiment in that capacity. August 29th, 1861, he was promoted Lieutenant Colonel. He took part in all the service of that command, until the 27th of June, 1862, when he was unfortunately taken prisoner, at the battle of Gaines' Mills, very near the close of the fight, and incarcerated in Libby Prison, until the 14th of August, at which time he was exchanged, and rejoined his regiment at Harrison's Landing. Lieut. Col. Varney's health at that time being much impaired, he was given leave of absence for twenty days, during which the regiment fought at the second battle of Bull Run. Rejoining his regiment about a week afterwards, he went through the Antietam campaign.

Previous to the battle, Colonel Roberts being on leave of absence, the command devolved upon Lieutenaut Colonel Varney, and this he retained through the march from Harper's Ferry to Fredericksburg, in the battle at which latter place he was wounded. On the resignation of Col. Roberts, Lieut. Col. Varney was promoted to be Colonel, his commission dating February 5th, 1863; and as such was engaged in the battle of Chancellorsville. He was mustered out with his regiment June 9th, 1863, and immediately entered active business life, in which calling he is engaged to-day.

Capt. Francis W. Sabine,

Was born in Bangor, August 7th, 1839. He entered Bowdoin College in 1855, and graduated four years afterwards, when he entered upon the study of law, which he was prosecuting when the nation was aroused to arms, in 1861. Imbued with patriotic feelings, he at once abandoned his studies, and enlisted in the Eleventh Regiment of Volunteers, in which, when organized he was made Second Lieutenant of Company E, and subsequently First Lieutenant. In McClellan's Peninsula campaign, at the battle of Fair Oaks, as the commander of a detached picket line, he held position of great hazard, in advance of any other portion of the army. His behavior, on that occasion, won for him honorable distinction for his gallant conduct. During the campaign he was advanced to the grade of Captain, and taken from his company, where there was no vacancy, and commissioned in Company G. While his regiment was in the Department of the South, he held the position of Provost Mashal of Fernandina, and at various times acted as Judge Advocate. During Grant's memorable campaign, from the Rapidan to the James, his regiment formed a part of Butler's army. At the battle in which it was engaged at Deep Bottom, Capt. Sabine was struck in the forehead, by a minnie ball, from the gun of a rebel sharp-shooter. He fell, with his sword raised, encouraging his soldiers to the attack. His wound was apparently slight, though sufficiently severe, to compel him to leave the field, and for a time occasioned no particular alarm. But in a few days, his symptoms assumed a more alarming type; his friends were sent for, and attended upon him during his few remaining days. He died at Chesapeake Hospital, Fortress Monroe, September 17th, 1864. His remains were brought to Bangor, and buried in the family cemetery at Mount Hope.

The regimental commander, in a tribute to his memory, says: "Through all the active service of the regiment, Capt. Sabine was with it, and one of its most efficient and respected officers, in every capacity in which he served, as Provost Marshal, Judge Advocate of Courts Martial, or Advocate for the accused, before the same, and, as commanding officer, he won an enviable reputation in the army, for ability, integrity and gallantry. The ability which he displayed, and the success which attended him, as advocate before the military courts, gave sure promise of high rank and a distinguished career for him, in his chosen profession of the law, had he lived. As a commanding officer, he had no superior of his grade, and few of any grade; his business capacity, his aptness for command, his high sense of honor, his genial disposition and courteous bearing toward all, secured for him the entire confidence and respect of his superiors, and the love and devotion of his men; a devotion which only the truly gifted can win from brave hearts."

As a man and a Christian, none have stood higher in the regards of the community, among whom he had his home, or wherever, for a time, his lot happened to be cast. A deep vein of religious feeling and liberal Christianity seemed to permeate his whole being, constantly exhibiting itself, as a ruling principal of thought and action. His friends have the proud satisfaction of knowing that the principles of life, which he cultivated at home, he carried with him, and maintained unimpaired in the camp, as in the sanctuary; in the conflict of the field, as in the peaceful avocations of business.

Lieut. Col. Daniel F. Sargent.

The material at hand for a biographical sketch of this brave officer is very scant. He commenced his military experience as Captain of Company G, Second Maine Infantry, in which capacity he proved himself an efficient officer, and was highly esteemed by his command. On the promotion of Major Chaplain, to the command of the Eighteenth Infantry, or First Maine Heavy Artillery,

Capt. Sargent was commissioned to fill the vacancy. He was engaged with his regiment in the battle of Manassas, (second Bull Run so-called), in which he displayed especial gallantry Col. Roberts, being at that time in command of the brigade, and Lieut. Col. Varney having been taken prisoner, Maj. Sargent led the Second Maine into and out of the battle in splendid style, and although wounded early in the action, refused to forsake his command until the conclusion of the engagement. Upon the resignation of Col. Roberts, Maj. Sargent received the promotion to Lieutenant Colonel, and as such was mustered out with his regiment on the expiration of their term of service. He subsequently received a Captain's commission, in the District of Columbia Cavalry, and was with that regiment in its early scenes of trial, until in one of its most severe engagements, he was fatally wounded. He was, in all respects, an energetic, faithful and efficient officer.

COL. AUGUSTUS B. FARNHAM,

Was commissioned First Lieutenant, of Company H, Second Maine Regiment, May 13th, 1861; Captain, September 14th, 1861; was commissioned Major, Sixteenth Regiment, August 9th, 1862; Lieutenant Colonel, February 5th, 1863; mustered February 16th, following; May 8th, 1863, Lieutenant Colonel Farnham was appointed by General Robinson, Inspector General and Chief of Staff, Second Division, and subsequently to the same position on Third Division Staff, Fifth Corps, by General Crawford, which position he held until wounded at Five Forks, Virginia, April 1st, 1865. He was breveted Colonel for gallant and meritorious services at battles of Gravelly Run and Five Forks, Virginia, April 1st, 1865. Mustered out, June 5th, 1865. Colonel Farnham, while leading the front line of his division in the charge of the Fifth Corps, at the battle of Five Forks, received a bullet in the lungs, about one and one-half inches from the heart, and fell from his horse; the latter was shot through the jaw, through both hind legs, and in the rump. The Colonel lay on the field until the next morning, when men carried him to the house of a Mr. Moody, the inmates of which rendered him such assistance and attention as was possible, for nearly a month, when a detachment of the Sixteenth, under command of Lieutenant George D. Bisbee of Company C, carried him six miles through the woods to the railroad station, whence he was conveyed by rail to Petersburg, Virginia, thence to City Point and Washington, and placed in Armory Square Hospital, under charge of Surgeon Bliss. He lay at the point of death for weeks; was finally carried to his home in Bangor, Maine, and months elapsed before he recovered a sufficient degree of health to resume business duties. During all his suffering and severe hemorrhages, which occasionally have occured to the present time, Col. Farnham has shown the same quiet fortitude which won for him the love and esteem of his comrades in the field.

Col. Farnham has, for many years, acceptably filled the office of Postmaster at Bangor, but with the change of administration, must of course, come a change in the office. He was succeeded by Capt. Fred A. Cummings, of whom a portrait and sketch are given in this book.

Brev. Brig. Gen. Charles Hamlin.

Before entering the service, this officer was engaged in promoting enlistments, in which he was highly successful, when at length, yielding to his patriotic impulses; he enrolled his name as a soldier for the war. On the 21st of August, 1862, he was com-

Brevet Brig.-Gen. CHARLES HAMLIN.

missioned Major of the Eighteenth Regiment of Volunteers, afterwards the First Regiment Heavy Artillery. While engaged in enlisting men for the field, he raised a large part of two companies for that regiment. On the arrival of his regiment at Washington, he had charge of seven companies of the Eighteenth, which were employed in felling trees, near Fort De Russy, and making abatis for the fortifications of the National Capitol, north of the Potomac. While the regiment was stationed at Fort Alexandria, now known as Fort Sumner, he was placed in command of Fort Franklin. Resigning his regimental commission, May 2d, the following year, to accept the commission as Major, and Assistant Adjutant General, which had been bestowed upon him, he was assigned to duty on the staff of the lamented Maj. Gen. Hiram G. Berry, commanding the Second Division, Third A. C., known as "Hooker's Old Division." Serving in this capacity until the Third Corps was broken up, and consolidated with the Second Corps, he was assigned to duty as Assistant Inspector of Artillery, on the staff of Maj. Gen. A. P. Howe, Inspector of Artillery, U. S. A., remaining on duty until leaving the service, save during the months of July and August, 1864, the time being when Gen. Howe relieved Gen. Sigel. At that time he commanded the military district of Harper's Ferry. He was breveted Lieutenant Colonel, June 18th, and Colonel and Brigadier General, September 28th, for faithful and meritorious services, to date from March 13th, 1863. In all the engagements in which his gallant division participated, from Chancellorsville to the campaign of 1864, he bore an honorable part, devoting himself with characteristic earnestness and fidelity to the work which devolved upon him.

At the battles of Gettysburg, Wapping Heights, Kelly's Ford, James City, McLean's Ford, Locust Grove, Mine Run, Mor ton's Ford, and other places at which his division met the enemy, he never shrank from danger, but met it with a moral courage and coolness, that gained him the approbation of his superior officers. In the official report of the battle of Gettysburg, at which his division suffered a loss of over forty per cent., the severest of the war, Maj. Gen. A. A. Humphrey, commanding the Second Division, Third A. C., thus refers to the subject of this sketch: "It was near dark, and the contest for the day was closed. Its severity may be judged, by the fact, that the killed, wounded and missing of my division, five thousand strong, were two thousand and eighty-eight, (2,088) of whom one hundred and seventy (170) were officers, and one thousand nine hundred and seventeen, (1,917) enlisted men. The missing numbered three officers, and two hundred and sixty-three enlisted men, the greater part of whom were wounded, though some were killed. The fortunes of war rarely places troops under more trying circumstances than those in which my division found itself on this day, and it is greatly to their honor, that their soldierly bearing sustained the high reputation they had already won, in the severest battles of the war. The fine qualities of many officers were brought out conspicuously. In some instances, their gallant conduct, fell under my own observation. I beg leave to express my sense of the obligations I am under, for valuable services rendered me in the field, by Major Charles Hamlin, Assistant Adjutant General."

In a private letter, dated December 17th, 1863, from the late Brig. Gen. William Blaisdell, commanding First Brigade, Second Division, Third A. C., to Hon. Noah Smith, of Calais, that distinguished officer pays a handsome voluntary tribute, to the gallantry and capabilities of Gen. Hamlin. Other testimonials, of a like character, were given by Generals Humphrey, Brewster,

Carr and Caldwell, when informed that he would be presented for promotion to the rank of Colonel of a regiment of infantry, then forming in Maine. In referring to this matter, Gen. Humphrey writes Major Hamlin, "that he would be very glad to see him at the head of a regiment from Maine."

He says: "Having served under my command, as Assistant Adjutant General of the Second Division, Third Corps, I have had the opportunity of learning how zealous, intelligent and efficient you were in the arduous duties imposed on you at all times, and especially in the campaign of Gettysburg, the severest I have yet experienced. I shall esteem myself as fortunate, if I can aid you in any way to advancement, since I consider it my duty to assist forward those of my command, who faithfully performed their duty."

Gen. Wm. R. Brewster, commanding Second Division, Third Corps, thus writes to his Excellency, Gov. Cony: "Major Hamlin has been for some time connected with this division, as its Assistant Adjutant General, and by his uniform good conduct on the field, his close attention to his duties, has won the respect of all, and it gives me great pleasure to bear witness of his capacity, and soldierly qualifications, for the position for which he aspires. He is a gentleman of unimpeachable character and agreeable address, and it is the influence and exertion of men like him, that contributes to elevate the tone and standard of the volunteer service." Brig. Gen. Joseph B. Carr, in his letter to Gov. Cony, of October 28th, 1863, recommending Major Hamlin, for promotion to Colonel, says: "Major Hamlin was assigned to the old veteran division in May, last. He participated in all its movements up to the present time, and on several occasions distinguished himself as an excellent administrative officer, combined with cool and undaunted bravery."

On his retiring from the service, a special order, complimentary to Gen. Hamlin, was issued by the General commanding.

BREV. MAJ. GEN. CYRUS HAMLIN,

Was born in Hampden, Me., April 27th, 1839. His early education was received in the schools of that town, and at the Hampden Academy. He afterwards attended the academies of Hebron, Bethel and Fryeburg, next entering Colby University. Here he remained one year, and then began the study of law. Being admitted to the bar, he practised nearly two years at Kittery, Me., entering the service at the outbreak of the war. He was made an Aid-de-Camp on Gen. Fremont's Staff, and took the field at once in Western Virginia. He was in what was known as the "Mountain Department," and served through the campaign of the spring and summer of 1862, participating in the battles at Strasburg, New Market, Cross Keys, etc. In August, he was ordered to Maine on special duty, but rejoined Gen. Fremont in October.

In January, 1863, he was put on duty as mustering and disbursing officer, being stationed at New York, leaving this position to take an active part in the raising of colored troops, and was made a Colonel of a regiment in the Corps D'Afrique. At the same time, John F. Appleton was made Colonel of a similar regiment, these two officers being the first from Maine appointed to the command of colored troops. The following March he was placed in command of the Second Brigade, Second Division, Corps D'Afrique, at Port Hudson. December 3d, he was promoted to Brig. Gen. Volunteers.

In February, 1865, after the breaking up the corps of colored troops, Gen. Hamlin was assigned to the command of the district of Port Hudson, and in December following was most deservedly

BREVET MAJ.-GEN. CYRUS HAMLIN.

promoted to Brev. Major General of Volunteers, "for distinguished services during the war."

After the war, Gen. Hamlin resumed the practice of law, locating at New Orleans. At this time, his system was thoroughly impregnated with malaria, and this was the cause of his early death.

There was a bright future before him. It was the intention to make him the Governor of Louisiana, which position was, after the death of Gen. Hamlin, given to Governor Warmouth. Modest as this record may appear, few officers in the service have earned a better reputation, or were more universally respected.

BRIG. GEN. CHARLES D. JAMESON,

Was, as Adjutant General Hodsdon says, "one of the best specimens of the chivalrous gentleman, soldier and patriot, which his native State has sacrificed to the Union during the war." As has been mentioned, Gen. Jameson left the State as Colonel of the Second Maine, and his military career, so long as he remained with that organization, is given elsewhere. At the first battle of Bull Run, he won his star as Brigadier. When he was commissioned, he was placed in command of choice regiments from New York and Pennsylvania, and the autumn of 1861 found them encamped on the farm of Hon. George Mason, a bitter rebel. This farm was on a slight eminence overlooking the Potomac, and about one and one-half miles from Alexandria. The camp was known as "Camp Jameson," and here the General endeared himself to his men. The history of the celebrated "Wild Cat," or One Hundred Fifth Pennsylvania Regiment, says:

"The General was a great favorite with the men. Himself a lumberman from the forests of Maine, he could appreciate the hardy, stalwart sons of the forest, who, in a great measure, composed the material of which the 'Wild Cat' regiment was made up."

With these men, Jameson fought at Yorktown, Williamsburg, Fair Oaks, and in other fields of battle. He was the first to enter Yorktown, and one of the first to enter Williamsburg. At the battle of Fair Oaks, it is believed that Jameson carried the stars and stripes, and by its side the Pine Tree banner of Maine. nearer Richmond than any other, either before or for a long time after. Capt. Craig, of the "Wild Cats," writing home soon after this, said:

"General Jameson is very sick, and looks very badly. I am afraid we may lose him; and if we should be so unfortunate as to do so, I fear we will hardly get his equal soon again. He is one of the *best men* I ever knew—as brave as a lion, and still as tender hearted as a child; as, for instance: On the day of the battle, (Fair Oaks), after fighting like a tiger through that terrible afternoon, and passing through that storm of leaden hail, as if he never knew of danger, when night came, and all our troops were called from the field, (or rather what were left), he came to me and told me what disposition to make of my company through the night, and asked me what I thought our loss would be. I told him I could not tell. He studied a little, and then looked up to me and said, 'Great God! my whole brigade is cut to pieces,' and then sat down on a log and cried like a child."

Alas! the fear expressed in the above, was only too well grounded, as soon after, General Jameson was obliged to return to his home in Stillwater, Maine. Some idea of the high regard entertained for him by his brother officers, and of their efforts to assist him in every way, can be gained by a perusal of the following order, the Capt. Smith mentioned, being Gen. Jos. S. Smith, of Bangor.

"HEADQUARTERS, ARMY OF THE POTOMAC,"
JUNE 13th, 1862.

GENERAL:

Under the peculiar circumstances of the case, the Commanding General desires that you will grant a leave of absence, for seven days, to Capt. Jos. S. Smith, Commissary of Subsistence, at General Sedgwick's headquarters, to enable him to accompany to the North, General Jameson, now very low at the White House.

Very respectfully, your obedient servant,

S. WILLIAMS, A. A. G.

To Brigadier General E. V. SUMNER,
Commanding Second Corps.

General Jameson intended to return again to the field; but it was not so ordered by Providence, and he sank gradually, until on the 6th of November, 1862, he died.

It sums up this narrative that Jameson was one of the first to volunteer, was the first Colonel from Maine in the field; that he was first at Yorktown, and among the first and foremost toward Richmond; one of the first in gallantry; one of the first in the love and admiration of his men. Alas! that he should be the first General of Maine to die. At thirty-five years of age, it was hard for the country to lose such a gallant spirit, but the State has gained the memory of a hero.

The Washington Republican speaks as follows of the qualities which distinguished our gallant General:

"Intrepid, enterprising, but withal judicious, Gen. Jameson had before him the prospects of a most brilliant military career. He was one of the fighting Generals.

As he, with others of the salvoed chiefs of fearless men, who lately have left us—when we could have better spared others of another mould than theirs—as he, and Kearney and Stevens, shall reach the shores of that dark river, made mournful by Cerberus' ceaseless howl, the waiting hosts of the bravest dead of all the past, will recognize their beaming blades, nor will they seek to dispute them place amid their front and foremost rank."

The funeral of the lamented Jameson took place at Upper Stillwater, November 9th, and was conducted by Bishop Burgess. A cold rain fell that day, but the attendance was large, and there were many others, yes, the State felt that she was putting away, to his last resting place, one of the bravest and best of her sons.

The remains were laid away in the village church-yard, at Upper Stillwater, where rests father, mother, and relatives.

Lieut. Col. Winslow P. Spofford,

Was a native of Georgetown, Massachusetts, where he resided until the year 1839, when, at the age of twenty-three years, he removed to Dedham, this State, residing there until the commencement of the Rebellion. Although at this time he held several offices of trust, and was, by age, exempt from military service, he felt it his duty to enter the service of his country, in her hour of peril. Early in the summer of 1861, he assisted to recruit a company, for the Eighth Maine Regiment, and in the autumn of the same year, recruited a company for the Eleventh Regiment, of which he received a commission as Captain. He was in the whole of the Peninsula campaign, and was highly complimented, by his superior officers, for his fidelity and bravery. In the fall of 1862, he was commissioned Major, and in November, 1863, was further promoted to Lieutenant Colonel, and as such, had command of the regiment for nearly a year previous to his death.

In a severe engagement at Bermuda Hundred, June 2d, Col. Spofford was wounded while on the picket line, and later was taken to Fortress Monroe, where he died June 17th, 1864. His brother officers always speak of him in the highest terms, and Gen. Plaisted says:

"Col. Spofford won his promotions by the zeal and faithfulness with which he performed every duty. He entered the service of his country from the highest motives, ready and willing to give his life, if need be, for his country's cause. We lost a brave and faithful soldier, and a Christian patriot in his death."

Major Joel A. Haycock.

This gallant officer was born in Calais, Jan. 11th, 1836, and was the first man to enlist in the first company of volunteers raised in his native city. Honest, patriotic and brave, burning with all the untamed ardor of early manhood, he was peculiarly fitted to render acceptable service to his country, in the terrible conflict for which she was buckling on her armor. When he enlisted, he left a lucrative employment, but his was too impulsive and generous a temperament to weigh pecuniary advantages against duty and patriotism.

On the organization of his company, he was chosen Captain, his command rendezvoused at Eastport, and afterwards at Portland, where it was assigned to the Sixth Regiment, as Company D, with which he proceeded to Washington, where they arrived on the 19th of July. Being too late to march into Virginia, and participate in the battle of Bull Run, they were stationed at Chain Bridge, to hold that important approach to the National Capitol in case of disaster. Here the regiment remained until the 1st of September, the interim being devoted to drill and discipline.

About this time, the second general movement of troops into Virginia commenced, under McClellan. Probably no officer in the army more earnestly hoped for an active campaign against the enemy than Capt. Haycock. Instead, however, of an advance, the fall was occupied in lining the south bank of the Potomac with fortifications, in grand reviews and in cautiously advancing from two to eight miles into Virginia. Nothing more was done until the army was set in motion early in the spring of 1862, by the famous War orders of President Lincoln himself.

The Peninsula Campaign which followed, unfortunate and disastrous though it was, was still a glorious struggle for success, by the rank and file of the army, and was far more consonant with Capt. Haycock's patriotic ardor. The Captain fought in command of his company at Lee's Mills; he skirmished and labored throughout the Siege of Yorktown; he participated in the brilliant and remarkable success of the regiment at Williamsburg; he marched with the command in the advance upon Richmond, and bore a conspicuous part in the ceaseless activity and exhaustive labor in front of the rebel capitol. He was foremost in the fight at Garnett's Farm, and his intrepidity was notable at Savage Station and White Oak Swamp during the Seven Days' battles, and when the army arrived at Harrison's Landing, he was specially commended by his commander in official reports, for gallantry in the above named battles.

When the Army of the Potomac was withdrawn from the Peninsula, he marched with his regiment to succor Pope's hard pressed forces, at the second battle of Bull Run. They arrived a few hours too late to take part in that desperate struggle. When the rebel hordes invaded Maryland, Capt. H. fought at the battles of Sugar Loaf Mountain, Crampton's Pass and Antietam. When the Army of the Potomac again marched into Virginia, Capt. Haycock fought with his men at Fredericksburg. This closed the active operations for 1862. His faithful services were rewarded, by his promotion as Major of his regiment, in March 1862, much to the satisfaction of his men. When the campaign was resumed in Virginia, in 1863, Gen. Hooker fought the battle of Chancellorsville with the greater part of his forces. The Sixth Corps was assigned to the duty of seizing the rebel position, in front of Fredericksburg. Their path lay right across the "Slaughter Pen," where Burnside's forces had been repulsed in December. Foremost among his comrades, Major Haycock rushed forward, to the terrible encounter, and half way across the "Slaughter Pen" he fell, pierced by a minnie ball, and expired almost instantly, thus sealing his devotion to his country's cause, by his heart's blood. The fierce, wild charge of his regiment swept away the opposing enemy, as chaff is swept before the wind, and their colors were planted in triumph upon the ramparts. But even in the first flush of victory, Col. Burnham, the commander of the regiment wept as a child, when he beheld the prostrate and lifeless form of this valiant and true hearted warrior. They buried him where he had fallen, half way up the green slope, which had drank so deeply of the Nation's best blood. He fills a soldier's grave and one ever to be honored.

BREV. BRIG. GEN. HARRIS M. PLAISTED.

On the 23d of September, 1861, this officer received from Gov. Washburn, authority to raise a company of volunteers for the Thirteenth Regiment, but on reporting at Augusta, was assigned to the Eleventh Regiment, of which he was commissioned Lieutenant Colonel, October 30th. He left the State November 13th, for Washington, where he was placed in charge of a school of instruction for commissioned officers. On the 28th of March following, he entered upon active campaigning. In 1862, he was in the Peninsula campaign, under McClellan; in 1863, in the siege of Charleston, under Gilmore; and in 1864 and '65, in the great campaign against Richmond, under Grant.

Lieut. Col. Plaisted was in the siege of Yorktown, and also in the battle of Williamsburg, in which he won deserved renown, being the first, on May 4th, 1862, to raise our flag over the rebel fortifications, at Lee's Mills. On the 12th of May, he was commissioned Colonel, and on the 22d, was mustered as such, to take rank from April 28th, the date of the vacancy. On the 20th of the same month, he drove the enemy from the railroad bridge, over the Chickahominy, and saved the bridge from destruction, after it had been fired by the enemy. On the 24th and two following days, Col. Plaisted led the advance from this point towards Richmond, and succeeded on the 26th, in establishing our outposts within four and a half miles of that city. On the 28th, 29th and 30th, he built a lumberman's bridge across the Chickahominy, thus connecting the two wings of the Army of the Potomac.

On May 31st, Col. Plaisted was in the hottest of the battle of Fair Oaks, unfortunately losing more than half of the men, and two-thirds of the officers under him. On the second day of that desperate battle, he was placed in command of the brigade, all the other Colonels of the brigade, and Gen. Naglee having been put *hors de combat*, on the previous day. On the 14th and 15th days of June, he held the Bottom's bridges against Stuart's cavalry, in his celebrated raid around the Army of the Potomac. During the battle of Chickahominy, or Cold Harbor, the decisive battle of the Peninsula campaign, he was placed in charge of the railroad bridge over the Chickahominy, with the Eleventh Maine, five companies of the Fifty-Second Pennsylvania, and a battery of artillery, with orders to hold the bridge at all hazards. On the appearance of the enemy, therefore, he burnt, and effectually destroyed the bridge, on the night of the 28th, and successfully resisted the passage of the enemy, until the following night, when he retreated with the rear guard across White Oak Swamp. At the same time, he had destroyed two locomotives and a train of cars, loaded with an immense quantity of ammunition.

On the 30th of June, the day following the retreat, Col. Plaisted commanded the Eleventh Maine and One Hundredth New York Regiments in the battle of White Oak Swamp Bridge, when he protected the Eleventh from loss by hastily constructed breastworks, although subjected to a terrific fire of artillery. At night, however, they were compelled to retreat to the James River.

July 1st, he supported the artillery in the battle of Malvern Hill. Being the only field officer with his regiment, the duties devolving upon Col. Plaisted during the Seven Days' battles were so arduous and exhaustive, that on the 2d of July he was compelled to go to the hospital. He rejoined his regiment at Yorktown, August 22d, but again, with health and strength most seriously impaired, he returned to the hospital, and on this occasion with but slight prospect of recovery. He was, however, enabled to resume the command of his regiment, November 1st. In the interim, while in Maine on sick leave for twenty days, he recruited upwards of three hundred men. From the 11th to the 15th inclusive, of December, he commanded his regiment in an expedition from Yorktown into the enemy's country, penetrating to within a few miles of the Rappahannock, and within hearing of the cannon at the battle of Fredericksburg. In this expedition, the Eleventh was distinguished for good conduct, for which reason all important prisoners were committed to its charge for safe keeping; whilst in the retreat, it was assigned to the post of honor, the rear guard. It was also complimented by Gen. Naglee in his General Orders.

In the latter part of December, the Eleventh was transferred to North Carolina, and thence to South Carolina, with the detachment of the Eighteenth Corps under Maj. Gen. Foster, reaching Hilton Head the last of January, 1863. After two months on St. Helena Island, spent in drilling, Col. Plaisted commanded the regiment in the expedition against Charleston, in April, under Gen. Hunter and Admiral Dupont. He was next stationed at Beaufort, S. C., until the 1st of June, when he was ordered to Fernandina, Fla., to command that post, including Fort Clinch. He also had charge of twelve hundred freedmen. Here he instructed his regiment in Light and Heavy Artillery tactics, and in the art of fortification. After this instruction, he furnished a detachment of the Eleventh to Gen. Gilmore, to serve as artillerists in the siege of Fort Wagner, and having charge of the Swamp Angel battery, threw the first shot into the city of Charleston.

On the 1st of October, Col. Plaisted was ordered with his regiment to Morris Island, and assigned to the command of the First Brigade, Gen. Terry's Division, consisting of the Ninth and Eleventh Maine, and the Second and Fourth New Hampshire Regiments. The Eleventh was then assigned to duty at the front, as artillerists, to serve the big guns and mortars at Forts Wagner, Gregg and Chatfield. As brigade commander, he was actively engaged in the siege of Charleston until the 16th of April, 1864. In December following, he received his second leave of absence, when, in thirty days spent in Maine, he recruited fifty-two men, and obtained two hundred others, by authority of the War Department, from the draft rendezvous at Portland.

Upon the re-organization of the Tenth Corps, and its transfer to Virginia in April, Col. Plaisted was assigned to the command of the Third Brigade, First Division, consisting of the Eleventh Maine, Tenth Connecticut, Twenty-Fourth Massachusetts, and One Hundredth New York. He landed at Bermuda Hundred, on the night of May 5th, and on the 7th commanded the brigade in the battle of Green Valley or Walthall Junction, fought on our side by five picked brigades from the Tenth and Eighteenth Corps. This was the first attempt of the Union forces to cut the Richmond and Petersburg railroad. By a flank movement, Col. Plaisted placed his brigade upon the flank of the enemy, drove him from the railroad, destroyed a trestle bridge, and tore up the track and four lines of telegraph, whilst at the same time, for two hours and a half, with a portion of his command, he was constantly engaged with the enemy.

On May 8th, Col. Plaisted was ordered by Gen. Gilmore to the command of three brigades, five batteries, and the Corps of Engineers, to construct a line of intrenchments as a base for the Tenth Corps. Within two days, with two thousand men working day and night, he succeeded in the completion of the original Bermuda Hundred defences. May 13th he led the advance of the Tenth Corps, with his brigade, in a brilliant flank movement to the rear of Drury's Bluff, which resulted, after a sharp engagement, in the capture of the enemy's outer line of intrenchments around Fort Darling. On the following day, he was engaged with the enemy's second line until 11 P. M., when his brigade severely repulsed a determined assault of the rebels. On May 16th, he fought the enemy in the bloody battle of Drury's Bluff, and in the retreat, with his brigade and the Thirty-Ninth Ill., covered the rear. The loss of the brigade in this battle was 404, but it never faced the enemy but to beat him. On the 17th, he was further occupied in the affair of Richmond Pike, when two regiments of his brigade made a night attack on Beauregard's trains, with a loss of twenty-seven men killed and wounded. On the 20th, he commanded the brigade in the battle of Bermuda Hundred defences, in which the Eleventh won an enviable reputation. It lost, however, forty men and five commissioned officers, including Lieut. Col. Spofford, fatally wounded, but was the only regiment on the Union front whose line was not broken by the enemy.

On the 16th of June, Col. Plaisted commanded the brigade in the battle of the Richmond and Petersburg Railroad, in which the rebel intrenchments were captured and the railroad cut. Lee's army, following Grant to Petersburg, having crossed the James River on the morning of that day, the Union forces were compelled to fall back. Having been notified early in the day that his command would cover the retreat, Col. Plaisted had "turned" the rebel fortifications and fortified Ware Bottom Church, and finally in the retreat made a stand at the latter place, and repulsed a fierce attack of Lee's veterans. He held the position against almost constant attacks of the enemy's infantry and artillery until the 18th, when he fortified a new line under heavy artillery fire, at night burnt the church, and fell back. On the night of June 20th, Col Plaisted, with his brigade, led the advance of Butler's descent upon the north bank of the James River, at Deep Bottom, and fortified that position.

On the 23d of July, Col. Plaisted commanded his regiment in a severe fight on Strawberry Plains, in which the Eleventh alone won an important position on the New Market Road, holding it until the following morning, when being relieved by a brigade of the Nineteenth Corps, Col. Plaisted returned with his regiment to

Deep Bottom. At midnight of the 25th, however, with the Eleventh Maine and Tenth Connecticut Regiments, he returned to Strawberry Plains, with orders to take command of the battery and seven regiments stationed there, and recapture the position on the New Market Road, the brigade of the Nineteenth Corps having been driven out. In this he succeeded after a hard fought engagement of ten hours duration, the position being finally won by a gallant bayonet charge of the Eleventh Maine and a portion of the Tenth Connecticut. He held this position during the night of the 26th, and on the morning of the 27th, he participated with Hancock's Corps and Sheridan's Cavalry, which arrived during the night, in the battle of Strawberry Plains; the Eleventh Maine and Tenth Connecticut capturing four pieces of artillery. In these engagements, the Eleventh won a reputation for gallantry second to no other regiment in the army.

On the 14th of August, Col. Plaisted commanded the Eleventh Maine in the battle of Deep Bottom, charging in skirmish order, carrying the enemy's position with a loss of nine killed and forty wounded, among the latter of whom were the gallant Maj. Baldwin and the lamented Capt. Sabine. On the 16th, he commanded the regiment in the battle of Deep Run, and charging two lines of rebel earthworks, captured them at the point of the bayonet, with a loss of ninety-six killed and wounded, out of less than three hundred of the Eleventh Regiment actually engaged. Of the officers, the brave Lieut. Col. Hill lost his right arm, and the noble Lawrence his life in this affair. In the charge upon the enemy's main line, the rebel General Gherrardie was killed and his body captured. The regiment was again in battle at Russell's Mills on the 18th, and repulsed the enemy in its attack on the Tenth Corps. At night, Col. Plaisted was selected by Gen. Berry to command the rear guard of one thousand picked men. On the 22d, having returned to Deep Bottom, he was placed in command of all the Union troops at that post and Strawberry Plains. On the 26th, he was further ordered to Petersburg with his brigade, to which the First Maryland Cavalry was now attached. He commanded the brigade in the siege of Petersburg until the 28th of September, whilst at the same time he acted at Engineer Officer, in charge of the construction of field fortifications, comprising six hundred yards of infantry parapet.

In the night of September 28th, Col. Plaisted crossed the James River at Deep Bottom with the Tenth Corps, and on the 29th commanded the brigade in the battle of New Market Heights or Chapin's Farm. On October 1st, while repulsing an attack of the enemy on the position held by this brigade, Col. Plaisted was struck from his horse by a minnie ball in the breast, but saved from a severe, if not fatal wound by a memorandam book in his pocket. On the following day, he made a reconnoissance up the New Market Road to the Laurel Hill batteries, in support of Gen. Gerry's dash up the Darby Town Road. On the 7th, he commanded the brigade in the battle of New Market Road, in which the enemy sought to turn the right flank of the Army of the James and dislodge it from its position before Richmond. In the heat of the action, Col. Plaisted moved his brigade to the extreme right flank of the army, and, receiving the brunt of the battle, repulsed the enemy with signal success and saved the flank from being turned. On the 13th of the same month, he again commanded the brigade in the obstinate fight of the Darby Town Road, which continued without one minute's cessation for ten hours. In this desperate encounter, one regiment of the brigade lost every company commander and one field officer, five of them being killed on the field. Col. Plaisted covered the rear in the retreat, and in repulsing the onsets of the enemy, captured the only prisoners taken by the Union army during the day.

On the 27th of October, the Colonel commanded the brigade in the battle of Charles City Road, or the second Fair Oaks, a general engagement of the Army of the James, from the New Market Road to the Chickahominy, in which the brigade fully shared the losses and honors of the day. He then covered the rear in the retreat, remaining in contact with the enemy until noon of the 28th. On the 29th, the enemy having captured the fortifications on the Johnson Plantation, held by our cavalry, Col. Plaisted was ordered to regain them. When, mustering his forces, he recaptured the works by a brilliant bayonet charge across an open plain of three hundred yards. This proved the last engagement of the enemy north of the James. Between May 7th and October 29th, Col. Plaisted's command was engaged with the enemy almost daily, having men killed and wounded on fifty-nine different days, and losing in the aggregate one thousand three hundred and eighty-five men out of two thousand six hundred and ninety-three. In this campaign, three hundred and sixty-three of the Eleventh Maine, sealed their devotion to their country's cause with their blood.

On the 2d of November, Col. Plaisted left the front, with the men of the Eleventh Regiment, whose term of three years service had expired, for Augusta, Maine, to be mustered out, when twelve commissioned officers, and one hundred and thirty-one enlisted men were finally discharged. Returning to the front the latter part of the same month, he was assigned, on the re-organization of the Army of the James, to the command of his old brigade, which, with the addition of another full regiment and squads of recruits, brought up its number to three thousand five hundred men, in the command of whom he remained during the winter.

On the 21st of February following, Col. Plaisted received from the President, the well earned promotion of Brevet Brigadier General of Volunteers. During the months of February and March, he was confined to his tent the greater portion of the time by sickness, and finally mustered out March 25th, after having faithfully served exactly three years and six months.

Gen. Plaisted has resided in Maine since the war, and when the Greenback wave swept over the State, became the standard-bearer of the party and was elected Governor. He now resides in Augusta, being the principal owner of, and interested in the management of the "*New Age*" newspaper.

Col. Jasper Hutchings,

Was born in the town of Penobscot, Hancock county, in 1835. When thirteen years of age, his family removed to Brewer, where, save during the time spent in the army, he has resided. Here his early education was gained, he finishing at Williams College, Mass. He then read law with the Hon. Abraham Sanborn, one of the best lawyers of his day, and on being admitted to the bar, hung out his modest shingle in Aroostook county, where it remained until the spring of 1862.

He now forsook the paths of law, and assisted in recruiting Company C, Twenty-Second Regiment, and in the fall of '62 was commissioned First Lieutenant of said company, of which George A. Boulton was Captain. With this regiment, Lieut. Hutchings remained during all its active service, and took part with it in the siege and capture of Port Hudson. The Twenty-Second, being a "nine months" regiment, and its term of service about to expire, Lieut. Hutchings resigned from this grade of the service, and immediately proceeded to organize the Eleventh Regiment, Corps D'Afrique (afterwards known as the Eighty-Third U. S. Colored

Infantry). Here he held the rank of Major, although he commanded. For Lieut. Col. this regiment had a medical man, Dr. J. V. C. Smith, who was attached to Bank's Staff. Strange to say, this gentleman of influence *never saw his regiment*, and was given the position only that he might gain the rank.

In the fall of 1864, while in Louisiana, Maj. Hutchings was commissioned Lieut. Col. of the Seventy-Eighth U. S. Colored Infantry, with which the Ninety-Eighth was afterwards consolidated. He continued with this rank and regiment until January 1866, when his regiment was mustered out of the service.

While in the service, Col. Hutchings was many times honored with positions of trust, and requiring clear judgment. He served several times in various capacities, on Courts Martial, on Military Commissions, and also as a member of the board to examine officers.

Relieved of his military duties, Col. Hutchings again resumed the practice of law, in Bangor, in 1866, where he has since remained, and where he has gained a position among the leading lights of the bar. He is one of the best known criminal lawyers of the State, and will be remembered as having been attorney for Calvin Graves, the murderer of the game wardens in Washington county.

Lieut. W. H. H. Rice,

Enlisted at Ellsworth, and was made Second Lieutenant of Company G, Eleventh Regiment. He participated in all the actions of that body up to the time of his wound, at the battle of Fair Oaks.

At the time of that battle, Lieutenant Rice was sick and in hospital, where there were a number of the men of the Eleventh.

After the fight grew warm, he exclaimed: "Boys, all who can hold up their heads, follow me," He then shouldered a musket, and they all joined the regiment and fought gallantly.

Rice, after firing seventeen rounds with deadly effect, for he was a crack shot, fell severely wounded, and was carried from the field. While he was in the hospital, he was promoted to First Lieutenant, "for his gallant conduct in the late battle." He died July 1st, 1862, the immediate cause of his death being consumption, brought on by his wounds, and by exposure. His body was embalmed by order of Chaplain Henries, and sent home to Ellsworth, for burial. He was a brave soldier, and a noble young man, and would undoubtedly have made his mark, high in military circles, had he lived.

CAPT. F. A. CUMMINGS,

Was born in Bangor, in 1838. His early life, after receiving his education, was spent on the ocean and in following his trade as carpenter. The year before the war found him in the South, in the State of Louisiana, where he was employed on a railroad. At the beginning of the war, his father organized Company I, Ninth Maine, and was made Captain, and afterwards promoted to be Commissary of Subsistence, and attached to the staff of Jameson. F. A., the subject of this sketch, at this time went to the front, acting as clerk for his father. The latter being taken ill, F. A. was given the power of attorney, acting in his place. After the battle of Williamsburg, Capt. Cummings, still a civilian, came home and, in conjunction with W. S. Clark, raised Company E, Eighteenth Maine, and was made a Lieutenant of it. When this regiment was transferred to the artillery, and two companies added, Cummings was made Captain. Previous to his de-

Capt. F A. CUMMINGS.

parture, it may here be stated he organized Company L. While in the service, Capt. Cummings passed an examination, and was offered a position in the Colored Service, which he declined. He fought with his regiment until November 17th, 1864, when he was discharged for disability. In one battle a bullet struck his watch in his vest pocket, breaking that instrument and also two of the Captain's ribs. His time of service was thirty-one months.

After the war, Capt. Cummings returned again to his labors, being for twelve successive years a scaler and surveyor for Messrs. Coe & Boynton. In 1883, he was elected Mayor of Bangor, being the working-men's candidate. In 1887, he was appointed Post Master of the city of Bangor; his fine war record contributing largely to his success. This office he now holds.

JAMES W. CLARK,

Was born in Sangerville, February 11th, 1839, and in early life moved to Great Falls, N. H., where, April 23d, 1861, he enlisted as a private in a three months' regiment. He afterwards enlisted for three years, and became a member of Company H, Second New Hampshire Volunteers, commanded by Col. (afterwards Brig. Gen.) Gilman Marston. The regiment left New Hampshire for Washington about the middle of June, previous to which time, Private Clark received his first promotion by being appointed Corporal.

With his regiment he marched into Virginia, in July, and participated in the disastrous battle of Bull Run, seeing what was then accounted severe fighting. For his gallantry in this engagement, he was shortly afterwards promoted to the rank of Sergeant. His regiment saw no more active service until the Peninsula campaign. Meanwhile it was assigned to duty with the original brigade of Gen. Hooker, and afterwards formed a part of his division in Heintzleman's Corps. Under this distinguished officer, Sergeant Clark labored and fought at Yorktown, participating in a brilliant and successful attack, upon an annoying outwork of the enemy. When at length the rebels were unearthed, he fought at the bloody battle of Williamsburg, when his regiment suffered severely, the brunt of the action being borne by Hooker's division. Marching up the Peninsula, he participated in all the operations of the army, in the vicinity of Richmond, fighting at Fair Oaks, battle of the Swamp, Peach Orchard, Savage's Station, White Oak Swamp, Glendale and Malvern Hill. During all this campaign he never left his company for a day, although worn down and weakened by the malarious diseases of the Peninsula, his indomitable courage kept him at his post of duty.

A single instance of his heroism deserves narration. At the battle of the Swamp, June 25th, Col. Marston, after a spirited and successful charge, found his regiment flanked, and virtually cut off from the co-operating forces. Determined to hold the hard won position, he called for a volunteer to carry a dispatch to Gen. Cuvier Grover, the brigade commander. The peril of the undertaking was sufficient to appal the stoutest heart. There was a momentary hesitation in the ranks, until Sergeant Clark stepped forward and received the dispatch. Gliding stealthily from tree to tree, he ran the fierce gauntlet of the rebel fire, reached Gen. Grover in safety, and executed his mission. Fresh troops were ordered up, and the position was held. His act of gallantry was not forgotten by the Colonel, and on more than one occasion thereafter, when the Second New Hampshire was hotly engaged with the enemy, he called for Sergeant Clark, and kept him by his side, or employed him in carrying orders and dispatches.

Just before the Peninsula was evacuated, Sergeant Clark received, from the Governor of Maine, a commission as First Lieutenant of Company E, Eighteenth Maine Volunteers, afterwards the First Maine Heavy Artillery. Application was at once made for his discharge, but it was not issued until his regiment had arrived at Alexandria, and was on the point of pushing out to the support of Pope's forces. He was not the man to part from his old comrades at such a time, but again shouldering his musket, he marched with them towards the enemy, and participated in Gen. Hooker's fierce fight for the railroad in the vicinity of Manassas, on the 29th of August, and in the second battle of Bull Run, a day or two later. In both of these engagements, he fought by the side of Col. Marston.

Lieut. Clark joined the Eighteenth Regiment at Washington, and entered upon his duties as First Lieutenant of Company E. His regiment remained in that vicinity until Grant's campaign from the Rapidan to Petersburg was inaugurated. Meanwhile, his intelligence and marked efficiency as an officer had attracted the notice of his superiors, and in April, 1864, he was promoted to be Adjutant of his regiment, now the First Heavy Artillery. In May, he marched with his regiment to join Grant's forces, and participated in the most terrific campaign of the war. He fought with his comrades in their bloody encounter with the enemy near Spottsylvania Court House, May 19th; at Tolopotomoy, at North Anna, at Cold Harbor, June 1st and 3d; and in the subsequent operations at the latter place up to June 12th. On all these occasions he displayed the same coolness, dash and bravery, which had given him so enviable a name among his old comrades of the Second New Hampshire Regiment; and these qualities did not fail to win for him the confidence and admiration of the officers and men with whom he associated.

When the army was withdrawn from Cold Harbor, he marched with his regiment in the movement upon Petersburg, and fought with them in their hot engagements at that place on the 16th and 17th of June. Foremost among his comrades in their most heroic but terribly unfortunate charge upon the enemy's works, on the 18th of June, he was severely wounded in his right arm, when he was conveyed to the army hospital, David's Island, New York harbor. After languishing in the hospital three weeks, during which time he suffered intensely, he submitted to the amputation of his limb, and died on the 31st of July. His remains were conveyed by his bereaved wife to his home, and there buried in an honored grave.

ADJUT. GEN. JOHN L. HODSDON.

It is universally conceded among military men, that Maine had, in the person of John L. Hodsdon, the most efficient Adjutant General to be found in the North.

At the age of sixteen, he enlisted in the Bangor Light Infantry, and subsequently became a member of the Major General's Staff of the Third Division of the Maine Militia, with the rank of Major, and in January, 1839 was officially with the troops, called into service for the protection of Maine's northeastern frontier, in the immediate vicinity of Fort Fairfield, Aroostook county. After occupying that point for some time, a treaty was effected between the two governments and the troops were withdrawn. During the period between 1839 and 1861, Gen. Hodsdon was filling the various military offices, from Major to Major General, passing up the numerous intervening grades, and was twice made Brigadier General.

January 9th, 1861, he was elected by the legislature, Adjutant

General, a most fortunate choice, retiring after seven annual and almost unanimous elections at the hands of the several legislatures, it being upon the completion of his six volume of "Official Reports" of some eight thousand pages, affording all participants in the war recognition by name, annually, while remaining in the service of our State's military organizations, for the entire period of the war.

His official services closed upon his resignation, March 31st, 1867, with the completion of his sixth volume of "Official Reports," embodying a most exhaustive history, in detail of Maine's part in the war. This is a volume of nearly fourteen hundred pages, and contains the name and rank of every individual mustered into the United States service in Maine, with its every organization, from April 1861, to March 31st, 1867. Gen. Hodsdon's reports were eagerly sought by all the United States Government officials of the military departments, the moment they came from the book-binder, so greatly did they facilitate the settlement of accounts with officers and soldiers, and the procurement of pensions.

Gen. Hodsdon still resides in Bangor, and is still authority on military matters. In addition to the position of Adjutant General, he held, during the war, the important trusts of Acting Quartermaster and Paymaster General.

BREVET BRIG. GEN. JOS. SEWELL SMITH,

Was born in Wiscasset, November 27, 1836, but removed to Bath when quite a young man. After passing through the common schools of that city, he attended and graduated from the Academy at Gorham. Soon after he went to Stillwater, Me., where he engaged with Wm. Jameson as book-keeper and clerk. In 1857, he went west, being engaged in lumbering at Stillwater, Minn., and Lyons, Iowa. Upon the breaking out of the war in 1861, he returned to Maine, for the purpose of enlisting and going to the front in a regiment from his native State. June 4th, he enlisted as a private in Company D, Third Maine Regiment, Col. O. O. Howard commanding, and it was not long before he was promoted to Corporal, Sergeant, Lieutenant, Captain and Lieutenant Colonel. October 27th, 1864, while serving on the staff of Gen. Hancock, he was breveted Colonel, "for gallantry in action at Ream's Station, August 25th, 1864, and at the battle of Boydton Plank Road, October 27th, 1864." On the 9th of April, he was breveted Brig. Gen. U. S. Volunteers, "for faithful and meritorious services, etc.," upon recommendation of Maj. Gen. A. A. Humphrey, commanding Second A. C.

Gen. Smith served continuously with the Second Army Corps, Army of the Potomac, from its organization to its dissolution, participating in the first battle of Bull Run, and nearly every other battle in which it was engaged, and was finally honorably mustered out of the service, July 11th, 1865.

In writing of Gen. Smith, Gen. Hancock said: "He was breveted for bravery in action. His conduct in the field was always marked for spirit and gallantry."

Gen. Humphrey said of him: "My estimate of him, as a faithful, skillful and efficient officer, whose long experience in the field, and sound judgment makes him a most valuable officer. The spirited manner in which he served as aide, in the action, shows him to be as soldierly as he is capable in administration."

In a letter to a brother officer, Gen. O. O. Howard said: "Col. Smith came into the service, as a private soldier, in the Third Maine, at that time commanded by me. He served on my staff at the first battle of Bull Run. While under my command, his services were of a very meritorious character, and his subsequent record is equally good. I have always considered him a capable, energetic and efficient officer."

Hon. Hannibal Hamlin.

Hannibal Hamlin, third son of Cyrus and Anna (Livermore) Hamlin, was born in Paris, Maine, August 27th, 1809. His grandfather, Eleazer Hamlin, of Massachusetts, was a Major in the Revolutionary war. He attended Hebron Academy, and was fitted for college, but the death of his father required him to take charge of the home farm, where he acquired that love of agriculture which he has since retained. In 1829, he and Horatio King bought the "Jeffersonian," a Paris newspaper, in the office of which he worked for several months, and then sold out. He then entered the office of Judge Cole, of Paris, as a student of law, for two years, and later in the office of Fessenden, Deblois and Fessenden, of Portland, and was admitted to the bar at Paris, January 1833. On the same day that he was admitted he tried a case and won it. The counsel on the other side was the Honorable Stephen Emery, whose daughter Mr. Hamlin afterwards, married. He first thought of settling in Bridgton, but decided to come to Lincoln, where he found Samuel F. Hersey and William R. Hersey, natives of his county, who gave him a cordial welcome. His father was one of the original proprietors of the town, and it was settled largely by families from Paris, Buckfield and Woodstock. After staying there a few weeks he concluded to settle in that place, and went to Paris for his library. On his way he met John Appleton, afterwards Chief Justice of the S. J. Court, who informed him that Charles Stetson was about to move from Hampden to Bangor, and advised him to go to Hampden, and settle there, which he did, commencing practice April 1st, 1833. He continued to live in Hampden until the spring of 1862, when he removed to Bangor, where he has since resided.

He was a Representative to the Legislature in 1836, '37, '38, '39, '40 and 1847; Speaker of the House, in 1837, '39 and 1840; Aid-de-Camp to Governor John Fairfield in 1839; Representative to the Twenty-Eighth and Twenty-Ninth Congresses in 1843 to 1847; U. S. Senator 1848 to 1856; Governor in 1857; U. S. Senator in 1857 and 1861; Vice-President of the United States in 1861 to 1865; Collector of the port of Boston in 1865 and 1866; United States Senator in 1869–1881; Minister to Spain in 1881, resigned in 1883, and returned to Bangor. The degree of LL. D. was conferred on him by Colby University in 1869. He also served as a private in Company A. State Coast Guards, Capt. L. J. Morse.

Since his return home from Spain, Mr. Hamlin has resided in Bangor, where, it is almost needless to say, he has the universal esteem and regard of all the people. In two things, outside of his domestic affairs, he seems to take a deep interest—the tilling of the soil about his pleasant home, and the affairs of the Grand Army of the Republic. He is always ready to assist this organization in any way, and, when on Decoration Day, he marchet to the cemetery and addresses his comrades, as he did last year, is is easy to see, from his fervid tones and solemn mien, that he fully appreciates the sacrifices made by those, who so well and faithfully represented, in the late Civil war, Eastern Maine in the Rebellion.

THE LOSS OF THE "EMMA JANE."

Some time ago, Capt. Elijah Low, of Bangor, had for a guest his brother-in-law, Capt. F. C. Jordan, and it was the good fortune of the author to meet him, and also to hear from his lips his experience with Capt. Semmes, late of the Confederate Navy. The story of the loss of the ship, as told by Capt. Jordan, is, in substance as follows:

During the war, Capt. Jordan, then commanding the ship "Emma Jane," touched at Singapore, where a portion of her cargo of coal was discharged, and, a few days later she sailed for Bombay, which port was made in due time, where the balance of the freight was taken out. As the ship was ready to return for another cargo, Capt. Jordan learned that the "Alabama" had followed him into Singapore, where some of the coal that he had left there had been taken on board, and that in all probability she was then hovering off the Malabar coast, in the track of merchantmen. In order to avoid her on his return trip, Capt. Jordan determined to keep away from the land, outside the usual track, and thus escape the enemy, but, as the sequel will show, Capt. Semmes, being a shrewd fellow, anticipated just such action, and he too "kept off." One morning Capt. Jordan discovered a stranger directly ahead, and, as the rising sun lit up the horizon, it was seen to be a steamer under sail. No uneasiness was felt, however, on board the "Emma Jane," as many English and other foreign steamers traded in those waters.

Gradually the two vessels approached each other, being propelled over the gently rolling sea by the light breeze of the morning, and, when half a mile apart, the steamer ran up the American flag, to which Capt. Jordan responded by sending aloft the stars and stripes also. Just as the Americans were congratulating themselves upon the fact that the stranger was a friend, boom! went the port gun to windward. This was a signal to "heave to," and with doubtful hearts the Yankee crew backed the main topsails, and soon a boat was seen to "lower away" from the steamer. With a glass Capt. Jordan made a hasty examination of the boat, and then, walking to the cabin door, said to his wife:

"Pack up your valuables and prepare to leave. Yonder steamer is the Alabama."

The experienced eye of the sailor had detected the fact that the lap-streak boat, which was now approaching rapidly, was of English build, and he knew that the steamer rolling to windward had no right to hoist the beautiful emblem of the Republic, and that he had fallen into the claws of the "Leaping Tarantula," as Semmes loved to call his handsome craft. With measured and strong strokes, the powerful crew sent the light craft along, now mounting the green glassy wave, and now going down between the swelling seas, until she came alongside, and her commander quickly mounted to the deck of the doomed ship. No time was lost by this man of business, who said:

"I represent Capt. Semmes and the Alabama, and I desire you to take your papers and go on board at once."

When Capt. Jordan arrived on board the Confederate steamer, he was met by Semmes, who was much disappointed on learning that the ship was in ballast only, and without any deliberation he said:

"I shall burn your ship, Capt. Jordan. You can have twenty minutes in which to bring off your wife and crew. I will allow you one trunk of clothing and the sailors one bag each."

At the same time, a portion of the crew of the steamer,—about one hundred and fifty in all—began to plunder the ship, searching in vain for money. They would not believe Capt. Jordan when he told them that all his cash—some $22,000—had been sent home from Bombay, and actually overhauled the ballast in search of it. The crew were under but little restraint, some drinking freely, others gathering about the organ in the cabin, singing ribald songs, others arraying themselves in the clothing of Mrs. Jordan, while the balance, as though possessed by a desire to destroy and mutilate, went about cutting and hacking the cabin furniture, breaking up the crockery, etc. All day long the work of removing the stores went on, and was not finished until night had thrown her mantle over the scene of destruction. The wind had gone down, the gently heaving ocean was like a sea of glass, save where it was broken by the splash of an oar, or by the fin of some monster of the deep as he rolled lazily along, leaving behind him a phosphorescent track that sparkled and glittered in strange contrast with the reflection of the black southern sky above. Before the last of the crew left the vessel, the broken furniture was gathered in a heap in the cabin and fired, and at the same time the torch was applied forward and the craft left to the destroying elements.

The "Alabama" lay by that night, as there was no wind, but it seemed as though she could not depart until the work of destruction had been completed, and all through the dark hours Capt. Jordan and his wife and crew sat silent spectators.

At first volumes of smoke only arose slowly, covering the whole scene as with a black pall. Later, forks of flame shot up through this as lightning darts through clouds, disappearing, however, the next instant. Then solid flame broke through the cabin woodwork, and, after seemingly resting for a moment, prepared for a swift flight. A fork of flames darts out and catches the standing rigging. The hot sun of the tropics had been beating down upon this all day, the tar that covered it was soft and warm, and the flame, catching this, went skyward with the swiftness of a rocket. It catches the sails, it divides itself at every intersection of rigging, shooting upward, outward and downward at the same time; weaving itself into zigzag trails as the gentle breeze—a thing of its own creation—wafted the small strands and ropes to and fro. Now and then it darted away from the rigging and the sails, carrying some portion of each along with it, and poising a moment in mid-air, whirled rapidly, and then dropped into the sea below. It roared too, and sent out weird sounds, as though it were a thing of life, giving expressions of glee as it hurried along on its errand of destruction. It bit through the to'gallant masts, the rigging which supported them, and they came tumbling from aloft, leaving a trail of sparks hanging in the Heavens. It bit through the topmast, darted over the bow-sprit, along the rail and quarter deck and down over the stern, shooting its thousand insinuating tongues into every crack and crevice, until the top hamper having all come down, the once beautiful craft lay a blackened wreck upon the ocean, while the symmetrical Alabama lay off, looking like some beautiful marine monster contemplating its prey.

The end was near at hand.

The flame ate its way through the stout timbers, that had so long and well resisted the restless ocean, weakening them and drawing the bolts until at last, the ship coming lazily and heavily down from the crest of the swell, they gave way, admitting the other element that was to complete the work. With the fury of a tiger this rushes in, filling the ship to its level, holding its own as she rose on the wave, and as the doomed craft came back creaking and groaning in every timber, gains a higher hold upon her, until at length the ship, as though she were a thing of life appealing to Heaven for mercy, threw her head high into the air, hung for an instant, and was then drawn into the dark unfathomed caves of old ocean's bed, while those who loved her so well shed tears as she departed.

The next day Semmes ran in towards the coast to land his captives. The place selected was a wild and uninhabited country, save by a few natives who lived along the shore. As the "Alabama" approached, the long line of breakers, through which the salt sea churned itself until it was white with foam, the dreary, barren land behind them, the black hills forming the back-ground, all looked anything but inviting, and Capt. Jordan appealed to the rebel commander to transport him to a civilized section of the country, but no; here they must land and at once.

"We want to get rid of you as soon as possible," was the answer. "Prepare to go ashore."

Words were useless, and soon they were being hurled through the breakers, thrown upon the shore by the violence of the sea, while the crew that had brought them in, forced the now light boats back with the ebb of the tide, and later the "Alabama," urged forward by both wind and steam, disappeared down the western horizon. Capt. Jordan watched her as she got under way, and as she grew smaller and smaller to the eye as the distance grew greater, he knelt under the cocoanut tree and prayed that the "Scourge of the Seas" might sink that night.

Here Capt. Jordan and his companions in misery were obliged to remain until the natives had grown to understand their signs, when they were taken in a flotilla of canoes, and carried to a point one hundred and fifty miles away, where connection was made for Bombay, at which place they arrived in due season. Here money was secured and the journey was then continued overland to Europe, and thence to America. The hardships were many, but Mrs. Jordan, with rare fortitude, bore up under them, while Capt. Jordan was in a measure rewarded for his sufferings and loss, by receiving a good round sum of English money for his ship.

INDEX

---- F A 378 Fred 180 181 Hal 80 Mr 192 Pat 108
ABBOTT, Capt 225 Chas B 30 L P 70 N 230 Rev Mr 266
ABERCROMBIE, Gen 250
ABLE, Charles 43
ACHORN, M A 214
ADAMS, James M 22 James W 43 Jas 200 Mr 194 Wm 28 215
ALDEN, H E 216
ALEXANDER, Capt 73
ALLEN, C L 207 Col 249-251 Dr 72 76 79 James 29 Maj 249 S H 221 Samuel H 246 Surgeon 54 60 W H 42
AMES, Gen 134 290 Geo P 235
ANDERSON, Horace 235 Hugh J Jr 234
ANDREWS, Ezekiel 112 John 30 T S 216
ANSON, Lt 280
APPLETON, Edward L 42 John 385 John F 360 Judge 203 Serg Maj 61
ARNOLD, 91 Benedict 65 Cyrus 29 Jesse M 91 93 Wm 29 177
ASHBY, Gen 259
ATHERTON, B T 204
ATKINS, Jeremiah B 43 Mrs 116
ATWELL, Capt 139 John W 113
ATWOOD, A P 29 Gilbert 29
AUSTIN, A A 216

AVERILL, F R 235 Frank 177
AYER, Benj 216 Lt 232 N C 28 Richard S 231 W O 29
B, Mr 88
BABB, Aaron 30
BABCOCK, F P 158
BACON, J A 30 John 200
BAILEY, Chas H 70 Isaac H 265 Noah 234 Thomas C J 102
BAILY, Thomas C J 123
BAKER, E W 235 John 68 125
BALDWIN, Maj 298 373 T W 29
BALLINGER, Capt 133 331 John H 69 330 Lt 330
BANK, Gen 260
BANKS, C A 235 Gen 249 250 259 280 348 Horace 234 Wm A 207
BARDEN, A F 23
BARKER, David 167 266 Lewis 38 116 167 268
BARLEY, Gilman 94
BARNES, A H 113
BARRETT, C 24
BARTLETT, Capt 138 163 Chaplain 256 Geo H 30 H 29 Hermon 42 I S 18 J 203 Jas 29 Joseph 19 Lydia A 29
BARTON, A L 94 269 Boynton 235 George 23 Mr 269 270
BASSFORD, L L L 69
BASSICK, E N 235

BATCHELDER, Jno 30
BATES, Andrew 235
BATTLES, Amory 30 Rev Mr 199
BAYARD, 250
BEALE, P J 236
BEAN, A D 234 Andrew D 99 B B 214
    C N 214 Capt 240 Joseph H 235
BEARCE, 241
BEAUREGARD, 82 296 372
BECKMORE, C F 235
BEECHER, Henry Ward 283 Mr 283
BENHAM, Gen 288 W H 329
BENNER, Lorenzo 45 Lorenzo D 66
BENNOCK, John E 113
BENSON, John 331 332 Mary E 138
    Seth E 62 William R 332 William
    Roscoe 332
BENT, J P 30 John P 33 34
BERGEN, E E 232
BERRY, 223 313 Col 213 G S 234 Gen
    102 217 219 220 222 312-317 373
    Geo W 215 Hiram 102 Hiram G
    218 311 357 John T 215 Maj Gen
    222 351 William 24 Z 235
BICKFORD, A D 247 W K 216
BIGELOW, E C 247
BILLINGS, Caleb 29
BIRD, John Jr 215
BIRNEY, Gen 152 Maj Gen 141
BISBEE, George D 356 Lt 100
BISHOP, N H 30
BLACK, Hiram T 93
BLACKMORE, Thomas M 158
BLAISDELL, H M 301 William 358
BLAKE, Eben P 235 Mr 185 P M 185
    S 28 235 S H 116 203 Samuel H 18
    W A 28 40
BLANCHARD, E 235 Geo P 69 Orias
    38 W H 235
BLUNT, Eben 29
BOARDMAN, S H 29

BODEN, Abner 23
BODWELL, A J 157
BOODY, D A 213
BOOTH, 182
BOOTHBY, Lt Col 256
BOULTON, George A 376
BOURNE, Geo F 99
BOUTELLE, C A 334 336 Capt 337 Lt
    336 337 Master 335 Mr 334-337
BOWEN, Geo W 235 John C C 247 L
    H 258
BOWLER, J H 203 J N 29
BOYCE, Michael 18 32 William H 44
BOYD, 91 Archibald L 91 93 Wm 29
BOYNTON, Capt 64 284 David 92
    Gorham L 92 93 194 Henry 288 J
    N 30 Lt 119 Mr 379 Warren H 41
    43
BRACKETT, Hiram E 23
BRACKLEY, B 210
BRADBURY, 159 B F 29 Bion 158 S
    P 29 200
BRADFORD, Lemuel 30
BRAGDON, Gardner 29 Z L 192
BRAGG, C S 29 Isaac M 30
BRANN, W F 30
BRANNON, Lt 298
BRASTOW, Billings 332 Capt 333
BREWSTER, Gen 358 Wm R 359
BRIDGES, Charles 43
BRIER, Geo F 235 Geo H 235
BRIGHT, J 30
BROOKS, Gen 129
BROWN, C 38 C P 28 235 Capt 66
    Cyrus 66 70 E E 94 Geo I 43 Geo
    M 247 George W 43 H M 215
    Moses 125 Moses W 66 69 S P 266
BRYANT, Jas 30 Samuel 207
BUCHANAN, Adm 336
BUCK, A P 66 Addison P 69 124 Benj
    J 69 Edward A 92 R P 54

BUDGE, J T 186
BUGBEE, D 29 162 203 David 18 33 62 157
BULIERS, Franklin 25
BUNKER, Capt 227 Lt 137
BURD, E D 235
BURGESS, Bishop 364 Geo W 234 T J 235
BURLINGHAM, Joseph A 44
BURNHAM, Capt 338 Col 126 127 129-131 134 339-341 345 367 Gen 338 341 343 344 Hiram 68 124 338 Lt Col 124 339
BURNS, Frederick 23 G J 99 207 Geo J 210
BURNSIDE, 122 367 Gen 132 160 349
BURR, C Chauncy 272 Chauncey 276 Mr 272 273 Thomas W 92 93
BURROWS, 240
BURTON, A G 66 Albert G 70 125
BUTLER, 353 372 E W 113 Gen 35 58 107 111 136 296 298 Henry A 29 J H 115 162 220 James H 35 37 Maj Gen 290 Nathaniel 220
BUTTERFIELD, W J 113
BUZZELL, Z 68
BYRON, 260
CABLES, Geo 213
CALDWELL, Col 293 Gen 359 John C 293
CALL, E 30
CAMBELL, James 24
CAMPBELL, A M 196 B A 69 Capt 293 J C 70
CANBY, Gen 307
CAREY, Theo 70 Theodore 125
CARLISLE, Capt 64 Geo M Jr 23 Robert 19
CARR, Charles C 292 Gen 359 John B 30 Joseph 29 Joseph B 359
CARROLL, John 27 44

CARTER, A W 236 C P 233 Horatio H 233 Lt 100
CARVER, A S 235 B 2d 235 L D 210
CARY, George 247
CASE, John S 221
CASEY, 293 312 Henry 27 44 Lt 79 Maj Gen 290
CASS, Capt 63 64
CATES, J C Jr 235 Timothy T 92
CATINAUD, V L 29
CHADWICK, John S 28
CHALMERS, Geo 30
CHAMBERLAIN, Col 57 Ira 30
CHAMBERLIN, C 266
CHANDLER, C H 177 Capt 64 Chas H 66 69 124 Col 177
CHAPLAIN, Capt 45
CHAPLIN, Col 137 138 140 143-146 Daniel 32 41 43 139 140 144 345 Maj 119 144 Mr 40
CHAPMAN, Calvin S 23 S H 208 212 Sewell 114
CHASE, A F 30 Alden 233 Alexander 25 Hooper 30 170 200 Joseph 38 Mr 37 Nathan W 30 S T 30
CHICK, Edwin 30 G H 162
CHIPMAN, N P 351
CILLEY, J P 213 247 Lt Col 257 Maj 256
CLARK, 28 64 83 84 90 91 96 161 163 A E 216 Augustus 234 Capt 137 139 320 Charles D 113 I R 29 J G 92 J M 235 James W 379 Lt 381 Maj 321 Mr 47 94 95 Plynn 38 Pvt 379 Ruel S 25 43 Sgt 380 381 W S 378 Whiting S 320
CLERGUE, J H 30
CLOSSON, A 236
COAN, William H 70
COBB, Geo S 228 J C 208 John C 210 Mrs 116 Surgeon 225

COBURN, 159 Abner 158 Gov 163 164 220 222
COCHRAN, W S 216 Wm S 208
COE, Mr 379
COLBURN, H G 157 Jonas 157
COLBY, Capt 139 George W 247
COLCORD, A P 235 B L 236 J S 235
COLE, Capt 255 Judge 385
COLEMAN, Wm P 247
COLLIMORE, Chas I 112
COLLINS, James C 43
COLTON, N H 29
COMSTOCK, Lt 125
CONANT, C H 226 Capt 225 284 O J 209
CONNORS, Edward P 111 William 27 Wm 112
CONWAY, Wm S 228
CONY, Gov 205 359
COOMBS, F S 234
COTTRELL, C T 235 Geo W 235
COUCH, 312
COUNCE, R H 216
COWAN, Albert L 44
CRAIG, Capt 362
CRAMMER, C 235
CRANE, Chas L 112
CRAWFORD, Gen 355 W E 216
CROCKER, Chas 207 William 24
CROCKETT, C S 214
CROSBY, Capt 348 Charles S 95 247 Charles W 19 George 235 Henry 280 347 John L 29 33 Mr 347 Mrs Jas 52 Timothy 28 W G 230 Wm 234
CROSS, Edmund 235
CROSSMAN, Capt 139 Christopher V 113
CROWELL, H P 24 Hartshorn P 42 Thomas 235
CROWLEY, Michael 44

CUMMINGS, Capt 378 379 F A 378 Fred A 356 Geo A 18
CUNNINGHAM, Albert E 234 Capt 232 H W 98 230 231
CURRIER, Capt 347 Edwin 43 William R 43 347
CUSHING, Lt Commander 336
CUSHMAN, Henry M 23 43
CUTLER, C F 227 C H 217 John L 30
CUTTER, Frank L 247
CUTTING, Jonas 30
D, Mr 88
DAGGETT, Capt 139 346 Samuel W 345
DAHLGREN, Col 255 256
DAKIN, Daniel 194
DALE, 21 Mayor 163 164 S H 18 34 Sam'l H 28 Samuel H 194 200
DALTON, A 30
DANA, 156 John W 155 Mr 155
DARBY, Hiram 234 Isaac 234
DARLING, J O B 29 Rev Mr 266
DAVENPORT, Fred S 112
DAVIS, 82 C M 214 Capt 293 Gen 255 Jeff 107 232 Jefferson 20 107 326 Mr 326 R 29 Robert O 200
DAWSON, Stephen W 25
DAY, 240 Charles 71 Warren 23
DEANE, 77 78 Pvt 81 Wm 75
DEANEO, James 42 William J 42
DEARBORN, R 266 Sam'l 23
DEBLOIS, 385
DEERING, Chas 161
DENACO, Henry B 302
DENNETT, W S 29
DETROBIAND, Brig Gen 143
DEVERAUX, Seth K 42
DEVREAUX, S K 41
DICKERSON, J G 230
DICKEY, 30
DILLINGHAM, 30 F H 200 N H 30

DINGLEY, James Jr 285
DOANE, W W 113
DODD, T S 30
DODGE, Ferdinand 236 Jas E 234
  John E 301
DOLE, 91 Charles E 36 37 67 93 115
  Chas E 200 H S 158 John 30
DOUTY, 261 263 264 266 Calvin S
  247 266 Calvin Sanger 259 Col
  250 252 253 259 260 262 265 Lt
  Col 250 251 Maj 249 259
DOW, D A 235 John 235
DOWNE, J N 30
DOWNES, Colin L 43
DOWNS, C L 24
DRAKE, Stephen 38
DREW, Mr 273 S S 272 273 Silas 197
DRINKWATER, Seth E 113
DRUMMOND, A 29 John P 25
DUCKWORTH, Mr 195
DUMMER, J G 30
DUNBAR, Ira 30
DUNHAM, J J 204
DUNNELLS, John 234
DUNNING, 161 C H 30 Col 207 Isaac
  94 James 18 21 28 36 67 92 162
  200 Mr 21 26 R B 30
DUPONT, Adm 370 S F 334
DUREN, E F 29 49
DURGIN, Taylor 29
DURHAM, F J 234
DUSTIN, Mr 268 N 267
DUTCH, Saml 235
DUTTON, Jesse 300
DWINEL, 92 Rufus 91 93 192 200
DWINELL, Chas 139
EATON, Luther H 19
EDDY, Jonathan 28
EDWARDS, 240 David W 239
EGERY, Marshall J 91 93 Mr 64 T N
  31 Thomas N 18 Thos N 28
ELDER, E W 194

ELLIS, C B 235 Charles J 44 F A 235
  O A 247
ELWELL, J H 214
EMERSON, Albert 29 Capt 21 41 47
  77 163 Geo W 69 Levi 22 43
  Moses W 235 Mr 21
EMERY, 90 92 269 Editor 82 92-94
  Harvey 24 J H 235 Marcellus 94 98
  193 198 273 Mr 85 87 88 93 273
  275 Seth 30 Stephen 385 W C 235
ESTABROOK, G C 216
ESTABROOKS, David N 113 J H 209
ESTES, 28 Gen 324 Llewellyn G 323
  Lt 323 Maj 324
EVERETT, C C 30
EWELL, 320 Gen 350
FAIRFIELD, Gov 32 John 386
FARNHAM, Augustus 44 Augustus B
  355 Col 355 356 Henry B 92 J G
  214 Lt Col 355
FARNSWORTH, B B 29 34 200
FARRAND, Eben 337
FARRELL, Patrick J 44
FARRINGTON, Mrs 116
FARRIS, 29
FARROW, William Jr 213
FARWELL, Joseph 208 219 N A 208
  225 226 326
FAUST, 80
FELLOWS, Albert G 44
FERNALD, G E 204
FESSENDEN, 385 J D 104 S C 219
  Wm 209
FIELD, Chas 235 Timothy 28
FIFIELD, 30 91 E B 158 Isaac E 91 92
  93
FISHER, Paul M 285
FISK, Mr 21
FISKE, J B 34 Jas B 28
FITZ, George 29
FITZGERALD, Chas 70
FLAGG, E W 29 Ed 198 Wm H 197

FLANDERS, Wm 235
FLETCHER, Samuel 30
FLINT, A C 30 Henry 215 John C 177
FLOWERS, Wm 30
FOGG, E N 29 H H 19 29
FOLSOM, Morison J 44 N D 30
FORBES, J 30 Joseph B 44
FORD, A 235 James 235 Wm 235
FOSS, Capt 119 Fernando C 44
FOSTER, J B 28 30 34 62 200 John B 21 33 Maj Gen 370 Thomas 23 43
FOWLER, A 235 C F 235 J S 236
FOX, E T 29
FRANKLIN, Gen 315 340 Maj Gen 340
FRAZER, Isaac 66
FRAZIER, Capt 302 Isaac 69 125 304 Milton 69
FREEMAN, Lt 317 R G A 29 Wm 345
FREEZE, D W 70
FREMONT, Gen 349 360
FRENCH, A S 30 Fred S 29 Hiram B 23 43 M S 94
FROST, B C 139 Benj C 112 J W P 29
FULLER, Capt 325 Col 325 David 29 Geo 66 70 125 George 125 324 Lt Col 324 325 Maj 135 Silas M 233
FURBUSH, Albert G 24 Fred 213 Jas 234
FURGERSON, Geo B 235
FURLONG, Capt 134 135 R W 69
G, Capt 316
GAMMON, A 235
GANNAN, M 234
GARCELON, Surgeon Gen 54
GARLAND, F 30 Frank 19 Henry 30
GARNSEY, Capt 172 Frank A 44 172 Lt 79 T H 19 Thomas 38
GERRY, Gen 374
GETCHELL, Edward L 33 44 Josiah 208 Lt 75
GHERRARDIE, Gen 373

GIDDINGS, M 28 Moses 67
GILKEY, P 235
GILLAN, Henry 30
GILLIGAN, M 19 29
GILLISPIE, Charles 92
GILMAN, Capt 280 E G 30 John 112 Jona 30 Rev Mr 163
GILMORE, 328 A T 236 Atwood 236 Charles D 350 Col 350 351 D P 234 Gen 288 295 332 349 370 371 Lt Col 331
GINN, Fred P 69
GLOVER, T B 210 Wm 235
GODDARD, 249 Col 248 John 246
GODFRED, E D 29
GODFREY, John E 30 177
GODFRY, Rev Mr 267
GOLDEN, Patrick 19
GOODELL, John Jr 30
GOODHUE, Ira 30
GOODWIN, I 30 Lewis 33
GORHAM, Christopher S 44
GOSS, Cyrus 30
GOULD, A P 209 Cyrus E 92 Daniel C 112
GRAFTON, Jennie 209
GRANT, 101 166 190 241-243 353 372 381 Gen 136 Geo 302 Geo W 158 George W 350 Isaac 240 Lt 350 U S 207 345
GRANVILLE, Henry 44
GRAVES, C W 23 Calvin 377 Lincoln 43 Robert S 112
GRAY, A H 235 Capt 133 E 214 Franklin 285 H C 234 M H 235 Sewall C 69 Sewell C 125
GREEN, Joseph 77 Leonard 214
GREENHALGH, J B 316
GREGG, C C 235 Col 252 Gen 251 Mrs 116
GREGORY, John 207
GRIFFIN, E L 236

GROSS, Stover B 44
GROVER, 279 Cuvier 380 Gen 380
GUILD, A P 30
GUNN, Geo 231 Lt 232
GURNSEY, Sam'l 30
H, Capt 366
HALCOM, Col 280
HALE, Charles 29 50 Eugene 304
HALEY, Geo W 247
HALL, Charles F 66 Charles J 42 E P 215 Francis P 43 O G 207 215 227 R W 24 Wm H 234
HALLECK, Gen 218
HALLOCK, Joseph 220
HALLOWELL, A R 29
HAM, John 208
HAMILTON, Geo 158
HAMLIN, A C 349 Anna 385 Asst Surgeon 60 65 Augustus C 42 Charles 38 104 139 356 358 Chas 247 Cyrus 360 385 Dr 349 E L 28 Eleazer 385 Gen 358 360 361 Hannibal 38 199 203 220 270 385 Maj 359 Mr 165 222 223 247 248 270 385 386 Surgeon 66 Vice-Pres 52 58 72 114 116 165 169 204 222
HANCOCK, 340 373 Gen 125 126 129-131 136 340 384 W S 339
HANRAHAN, C 215 Cornelius 223
HANSON, Dr 57 119 H F 55 William H 44
HARBACK, Philip 25
HARDEN, John F 213
HARDING, Col 221 H F 345 Rev Mr 345
HARDY, R K 200
HARLOW, 91 A D 162 Capt 266 Mr 193 N S 29 34 62 92 Nath'l 28 193 Noah S 91 93 Sam'l G 30 W H 92
HARMON, John C 42
HARPER, Wm 291
HARRIMAN, Jesse 114

HARRIS, Benj F 69 Benjamin F 125 Lt Col 132 134 135 Maj 131 Prof 199 Rev Dr 167 Sam'l 30
HART, H A 220 H B 235
HARVEY, Capt 293
HASEY, Elijah W 92
HASKELL, Albert 113 Elbridge F 44 Lewis R 43
HASKINS, R 30
HASSELTINE, Timothy 38
HATCH, 161 249 Alderman 163 Horatio N 177 Mr 161 S C 29 49
HAVENER, A 236 C M 234 R H 214 T O 235
HAWLEY, T W 160
HAWS, H H 235
HAYCOCK, Capt 366 367 Joel 133 Joel A 69 125 365 Maj 367
HAYDEN, Mr 267
HAYFORD, Maj 40
HAYNES, Henry P 94
HAYWARD, Charles 29 33 203 Chas 123
HAYWOOD, Charles 34 Chas 200
HEATH, Mr 21 Willard B 192
HEINTZELMAN, 129 Gen 105
HEINTZLEMAN, 380 Gen 312 313
HELLIER, W S 30
HEMINGWAY, Capt 284 286
HEMMINGWAY, G 30 J 30
HENDERSON, Q M 234
HENRIES, Chaplain 378 Henry C 285
HERRICK, S B 234
HERRING, Rev Mr 266
HERSEY, Gen 50 Roscoe F 112 S F 31 Sam'l F 28 Samuel F 385 Thomas 115 162 189 Thos 37 W Prince 279 William R 385
HEWETT, A E 214
HIGGINS, N G 112
HIGHT, Chas 30 Lt Col 250 Thomas 211 246 285

HILL, A P 254 315 Capt 293 Fred A
69 John M 158 Lt Col 373 T A 30
Warren H 292 Wiggins 26 28
HILLIARD, Wm T 30
HINCKLEY, E B 216 Mr 64 Samuel B
42
HINDS, Nimrod 38
HINKLEY, Capt 139
HITCHBORN, R H 29
HODGDON, C F 208
HODGKINS, J M 29 R 29
HODGMAN, F H 29
HODSDON, Adjt Gen 163 164 220
221 316 326 361 Gen 382 383 John
L 65 94 327 382
HOGAN, Michael 25
HOLDEN, 76 Henry 75-77 Mrs 76
William P 44
HOLT, Charles 113 George E 44 T K
94
HOLTON, A 29
HOOKER, 312 380 Gen 56 122 123
313 315 316 317 323 349 367 380
381
HOOPER, Otis F 23
HOPKINS, Nathan 29
HOUGHTON, Jno S 285
HOUSLON, H H 236
HOWARD, D M 174 Gen 116 169 316
J C 235 O O 384 R S 217
HOWE, 29 91 A P 357 Amasa 91 93
Gen 357
HOWES, L W 227
HUDSON, Henry 271
HULL, 228
HUMPHREY, A A 358 384 Gen 358
359 384 S F 30
HUNKIN, Surgeon 225
HUNT, A G 214 J W 207
HUNTER, Benj F 321 D 329 330 Gen
288 289 370 Maj Gen 288
HUNTLEY, W C 234

HURD, 242 243
HURLEY, P 28
HUSSEY, Lt 255
HUTCHINGS, Capt 284 Col 377
Jasper 376 Lt 376 Maj 377
HYDE, Col 321 Gen 322 Thomas W
322
ILLSLEY, Chas E 301
INGALLS, 91 Oliver H 91 93
INGRAHAM, J N 215 J S 85 88 196
IRELAND, Benj 30
IRVIN, Geo C 69
JACKSON, Albert M 44 Col 56 John
H 113 M S 186
JACOBS, Geo H 70
JAMESON, 159 362 378 C D 37 158
Charles D 37 42 361 Chas D 36
Col 52 61 80 81 155 Gen 105 165
361-363 Wm 383
JAQUITH, J G 114
JEFFERDS, Capt 266
JENKINS, 242 243
JENNINGS, Stephen D 272
JERRARD, Col 279 280
JEWETT, A G 67 230 E J 69 G K 28
Representative 26 Ruel 23 Samuel
93
JOHNSON, 28 Arbella 232 Geo H 234
I S 29 J S 235 T C 112 Theo C 111
Wm H 44
JOHNSTON, 82 258
JONES, 90 197 198 Amos 30 Capt 77
78 212 Elisha N 43 J 84 J Wesley
272 Joseph 83 Mr 85 Nath'l 215 S
F 30
JORDAN, Capt 387-389 391 392 F C
387 Mrs 391 Sabin 23
JOSE, Martin 78
JOY, John G 25 S D 302
KEARNEY, 364 Gen 312-314
KEEN, Elden 23
KEENE, Capt 225

KELLEHER, Patrick 92 Richard 44
KELLER, J A 235
KELLOCK, John 234
KENDALL, Steadman 38
KENNEY, A C 235 Mrs 116
KENT, Judge 273 O W 301 Otis 66
    Otis W 69
KEYES, Col 74 80 E D 339
KILLGORE, H L 235
KILPATRICK, 261 262 Col 251 256
    Gen 255 323 324
KIMBALL, C E 266 Capt 293 Charles
    E 38 Chas 235 D H 29 G W Jr 221
    J K 207 John S 29
KING, Horatio 59 385
KIRKPATRICK, A 34
KITTREDGE, James P 43 John H 43
    Lt 266 N 30 Sumner R 43
KNOWLES, 241-243 Abner 67 68 125
    Charles 240 Col 124 Lt 280
    Percival Jr 68
KNOWLTON, Jabez 94
KUHN, G O 210
KYES, Albert F 292
LADD, Geo W 40 92 196
LAMPHER, L 235
LANCASTER, Mrs H N 239
LANCEY, J A 139 John Q A 42
LANCY, John A 111
LANDERS, Patrick 92
LANE, Jas S 70 John 28
LANG, Mr 65
LARRABEE, G W 29 Mr 231 Samuel
    92
LAWRENCE, 373 Capt 298 Will 77
    William H S 44 Wm H S 33 72 177
LAWTON, S 30
LEAVITT, D F 94
LEBROOK, A G 266
LEE, 82 134 190-192 202 243 244 258
    291 304 372 Gen 151 345
LEIGHTON, A 29 Geo W 70 I E 177

LELAND, Benj 70
LENFEST, C W 113
LEONARD, Charles S 43
LESLIE, Jim 176
LEWIS, J C 235 James 235
LIBBY, Capt 225 D W 158 Hall J 23
LINCOLN, 176 182 190 203 228 244
    277 305 Dr 147 348 John M 70
    Pres 17 55 66 67 104 202 218 219
    230 277 311 366 Theo Jr 70 Wm H
    70
LITCHFIELD, J B 209
LITTLEFIELD, J B 235 James 34 Jas
    28 200
LIVERMORE, Anna 385
LORD, Alvin 302 Charles V 42 Chas B
    200 Geo 302
LOUD, W J 29
LOVEJOY, C C 215 Geo C 223
    Samuel C 247 Wm 77
LOW, Capt 173-176 179-182 Elijah
    172 176 387 Fred C 152 Maj 152
    Mr 173-175 Provost Marshal 190
LOWELL, Chas 177
LUCE, Alonzo B 25
LUFKIN, D 235
LYFORD, Rev Mr 272
LYNDE, 29 Mr 170
LYON, William 23
LYSER, William N 125
MACE, B H 38 Benj H 19
MACMICHAEL, C 298
MADDOCKS, J P 235 John S 244
    Lewellyn 244 Otis 235
MAHONEY, 242 Dennis 44 John 241
    Mr 241
MANN, 91 Samuel S 91-93 Wm 30
MANSILL, Capt 162
MANSON, 29 A D 62 R D 203
MARA, John O 2d 24
MARDEN, F M 38
MARINER, Rev Mr 210

MARSHALL, Capt 231 232 Col 102 T
    H 230 Thomas H 102
MARSTON, A B 112 Col 380 381
    Gilman 379
MARTIN, 118 A P 144 Gen 144 Geo
    W 125 Washington I 24
MARTINDALE, Gen 120
MASON, Dr 22 George 361 J 30 John
    B 235 Thomas 203 Thos 30
MATHEWS, E 235 Geo 235 Wm 234
MAXFIELD, John B 158
MAYHEW, Miss 209 Ruth S 209
MAYO, Capt 282 E N 177 E R 281
MCALLISTER, Robert 152 154
MCARTHUR, Capt 284 288
MCCABE, Wm H 69
MCCLELLAN, 160 184 353 366 368
    Gen 125 126 158 313 339 340 349
    Geo B 167
MCCLURE, Geo A 23 Jacob 104 226
MCCRILLIS, William H 95 Wm H 19
    26 30 116 212
MCDONALD, H M 234 Moses 271
    Wm 92
MCDOWELL, 120 339 Gen 250 281
    349
MCFARLAND, John D 66 68 69 124
    Thos H 234
MCGAW, Jacob 30
MCGREGOR, John 70
MCKENNEY, 242 243 Charles O 241
MCKINLEY, Lt 135
MCLAIN, Geo W 69
MCLAUGHLIN, Henry 197 James 30
    Jas 29
MCLELLAN, Gen 119 120 George A
    44 Samuel 94
MCLOON, Wm 207 218
MCNAMARD, John F 112
MCNEIL, John 24
MCQUESTEN, Chas A 68
MCQUESTION, James F 105

MCRUER, Dr 29 Miss 52 53 Mrs 116
MEADE, Maj Gen 345
MEADER, Dan'l G 69
MEARS, C W 235
MEINECKE, F 18 49
MEINICKE, Frederick 44
MERRIAM, Capt 137
MERRILL, 29 Addie V 30 Charles W
    25 43 Elias 30 Geo E 235 Geo W
    192 George W 192
METCALF, 28
MICHAELS, Samuel 235
MILL, 249
MILLER, C A 207 Charles A 221
    Charles W B 42 Chas K 29 G A
    217 James B 235 N W 241 W M R
    94
MILLETT, Samuel V 43 Stephen D 43
MILLS, W H 203 Wm H 162
MINES, Chaplain 61 John F 42
MINK, Chas 212
MITCHELL, Capt 256 D Y 235 Gen
    289 J C 30 O P 209 Robert B 351
MOGAN, Peter 44
MONROE, Charles F 292 Richard A
    43
MONTGOMERY, Wm 247
MOODY, Mr 356
MOOR, Abram 29
MOORE, A S 233 Americus W 44 Asa
    158 John 24 May E 232 Richard
    114
MORELL, Gen 120 122
MOREY, H S 68
MORGAN, Col 280
MORRILL, Eliphalet S 43 Gov 327
    Lot M 220 325 W G 69 W P 235
MORRIS, 29
MORRISON, Dr 183 John 38 R S 269
    S B 29 S D 177
MORSE, 28 91 92 Capt 220 L J 112
    137 162 200 386 Llewellyn 195

MORSE (continued)
    Llewellyn J 91 93 194 Lt 75 Ralph
    33 Ralph W 44
MOSEBY, 255
MOSES, J C 160
MOSSMAN, E W 236
MOTT, Brig Gen 141 Gen 152 153 316
MU??H, Albert M 69
MULDAUR, A W 336
MURCH, Isaac 216 Levi 112 Simeon
    C 43
MURPHY, S J 29
MURRAY, 47
MUZZY, F 19 28 200
MYRICK, 242 243 Hall C 233
NAGLE, Gen 295
NAGLEE, Gen 368 370
NANSON, G G 216
NAPOLEON, 275
NASH, Capt 293
NEALEY, Mrs 116
NEALLY, John 241
NEWENHAM, Wm R 322
NIAM, Samuel 24
NICHOLS, A D 207 A J 235 J B 235 J
    H 235 J L 235 P 235 W G 236
NICHOLSON, James 43
NICKERSON, Capt 207 E V 235 F S
    232
NORCROSS, Col 185 I B 115 Israel
    194 195 Israel B 19
NORRIS, J H 70
NORTON, Freeman 23
NORWOOD, W E 216
NOYES, Charles 113 Geo E 43 Joseph
    S 231 Wm F 112
NUTE, Lt 137
NUTTING, Jesse 272
O'BRIEN, E K 216
O'DONOHUE, 161 James 18 Jas 28
OAKS, S J 282 Sanford 158
OLIVER, Orren 91 93

ORCOTT, Warren H 42
ORFF, Fuller 77
OSGOOD, Col 163 Lt Col 221 T K
    207 208 212 215 217
OTIS, Albert J 24
OWENS, Thomas 235
P, C 30
PACKARD, Miss 209 O A 209
PAGE, A L 24 John L 235
PAINE, A W 40 203 Albert W 29 R E
    139 Seth 29
PALFRY, Rev Dr 233
PALMER, 28 Alden L 42 Dr 79 Geo
    29 Lient 47 Steward 60
PARK, Horace 235 R R 104
PARKER, H H 235 W T 158
PARKS, Nichols 236
PARSONS, I 29 N H 30 Solo' 30
    Solomon 18
PATCH, O R 29
PATTEE, W S 30
PATTEN, 202 A 201 Amos 194 195
    198-201 Edward M 247 Edwin 196
    198 Edwin B 195 Isaac 196 Isaac
    W 195 J S 30 177 John 30 John F
    92 M H 113 Marion B 94 Z S 29
PATTERSON, Andrew 235 Frances V
    235 Geo H 71 R P 160
PAUL, Silas 266
PAYSON, C A 217 S A 235
PEABODY, Mr 37
PEARSON, S T 29 Wm T 29
PEASE, Burleigh 29
PENDLETON, 184 194 N P 30 T C
    235
PENNELL, Capt 293
PERKINS, D P 235 Elisha S 43 J W 40
PERRY, A W 215 Edgar G 285 John F
    216 Mr 240 O H 208 P W 301 303
    304 W H 30
PETERS, John A 29 116 196 199 200
    Patrick 25

PETTINGILL, Byron 302
PHILBRICK, J 235
PHILBROOK, Augustus 234 R 216
PHILLIPS, Chas E 29 Geo H 24 Geo L 29
PICKERING, G W 28 Geo C 29 George 267 George W 18
PIERCE, Frank 68 124 Frank C 70 Franklin 66 John L 69 Luther A 42 W T 30
PIKE, F A 167 Mr 37
PILLSBURY, C E 70 Daniel 234 Evans S 247
PINKHAM, M B 157
PIPER, C R 235 H I 157
PITCHER, A A 235 Horatio 139 204 Oscar W 234 Thos W 235 W H H 93 162 Wm L 99
PLAISTED, Col 294-296 368-375 Gen 365 376 H M 29 293 Harris M 298 367 Lt Col 293 368
PLUMMER, B 30 Daniel 158 Watson E 92
POMEROY, Capt 293
POND, Enoch 30 203 Rev Dr 203
POOR, Benj F 113
POPE, 366 381 Gen 121 349
PORTER, 120 C G 30 F J 105 Fitz John 251 Gen 119 120 Joseph 18 S A 176 T W 30 33
POTE, Geo 204
POTTER, J W 13
POTTLE, Simon 70
PRATT, David 213 Gen 340 O W 23
PRENTISS, Henry E 28
PRESCOTT, Constable 241
PRINCE DE JOINVILLE, 312
PRINTISS, Henry E 95
PULLEN, Thomas 38
PURINGTON, Chas 114
PUTNAM, Lt Col 279 Z B 70
PYSELL, Wm N 70

QUIMBY, 78 Daniel Jr 44 Geo T 235 John C 44 Robert 25 Sgt 77
RAMSDELL, C V 104 J H 37 Seth B 44
RANDALL, John J 43
RANKIN, Quartermaster 225
RAY, Joshua 23
REDMAN, Ed 100
REED, Alvin A 216
REEVES, W H 235
REEVIL, David 44
REMMINGTON, J 299
RENO, Gen 250
RENSHAN, Lt 228
REYNOLDS, Adjt 61 John 47 80 John E 42 Lewis 198 Sam'l 30
RHIND, A C 337
RICE, 378 Capt 284 J S 38 James S 300 John 266 John H 72 Jos S 285 Lt 302 377 P H 38 W H H 302 377 Wm 236
RICH, 78 Col 158 Geo 78 Moses W 235 Sylvanus 29 63
RICHARDSON, J R 215 Lt 77 Lyman E 24 43
RICKER, George W 157 J S 63 John S 19 197 Josiah S 203
RILEY, Philip 24
RING, F W 112
ROACH, Henry 23 Thos P 71
ROBBIN, 223
ROBBINS, John M 285 M 234 Mr 37
ROBERT, Capt 64
ROBERTS, 29 A M 40 106 B F 158 C W 41 105 Charles W 18 42 58 122 333 Col 105 120-123 161 163 167 170 334 352 355 Gen 105 J G 66 70 Lt Col 80 Mr 49
ROBINSON, 92 A M 38 Benj F 70 Bradbury 94 C H 233 C R 25 F E 204 Gen 355 J F 30 J H 138 J J 104 James A 91-93

ROE, F A 336
ROGERS, Cyrus 23 Levi 235
ROLLINS, Chas A 209 E H 29 H 29
ROSE, E 310
ROSS, Charles W 113
ROUSE, J 208 James 223
ROWE, 91 Frank M 91-93 James L 43
    James S 29 Joshua 213
RUSS, 194 Albert S 24 Geo A 234
    Robt F 234
RUSSELL, A P 247 Gen 134 J J 93
RUST, Capt 284 Col 286-290 326 327
    329 330 Gen 327 328 330 J D 327
    329 John D 212 285 325 329 Wm
    M 230
SABINE, Capt 139 298 353 373 F M
    29 63 Francis W 352 L E 30
SALMON, Edwin 235
SAMPSON, John S 43
SANBORN, Abraham 94 271
SANDBORN, Abiathar 23
SANFORD, Capt 240 M 49
SANGER, E F 68 Eugene F 125
SARGENT, Capt 45 74 75 79 355
    Daniel 33 Daniel F 44 354 Maj 122
    355
SAWTELL, A V 234
SAWTELLE, Chas F 225 Jerome W
    113 O P 30
SAWYER, Capt 64 Frank L 24 G W
    266 N K 38
SAXTON, Rufus 329
SAYWARD, A 215
SCHMELL, Henry 44
SCHRYVER, Lt 307
SCHWARTZ, Michael 28
SCOBLES, W H 234
SEAVEY, Calvin 197 E W 235 Wm W
    112
SEDGWICK, Gen 341 363
SELLERS, Henry E 111
SEMMES, 391 Capt 387 388

SEVERANCE, Wm 77
SEWALL, Geo P 156
SEYMOUR, Gov 274
SHAW, 29 194 F E 146 Fred E 62 G J
    158 Peltiah 234 T H 235 William H
    293
SHEPARD, George 30 Maj 147
    Russell B 111
SHEPHERD, Col 148 R B 148 Russell
    B 139
SHERER, J T 214
SHERIDAN, 373
SHERMAN, 73 Gen 323 324
SHUTE, Alonzo 235 F 235
SIDELINGER, Geo 217
SIDES, Edwin 235 Isaac 235
SIEGEL, Gen 349
SIGEL, Gen 357
SIMONTON, T E 214 T R 212 226
SIMPSON, A K 235 A L 19 Editor 239
    James M 43 Wm H 234
SINGHI, F 98
SKINNER, John K 43 Lt 78
SLAVE, Sambo 110 111
SMALL, A K P 30 G C 235 Gilbert M
    302 John S 43 L P 235
SMART, E C 29 E K 213 326 Edward
    235
SMITH, 30 A C 18 38 Albert 30 305 B
    C 235 C Edwin 112 C F 30 Capt
    139 249 362 Charles 44 Chas H
    247 Col 252 253 339 384 D T 30 E
    S 207 G P 29 Gen 128 340 341 384
    Geo H 235 Geo R 177 J V C 377
    Jacob 196 Jacob C 196 Jas Jr 30
    Jos A 302 Jos L 36 Jos S 362 363
    Jos Sewell 383 L 70 L W 70 Lt Col
    204 264 Maj 148 Noah 358 S
    Wilson 24 Samuel 93 W F 339 W
    H 19 28 Warren G 112 William H
    92 Wm A 200 Z A 158
SNOW, A J 24 Chas W 213 H C 303

SNOW (continued)
    Joseph F 111 113
SNOWMAN, Geo 70 J W 68 Jos 69
    Joseph 66 125
SOMERBY, A T 69
SOPER, Henry R 70
SOPHER, Henry R 66
SPAULDING, A C 207
SPEAR, Col 256 Elk 207
SPENCER, Albert L 99
SPICER, Horatio 234
SPOFFORD, Capt 293 Col 365 Lt Col
    296 298 372 W P 301 Winslow P
    364
SPRAGUE, A 227 Alden 207 Edw 207
SPRATT, G W 30
SPROUL, Hiram B 70
SPURLING, 248 Andrew B 247 Lt Col
    307
STANCHFIELD, John R 43 William H
    125 Wm H 70
STANLEY, A 207 Mr 65
STANTON, 223 Edwin M 173
    Secretary of War 261
STAPLES, Daniel 44 Horatio 44 Sgt
    77
STARR, Geo A 213
STEEDMAN, Capt 337 Rear Adm 337
STEELE, Gen 307
STEPHERSON, C B 235
STERLING, E L 23 Edwin L 43
STETSON, Charles 28 203 385
    Charles P 33 62 Chas P 200 E W
    221 Geo 200 George 28 192 Isaiah
    18 28 52 94 Mayor 53 83
STEVENS, 364 A L 70 Alex 70
    Andrew 234 Edmund Jr 234 G W
    29 177 Gen 66 Geo W 111 John
    292 Jos E 234 S S 29
STEWART, A T 188 H B 29 T J 34
    Thos J 28

STICKNEY, 29 Amos 29 M T 30 Mr
    49
STILES, George H 91 93
STINCHFIELD, L H 66
STOCKMAN, E N 94 John 113
STOCKWELL, David R 28 L 30
STONE, 49 Chas F 69 Sam'l B 29
STONEMAN, 251 Gen 251
STOWELL, David P 246 Maj 249 250
STRATTON, Lewis F 158
STRAW, Capt 293
STRICKLAND, 28 161 194 A H 285 C
    L 210 Capt 284 Col 286 Gen 58
    Hastings 18 Isaac 68 125 Lee 285
    326 Mr 161 S P 18 28 203
STUART, 101 251 Gen 262
STUDLEY, G E 217
STURTEVANT, Walter W 43
STYLES, Geo A 162 George H 93
SULLIVAN, Geo S 24
SUMNER, E V 363 J F 217 M 207
SWAN, J A 113
SWEENEY, J 28 Miles J 44
SWEET, A S 30
SWEETSER, C W 234
SWETT, Benj 94 Benjamin 92 Capt
    281 Cyrus 43 E C 113 James G 281
SYLVESTER, Joseph H 43
TABOR, 91 92 John 93
TALBOT, Lt Col 138 T H 139
TARBOX, M H 30
TAYLOR, 83 Capt 255 Col 255
    Loomis 49 Lt 250 T A 32 Thomas
    A 32 Thos A 29 W W 162 Wilder
    H 177
TEFT, Benj F 247 Dr 248 249
TENNEY, 49
TENNY, Rev Dr 305
TERRY, Gen 370
THATCHER, Adm 336 Benj B 112
    Geo A 30

THAXTER, H G 29 Sidney 19 29 34 Sidney W 247
THISSELL, James 29
THOMAS, Gen 349 Geo E 69 Joel 214 John 234 Maj Gen 349
THOMBS, Ambrose 235
THOMPKINS, 29
THOMPSON, A 29 216 E H 177 G W 30 Hannibal 158 William 92 Wm 207 Zenas 68 125
THORNDIKE, J C 112 R S 217
THURSTON, 28 E G 30 200 J D 33 John R 25 S D 34 62 Samuel D 28 33
TIBBETTS, Daniel Jr 24 Richard 43
TILDEN, Charles W 42
TILLSON, Davis 208 Gen 213
TISDALE, Mrs Seth 301
TITCOMB, Gen 211 Wm H 220 221
TOLMAN, O P 215 Walter 215
TORAY, John 24
TOWLE, Josiah 30
TOZIER, Henry E 292
TRASK, J E 235
TREAT, Adams 271 D 235
TRICKEY, 161 John 92 Thomas 203 Thos 30
TRUE, Capt 288 Jabez 29
TRUSSELL, Moses 234
TUCK, M G 94
TUCKER, Benj F 247 Mr 300 Sheriff 241 242
TWITCHELL, Capt 284 286
TWOMBLY, Isaac S 113
TWOMEY, William 44
TYLER, 194
UPTON, E A 29
V, F F 110 Mr 110 111
VARIAN, 73
VARNEY, Col 56 57 122 163 164 Geo 266 George 42 352 Lt Col 123 352 355 Maj 61 77

VEAZIE, Gen 189 J P 30 Sam'l 28 Samuel 18 106
VIELE, Egbert L 285 328 Gen 286
VINAL, E 217
VOSE, Thatcher 71 Z Pope 207
W, 88
WAID, John B 71
WAITE, B F Jr 69
WAKEFIELD, A G 29 201 Mr 202
WALKER, Elijah 209 212 213 225 James 29 S 90 Simon F 92
WALL, Patrick 29
WALLY, Roscoe G 24
WARDWELL, David D 42 V P 69 Virgil P 66
WARMOUTH, Gov 361
WARREN, A 235 Ambrose C 197 Geo W 235 Henry 23 Lorenzo 292
WASHBURN, Gov 18 19 25 26 32 34 35 47 54 164 220 222 247 326 327 367 Horace B 23 Israel H 351 Israel Jr 25 155 John 68 W H 217
WASHINGTON, 87
WATERHOUSE, R T 235
WEATHERBEE, Washington 94
WEBB, 29
WEBBER, Payson C 92
WEBSTER, Daniel 64 211 John 30
WEED, 161
WEEKS, Jason 28 Wm H 230
WEITZEL, Gen 333
WELCH, Peter 79
WELLINGTON, Geo 30
WELLS, Secretary 336
WELMAN, J 234
WEST, A B 235 S 160 W W 285 Wm H 69
WEYMOUTH, Jas M 38
WHEELER, 29 John A 235 Mr 170 195 S H 71
WHEELWRIGHT, 28 64 83 84 90 91 94 96 163 J S 18 34 163 195 200

WHEELWRIGHT (continued)
Mr 47 95
WHITAKER, B B 235
WHITCOMB, Arthur C 43 Eben 240 H 235 H V 25
WHITE, A 113 160 Daniel 205 Geo N 234 H H 69 J C 29 188 O G 235 Thomas A 49 Thos A 28
WHITMAN, P M 29 Wm S 30
WHITMORE, Otis 235
WHITNEY, Benjamin D 43 C N 24 G W 30 George F 43 George W 92 Maj 250 Mr 37 S 207 W L 30
WHITTIER, 28 A J 70
WIGGIN, C P 177 Mayor 207 Rinaldo B 42 Sullivan D 112
WIGHT, J P 235
WILKINS, Lt 135 Lyman H 69
WILLEY, B F 25
WILLIAMS, 29 161 Edward 69 James W 112 S 363 T 207
WILLIAMSON, Caro 232
WILLIS, H S Jr 24
WILSON, A P 41 Albion P 43 Capt 119 163 F A 19 29 200 J B 41 Mr 156

WING, A A 28 Aaron A 18 28 177
WINGATE, Collector 19 D P 30 J J 40 John 88 Mr 88 W P 28 Wm P 200 201
WISWELL, Arno 38 J B 236 John B 232
WITHAM, E P 215
WITHERELL, Chas T 71
WITHERLY, Thos J 30
WOOD, Henry A 269
WOODARD, A 29 Abram 28 N C 207
WOODBURY, C H B 38 Charles A 24 Eben 177
WOODMAN, Capt 284 286 T C 38
WOODWARD, Abram 40 N C 213
WOOL, Gen 56
WOOSTER, Thomas H 43 Wm M 234
WORCESTER, Galen 25
WORTMAN, E E 215
WYER, Miss 187
WYMAN, J P 30 John 28 83 84 197 200 201 Mr 83 84
YEATON, 29
YORK, George 24 John B 44
YOUNG, Capt 133 Jonathan 18 Ralph W 70 125

www.ingramcontent.com/pod-product-compliance
Lightning Source LLC
Chambersburg PA
CBHW050325230426
43663CB00010B/1741